Jewish Radicals

Frontispiece 'The vampire of the sweatshop'. Frontispiece to *Songs of Labor,* by Morris Rosenfeld, a book of poems translated from Yiddish, published in Boston in 1914.

Jewish Radicals

From Czarist Stetl
to
London Ghetto

by

William J. Fishman

PANTHEON BOOKS

A Division of Random House, New York

First American Edition

Copyright © 1974 by William J. Fishman

All rights reserved under International and Pan-American Copyright Conventions. Published in the United States by Pantheon Books, a division of Random House, Inc., New York, and simultaneously in Canada by Random House of Canada Limited, Toronto. Originally published in Great Britain as *East End Jewish Radicals 1875-1914* by Gerald Duckworth & Co., Ltd.

Library of Congress Cataloging in Publication Data

Fishman, William J.
  Jewish Radicals.
  Bibliography: pp. 322–25.
  Includes index.
  1. Jews in London. 2. London. East End.
3. Radicalism—Jews. 4. Lieberman, Aaron Samuel,
1844-1880. 5. Rocker, Rudolf, 1873-1958. I. Title.
DS135.E5F5   1975   914.21′06′924   74-26194
ISBN 0-394-49764-3

For Barney Shine
without whom this would not have been possible

Contents

List of Illustrations

Frontispiece 'The vampire of the sweatshop'. Frontispiece of *Songs of Labor*, by Morris Rosenfeld, a book of poems translated from Yiddish, published in Boston in 1914.

Illustrations are reproduced by the kind permission of the following: 2, Mr J. Barnett; 4, The British Museum; 11 and 12, Alfred Wess; 14, 15, 17, 18, 19, 20 and 21, Fermin Rocker. Photographs 5, 8 and 9 are by R.C. McCormick; 16 is by Ray Davies.

Preface to the North American Edition

The immigrant story told here has inbuilt elements of dupli-
cation, of universality. It cannot stand on its own. The East
Side of New York, like London's East End, was the main re-
ceptacle for the incoming 'greeners'. It is easy to read Delancey
Street for the Whitechapel Road, Orchard Street for Brick
Lane; the tenement blocks between Cherry Street and Chath-
am Square are but larger replicas of the decaying Charlotte
de Rothschild Dwellings, grim barracks pressed between
Whitechapel's Wentworth Street and Flower and Dean Street.
In both, sweating, overcrowding and insanitation were a way
of life, with a proliferation of *landsleit*-based *stieblech* and
shools, their dubious hours of glory sustained during this
period, to suffer a dying fall after World War II.

The parallels are consistent. For the Jewish immigrant,
Arnold Toynbee Hall on East Broadway performed a similar
educative rôle to its counterpart in London. Both cities
spawned a mélange of labour leaders with charisma. Through
the advocacy of the *mame loshen,* Yiddish political sheets were
sponsored by a common readership on both sides of the Atlantic. The ubiquitous Feigenbaum thundered his irreligious
polemics to packed audiences, from the Christ Church Hall,
Whitechapel, to the Clinton Street Hall, East Side; while the
great Emma, with her amalgam of club oratory and rabbinical
pilpul, urged the immigrant poor of America to take to the
streets in direct action. In recalling for us the annual Yom
Kippur comedies when 'speeches on free thought, dances and
plenty of eats took the place of the traditional fast and prayers.
Religious Jews resented our desecration of their holiest Day
of Atonement, and their sons came down in strong force to
meet our boys in pitched battle', she might well be reporting
the same fracas, on the same day, 3,000 miles away in the heart
of Spitalfields. For Morris Hillquist, New York, read Yud

Kaplan, London. The names may differ, but the liturgy remains the same.

In radical legend, the transatlantic life-line remained unbroken during these years. From the common point of departure (Eastern Europe), in the earlier period, London provided the preparatory and New York the finishing schools for socialist and libertarian education. Rocker suggests that 'London was a clearing-house for the Jewish revolutionary labour movement . . . They [the Russo-Polish immigrants] formed groups in their new homes [in America], and maintained contact with the original group in Britain, which remained the motherland of the movement'. There is evidence to validate this. Yet there is a diversity within this common experience which poses more questions rather than giving clear-cut answers; we are, perhaps, at the start line of the enquiry, which offers a challenging task for scholars of varying disciplines.

For example, why did the ghetto in East London last longer than that of New York? One explanation could be that the Jews' position was more clearly prescribed in London than in, say, New York or Chicago. They were the *only* immigrant minority (against those in the USA who were one of many) and, therefore, more easily pinpointed as a scapegoat in the current anti-alienism, engendered by Trade Union leaders voicing uninformed working-class prejudices, and political demagogues on the make. The London Jewish immigrant remained bound to the ghetto far longer than his US counterpart, since the latter enjoyed a *comparatively* easier and earlier mobility—upward and outward. In the short term there were far more possibilities open to the New Yorker in terms of terrain and socio-economic opportunities; in contrast to Britain, which was already receding as an industrial power, there was an ever-expanding market, fed by a rising population accruing from diverse ethnic groups, and by vast deposits of raw materials available for industrial exploitation. Yet there are still difficulties in quantification in defining the British-US comparison. One problem arises from the relatively minuscule percentage of Jewish immigrants per host population in Britain against that in the USA.

Another question posed is: why did London Jewish radicalism veer towards Libertarianism while the New York movement was predominantly Social Democrat? The London transmigrant and Yiddish poet Morris Winchevsky carry the banner bearing the prophet Hillel's prescription, 'If I am not for myself, who will be? And if not now, when?' When may be too late.

William J. Fishman

Acknowledgments

I must record the debt I owe to the many friends who helped by deeds or patiently endured my verbal ramblings during the gestation of this book. My thanks are particularly due to Barney Shine, whose encouragement and generosity to a fault brought this to fruition; to Trevor Smith, whose devoted and practical aid in all ways I can never repay; and to Martin Paisner, for his many kindnesses and for embracing this venture as though it were his own. I am grateful, too, to Sybil, for her stoicism in the face of interminable enthusiasm at our Baker Street rendezvous.

I must also express my gratitude to the many others who, actively or passively, helped me on the way, especially Professor Richard Cobb who, in one of our earlier trips together round the East End, implanted the idea when he urged me to 'write this down before it is too late'. I have also benefited from the advice, criticism or example of certain friends and colleagues, namely Dr Christopher Hill, Professors Harry Hearder, James Joll, Georges Haupt, Paul Avrich and Jeffry Kaplow, Maureen and Jeff Mandler, Charlotte and Reuben Klate, May Maccoby and, not least, the dedicated libertarian Nicolas Walter. My brothers Morris and Al have positively abetted by sustaining with me, through conversation, a love for the *mame loshen*, a knowledge enhanced by my acquaintance with that superb Yiddish poet, Avraham Stencl. I also pay tribute to the staff librarians of the British Museum, Tower Hamlets and Mocatta libraries, the International Institute for Social History, Amsterdam and YIVO Institute, New York (especially Miss Dina Abramovich), and to my editor Emma Fisher, for their painstaking guidance.

In addition there were those who gave generously to facilitate my research. My friend Fermin Rocker offered invaluable records and information on his father, as did Alfred Wess. The quality of life of the pre-1914 immigrant poor was conveyed to me through the reminiscences and contemporary material, freely submitted by those charming old survivors, *Arbeter 'Frainter* Sam Dreen and littérateur Joseph Leftwich. I recall, with reverence, those old *chaverim*, now gone, who opened up their homes and their most cherished books and documents to me: Aron Rollin (trade union leader and social historian), Jacob Fine JP, Louis Bailey, Rose Robins, Millie Sabel (Sabelinsky) and Karl Lahr.

My thanks are also due to the trustees of the Acton Society, who initially sponsored this research, with special appreciation for the assistance of Mrs Sue Rayner and Miss Jackie Eames, who typed the complete draft with consistent skill and accuracy; and to Colin Haycraft of Duckworth, who willed its publication. To which must be added my gratitude to Vic Thorpe and Christopher Martin, for their detailed criticism and advice on form, content and syntax during every stage, and to Professor Maurice Peston for welcoming me to Queen Mary College and providing me with the facilities that have made writing and teaching there so pleasurable. My deepest gratitude is to Doris, who prodded, cajoled, but cared absolutely until the last word was written.

No book like this could have been conceived without constant reference to the classic text, *The Jewish Immigrant in England (1870-1914)* by Professor Lloyd Gartner, to Dr Boris Sapir's pioneer research on Aron Lieberman, and the works of Elias Tcherikover and Kalman Marmor. I am always conscious of the debt I owe to their scholarship.

The reader will soon detect that this is a labour of love, and will, I hope, bear with my prejudices. The East End was my home in the 1920s and 30s, when conditions differed only marginally from those during this period. I breathed, ate, laughed, wept and dreamed dreams with the immigrant poor. For better or for worse they were my people. As long as there is one cobbled alley, one undeserted tenement left, which recalls the voices and images of the *chaverim*, I still walk with my father.

W.J. Fishman

London, 1974

Part One
Exit and Entry

1. In Bondage

'Russian Tsardom began its consistent role as a persecutor of the Eternal People when it received, by way of bequest, the vast Jewish population of disintegrated Poland.'[1] The first partition of Poland in 1772 brought unwelcome guests, a vast influx of Jews, into Russia. To the traditionally anti-Semitic Tsars this was the prime deficit in the balance-sheet of territorial acquisition. The Empress Elizabeth had personally issued a general order for the expulsion of the Jews in 1742.[2] According to legal record, there were therefore comparatively few survivors in 1772. The dismemberment of Poland by the imperial predators meant compulsory return for the unhappy Jews. Henceforth they would face the worst era of persecution in the annals of Jewish martyrology until the German holocaust.

It was the advent of Nicholas I (1825-55) that brought about a systematic plan from the top to de-Judaise Russia. The schemes evolved according to the whims of the Tsar. Nicholas had revealed himself as an anti-Semite, when on an official tour through Russia in 1816 he made note of his personal reaction to Jews in his diary:

> The ruin of the peasants in these provinces[3] are the Zhyds [Yids]. As property holders they are second in importance to the landed nobility. By their commercial pursuits they drain the strength of the hapless White Russian people . . . They are everything here: merchants, contractors, storekeepers, mill owners, ferry holders, artisans . . . They are regular leeches, and suck the unfortunate governments to the points of exhaustion.

1. S.M. Dubnov, *History of the Jews in Russia and Poland*. Three vols, Philadelphia, 1916-1918.
2. In 1749, on discovering that her physician Sanchez, who had attended her for eighteen years, was a Jew, she banished him forthwith.
3. i.e. White Russia.

This accorded with governmental attitudes. In the villages the Jews had been forced into the unpopular role of economic middleman between landlord and peasant. In Poland they had administered the estates of the nobility (*slachsa*). The historian of Lithuanian Jewry wrote that by 1792 '*all* the trade and industry of Lithuania was controlled by this population'.[4] In the south-western provinces their widespread employment as agents and administrators of land-owning property made the titles Jew and leaseholder (*arendator*) synonymous. A major involvement was in the liquor trade, which appeared to register widespread control by Jews in rural areas through leasing distilleries and monopolising sales in taverns and inns. This was the superficial picture. There was no fully quantified record of Jewish economic activities at this time.

But for Nicholas the surface picture sufficed. Imbued with xenophobic sentiment, he regarded the Jews as a cancerous foreign body. He was resolved on their spiritual and physical destruction; a less sophisticated progenitor of genocide, he would at least set the example to his Russian and German successors. To this end he first conceived of a scheme to replace the exemption tax imposed on Jews by personal military service. Throughout 1826 he drew up a military statute outside normal legislation. On 26 August, 1827, he issued his recruiting ukase. Ostensibly it was 'to equalise military duty for all estates', but the reality was a cruel, discriminatory act against the Jews. Against them were arrayed ninety-five clauses and sixty-two supplementary instructions. Clause eight was a permissive note for child murder. Youths of between twelve and twenty-five years were to undergo selective conscription, on the basis of ten for every thousand of the Jewish population. The duties of selection and ensuring correct numbers fell on the local Kahals (Jewish communes) by way of a responsible committee of three to six trustees. Failure to secure the requisite enlistment would mean fines or even conscription imposed on the trustees themselves.

Under clause seventy-four, 'Jewish minors (i.e. under 18)

4. S.A. Bershadskii, *Litovskie evrei*, St. Petersburg, 1883.

were to be placed in preparatory establishments for military training'. These were named 'cantonists'; and whereas all Jewish youths faced compulsory service, it only applied to those Gentiles categorised as 'sons of soldiers on active duty'. And these years of preparation were to be excluded from the total term of service, so that a Jew could be forced into thirty-one years with the colours — if he survived. It was therefore common for the ritual *kaddish* (prayer for the dead) to be pronounced on the young conscript. Few would ever return. For a terrible ordeal faced the child soldiers. Under brutal NCOs they were marched to recruiting centres where they were segregated and despatched to their respective units. These were more often sited in the remote corners of empire, such as the eastern provinces of Siberia, where, it was surmised, Jewish de-culturisation could be more easily enforced. Fortunate were those who even survived the journey. The roads to Siberia were littered with the corpses of young Jews; and not all perished from the cold or epidemics. After medical examination at the centres they were packed into wagons like cattle. *En route* they were billeted in Gentile houses, so that they must eat forbidden meals (*trefa*) or starve. The traumatic shock of exposure to such conditions could alone prove fatal. Alexander Herzen, on the road to exile through Viatka in 1835, presents us with a horrifying picture, when he caught up with a column of 'cantonists'. He asked the officer in charge what was happening. The latter explained, adding that half of them would not reach their destination. 'Epidemics?' suggests Herzen.

> No, not exactly epidemics; but they just fall like flies. Well, you know these Jewish boys are so puny and delicate. They can't stand mixing dirt for ten hours, with dry biscuits to live on. Again everywhere, strange folks, no father, no mother, no caresses. Well then again, you just hear a cough and the youngster is dead. Hello, corporal, get out that small fry!

Herzen, appalled, goes on:

> No brush, however black, could convey the terror of this scene on canvas.

Pale, worn out, with scared looks, this is the way they stood in their uncomfortable, rough soldier uniforms, with their starched turned-up collars, fixing an inexpressibly helpless and pitiful gaze upon the garrisoned soldiers, who were handling them rudely. White lips, blue lines under the eyes betokened either fever or cold. And these poor children, without care, without a caress, exposed to the wind which blows unhindered from the Arctic Ocean, were marching to their death.

For the survivors there was little respite. On reaching their destination they were immediately subjected to the initial process of de-Judification — forced baptism. A combined plan, under the jurisdiction of NCOs and Greek Orthodox priests, was put into operation. The outcome was a systematic brutalisation of the child. The stubborn, who resisted the holy water, was in succession flogged, forced to eat pork and salted fish, then deprived of water. Exercises in religious brainwashing were performed by the holy fathers. Those who persisted ended up in military hospitals, where they died. In the many attempts at genocide prior to the holocaust, none were so manifestly depraved as this exercise in the moral and physical destruction of Jewish children.

There was no amelioration for the over eighteens. Almost certainly married, they were torn away from their wives and children. It was customary for them to offer their wives a *get* (divorce) in anticipation of twenty-five years' absence and forced conversion to boot. In the army they were beaten and tormented as an alien group. Their inability either to speak Russian (Yiddish was their lingua franca) or adapt to the barrack-room mentality accentuated the hazards of army life. Nor could any practising Jew rise above the rank of NCO. The apostate might; and on completion of service could enter a post in the civil service. The obstinate ones, their ordeal completed, could only return to the Pale of settlement. Yet there was no guarantee that conversion provided an open door. To the majority of Russians, a Zhyd remained a Zhyd.

Within the *stetl* — the small town or village — there remained other unpleasant effects of the recruiting ukase. The means employed in choosing draftees bred suspicion and insecurity and, periodically, strains in personal relationships brought communal discord. The Kahal, burdened with the responsibility of recruitment, was forced into the role of police agents. In many cases their zeal in enforcement went beyond the limits of necessity. For they were continually faced with the problem of runaway conscripts. Parents anticipating the call-up of their sons connived at their escape into the neighbouring forest or large towns. The Kahal hired professional 'hunters',[5] who either tracked down their victims or, in default of those absent, made up the quota by means of kidnapping or paying a desperately poor parent to submit a substitute. It was the poor, the majority Jews who provided the main supply of 'cantonists'. Many of the sons of the rich, of rabbis and members of the guilds, eluded the draft, so long as their parents held rank or influence within the Kahal.[6]

Almost simultaneously came the second blow. On 2 December, 1827, two ukases ordered the expulsion of Jews from two locales. The first forced thousands of Jews to quit the villages in the government of Grodno for the towns. The second decreed the wholesale banishment of Jews from Kiev. There was a dual aim in the action: the elimination of Jews from the countryside and their subsequent concentration in urban ghettos.[7] By 1829 the squeeze was on. Tighter

5. Called 'chappers', i.e. catchers.
6. This evidenced an early class struggle within the Pale assuming sharply defined antagonisms, and the legend of popular hatred against the Kahal is reflected in a contemporary folk song (cited in the English translation of Isaac Levitats, *The Jewish Community in Russia 1772-1844*, New York, 1943, p.65).

Tots from school they tear away
And dress them up in soldiers' grey.
And our leaders and our Rabbis
Do naught but deepen the abyss.
Rich Mr Rockover has seven sons,
Not even one a uniform dons;
But poor widow Leah has an only child,
And they hunt him down as if he were wild.
It is right to draft the hardworking masses
Shoemakers or tailors — they're only asses!
But the children of the idle rich
Must carry on without a hitch.

7. Catherine the Great was more tolerant. With the accession of White Russia in 1769 she also gained hundreds of Jewish concerns in the forefront of trade and commerce, which, for the sake of expediency, she left well alone. But her attempts to get the Jews rights enjoyed by other communities were undermined by

measures of enforcement reduced Jewish settlement in specific areas of the Baltic and Black Sea. In Courland all Jews not born there had to go. Those who had not registered within six months in a municipality would be conscripted or, if unfit for military service, despatched to Siberia. For that year, new legislation introduced declared Jews a security risk. It decreed that, since the cities of Nicholayev and Sevastopol were of military and naval importance, continued residence by Jews there was inconvenient and injurious. An expulsion order was issued. Those with considerable real estate were granted two years' stay of execution, others a maximum of one year to settle affairs. The Polish uprising of 1830-1 delayed the exodus from Kiev. It was a case of political and economic expediency. The local military commander feared that the oppressed Jews could constitute a fifth column for the insurgent Poles and it was discerned that prices rose dramatically as the Jews quit a locality. A halt was called for three years, after which the Governor issued a personal plea to the Tsar for further postponement, 'this being found useful also in this respect, that, on account of their temperate and simple habits of life, they are in a position to sell their goods considerably cheaper, whereas in the case of their expulsion many articles and manufactures will rise in price'. Nicholas rejected this but agreed to delay expulsions until February 1835, while a Jewish Committee was set up to codify statutes of oppression, with the sinister rider that 'a reduction of the number of Jews in the monarchy' was the prime objective. Elsewhere, goaded like animals, they were driven across the Pale.

The new code, submitted in 1834, was signed by the Tsar in April 1835. It was agreed by all ministers except that of Finance to transfer all Jews from villages to towns. But the Department of Laws, as part of the Council of State, had

---

the Senate. Under the guise of interpreting her wishes, they imposed restrictive measures by the Senatorial ukases of 1786, 1791, and 1794 — the mainspring of all later oppressive acts. Under these, the Jews were forbidden to inhabit seaports and excluded from corporations into which the Tsarina had previously granted them admission. Residence of Jews was to be limited to White Russia and those areas acquired by the partition of Poland. This was to constitute the Pale of Settlement and Jews were forbidden egress from here except under special circumstances. Thenceforth restrictions grew also in employment and professions.

pointed out the risks in the operation, as in the case of earlier expulsions in White Russia (1823), which 'while it has ruined the Jews, does not in the least seem to have improved the condition of the villagers'. It was finally confirmed that the proposed exclusions would be extremely difficult to execute and 'should be eliminated from the Statute; and . . . stopped even there where it had been decreed but not carried into effect'. The Tsar intervened. He appended the resolution, which would be enforced, in his own hand. 'Where this measure has been started it is inconvenient to repeal it, but it shall be postponed *for the time being*, in the governments in which no steps towards it have as yet been made.' The threat remained imminent. There was to be no respite for the outcast Jew.

Extension of settlement was forbidden and conscription was 'to be left as heretofore' (the Tsar's personal verdict). Protests to the Council of State were ignored and a 'Charter of Disabilities' codified all discriminatory laws hitherto enacted against the Jews.[8] It would remain until the 1860s. In line with official policy, scrutiny of all Hebrew literature was undertaken by government-appointed Christian or proselyte censors. To facilitate the supervision of new publications, all Jewish printing presses were closed except those of Vilna and Kiev, traditional centres of Jewish learning. In 1837 the Tsar instructed that Hebrew books of antiquity were to be 'delivered to the flames on the spot'. To prevent

8. The Charter of Disabilities imposed stringent rules against the Jews. It defined conclusively the Pale of Settlement. Rural settlements in the 50-*verst* zone along the western frontier were closed to newcomers. Furloughs for Jewish residents were limited to six weeks only for execution of legal and business affairs, provided they were in Russian dress, and movement was restricted to interior provinces only. Merchants of first and second guilds were privileged to visit the two capitals, seaports, the fairs of Nizhni Novgorod, Kharkov and other fairs for wholesale buying and selling. Visits for first-guild members were extended to three months. Other discriminatory laws included the following: Jews were forbidden to employ Gentile domestics permanently. The minimum age for marriage was eighteen for men, sixteen for girls. Jewish public documents were to be printed in Russian or the local dialect, but 'under no circumstances in the Hebrew language'. The constitution and use of the Kahals was laid down as a means of importing and executing 'instructions for the authorities'. Synagogues could no longer be built near churches. Russian schools would be open to Jewish children, 'who are not compelled to change their religion', but coercive baptism under the Statute on Conscription was 'to remain in force'.

'dependable' rabbis acting as self-censors and passing books as harmless, all literature was to be transferred for assessment to censorship committees located at Vilna and Kiev. Convoys of wagons packed with confiscated books trundled their way ceaselessly towards the two centres. A formidable attack on the bastions of Jewish culture had been mounted. It failed. On the contrary, the result was a consolidation of Jewish identity by way of rigid adherence to orthodoxy. To sustain themselves against the social and political vicissitudes from which there was no respite, the Jews turned inwards to the illusions of warmth and security within their *stetls*: to the authoritative dispensations of their rabbis, the poignancy of the *stiebel* prayers and the soul music of their *chazanim*.[9] A hardening of the ranks under religious discipline was the countervailing force against the autocracy.

By 1840 government failure spoke for itself. Entries in the military files of the imperial records deplore 'privates from among the Jews remaining in the same faith' and in civilian matters 'apostasy is a very rare phenomenon'. With conversion in mind, the Council of State debated the Jewish question by invoking new methods which could practically effect 'a radical transformation of this people', namely assimilation. The stick and the carrot would be applied. Secular schools for Jewish youth would be set up to compete against obscurantist *melammeds* and *cheders*[10] — inbuilt forces resisting Russian 'enlightenment'. The rabbinate was to be re-structured and Jewish dress prohibited. An end to Jewish autonomy would accrue from the dissolution of Kahals and changes in the system of taxation. The Minister of Public Instruction, Sergius Uvarov, was the first to recommend more refined methods of enlightenment. He drew attention to the attitudes of Western governments, who no longer persecuted, with the suggestion that 'this period has also arrived for us'. Stern measures had failed. 'Nations are not exterminated, least of all the nation which stood at the foot of Calvary.' A more humane approach would facilitate 'a purification of [the Jews'] religious conceptions'. Once the

9. Cantors.

10. *Melammeds* were untrained teachers of religion. *Cheders* were children's religion schools usually attached to the local synagogue.

armour of religious orthodoxy was pierced, assimilation would inevitably break through.

To soften up the Jews to accept the reform dictum, the Committee sent an 'official' rabbi — a German, Dr Max Lilienthal, director of one of the three most modern Jewish schools in Russia. He was the ideal candidate to act as a government public relations man. When ordered to St Petersburg (February 1841) to be given details of his assignment, Lilienthal agreed with the abolition of *cheders* but added that the re-education policy would be far more acceptable if the Tsar would remove all discriminatory laws against Jews. Uvarov declared that they must first 'try to deserve favour of the sovereign' — an inconceivable assumption. The Rabbi's task was doomed from the beginning. He was to tour the Pale, and organise the few *maskilim*,[11] who would assist him in spreading the gospel of school reform amongst the orthodox-ridden *stetls*. But a government which seized Jewish children for its army, that destroyed them physically and mentally, could expect the inevitable response. At Vilna, Lilienthal was confronted with open animosity and distrust. The elders got the message: 'The Government intends to have but one Church in the whole Empire . . . We are sorry to state that we put no confidence in the new measures proposed by the ministerial council, and that we look with gloomy forebodings on the future.'[12] At Minsk he was widely abused and sent packing. Reporting back to Uvarov, Lilienthal explained the difficulties he had encountered. A second tour of the south-western provinces provided some grounds for optimism. He was accorded a friendlier reception in Berdychev, Odessa and Kishinev, where he appeared to have won more confidence amongst the Jewish communities. He returned to St Petersburg to partake in the Rabbinical Commission, a body instituted by a ukase of 22 June, 1842, to help implement government policy by

11. *Maskilim*: these were Jewish intellectuals who embraced the rational precepts of the French Enlightenment and eschewed religious obscurantism. They urged that Europeanisation and local Russification of Jewish culture were the prerequisites for emancipation.

12. David Philipson, *Max Lilienthal, American Rabbi: Life and Writings*, p.264.

putting the face of respectability on the forthcoming 'reforms'.

The outcome was a compromise. The *cheders* were to be retained temporarily while new secular schools would be introduced to compete with them as a viable alternative. In an earlier report on policy (17 March, 1841), Uvarov had declared: 'In directing the instructions in these schools against the influence of the Talmud, it is not necessary openly to proclaim this intention.' The final policy-making ukase of 13 November, 1844 reflected this duplicity. New Jewish schools were to be established in two grades. The junior grades were to house a mixed Jewish and Christian staff under the authority of a Christian superintendent. Mixed school boards would organise and administer reforms and school graduates would be granted a reduction in military service. Teachers' licences would be withheld from *melammeds* who had received no secular education or training; and after twenty years no one could hold the post of teacher or rabbi without having obtained a qualification from one of the official senior grade rabbinical institutes. A confidential rescript confirmed that the real 'aim in training the Jews is that of bringing them nearer the Christian population and eradicating the prejudices fostered on them by the study of the Talmud'. It was anticipated that the benefits afforded to the Jews in the new schools would cause gradual closure of the *cheders*. With that event, compulsory attendance could be implemented. The elders of Vilna and Minsk had been far more perceptive than the gullible Lilienthal. He finally realised that he had been used for the very purpose of which the old men had warned him, namely that the Tsarist way to Jewish 'liberation' was 'by [their] bowing down before the Greek cross'. He quit Russia abruptly for the USA and never returned.

The proposed educational reforms proved difficult to impose in practice. There were, by definition, not enough qualified Jewish teachers. The system was obstructed by the *melammeds*. Few attempted to learn Russian, and many of those who did, passed the test by bribing the examiners. The Christian superintendents appointed were more concerned with their pockets than with syllabuses. The call of the rouble encouraged them to play a dual role. They received official pay from the ministry to disseminate Russian culture, and unofficial pay from the local Jewish community to do the reverse. Since there was little danger of inspection and a more lucrative income to be derived from the latter, curriculum reform was, not surprisingly, slow to take on. By 1857 a mere 3,293 Jewish pupils were registered in Crown schools; in 1864 the total was 5,711 with an additional 1,561 enrolled in Russian institutions. But Jewish demand for higher education promoted the opening of the two rabbinical seminaries of Vilna and Zhitomir in 1847. At first they were badly financed and ill-supported. But in the freer climate of the 'reforming' Tsar Alexander II they provided the training-ground for social revolutionaries.

The subtleties of the autocracy's educational policies proved illusory. On the one hand the government curtailed peasant education beyond the primary level so that they would remain unthinking hewers of wood, while opportunities were extended for Jews in order to Christianise them. The more immediate failure to de-culturise the Jews called for more repressive measures. Laws to annihilate the last vestiges of communal autonomy were published on 19 December, 1844. The Kahals were abolished. Their administrative duties were transferred to the police, while their economic and financial responsibilities were turned over to town councils and municipalities. Superficially this put the Jews on a par with the rest of the community, but separate treatment was maintained in the areas of taxation and conscription. 'Conscription trustees' and tax collectors were to be elected by Jewish communes 'from among the most dependable men'. In turn these were scrutinised by a special department for Jewish affairs set up in every locality. A basket tax (*korobochny sbor*) was imposed in which proceeds from kosher meat were farmed out to the highest bidder under gubernatorial control. Income from this source would be applied to cover payments of Jews in arrears, the maintenance of Crown schools, official promotion of agriculture among Jews, and any surplus was to be diverted to local charities. A candle tax, a toll on Sabbath candles, was re-instituted, ostensibly to help finance Crown schools. These new impositions were the scourge of Jewish economic and communal existence. A more terrible blow had already fallen. On 20 April, 1843, a ukase in the Tsar's own hand decreed the expulsion of all Jews from the hamlets and villages within the fifty-*verst* zone along the Austrian-Prussian borders. It roused a universal cry of horror including movements of condemnation and protest in France, Germany and England. They were ignored. The order was stayed only because the financial disruption resulting from its execution would have meant vast losses to the exchequer. The homes and means of livelihood of hundreds of thousands of Jews living on the borders of the Pale were henceforth in jeopardy. It only needed a stroke of the pen.

There was no let-up from Tsarist persecution. Perhaps the most sinister crime perpetrated against the Jews was the recurrent accusation of child murder. This was derived from medieval superstition that Christian blood was required as part of the Passover ritual. Tsarist sympathy, if not collusion, with these trumped-up charges is reflected in the two trials, which significantly began and ended the reign of Nicholas I. The first was the Velizh case, which emerged on Passover day 1823 with the discovery of the corpse of a Russian boy stabbed to death in a swamp. At a judicial enquiry the evidence of a prostitute and an imbecile was accepted as valid, and as a result two prominent Jews were accused of ritual murder. The Supreme Court of Vitebsk quashed the case, but in 1825 Alexander I instructed that it be re-opened, and subsequently forty-two Jews were jailed and tortured. The next year his successor extended the punishment by ordering the closure of all Jewish synagogues in Velizh. But a spate of false rumours on additional murders roused suspicion in an anti-Semitic Tsar, and he demanded careful police investigation, which continued for seven years whilst the accused rotted in gaol. In 1834 the Council of State decreed that the charge was a tissue of lies. They demanded the release of the prisoners with an award for unjust imprisonment and that the perjured informers be exiled to Siberia. This was endorsed in a ukase of 17 January, 1835, issued by a reluctant monarch, who appended his own prejudiced comment: 'I do not have and indeed cannot have the inner conviction that the murder has *not* been committed by Jews. Numerous examples of similar murders ... go to show that among the Jews there probably exist fanatics or sectarians who consider Christian blood necessary for their rites.'

His presumptions had ominous repercussions. A perennial threat of the recurrence of the accusation made Passover, for the Jews, a time of fearful anticipation. After some minor abortive attempts, a second charge – the ritual murder trial of Saratov – revived old nightmares. In 1853 the bodies of two Russian boys, who had disappeared three months before from Saratov, were recovered from the Volga. Their bodies bore traces of crude attempts at circumcision. Although the city was outside the Pale, it harboured about forty Jewish soldiers and a handful of Jewish tradesmen and artisans, who had settled, with police connivance, in a prohibited area. It was a ready-made opportunity for an anti-Semitic 'happening'. There was no shortage of crooks and Jew-haters, who could invoke the popular myth to cover up their own tracks or indulge in some real Jew-baiting. It came by way of a soldier, Bodganov, charged with vagrancy, and a drunken official, Krueger. They volunteered evidence that they had observed the murder carried out by Jews who had subsequently squeezed blood from the corpses. They named the leaders as one Shlieferman, a local soldier *mohel* (circumciser), and an orthodox Jewish farrier, Yushkevicher. The accused were promptly thrown into gaol and, in spite of torture, persisted in declaring their innocence. As before, the case began to mushroom, involving more and more people and gaining widespread notoriety, such that by July 1854 the Tsar himself, always on the alert for 'investigating the dogmas of the religious fanaticism of the Jews', set up a Judicial Commission to assess evidence and pass final judgment on the feasibility of ritual murder. He died before the findings were published. These significantly recorded that, as there was no positive evidence to associate the accused with that crime, they were to be freed but left under strong suspicion. The bureaucrats at the Council of State would not have it. The verdict was reversed and the Jews sentenced to penal servitude. And the new, 'reforming' Tsar confirmed it.

Social ostracism coupled with political oppression ensured a steady deterioration in the economic life of the Jewish masses. Only a minority of Jews — the *haute bourgeoisie* — maintained themselves against the general attack on their co-religionists. Such were the Poliakovs (railway builders and bankers), Herman Epstein (Polish banker), the Gunzburgs (bankers) and Brodskis (sugar producers and exporters). The liberal responses of Alexander II were grossly exaggerated by his contemporaries. His views on Jewish 'moral turpitude' were well known to the wealthy and professional parvenus, who were out to extract special privileges for their own class. Although they consistently defended their religious identity against government onslaughts, they made a sham of that unitary conception of a Jewish folk. They were prepared to employ the legend of Nicholas I's arbitary division of Jews into the useful and useless, for their own advantage. Both the autocrat and Gunzburg were at one in their definition of the useless: they were the poor and dispossessed of the Pale. In 1856 Baron Erzel Gunzburg pleaded for those Jews 'who for many years developed the life, activities and resources of the country' against 'the other classes of Jewry, who have not as yet given any evidence of their good intentions, usefulness and industry'. This peculiar sycophant went on to beg 'the gracious monarch to distinguish the wheat from the chaff, and, as an encouragement to good and praiseworthy activity, to bestow a number of modest privileges upon the deserving and educated'. Amongst other pleas, this time from the intelligentsia, was that by thirty-four medical students requesting civil enfranchisement in order to serve in the army: 'Having discarded the errors of our co-religionists and finding the company of our Christian colleagues and learned teachers so congenial, we find it painful to be reminded at the outset of our career of our unfortunate origin.'

Alexander II, after some vacillation, agreed to the policy of easing restrictions on the minority elect — that useful section constituting the merchants of the first guild, university graduates and incorporated artisans. He acquiesced according to the proposition that hidebound oppression could only lead to the disruption of his empire. Right of residence outside the Pale was granted to top merchants, qualified doctors and graduates (1861). The latter were also allowed to serve in government departments. Later (1879), this was extended to those qualified in other higher educational institutions, medical aides and midwives. A few crumbs were tossed to the lesser fry — a gesture dictated by practical or immediate necessity, for instance a limited exit for sutlers from the Pale during the Crimean War, and one Jewish tailor or cutter attached to each regiment or academy located outside; but not many. The Tsar refused permission for those tough 'Nicolai' soldiers who had served their time to settle where they wished (1858), and underlined the Jewish Committee's rejection of the Minister of the Interior Lanskoi's proposal to abolish the Pale with the curt note 'entirely correct' (1861). He discarded a memorandum compiled by Governor-General Nazimov ascribing the miserable conditions of Jews in his province (Vilno) to the disproportionate number forced to engage in petty trading. It was this abnormal competition which limited the possibilities for making an honest living. According to this perceptive official the 'ignorance and low moral level of Jews' was derived from legal disabilities which deprived them of choice of locality and occupation. The message was clear. Lift those restrictions and the Jews would become more conducive to moral education and civil usefulness. The outcome of the Polish insurrection (1863) was to turn the wheel full circle back to anti-emancipatory legislation. By 1870, so-called municipal reforms included limitations on Jews to a maximum of one-third the number of representatives, adding that no Jew could be elected mayor, notwithstanding a predominance of Jews in the town concerned. The rising barometer of anti-Jewish sentiment registered dramatically with the pogrom[13] which broke out in Odessa on Palm Sunday 1871. It was a warning of things to come. This time an organised mob, with the active or tacit approval of the authorities, had been let loose on the Jewish quarter. For three days a horde of Greeks and Russians, undisturbed by police or troops, roamed the city burning, looting and beating up Jews. On the fourth day the troops intervened to prevent a massacre and

---

13. Pogrom: an organised massacre for the annihilation of any body or class.

soon pacified the mob by the novel method of seizing and whipping rioters on the spot. It was confirmed that the outburst lacked political motivation (the events coincided with the news of the Paris Commune) so the message was not lost on the government. They could turn the pogroms to their own political advantage. In a climate of growing political opposition, the pent-up hatred and frustration of the peasantry could be diverted to a ready-made scapegoat — the Jew. From 1881 this inbuilt safety-valve for the autocracy would be resorted to with success. For many of the victims it provided that final spur, which drove them to join the great exodus from the land of torment.

In the crowded ghettos pauperisation and its concomitant hazards were widespread by the 1860s. Over-concentration meant cut-throat competition for existence. Tailoring, the traditionally over-subscribed occupation, was wide open to underbidding for custom. For although Jewish artisan guilds would try to apportion jobs to each of their members, there was no monopolistic control. Any non-guild member could, and did, compete on equal terms. The sharp-witted made out, the rest barely survived. After 1861 conditions worsened with the influx of 'liberated' peasants, poor and unskilled, pouring into the urban centres of the Pale. In the rural areas Jewish services were being dispensed with by both landlord and peasant. A 'free' peasantry meant reduced demand for land and sales managers. Rural credit institutions were set up to grant financial aid to those enterprising landlords who began to manage their estates personally. Also more peasants were now at liberty to engage in selling their own products and were, therefore, becoming more frugal and business-minded. This, in turn, further diminished the need for Jews as middlemen, who were forced to join the vast armies of unemployed mobilising in the towns and *stetls.* Aggravating the problem was the incidence of Jewish entrepreneurs preferring to employ Gentiles;[14] and expanding factoris-

14. With the arguments that: (a) one could keep one's distance with Gentile employees, but not with those who attended your own synagogue; (b) Jewish workers were noted as labour organisers and agitators; (c) Jews were not prepared to work on the Sabbath which could mean vacant capacity and uneconomic use of plant.

ation, which was eroding small concerns, ensuring, in the long term, the elimination of independent artisans. There was temporary alleviation after 1865, when selected Jewish technicians were allowed into the Russian interior, as part of the drive towards industrialisation. But here again, bureaucratic harassment was rife. They were periodically subjected to a trade examination, which, as an English observer noted, was so constructed that 'even the cleverest artisans have no hope of passing'. A major deterrent for the family worker was that security of tenure was not passed on to his widow and children. Should he die, they would be forced to return to the Pale. It appeared that the only right to residence was limited to Jewish prostitutes, who had to carry a yellow card. This was often employed by widows or others wishing to visit relatives or live in a forbidden area. There is the traditional story of a poor girl eager to become a secretary, who procured a yellow card to settle outside her *stetl*. The police caught up with her ensconced in a respectable occupation and she was summarily expelled for not plying her 'legal' trade. The Alexandrine 'reforms' brought about retrogression in traditional occupations and incomes, which was not relieved by the transference of small numbers into new occupations.

In 1849[15] B. Miliutin estimated that only three per cent of the Jews had any capital, while the rest were living on the margin of subsistence. The situation had been aggravated by Nicholas I's imposition of high tariffs on incoming goods to protect and boost home industries. It hit the border folk, especially the Jews. For as the tariff bit, it quickly curtailed entrepreneurial activity among those Jews engaged in import and export. Thousands faced ruin. It was natural for them to join the ranks of smugglers who were engaged in Austrian and Prussian contraband, which sold cheaper than the home product. In turn it roused the energies of the police and higher authority to plug the leaks in revenue. The ukase of 1843 willing the expulsion of Jews from the western frontier was the Tsar's private remedy. Evidence of the Jews as a

---

15. B. Miliutin, *Ustroistvo i sostoianie everiskitkh obshestv v Russii* (Structure and Status of the Jewish Communities in Russia), St Petersburg, 1849, pp.225 ff.

nation of paupers is derived from governmental and academic sources; but here one must treat those registered as 'merchants' with reserve. Of these the majority were unregistered peddlers, agents, tally-men and the like, *luft-menschen* who scraped a bare existence from casual trading. A picture of the male-less *stetl* before the Sabbath is given by a contemporary:[16]

> The hamlet looks dead during the whole week; it has the semblance of a gynocracy, that is a kingdom inhabited only by women. Men spend the week until Friday in the country, they wander from village to village and court with all sorts of notions, which they exchange there against flax, linseed, rabbit and calf skins, pig bristles and feathers. They sell that to . . . the rich man of the community. In the hamlet itself remain only women, children, communal officials, students of the academy and a few unemployed (*batlanim*).

There is ample quantitative evidence of the economic deterioration of the Jewish masses. Official government statistics of 1844-7 reveal that the death rate amongst Jews was twice that of non-Jews. Overcrowding, disease and want were the norms. The trade cycles made their bow in the years 1858-68 and 1873-6. The Jews were the more vulnerable, and consequently the easiest victims in times of dearth. Non-Jewish researchers provide the testimony. The 1857 survey of the Provincial Branch of Finance in Minsk (which assessed Jewish occupations percentage-wise as 2.3 merchants, 4.3 agricultural peasants, 48.4 burghers with definite trades etc., and 22.4 no fixed occupation) is challenged by the contemporary scholar Zelensky. His criticism is that no account was taken of the *luftmenschen*, who registered themselves as occupied for fear of being conscripted, and contends that 50 to 70 per cent were in this category because of lack of job opportunities. That a disproportionally large body of Jews were engaged in commercial and industrial concerns was a myth. In a later official enquiry (1864) the number of Jewish entrepreneurs was well below the proportion of Jews per population in western Russia. For instance, in Vilna, Jews constituted 8/13ths of the urban population but owned only 1/4 of the shops and industrial plants; in Mogliev they were

16. Isaac Meier Dick, *Feigele der Maggid*, Vilna, 1860.

6/7ths owning 1/6th, and in Vitebsk they constituted 1/3rd but owned only 1/4 of the shops etc. Even under the more favourable conditions of the south-western provinces, the Jews were under-represented. For example in Kiev, where the Jews constituted 4/5th of the city population, the proportion of Jewish factory owners was approximately 1/6th, and many of the so-called factories included small one-man concerns. At this juncture statistical evidence suggests that the bulk of Jewish enterprises were those which required little capital, simple machines and few employees, in other words artisan workshops.

Most of the Jews were forced to live in a permanent state of congestion and squalor. Again the averages of large-scale concentration could be underestimated, since many failed to register themselves or new births so as to avoid taxation and military service. The plight of the Jews of Grodno exemplifies the issue. Between 1855 and 1857 even the government was obliged to cancel taxes for the province as the Jews were unable to meet their commitments. In 1860 the Jews of Minsk, who constituted 1/12th of the provincial population, could not meet their tax arrears through two causes. First, the heaviest burden of taxation (one-quarter of the total) fell on their community. Secondly more than half of the Jews themselves were existing on charity. Problems of overcrowding were such that by the 1880s Jewish habitations were reported by a government housing committee to be usually 'dangerous for occupation'. Earlier, in Grodno, the statistician P. Bobrovsky noted:[17]

Death was more successful in the crowded dirty hovels inhabited by Jews who comprise one-eighth of the population of the state. Look into one of these hovels, which is about to collapse and bury as many as fifteen male and fifteen female souls, and you will be struck by the filth and stench. The swarm of half naked children can hardly find room in this dark hut, three quarters of which is taken up by the stove, bed and table . . . Tuberculosis, asthma, nervous fever, nose bleeds and haemorrhoids find not a few victims among these Jews.

Others confirm this as typical. An observer reports on a

17. P. Bobrovsky, *Grodnenskaia Gubernia*, St Petersburg, 1863.

household in north-west Russia, noting: 'families crowd into a rickety hovel. Half naked . . . hungry children huddled on an unheated oven . . . The riotous joy of children when the father comes home with a loaf of bread in his hands . . .'[18] We read elsewhere of Grodno province where 'a three or four roomed hovel sometimes accommodates up to a dozen families . . . a pound of bread, a brown herring and a few onions constituting the daily food for one family . . . and the average earnings 15 kopeks a day.' Widespread congestion is commented on quantitatively by Prince Demidoff San-Donato, who in his report on the provinces of the Pale estimates an average of 1584 persons per square mile, compared with the excluded provinces, where the figures range from the 1,154 at the highest to 10 per square mile at the lowest.[19] In the government of Kiev, the mean number of Christian inhabitants in one house over forty years was 410 to 510, while for Jews it was 1,129, and at Berdychev it rose as high as 2,287![20] Poverty, with its accompanying overcrowding and ill-health, was endemic.[21] By 1870 an estimated forty per cent of the Jewish people consisted of *luftmenschen* who lived from day to day, dependent on occasional labour from their relatives and members of the community or on peddling and 'fiddling' outside. By 1894 the increase in pauperism reached a peak when 85,183 Jewish families were registered as such with charitable institutions.

Extreme want is often accompanied by a prolific birth rate. Over the six decades (1820 to 1880) the Jewish population in Russia and Poland rose by approximately 1,600,000 to 4,000,000, that is by 150 per cent compared with 87 per cent by the non-Jewish majority.[22] Although

18. Levanda, *Razsvet*, 1860, no.1., p.8.
19. Prince Demidoff San-Donato, *The Jewish Question in Russia*, London, 1884.
20. Souravski, *Description du Gouvernement de Kiev*, vol.7, p.247.
21. In 1875 the War Department reported twice the number of physically unfit Jews as that of non-Jews. That year two-and-a-half times as many Jews compared with Gentiles were declared unfit for military service.
22. Official population figures record Jews as follows. They are approximate figures:

1820	1,600,000
1851	2,400,000
1880	4,000,000

there was a higher death rate, religious exhortation to procreate, early marriages and absence of contraceptives ensured a higher birth rate. A more sophisticated cultural level, and communal concern for the individual which emphasised strictest care for the young, minimised infant mortality. Certainly losses occurred and were sustained through two wars (the Crimean and Russo-Turkish), epidemics (especially the cholera outbreaks of 1848 and 1869) and famines (1820, 1821, 1833, 1839-40, 1843-6, 1890-1). Many Jews were siphoned off by conversion to Christianity and lost by emigration. But these had only marginal effects on the steady rise in Jewish numbers, which was maintained by urban Jews — the pauperised majority — who, perhaps because of their appalling conditions, found respite in sexual activity and maintained this rise.

It must be reiterated that the social and industrial reforms of the 1860s worsened conditions for most Jews. Industrialisation might advance the development of rail and modern transport techniques. A handful of major Jewish entrepreneurs did profit. The Jewish innkeeper and coachman, however, was edged out of existence. Yet there were a considerable number in high places who saw the folly of confining Jews to specific areas, which bound them to poverty from which there was no escape. They called for the dispersal of Jews on the basis that, where Jews were allowed to settle in limited groups, incomes generally rose and therefore there was a greater potentiality accruing from taxation. So argued Governor-General Vasilchikov of Kiev in a memorandum (1861), in which he supported the extension of rights of residence outside the Pale. Postels, a senior official in the Ministry of Public Education, repeated this in his report.[23] But a reactionary bureaucracy and press would not have it. 'Syn Otechevesta' replied, 'It is evident that if civic equality should be granted to that mass of usurers and hucksters of doubtful honesty, the Jewish tribe will burst *en masse* into the centres of industry and into the untrammelled patriarchal regions enriching themselves at the expense of the gullible Russians.' It was a fair example of the official

23. *Otchot Postelsa po Obozreniiu Evreiskikh Uchilishch*, pp.64-5.

response, although official surveys showed that good sense and profit would result were the government to relax the bonds it imposed on its Jewish citizens. V. Pavlovich, in his study *Ekaterinoslavskaia Guberniia* (p.263),[24] noted that the small towns of New Russia and Ukraine were kept alive by Jewish enterprise. Otherwise they would have been reduced to villages. The Russian economist S. Maksimov asserted that the Jews were bringing a great deal of industrial life into Siberia, therefore 'the Jew is both fit and useful for Siberia'. The financier and author I. Blioch, in his *Comparative Study of the Material and Moral Status of the Western, Great Russian and By-Vistula Provinces* (5 vols), produced a scholarly accumulation of evidence on the economic and legal enactments against Jews and their subsequent changes in status over a century. He pointed out that wherever Jews settled, the economic effects on the indigenous people were profound. The Russian peasants increased in numbers. There was four times the increase in livestock in Jewish areas (1856-85) and fifty per cent less debt incurred as compared with that in non-Jewish provinces. In 1877 (during the Russo-Turkish War) there was two and a half times more reserve food supplies in Jewish provinces than elsewhere. So even when the Jews were at minimum capacity to fulfil themselves, they still acted as a catalyst for a higher elasticity of prosperity for others. Other accusations were refuted. The anti-Semitic press condemned Jews for thriving on the liquor trade (which was one of the 'fixed' occupations for Jews anyway) and therefore being responsible for drunkenness and early death amongst the Russian peasants. But statistics and other official data prove the reverse, that is less drunkenness and higher longevity! In 1844 Jews were expelled from the villages on the part excuse that the peasants were demoralised and exploited by Jewish liquor salesmen, innkeepers and the like. But a follow-up study by I. Funduklei[25] in 1852 reported that both the price and consumption of liquor went up after the Jews left. The landlords, who replaced them, recorded double the profits of their predecessors. An equally

24. St Petersburg, 1862.
25. *Statisticheskoi Opisanie Kievskoi Gubernia* (3 vols), St Petersburg, 1852.

potent argument for emancipation was the manifest Jewish gift for cultural enrichment. In spite of the extremely limited educational and occupational areas in which Jews could operate, their contribution to Russian art, music and literature was well out of proportion to their numbers. It is true that many of the Jews who made it were proselytes or those *maskilim* who identified themselves as Russians first. The convert Daniel Khvolson (1819-1911) added scholarly grace to Russian theological commentary. Although a fallen Jew, he persisted in defending his people and the Talmud against the scurrilous attacks of the anti-Semites during the ritual murder trials at Saratov (1857) and Cutais (1877). It was disclosed at his death (from a letter bearing his instructions that it was not to be opened till his demise) that the great poet Fet was born illegitimate of Jewish parentage. Another famous proselyte, Anton Rubenstein (1829-94), the founding father of musical education in Russia, received the title of *Excellenz* by Alexander III. He wrote to his mother, 'I have a presentiment that I shall need this *Excellenz* some day against the very powers that gave it to me. For all your baptism at Berdychev, we are Jews, you and I, and sister Sophie.' His aversion to Wagner, and his emotional reaction to Wagner's anti-Semitic pamphlet *Judaism in Music* compelled Rubenstein to concentrate on Judaic themes. The outstanding sculptor of his age, Mark Antokolovsky (1842-1902), derived his early creations from his Jewish milieu, for instance the 'Jewish Tailor' earned him a silver medal. But he remained the poor boy from the Vilna ghetto, always concerned with his Jewish roots. He would never convert and was deeply committed to the welfare of his co-religionists, especially the young, aspiring artist. But, in the main, for the unconverted there was little possibility of fulfilment. How many men or women were there, whose talents remained unrealised because of their refusal to renounce either their people or their creed?

Why did the Jews fail to achieve emancipation by 1881? The lifting of the Pale would have been the first logical step, but this had been halted by the solid rock of Tsarist bigotry. No Tsar or bureaucrat would move one step without the promise of mass proselytisation. Many of the so-called reforms affecting Jews were open or subtle attempts at conversion. The Alexandrine liberalisation was, for them, a temporary loosening of bonds, owing more to pragmatic necessity than enlightenment. Anyway, for the autocracy the persistence of Jews as an 'alien' body was a safeguard. They provided a ready-made scapegoat — a built-in focus for peasant discontent should political or economic circumstance require it.

In one sense, this ensured the failure of the *maskilim*. To them the Liberal Enlightenment and Russification would provide keys to the closed door. In following this ploy, they could not avoid being tainted with opportunism and sycophancy by their implicit acceptance of the Tsarist maxim that the Jews must earn those basic freedoms enjoyed as a birthright by non-Jews. On the other hand they were the pioneers of opening up the ghettos to secular learning, thus importing a broader intellectual experience as a challenge to the claustrophobic obscurantism of the rabbis. They stimulated the return to the land and sponsored agricultural colonies. This, together with their enthusiasm for Hebrew, against Yiddish, as the mother tongue, gave an impetus to that movement which envisioned ultimate freedom for the Jew in the return to Zion — the ancient homeland — in the foreseeable future, the Messiah notwithstanding.

From the *maskilim*, too, emerged a smaller minority of intellectuals who embraced social revolution as the only liberating force. To them the panacea for all freedoms, for Jew and non-Jew alike, was joint revolutionary activism with their Russian comrades. They 'went to the people' in the seventies and eighties as martyrs and were duly broken by peasant superstition and hatred as well as by the Judophobia of their own Russian Socialist 'brothers'. They were indeed the alienated ones. Yet, paradoxically, it was they who produced the legendary hero of Narodnaya Volya and the first protagonist of Jewish Socialism, as we shall see.

The hardening of religious orthodoxy proved both a boon and a disaster. It was the binding force which acted as solid armour against continual assault. In the ghettos the old faith meant hope, a spiritual euphoria which daily helped overcome a never-ending round of mental and physical suffering.

On the other hand it strengthened Tsarist hatred and suspicion, which brought on further oppressive measures. So neither the Haskallah nor Orthodox resistance could ensure the millennium. A radical change in heart and will, not only by the government, but of the majority of Russians, was an unlikely proposition. The transitory illusions of reform from above were brought home dramatically with the accession of the new Tsar Alexander III. For the imaginative and the adept as well as the desperate and outraged, enough was enough. Then the great diaspora began.

On 1 March, 1881 Alexander II was struck down by the terrorist group Narodnaya Volya. One young Jewish seamstress was involved — Jessie Helfmann. She was 'the letter carrier, messenger, and sentinel' of the St Petersburg group.[26]

The *Jewish Chronicle* of 6 May, 1881 issued news of the first pogrom, which broke out at Elizavetgrad on 27 April. It also included the report of the correspondent of the *Daily Telegraph*, who was already confirming that 'agitation against the Jews in Southern Russia has assumed proportions of which Western Europe is not yet aware'. He blamed the revolutionists, whom he accused of attacking the Jews as part of their political tactics. He continued:

> They are held up to popular reprobation as the assassins of the late Czar, and Jessie Helfmann, the Jewess, who was implicated, as having been the soul of the whole plot. The Czar's assassination happening on a day that is kept up festively by Jews in Russia, they were charged with having made merry in anticipation of what was going to happen. The object of the revolutionists is to create a popular rising, in which the troops would be called upon to defend the Jews against the Christians. They anticipate that either the troops would, under such circumstance, refuse duty, or that the people would be so infuriated that a general rising would ensue. The officers themselves apprehend the former contingency; but in either case the opportunity would be favourable for the revolutionists and they would know how to turn it to account.

There might be some truth in this, but the emphasis was in the wrong place. A more potent brew was being prepared in

26. See Stepniak (pseudonym of S. Kravchinskii), *Underground Russia*, London, 1890, pp.111-15, for a profile of Jessie Helfmann.

high places. More sinister was the revelation of the Vienna correspondent who, remarking on the scarcity of news from that part of Russia, explained it 'by the fact that the telegraph official will not accept messages in any foreign language, whilst those written in Russian are revised by the censor prior to transmission'. Immediately after the assassination mysterious emissaries from St Petersburg appeared at police headquarters in the large cities of southern Russia including Elizavetgrad, Kiev and Odessa. Their assignments were concerned with a common presumption — the anticipated 'outburst of popular indignation against the Jews'. Simultaneously, there appeared an unusual number of *katzaps*[27] at southern railway stations, attracting crowds of peasants to them with their talk of the forthcoming attack on the Jews to be confirmed by an imperial ukase exhorting all Christians to punish the Jews at Eastertide. It was too much of a coincidence. The same month (March), 'the Sacred League' had been founded, a reactionary secret organisation ostensibly set up to defend the Tsar, among whose members were the current anti-Semitic minister Ignatiev, and the future Torquemada of the Holy Synod, Pobyedonostzev![28]

The pogrom thus provided its own outriders. Outbreaks of violence occurred simultaneously all over southern Russia, the destructive urges receding only in early May. They followed a prescribed pattern. Agitators of the Greater Russian 'barefoot brigade' moved in, roused the local mobs into a frenzy, then disappeared without trace. Jewish liquor stores, pin-pointed for looting, were first attacked and sacked. The drunken rioters then went on to burn, loot and rape at will in the Jewish quarter, encouraged by what appeared to be the deliberate inactivity of troops or *gendarmerie*. Only on the third day did the combined police and military take forceful action, which quickly restored public order. The new barbarism struck with the virulence of a plague. From April to May, over fifty villages and hamlets

27. Great Russian artisans and labourers.
28. Pobyedonostzev, once questioned about Jewry's future under constant persecution, retorted hopefully: 'One-third will die out, one-third will leave the country, and one-third will be completely dissolved in the surrounding population.' He, personally, may have been inclined to have gone to the limit with a warrant for genocide.

in the governments of Kiev and adjacent Volhynia and Podolia succumbed to the epidemic. Only once did the Jews, in armed self-defence, abort an attack. At Berdychev station invading rioters, met by an advancing cordon of Jews carrying clubs, turned tail and fled. This was only possible due to a sympathetic (and well-compensated) police chief. The culminating point of the holocaust was the Odessa pogrom (3 to 5 May) when an immense mob invaded the ghetto containing 100,000 Jews. A massacre was averted by the timely intervention of the police, who quickly arrested both attackers and defenders. It would appear that it was just as illegal for the Jew to carry clubs for defence as it was for his attacker who used firearms.

Any lull in persecution proved short-lived. Anti-Semitic action, on the contrary, received top sanction by the bureaucracy. 'The street pogroms were followed by administrative pogroms *sui generis*.' Battalions of police, given *carte blanche* by their authorities, moved in to oust all Jews 'illegally' resident in the cities and overnight expulsions of 'criminals' took place, by thousands, with all the attendant horrors. In the law courts, instigators of pogroms received light sentences, with their victims, who had had the audacity to take up arms to defend themselves. The new Minister of the Interior, Nicholas Ignatiev, set the pace. The early official explanation that the riots were Nihilist-inspired was soon replaced by the theory of Jewish 'exploitation', which not only justified pogroms but also the new repressive measures being prepared against the Jews. The *reductio ad absurdum* in arbitrary rule was reached when the Minister of the Interior could secretly demand the sum of one million roubles to except St Petersburg from the forthcoming expulsion of Jews. He was refused. On 15 May, 1882, the May Laws were instituted. On the surface they appeared relatively mild. All Jews within the fifteen provinces of the Pale had to live within certain prescribed towns. Mortgages or leases on landed estates were suspended and Jews ceased to have powers of attorney for managing estates. Finally Jews were forbidden to carry out business on Sundays and principal Christian holidays, that is on those very days that the *luftmensch* could make that extra rouble which enabled him to maintain himself on the margin of subsistence. The overt support of the all-Highest himself was ominous. The new prescriptions were issued under the Tsar's own signature. And this after a year of the most fearful pogroms ever suffered by a people now goaded beyond the peak of endurance. The Imperial seal was irrevocably stamped on ministerial Jew-baiting legislature. It was the shape of things to come. Expectations of a savage orgy of official violence meant little hope for the Jew in the Russian Empire.

Between April 1881 and June 1882, 225,000 Jewish families fled from Russia.[29] It was the first mass exodus from the land of bondage. The majority set their sights on 'the *goldene medina*', the United States, but a substantial minority sought immediate refuge in the nearer land of promise. And so the *stetl* came to East London.

---

29. See *History of the Year October 1881 — October 1882*, London, 1882.

2. A Stetl *Called Whitechapel*: the Social Milieu

Formerly in Whitechapel, Commercial Street roughly divided the Jewish haunts of Petticoat Lane and Goulston Street from the rougher English quarter lying in the East. Now the Jews have flowed across this line; Hanbury Street, Fashion Street, Pelham Street, Booth Street, Old Montague Street, and many other streets and lanes and alleys have fallen before them; they fill whole blocks of model dwellings; they have introduced new trades as well as new habits; and they live and crowd together, and work and meet their fate almost independent of the great stream of London life surging around them.

> Charles Booth (ed.), *Life and Labour of the People of London*, 1889.

The Jews of Poland are the smeariest of all races.

> Karl Marx, in *Neue Rheinische Zeitung*, 29 April, 1849.

... there exists yet another class of workers, who are still more oppressed, exploited and ill-treated than all the others; this pariah is the Jewish proletariat in Russia.

> Karl Kautsky, 1901.

By the 1870s the Russo-Polish Jew was no stranger in East London. The influx of Dutch Jews was already receding by the mid-1860s. Hollingshead, in *Ragged London*, 1861, had taken note of the side alleys on both sides of the broad road from Aldgate church to Old Whitechapel church, where 'you may pass on either side about twenty narrow avenues, leading to thousands of closely packed nests full to overflowing with dirt, misery and rags'. Among these Thornbury located Tewkesbury Buildings as a colony of Dutch Jews, generally declaring 'the residents of the environs ... thieves, coster-mongers, stallkeepers, professional beggars, rag dealers, brokers, and small tradesmen'. But he noted well that 'the Jewish poor are independent and self-supporting and keep up the ceremonies of their nation under the most adverse circumstances'.[1] Even then, Old Jewry was being infiltrated by the new immigrant from the east.

The realities of life under the 'liberating' monarch Alexander II had already provided the spur for movement. Periodic sharp pulses of immigration followed. Defeat in the Crimean War and its aftermath of economic depression caused the exit of hundreds of Jewish artisans. Many of the Jews, who had taken up arms with the Poles in the uprising of 1863 and had eluded capture by the Russians, fled to London. The epidemic of cholera in the Pale (1867) and famine in Lithuania (1866-9) brought refugees streaming westward across Europe. Committees were set up in London, and the enlightened Reverend Albert Löwy, Secretary of the Anglo-Jewish Association, was sent on a fact-finding mission as combined representative for the Alliance Israélite Universelle and his own organisation, and returned with horrifying accounts. The net result was an additional inflow of Jews from that region. In the south the great pogrom of Odessa (1871), and the threat of compulsory service preceding the Russo-Turkish War, brought further numbers. The last was accompanied by a small élitist group of politicised intellectuals fleeing from the Tsarist police, who settled in London and brought to the Whitechapel ghetto an awareness of its ethno-cultural unity; revitalising it with a secular dialectic, creativity in language and political dynamism.[2]

The new contingents continued the legacy of poverty, but with a difference. By 1872 the Board of Guardians' report suggests that 'the poor Jews in England are almost exclusively recruited from Poland'. The statistician Joseph Jacobs adds: 'This had doubtless been due to the cheapening of the fares from the Continent. German Jews have quite got into the habit of "passing on" their Polish Jews to England.' He contrasts the resilience of the easterners with the karma-like acceptance of pauperism by their Dutch co-religionists.[3] A

1. Thornbury, *Old and New London*, London, 1865, vol.2, p.145.
2. See the informative address by A.R. Rollin, 'Russo-Jewish Immigrants in England before 1881', *Transactions of the Jewish Historical Society of England*, vol. XXI, pp.202-13.
3. Joseph Jacobs, *Studies in Jewish Statistics*, London, 1891, p.20: 'Whereas the former (Dutchmen) rarely raise themselves out of a state of pauperism if they

compulsive tenacity proved an inbred asset for survival.

For the majority of these eastern immigrants, the way to the new land had been beset with uncertainties and tribulations. Although the guaranteed civil and political freedom was the main spur, what of security — job prospects and the maintenance of one's cultural and religious identity? Garbled versions, often contradictory, reached the parochial *stetl*-dweller poised to depart. 'The Jew who left Russia or Poland had nothing fuller to advise him than meagre letters (from friends and relatives who had already emigrated), ambiguous word of mouth and the often inaccurate press. For some emigrants the only tangible information was an address in England.'[4] From the evidence of Ellis Franklin to the House of Commons Select Committee (1888) 'the address of the [Poor Jews' Temporary] Shelter was bought and sold' in eastern Europe.[5] By 1892 reports from the correspondent of *HaMelitz*, the St Petersburg and Odessa Jewish newspaper, reveal ominous signs of anti-Semitism in England where 'the spirit of the native workers and farmers is very bitter against the aliens (especially our co-religionists from Russia) in a very terrible and alarming way'; and underline the alternative prospects of unemployment or cheap 'back-breaking' labour in the struggle for existence. 'Bitter and evil is their fate here in England and America, where they must stand upon their feet to perform labour which exhausts them and breaks the body; all this for meagre bread and water of affliction.' Early warning signals of unwelcome from established Anglo-Jewry were registered through publicity agencies employed to deter would-be immigrants. This was reinforced by British consular officials who strongly advised against making England their goal, since it 'is overcrowded with unemployed', and religious bigots who warned that emigration might lead them 'to lands where they are religiously dissolute and transgress the

---

have once sunk to that level, the recuperative powers of the latter (Easterners) are remarkable.' See also Israel Zangwill, *Children of the Ghetto*, London, 1892, vol. 1, pp.37-8, on Jewish 'caste' distinction; 'Next to a Christian, a Dutch Jew stood lowest in the gradation.'

4. Lloyd P. Gartner, *The Jewish Immigrant in England (1870-1914)*, London, 1960, p.27.

5. House of Commons Select Committee on Alien Immigration, First Report 1888. Min. 1683-86, cd. 1742, Min. 3410.

commands of the Torah, such as shaving the beard and so forth'! But the cry for life and the realities of cash emoluments from relatives in London proved the more persuasive.

That there was to be no easy exit for the persecuted is a recurrent theme in Russian policy. The legal departure of a Jew was made difficult and cumbersome, so that the applicant was kept in a constant state of suspense. It was a lengthy and tenuous procedure. The would-be emigrant had first to present himself to the local magistrate or mayor for 'legitimation', a document proving that he was the person he represented himself to be, with the correct domicile underlined. This was supposedly free but a bribe normally expedited its receipt which, in turn, was passed to the local police chief, who had to endorse the applicant's character — political or otherwise. This was facilitated by a further crossing of the palm so that the police official could confirm that, from his point of view, he had no objection to the applicant's leaving the country. The next stage was the presentation of the document in the *Reichskasse* (Revenue Department) with a fee for passport and receipt. (The price rose significantly from ten to twenty-five roubles from 1880 to 1902). Thenceforth the papers had to be sent or taken to the nearest provincial governor with a supplication for permission to leave the country — the petition bearing two one-rouble stamps. Delay in postage back of the passport (if granted) to the police chief of the district in which the applicant resided could take two or three months. Final delivery was made by the police, again at a price. At the end of this tortuous and frustrating experience, permission to leave Russia was limited to three weeks only. If the permit was not used by then, it became invalid, and the whole process had to be repeated. It was an exercise in legal parasitism at the expense of the miserable Jew. The passport broker or agent was the additional benefactor from his misfortune. For a fee he undertook the whole process for his client, and this alone, by 1902, had risen to thirty roubles.[6]

'The possession of a passport is a *sine qua non*. To avoid

6. Three pounds in current English money.

the expense and trouble of obtaining these documents many subterfuges are resorted to, to enable the Jews to leave unnoticed.'[7] So wrote a virulent exclusionist, who continues to present a valid account of the dangers facing the Jew who chose the alternative — the illicit crossing of the *granetz* (border). 'On arriving at the frontier en route to Hamburg, and being found without these documents, many of the emigrants are subjected to the grossest maltreatment and robbery.' If caught, the guards fleeced them both sides of the border. If not, the smugglers hired to aid them did their fair share of extortion. 'It is said that many of them have been robbed of every coin, and almost every article they possess, and are sent across the frontier in an absolute state of beggary and destitution.'[8] The few, with more resources, or reliable political contacts, fared better. A Myer Wilchinski, who later presented a modified account of his escape from Russia before the House of Lords Committee (8 August, 1888) was one of the minority:[9]

> To escape was a comparatively easy task, as I had money, and was generally liked because of that; and so corrupt is Russian officialdom that it is a byword with the people that you can buy a policeman or sentry for a salt herring or a drop of schnapps and their superior for a silver rouble. To change my clothes and bribe the sentry was a very easy matter, to bribe another on the outside also not a risky job. Once on the road, to get a lift from a kindly waggoner, and tell him my tale, got me a long ride and a little rest. I rewarded him, to his entire satisfaction, as he understood my motives and sympathised with me. We soon reached a part of the road where a small wood was all that was between me and the *granitz*. I here parted company with my good friend, who, after warning me to be cautious, cracked his whip and went. I had really to be very careful, as it was getting daylight and the sentries were looking to be relieved; but a few more small bits of silver did the trick, and at last I was off Russian territory.

With the aid of a bottle of good rum, the resident German border official completed all that was necessary for him to proceed on to Hamburg and thence to England.

7. W.H. Wilkins, *The Alien Invasion*, London, 1892, p.38.
8. Ibid., p.38.
9. Myer Wilchinski, 'History of a Sweater' in *Commonweal* 26 May, and 2 June, 1888. This was found to be literally fictitious but circumstantially true.

But the majority were forced into the more hazardous routine traditionalised by escapees from military service or political *émigrés*. Frontier villagers and townspeople were entitled to a 'halb' pass (*polupasck*), gratis. The refugee could borrow one for a price. The pass was returned and used again and again. The danger of crossing the open frontier is exemplified in the experience of the sixteen-year-old Thomas B. Eyges (Mot) on the Russo-Prussian border in late 1889.[10]

> He arrived in Vershbolova — a small town on the Russian border; there a man was to cross the border with Mot early in the morning and the baggage was to be transferred by train to Prussia. At dawn, the next morning, a big heavy Russian peasant came for Mot. They took their shoes off and walked a short distance and when they came to a shallow stream they waded in.
> 'Hoy, Stoy, Kuda?' (Stop! Where are you going?) someone suddenly shouted from somewhere. The 'smuggler' did not stop but instead he quickly grasped Mot, set him on his back and ran. Mot heard a few shots then in a few minutes he was across the boundary in Yatkun, Prussia.

Mot was thenceforth fortunate in having the wherewithal to stay at an inn and leave by train for Hamburg. Whole families, wide open to the robber and blackmailer, trailed their way painfully on foot across Germany to reach the same port. There, the authorities devised some protective schemes. Shipowners administered hostels which carried out health inspections and prevented swindling and extortion. Elsewhere along the Baltic port centres an army of parasites was assembled to batter on the innocents:[11]

> ... keepers of immigrant hostels, railroad employees, ships' officers and crews, and pre-eminently, ticket agents. Many of these dealers were Jews who spoke Yiddish, and exploited their victims' trust in them. Stolen baggage, exorbitant lodging rates, misrepresentation of ships' facilities, and capricious shifts of sailing schedules occurred daily. One also hears of tickets sold to the wrong destination by unscrupulous agents.

10. Thomas B. Eyges, *Beyond the Horizon*, Boston, 1944, p.48. A similar experience in 1904 was recalled by J.L. Fine OBE, JP (1883-1971), in conversations with the author, June 1965.

11. Gartner, *The Jewish Immigrant in England, (1870-1914)*, p.34. See also *YIVO Bleter XXVI* (1945), pp.112-20.

The ports were but the beginning of another ordeal. There is ample qualitative evidence of the conditions of steerage for the immigrant in transit. A special commissioner of the *Evening News and Post* travelling as a 'destitute alien' in 1891 — a peak year of influx — reports on his experience during the voyage. There is some deliberate overcolouring of the issue, since his assignment purported to evidence the health dangers accruing to Britain from the free entry of alien 'paupers', at a time when the issue was being forced by exclusionists on a generally uninformed public. But the overall picture is valid. The passengers faced a voyage lasting from forty to sixty hours, depending on the weather. The ship resembled a cattle boat, with the passengers herded together as such; sleeping on fouled rags or blankets in a small space between decks. All had to bring their own food and bedding, and the commentator drily records that accommodation was certainly not up to British Board of Trade health specifications.

> Most of them [i.e., the passengers] were young women, wearing shawls on their heads and clad in soiled, faded and torn finery. Some of them were men, young or middle-aged, but so enfeebled and spiritless that one might have fixed their age at nearer seventy than thirty. A few were old women, bent, emaciated and almost lifeless. All, with few exceptions, were yellow with dirt and smelt foully.

The steerage cabins presented a scene which recalled to him the miseries of the damned.

> The stench which issued from the semi-darkness beneath was pretty unendurable, and it was even worse downstairs, when blended with the heat from the bodies of the emigrants . . . The apartment was about the breadth of the ship near the narrow end in width, and scarcely so long. In the centre a single oil lamp was hanging, which threw out a feeble flickering light. On each side a couple of platforms were erected, one over the other with about two and a half feet between them, divided into spaces in some places a little over two feet broad, and not divided at all in others. Here men, women and children were lying on the bare boards partly undressed, some in one direction, some in another. Young men lay abreast of young unmarried women, chatting jocularly and acting indecently, and young children were witnesses of all that passed. The greater portion of the floor was taken up with boxes, on which such of the

emigrants of both sexes as had not been able to obtain the ordinary sleeping accommodation were reclining as best they might.

On the second night 'the horrors of the place were increased by the accumulation of filth, which had taken place by the ever-increasing indisposition of the passengers the longer we were at sea . . . through the long weary hours I sat there sleepless.' Mrs Rose Robins, a surviving member of Rocker's *Arbeter Fraint* group, recalls vividly her own journey, steerage *en route* to London, ten years after the commissioner (1901).[12]

> We came by cattle boat. All of us slept overcrowded in bunks, stretched side by side over the whole length of the ship. We lived in hot, stuffy, filthy conditions. We ate salt herring out of barrels distributed by ordinary seamen. My young brother, one year old, was sea sick, in agony all the time. We scratched whilst we slept. For the nights were a nightmare.

It was no wonder that at the port of arrival the embarking immigrant - presented a squalid and unsightly spectacle; shabby, bowed, pale and unshaven, with eyes watering from the insanitary atmosphere below deck (a common-place feature which provided alien-baiters with a weapon of accusation, namely that the immigrant imported eye disease!). The point of disembarkation was not the end of their long and troubled journey. It could be the most hazardous. Beatrice Webb provides us with a colourful and perceptive view of new arrivals at a dock in the Pool of London. Underneath the objective reporting there is a sense of compassion for the 'greener', a rare sentiment at that time.[13]

> The scenes at the landing stage are less idyllic. There are a few relatives and friends awaiting the arrival of the small boats filled with immigrants; but the crowd gathered in and about the gin-shop overlooking the narrow entrance of the landing stage are dock loungers of the lowest type and professional 'runners'. These latter individuals, usually of the Hebrew race, are among the most

12. Interviewed by the author 5 March 1971.
13. In Charles Booth (ed.), *Life and Labour of the People in London*, London, 1889, vol. 1, pp.582-3.

repulsive of East London parasites; boat after boat touches the landing stage; they push forward, seize hold of the bundles of baskets of the newcomers, offer bogus tickets to those who wish to travel forward to America, promise guidance and free lodging to those who hold in their hand addresses of acquaintances in Whitechapel or who are absolutely friendless. A little man with an official badge (Hebrew Ladies' Protective Society) fights valiantly in their midst for the conduct of unprotected females, and shouts or whispers to the others to go to the Poor Jews' Temporary Shelter in Leman Street. For a few moments it is a scene of indescribable confusion: cries and counter-cries; the hoarse laughter of the dock loungers at the strange garb and broken accent of the poverty-stricken foreigners; the rough swearing of the boatmen at passengers unable to pay the fee for landing. In another ten minutes eighty of the hundred newcomers are dispersed in the back slums of Whitechapel; in another few days, the majority of these, robbed of the little they possess, are turned out of the 'free lodgings', destitute and friendless.

The dangers were real indeed. The white slave agent was on the prowl for the single, unaccompanied girl, who could be cajoled or manoeuvred into a life in the bordello. More often there was the 'crimp' or foreign shark in the pay of unscrupulous boarding-house keepers. Taking advantage of the ignorance and friendlessness of the 'greener', the victim could be conned into believing that his newly-found aid, who spoke Yiddish, was involved in Jewish charities. The latter would collect his luggage and escort him to a lodging house in Whitechapel. Here he was scrutinised by the keeper to see if he had sufficient resources to be of temporary value. If not, he was quickly disposed of by being sent in charge of a boy to the Jews' Temporary Shelter. The more lucrative victims were inveigled into staying a day or two so that they could 'look about them' ostensibly for a permanent job and accommodation. Then the extortion began. The exorbitant charge of two to five shillings a week for a filthy bed was imposed, which had to be paid one week in advance, even if the lodger stayed for one night only. Food charges were high. After breakfast a dubious assistant was detailed to march his victim round London, to help him job-hunting. Needless to say, work was never found, but the poor dupe had to pay five shillings a day for this 'service'. The routine was repeated until the lodger was deprived of everything but his luggage.

This could finally be accepted as a guarantee against a small loan from the boarding-house keeper to pay for food. Inevitably the victim was turned out into the streets without money, or shelter — a 'destitute pauper'.[14]

In the early years the greener had to fend for himself to survive. He could be the recipient of Jewish charity, which was at times extensive, but he was also its donor. 'Giving without a murmur' was the admiring epithet for the unusual open-handedness of the immigrants' response to the many calls on their minuscule philanthropic resources.[15] As we shall see, the established Anglo-Jewish community adopted an ambivalent attitude to the newcomers who, for basic needs, had to seek help from their own. Out of this relationship emerged an important institutional aid, other than the Jewish Board of Guardians. This was the Poor Jews' Temporary Shelter, conceived as an act of pious generosity by the immigrant baker 'Simha' Becker. He maintained his premises in Church Lane (near the point of confluence of Whitechapel and Commercial Roads) as an improvised short-term free board-and-lodging house for needy immigrants. Here one could eat, sleep in the warmth of the bakers' ovens, pray or read from the customary holy books, and even obtain clothing. This reached the ears of members of the Anglo-Jewish hierarchy, and in April 1885 Lionel Alexander and Frederic P. Mocatta made a surprise inspection of the house and declared the facilities 'unhealthy', which led to its closure by the intercession of the official Board of Guardians. The response was a large meeting of protest organised by immigrants at the Jewish Working Men's Club in Whitechapel High Street, at which Mocatta received rough handling as defender of the action; but the outcome was positive help from another quarter. A more solid replacement was sponsored by three wealthy supporters: Herman Landau, a Polish immigrant of 1864 and successful stockbroker; Sir Samuel Montagu, MP for Whitechapel, and the orthodox bene-

14. The *Jewish Chronicle* reports 21 August 1891: 'The process of robbery and chicanery . . . is quite as active in London as it is on the Russian frontier.' See also evidence of Herman Landau to House of Commons Select Committee. First Report of 1888, Minutes 2163-2190.

15. Gartner, *The Jewish Immigrant in England (1870-1914)*, pp.162-5.

factor Ellis Franklin. They jointly financed the re-opening of the Shelter in a more congenial building located in Leman Street, and named it as the Poor Jews' Temporary Shelter (October 1885). It developed as an entrepôt for immigrant and transmigrant, particularly operating as a dispersal agency, in which 'greeners' were protected from dockside crimps and land sharks. From the beginning it worked in close co-operation with local and government authority and thus attained official respectability. When an outbreak of cholera was registered on the Continent, it acted promptly as a quarantine centre for both immigrants and transmigrants. It kept a check on addresses of recent arrivals who had taken up residence with a relative or 'landsman'.[16] But it was no ultra-philanthropic institution. In accordance with the current philosophic duality of Samuel Smiles and *laissez-faire*, those who had the means must pay for the service. This was also to allay the fear that an over-hospitable centre would focus London as a point of attraction for alien immigrants, a nightmare that continued to haunt established Anglo-Jewry; and this would account for the stance of the Jewish Board of Guardians, which for fifteen years refused to come to terms with the Shelter.

For the Shelter provided more than an *ad hoc* palliative to the poor and weary stranger. After the long voyage beset with every form of tribulation, it gave some form of welcome to those already demoralised by the recognition that they were universal pariahs. Hospitality and easy aid would be the last things that the Jewish Board of Guardians would volunteer. This would open up the floodgates for the invasion of an army of Jewish paupers. The Shelter opened its doors to an influx of 1,000 to 4,000 immigrants and transmigrants annually up to 1914. It offered two full meals a day (three after 1897) and, for a short period, imposed a labour test upon every fit applicant. The maximum period of residence was fourteen days. Eyges paints an austere picture of his own brief experience, not without a sense of pathos and of the basic humanity underlying official postures:[17]

16. An immigrant from the same home town, etc. in Russia or Poland.
17. Eyges, *Beyond the Horizon*, pp.50-1.

Inside the entrance the emigrants were met by a tall man, in eyeglasses, with a short blond beard and a satin skull-cap on his head. He counted every one as they passed him. It was morning. The new arrivals, together with the others, had to say the morning prayers, and then breakfast was served. After breakfast, each new arrival was called to the office of the superintendent for registration. Each in turn was asked his name, where he came from, his trade, whether he had any relatives or friends in London, or elsewhere in England, and how much money he had. Every answer Mot gave was in the negative — he had no trade, no friends, or relatives, and was penniless.

Soon after the registration, all new arrivals were marched off to a Russian vapour bath and on return to the Shelter, dinner was served. Then followed the afternoon prayer (Mincha) and later at dusk, the evening prayer; then supper, and at nine in the evening everybody was ordered to bed. Although it was some time since he had a good night's sleep and he needed the rest badly, Mot was too excited to sleep.

The next morning, after the usual routine of morning prayer and breakfast, the door of the shelter opened wide and every immigrant was told to go and look for work.

The door of the shelter closed behind Mot, and for the first time he found himself alone in the world — alone in the biggest city in the world — without a friend, without money, without a trade and without a language.

In seeking a job, the immigrant found himself faced with a number of harsh realities. Opportunities were strictly limited. The system was periodically choked with high static and frictional unemployment. Language and cultural differences bred suspicion and hostility among his unwelcoming hosts. There were, in any case, rigid trade-union regulations for accepting new entrants. In the homeland they had lacked the occupational experience of working in a factory, since factorisation of industry had only recently extended into Russia and Poland. They were, therefore, forced back on the old trades. Hence the initial expansion of small workshops, where craft division of labour was the norm with its concomitant individual specialisation of function. In the long term this was a dying concern — against an age veering towards economic rationalisation, that is, large-scale production with the elimination of small, uneconomic units on the way.

But the majority remained faithful to the small workshops

both by choice and by design: to the sweated trades, which according to Beatrice Webb employ 'those who are incapable of the disciplined factory system'. In the process 'one hand, one job', was the maxim, with pay differentials according to recognised skills. By 1882, the reports of the Jewish Board of Guardians confirmed the order of attractiveness of immigrant occupations with tailoring at first place. Of a total of 1,528 classified applicants, 384 were tailors – the largest contingent. This is confirmed by a wealth of evidence. Attached to the first report of the Jewish Working Men's Club 1875, are details of 1,459 members (1,107 men and 352 women), 300 of whom are unspecified. Of the remainder distributed among 32 trades, tailors came first at 305. By 1891, Joseph Jacobs could report that from his investigation, 'the Jewish tailor, both as master and as workmen, is by far the commonest figure among the occupations of the Jews of London.'[18] This primacy was maintained throughout the period 1881-1914. In August 1903, the Aliens Commission report enumerates 64 occupations. Tailoring tops the list at 25,698, almost four times that of the number of bakers – second on the list at 6,334.[19] The main inflow was to a virtually new industry of cheap ready-made clothing to meet the demands of a 'huge and constantly increasing class . . . who have . . . wide wants and narrow means'. The same observer tended to exaggerate the existence of a phenomenon, which only later became more valid with the rise of

18. See section V, 'Occupations of London Jews' in Jacobs, *Studies in Jewish Statistics*, pp.33-40.
19. Table LXI of Statistical Appendix to the Royal Commission's Report, cd. 1741, pp.72, 75 (August 1903), shows the top nine occupations as:

Industry	Numbers	
Tailoring	25,698	
Bakers	6,334	
Hawkers, costers	5,372	
Cabinet Makers	4,815	
Boot & Shoe Makers	4,770	(incl. 715 slipper makers)
Hairdressers	3,355	
Dressmakers	3,068	
Hat & Cap makers	2,022	
Textile Dealers	1,825	

Lowest on the list were grocers – 1,015.

such enterprises as Montague Burton and Marks and Spencer — cheap and functional clothing appealing to all classes and tastes. This was the 'democracy of modern dress. It is no longer possible, as it was even thirty years ago [i.e. 1858] to tell with tolerable accuracy what a man is by his dress.'[20]

The multiplication of small workshops was identified with the perpetuation of the sweating system. These were already located by Beatrice Webb in 1887.[21]

> Between factories proper and home work lie a class of home workshops: these are usually built in the yard or garden behind the dwelling house, sometimes connected with and sometimes detached from the house ... the plan seems to be on the increase ... It is applicable to industries where no power machinery is needed and it is a great improvement on employment in city houses.

Elsewhere she gives fuller definition of her subject and submits a detailed analysis of social causes and the function and structure of these establishments in response to the needs of the immigrant producers and their market.[22]

After 1860 the transformation of a large section of the tailoring trade from retail to wholesale enterprises was possibly due to several mutually inclusive factors. The introduction of Isaac Singer's sewing machine together with the growing subdivision of labour coalesced to meet the demands of an expanding middle- and working-class and colonial market. With the reality that 'wholesale distribution needs wholesale production' the individual journeyman had to go. East End tailoring was developing

> a new province of production inhabited by a peculiar people working under a new system, with new instruments, and yet separated by a narrow and constantly shifting boundary from the sphere of employment of an old established native industry. On the (Jewish) side of the line we find the Jewish contractor with his highly organised staff of fixers, basters, fillers, machinists, button-hole hands and pressers, turning out coats by the score, together

20. A.A. Baumann, MP, 'Possible Remedies for the Sweating System', in the *National Review* XII, no. 69, November 1888, pp.292-3.

21. Charles Booth, *Conditions and Occupations of the People of Tower Hamlets 1886-1887*, London, 1889, p.50.

22. Booth (ed.), *Life and Labour of the People in London*, vol. 1, pp.209-40, 'The Tailoring Trade'.

with a mass of English women, unorganised and unregulated, engaged in lower sections of the trade.

This 'new province' became popularly associated with the 'sweating system', while the declining hand-sewn garment was identified with the high-class product of the individual journeyman tailor. Beatrice Webb was highly critical of the East End products: they were 'bagged together', shapeless against those made by English craftsmen, which were tailored to personal requirements and would wear three times as long. To her 'the English home worker was a good instrument out of repair, the Jewish "bespoke" workshop an inferior instrument sharpened to its highest pitch'.

Wholesale traders requiring contractual production and clothiers drew on two sources — provincial factories supplying cloth design and labour, or contractors, large and small, mainly concerned with organising labour in production. In the latter category the East End domestic outworker would find his niche. There was no deficiency in labour supply. On the contrary, the pulses of immigration ensured a reservoir of men and women seeking work. The overall picture was a cut-throat struggle for existence. Small workshops proliferated, each one facing an ephemeral existence dependent ultimately on the cost of the most vital factor of production — labour. Price competition at all levels was the maxim. In human terms, the story of humiliation and exploitation experienced by the majority of immigrant workers is given voice and image by the sufferers themselves. To obtain work, the 'greener' made his way to the *chazar mark* (pig market!) — an open thoroughfare where the masters came to select 'hands' seekings employment. Wilchinski, as early as 1882, evokes the desperation of hungry men: [23]

Many of them, like myself, 'greeners', willing to work at anything, that would bring them the scantiest means of existence; some married and with families and all with that enquiring, beseeching look, that half starved, helpless, hopeless beings must of necessity possess . . . the majority . . . looked like so many unwashed corpses.

23. Wilchinski, 'History of a Sweater'.

Eyges (1889) gives us an early site of the sweaters' 'hire parade', 'where every Saturday morning the gathering of the boot finishers took place. This was at Whitechapel, near Black Lion Yard, a narrow alley that led into Old Montague Street'.[24] In 1892, the venue is located by W.H. Wilkins,[25] the anti-alien propagandist, who records the scene. The new arrivals take work on any terms to live. They line up against a wall at the corner of Goulston Street, Aldgate, where they are inspected by a less shabby individual, who may be the sweater himself or his agent. They stand there 'with the high boots and fur caps of the peasant'. The degradation is complete as each attempts to barter away his labour for the lowest price to ensure an immediate pittance. The single man often faced the prospect of receiving only food and lodging until he had learned the trade. This accords with the evidence of Wilchinski ten years earlier.

I determined to chance my luck, and closed with a tailor who offered to teach me the trade and give me lodgings and coffee for three weeks, and six shillings a week afterwards, until I learned one branch of the trade (coat-making) when I would be able, he said, to demand from four to eight shillings a-day for my toil. He lived in one of the many dirty streets in Spitalfields, and the work he made was railway and seamen's coats — hard heavy work, that required more brute strength than skill. He occupied two rooms on the second floor, for which he paid seven shillings a week; had a wife, and three children aged respectively seven, four, two; very intelligent, almost crafty.

The room we worked in was used for cooking also, and there I had to sleep on the floor. The wife helped as much as she could at the trade, besides doing all the work of the house and the children. A young woman worked the machine from eight in the morning till nine at night, for three shillings a day; not very often making a full week's work. My work at first was to keep up a good fire with coke, and soap the seams and edges; and the elbow grease I used was considerable. I had to get up in the morning about half past five, and we finished at night between ten and eleven, and turned out every week about thirty coats, which came to about four pounds. The master himself worked very hard indeed; and he himself told me

24. See also description by Isaac Stone in the *Poilishe Yidl* 1,9 (September 1884). This alley is recalled later as a rendezvous for tailors 'for hire' by Sam Dreen. He also locates a warehouse near Black Lion Yard as the headquarters of the Tailors' Strike Committee during the seven weeks' strike in 1906.

25. Wilkins, *The Alien Invasion*, p.44.

afterwards that he had left the old country for the same reason as myself, and that a few years previously he had been a cowkeeper and dairyman, but was now a 'tailor'.

... The three weeks passed, and I had learned to make myself tolerably useful; and my master told me that if I was willing to work the machine he would give me the six shillings a week he had promised me. I was rather pleased at this, so I consented; but the young woman who had previously done the work was sent away. For the next few weeks my life was anything but pleasant; but my master was most patient with me, and I learned to operate the machine.

There was, therefore, little sentiment in this day-to-day competitive struggle where dog ate dog. As he became more proficient he demanded and received fifteen shillings a week, with no scruples about moving on to the highest bidder. But he was still tied to 'proper hours' which, by common consent of masters and men, were 'seven in the morning till nine at night'.

Long-term persistence in work conditions and life-style is evidenced in the recollections of the surviving members of the *Arbeter Fraint* group and others. Sam Dreen,[26] later protégé of Rocker, arrived in London in 1900 as a fifteen-year-old immigrant. Conditions had hardly changed since 1882.

A group of twenty of us were met by Jewish shelter officials. We walked through a rough area, where the inhabitants hated immigrants and threw stones at us all the way to Leman Street.

Landsleit [fellow countrymen] brought us thence to Little Turner Street, off Cannon Street Road in the Commercial Road. Two small rooms were ready for three of us and I started work on the premises. At that time the Boer War was on and uniforms were in demand. My employer came from my own home town, Vitebsk, and made military uniforms. I helped as a 'hand' to make soldiers' trousers out of blue material and red piping — specialising in piping. I got thirty shillings a week, good wages then. But the hours were from eight in the morning till ten at night. I didn't like working so late so I made a habit of stealing out with the women workers who left at eight. That cost me my job ...

There were plenty of workers unemployed, glad to come in if any of the others worked out. The employer stood no nonsense. At the

26. Interviewed by author in Milwaukee, November 1969.

least sign of dissatisfaction out you went. For talking in working hours, for coming late, for going early the penalty was the sack.

Dreen then turned to making breeches in a small workshop in Quaker Street where, on piece-work, he was forced to work sometimes till two and three in the morning to meet the schedule of an exacting master.

In quantitative terms, a reasonably objective picture which persists throughout our time-scale is proffered by Booth from his case studies in 'The Tailoring Trade'.[27] Out of 901 workshops surveyed by his research workers, 685 employed under ten people and provided the worst conditions of sweating industry, although the 'presence of bulky machinery and the marketable value of light are physical impediments to the cellar accommodation and huddled misery of the lowest class of boot finishers'. 'Proper' hours were confirmed. For men, the working day registered 13-14 hours, with wages reckoned on a daily basis but paid weekly. Women worked an average 12-hour day but payment received was based on 10½ hours, since this was the legal limit imposed by the Factory Acts. Overtime was sustained in two ways. The hand was granted extra payment per hour, or a very long day might be joined to a short day, that is, 17 hours' working on Thursday would be compensated by early closure on Friday, before nightfall, to meet the eve-of-Sabbath requirement. These terms were not applied to unskilled learners, who were expected to 'convenience' their masters for the privilege of learning the trade, when they worked the same hours for a ceiling 10 to 13 hour wage rate. Thus cheap labour was perpetuated under a crude form of apprenticeship.

There was an unwritten 'scale of progress'. A greener received a nominal wage in the slop shops for three months in his role as 'learner'. In six months he could graduate to a wage of three to five shillings for an indefinite day's work. In one year, depending on the class of work he had attained to, he could command six shillings to ten shillings and sixpence for a day limited between 13 and 14 hours. Coat-making offered rates of four and a half pence an hour for male and

27. Booth (ed.), *Life and Labour of the People in London*, pp.221-5.

two and a half pence for female workers with the high-water mark of normal mature labour standing at ninepence an hour for men and sixpence for women, the latter accruing to top skilled workers. The trade has till recently been bedevilled by seasonal demand. In bespoke concerns, the peak of work was March to August, then October to Christmas. Workers laid off during the interim months faced starvation. In the stock and slop workshops work was still irregular due to seasonal demand and competition between masters for orders. Only the highly skilled faced the prospect of continuous employment, since they were maintained during the slack season, partly to prevent them being 'poached' by competitive employers but mainly to cope with rush orders. During the busy season there was constant price competition between masters to bag the highest skilled workers. But rarely did a workman complete a full week's work. Booth analyses the average week's labour per year according to the class of employer. Skilled workers with large contractors averaged a 4 to 4½ day week; ordinary skilled workers in medium shops 3 days and the majority — learners or permanently unskilled — only 2½ days.

For the ordinary Jewish workman this spelt out a precarious living, always poised on the margin of subsistence. The difficulties of adjustment to his new land, the tensions inherent in insecure employment, the financial and legal problems to overcome before he could bring over his family from the *heim* (Russia or Poland), forced him to an unlimited application to work. As Professor Gartner rightly observes: 'His individualism in part reflected the instability of the immigrant trades, where the bridge from the entrepreneur to workman and back was a short one, frequently trodden many times by the same person.' The new dimension of freedom provided additional momentum for the fulfilment of one's innate potentiality, which, in the immigrant's rationale, would be directed towards material success as a prerequisite for security. For most it proved elusive. The ease with which workman became master and vice versa is legendary. The would-be entrepreneur turned his living-room into a workshop, with a friendly landlord or butcher pledged as security. He could call on the aid of a brother Jew (whose task was to supply pattern garments as samples to wholesalers) for a price. With a small down-payment he obtained hire of a sewing-machine and presser and tailor's tables.

> At first, the new master will live on 'green' labour; will, with the help of his wife or some other relative, do all the skilled work that is needed. Presently, if the quantity of his work increases, or if the quality improves, he will engage a machinist, then a presser. His earnings are scanty, probably less than those of his skilled hands to whom he pays wages, and he works all hours of the day and night. But the chances of the trade are open to him; with indefatigable energy and with a certain measure of organising power he may press forward into the ranks of the large employers, and if he be successful, day by day, year by year, his profit increases and his labour decreases relatively to the wages and the labour of his hands.[28]

But only a ruthless minority made it. Until the 1930s the tragi-comedy would be repeated *ad nauseam*. The majority who tried, suffered their dubious hour of glory as master, then sank back into poverty and debt. In the jungle of cut-throat competition which proliferated, they were overwhelmed one by one.

Physical conditions of labour were, to say the least, socially and medically hazardous. Workmen slept in the workrooms, particularly newly-arrived greeners with no fixed abode, and breathed in an atmosphere already foetid with the sweat of congested day workers and the steam of the press irons. Wilchinski's comments referred to conditions in 1882. There is a wealth of subsequent evidence that such conditions were the norm well into the next century. A 'Report of the *Lancet* Special Sanitary Commission on the Polish Colony of Jew Tailors', issued on 3 May, 1884, made an immediate impact, especially on the editor of the *Jewish Chronicle* and the officials of the Jewish Board of Guardians. Both regarded it as exaggerated although basically true, with the *Jewish Chronicle* calling on the Board (editorial, 16 May) to deal with 'unscrupulous masters' and to 'see that the sanitary authority does its duty'. The report declared that 'the principal grievance to be brought against the Jew tailors of

28. Ibid., p.232.

the East End is that they work in unwholesome, overcrowded houses where girls and women are kept toiling long after the hours prescribed by the Factory and Workshop Act'. Jewish Spitalfields assumed the gloomy somnolence of a city of dreadful night. 'At all hours of the day and night the [Pelham] street resounds with the rattle and whir of the innumerable sewing machines, the windows shine with the flare of gas, but the street is comparatively deserted.' Police evidence the continual hum of heavy machinery going on as late as 2 a.m. and beginning again at 7 a.m. 'In one street there was a house where women worked from 7 a.m. till 1.30 a.m. at night', presumably a shift system, as the weird comings and goings of shawled females were observed by a suspicious constable. The once splendid three-storeyed dwellings of Huguenot silk merchants had been subdivided into lodging-rooms and/or workshops, all reduced to a condition where decay and foul sanitation were commonplace.

> In Hanbury Street we found eighteen workers crowded in a small room measuring eight yards by four and a half yards and not quite eight feet high. The first two floors of this house were let out to lodgers who were also Jews. Their rooms were clean but damp, as the water was coming through the rotting wall. The doors fitted badly, and the locks would not act. In one room the window frame was almost falling into the street; in another the floor was broken and the fireplace giving way. The boards of the stairs were so worn that in some places they were only a quarter of an inch thick and broke under extra pressure.

In accord with recent demolitions[29] to effect slum clearance, expansion of railway facilities, street improvements and school building, the time lag in constructing new accommodation meant that overcrowding was rife and rents were high.[30] This escapes the *Lancet* commentator, who is appalled at the inflated rent paid by the master tailor, although he captures the milieu of the sweatshop admirably.

29. See H.J. Dyos, 'Railways and Housing in Victorian London', in the *Journal of Transport History*, 11, 1, May 1955, pp.11-21. 2 November 1955, pp.90-100.
30. In Whitechapel the number of houses dropped from 8,264 in 1871 to 5,735 in 1901 although the population rose from 75,552 to 78,768. *Census of England and Wales 1901*, cd. 875, 1902. Table 9.

Yet the tailor who hired this miserable abode showed us a receipt for seventeen pounds in payment of only one quarter's rent. It seems preposterous that sixty-eight pounds should be charged for a house literally falling to pieces, and containing only six rooms. When further we consider that the top room, though the largest, had at times to hold eighteen persons, working in the heat of the gas and the stoves for warming the press irons, surrounded by mounds of dust and chips from the cut cloth, breathing an atmosphere full of woollen particles containing more or less injurious dyes, it is not surprising that so large a proportion of working tailors break down from diseases of the respiratory organs.

He revealed the discriminatory exploitation of women, which Beatrice Potter (Webb) later confirmed when, during spring 1888, she worked as a 'plain trouser hand' to investigate their condition.[31] Since women were only paid for three-quarters of their legal day, to ensure a full day's pay they were forced to work from eight in the morning till eleven or twelve at night, a practice which contravened the Factory Act. A shortage of inspectors, non-registration of workshops and cunning evasion resorted to by masters, negated any attempt at effective labour inspection.

The workshops are but rarely inspected either early in the morning or late at night, and our appearance after nine caused quite a panic; the master tailors freely expostulating that visits at such hours were illegal. *BUT AT EACH CALL WE FOUND WOMEN STILL AT WORK.* On the appearance of any stranger the women are often distributed throughout the private parts of the house — in the bedrooms, kitchens and so forth. If any question is asked there is always a ready reply — the one is a niece, the other is a daughter; and if they are working, it is only for the family and not in pursuit of their trade. These explanations are often absolute falsehoods, but the foreign Jew workwomen are . . . in so dependent a position that they dare not rise and contradict their employer. They will even answer questions falsely so as to avoid the application of the Factory Act. It is absolutely useless to question the workwomen in the presence of their employers; they cannot say how long they work, how little time is allowed for their meals, unless they feel certain that such revelations will not be brought home to them, entailing the loss of their means of livelihood. The evil cannot be uprooted by official visits paid in the broad daylight; it must be dealt with by the same methods as those employed in the detection of crime.

31. See article, 'The Pages of a Work Girl's Diary' in *Nineteenth Century*, October 1888.

There is, of course, overwhelming evidence on the enslavement of women from diverse sources. Later that year Lewis Lyons, an early Jewish trade-union leader,[32] publicised the 'Deplorable Conditions of the East London Tailoresses' in an article in the *East London Observer.* He commented on the lack of sanitation in cramped rooms containing

> tables four feet by two feet, round which are placed eight or nine girls . . . If any complaints are made, the reply of the sweater is, 'If you don't like it, go!' . . . I ask whether the voice of the public will not be raised against such vile slave drivers, who keep young females ranging from nine years upwards in captivity.

In response to this a W. Ingham Brook, of 3 Sidney Square, Stepney,[33] added his own observations on tailoresses making lawn-tennis aprons with trimming complete for five pence a dozen, and large ulsters requiring twelve buttons and button-holes made for six pence to one shilling total labour price and sold for one guinea or thirty-five shillings. 'And we must bear in mind that these women — many of whom work twelve hours a day for such a miserable pay — have to supply their own needles, cotton, silk twist, gimp, oil, soap and firing.' Women continued to constitute a vast reservoir of 'slave' labour in most trades where cheap labour was an overall feature in production. Thus they posed a threat to the livelihood of their menfolk in their role of depressing the price of labour generally. In 1908 James Samuelson makes the oft-repeated appeal to men to insist upon women receiving a 'living' wage on the precept of self-interest, if nothing else. ('For as much as women's labour competes with their own, it is to their advantage that their [the women's] wages should be raised as high as possible!') He followed with an optimistic plea for 'the formation of women's unions under State sanctions'.[34] That same year, Mary MacArthur made a devastating report on women's labour before the Select Committee on Sweating, warning that 'the overcrowded and undernourished woman is the greatest menace

32. *East London Observer*, 6 December, 1884.
33. Ibid., 10 December, 1884.
34. James Samuelson, *The Lament of the Sweated*, London, 1908, p.44 ff.

to the prosperity of the nation as a whole'. East End tailors and other minor immigrant concerns would be following prescribed practice in a male-oriented society, with perhaps a difference. Booth notes that 'the Jewish wives of every grade seldom work for money; they attend to cooking and household duties . . .' as part of the conditioning to preserve the pattern of family life. The Webbs were quick to note that the 'moral precepts of Judaism are centred in the perfection of family life, in obedience towards parents, in self-devotion for children, in the chastity of the girl, in the support and protection of the wife';[35] and this contrasted sharply with the *mores* of many of their Gentile neighbours, who, although equally subjected to poverty and degradation, were unencumbered with theological nuances which would restrain their indulgence in drunkenness, wife-beating and child neglect.

As the Jews pressed eastward from Aldgate, so did their life-style begin to project a bizarre quality on the immediate environment. Slowly the narrow streets and courtyards of Whitechapel, Mile End and St George's filled up with *landsleit.* They formed their own self-contained street communities with workshops, *stiebels* and all-purpose stores where the men would foregather on Sundays to discuss the 'rebbe's' sermon, politics, and local scandal or indulge surreptitiously in the immigrants' vice – gambling.[36] During the whole life of the East End ghetto the familiar figure of the bookie, recognised at close quarters by his loud, outlandish clothes and rubicund *bonhomie*, could be seen working his pitch outside some corner shop. On Fridays – the eve of Sabbath – the cloistered alleys and thoroughfares came to life as candles blazed from the front parlours of shabby one-storeyed dwellings or tenements. In their week-end finery, the young of both sexes were led with reluctance to 'shool'. On high holy days the young men, garbed in dress

35. Beatrice and Sidney Webb, *Problems of Modern Industry*, 1898, Chapter 11, 'The Jews of East London', pp.20-45.
36. Gambling in cards, dice and horses remained the vice which replaced drink in the Jewish idiom. Coffee houses, restaurants and clubs were plagued with gambling schools. See Minutes of Stepney Jewish Lads' Club, 6 January, 1901, which reveals fixed regulations against gambling.

coats and flaunting their manhood along the main streets and high roads of the ghetto, 'were epitomes of one aspect of Jewish history, replacing the primitive manners and foreign piety of the foreign Jew by a veneer of cheap culture and a laxity of ceremonial observance'.[37] But in most cases the young man stayed tethered to his people, since 'whether he married in his old station or higher up the scale, he was always faithful to the sectarian tradition of the race, and this less from religious motives than from hereditary instinct'.[38] While the first-born generation viewed themselves with pride as Britishers, the old, like the immigrant Reb Shmuel, could 'never quite comprehend the importance of becoming English. He had a latent feeling that Judaism had flourished before England was invented.'[39]

For those who had just arrived or were impervious to change and circumstance, the *stiebel* sustained their ambiguous response to the new environment. It was a confirmation of their identity in *goles* (exile), yet reflected a poignant attachment to the *heim* which had dealt with them so harshly. The detached social observer confirmed that these *chevras* (religious associations) supplied 'the needs of some 12,000 to 15,000 foreign Jews'. They combine

> the functions of a benefit club for death, sickness and mourning rites with that of public worship and the study of the Talmud. Thirty or forty of these *chevras* are scattered throughout the Jewish quarters . . . Usually each *chevra* is named after the town or district in Russia or Poland from which the majority of its members have emigrated . . . from ties of relationship or friendship or, at least, from the memory of a common home . . . the new association springs.[40]

Yet Beatrice Webb responds to some degree to the emotional manifestations of the participants:

> Here, early in the morning or late at night, the devout members meet to recite the morning and evening prayers or to decipher the sacred books of the Talmud. And it is a curious and touching sight to enter one of the poorer and more wretched of these places on a Sabbath morning.

37. Zangwill, *Children of the Ghetto*, p.233, 'The Purim Ball'.
38. Ibid., p.237.
39. Ibid., p.163.
40. Beatrice and Sidney Webb, *Problems of Modern Industry*, London, p.23.

But it is Zangwill, who was involved and understood, who presents the reality with an amalgam of wit and pathos, unrivalled in its imagery:[41]

> The *stiebel* [consisted of] two large rooms knocked into one, and the rear partitioned off for the use of bewigged, heavy-jawed women who might not sit with the men lest they should fascinate their thoughts away from things spiritual. Its furniture was bare benches, a raised platform with a reading desk in the centre, and a wooden curtained ark at the end containing two parchment scrolls of the Law, each with a silver pointer and silver bells and pomegranates. The scrolls were in manuscript, for the printing press had never yet sullied the sanctity of the synagogue editions of the Pentateuch. The room was badly ventilated, and what little air there was was generally sucked up by a greedy company of wax candles, big and little, stuck in brass holders.

Here the worshippers came

> two and often three times a day to batter the gates of heaven and to listen to sermons more exegetical than ethical. They dropped in, mostly in their workaday garments and grime, and rumbled and roared and chorused prayers with a zeal that shook the window-panes, and there was never lack of a *minyan* — the congregational quorum of ten.
>
> This synagogue (Sons of the Covenant) was all of luxury many of its Sons could boast. It was their salon and their lecture hall. It supplied them not only with their religion, but their art and letters, their politics and their public amusements. It was *their* home as well as the Almighty's, and on occasion they were familiar, and even a little vulgar with Him. It was a place in which they could sit in their slippers — metaphorically, that is; for though they frequently did so literally, it was by way of reverence, not ease. They enjoyed themselves in this *Shool* of theirs; they shouted and skipped and shook and sang, they wailed and moaned; they clenched their fists and thumped their breasts, and were not least happy when they were crying. There is an apocryphal anecdote of one of them being in the act of taking a pinch of snuff, when the confession caught him unexpectedly.
>
> 'We have trespassed,' he wailed mechanically, as he spasmodically put the snuff in his bosom, and beat his nose with his clenched fist.

The 'other' immigrants and pariahs of today — the blacks in their homespun revivalist chapels — would know what this is

41. Zangwill, *Children of the Ghetto*, pp.254-6.

all about. For the rejected and dispossessed the language may be different, but the liturgy is the same.

The street society of the Jew contrasted vividly with his gentile neighbour. In 1895, the environs constituted, according to Rocker, 'an abyss of human suffering, an inferno of misery'. It appeared finally to dispel his illusion that, as social conditions became worse, those who suffered so much would come to realise the deeper causes of their harsh existence. In the East End he found 'a pitch of material and spiritual degradation from which a man can no longer rise. Those who have been born into misery and never know a better state are rarely able to resist and revolt.' Yet the exception was there. Among the Jewish labouring poor he would discern the social dynamic for questioning and change. In this and other ways, the newcomers offended their more stolid neighbours — native-born Jews and Gentiles alike. A notable exclusionist, commenting on the 'invasion' of Spitalfields between 1881 and 1891, lamented the influx of foreign habits, of shops where 'smoked beef and sausages from Warsaw' were the staple foods sold, and where Yiddish placards, handbills and newspapers had usurped English print. 'There are Yiddish clubs and gambling halls, and little Jewish lodging houses without end . . . like the ghetto of a continental city.'[42]

The chorus was joined by two home-born Jews, in their evidence to the Immigration Committee (1891). A Mr Henry Deyonge, Whitechapel cigar-maker, deplored that 'there has been a very large increase (of immigrants) in the last eight years. In Wentworth Street out of eighty-five shops there are forty-eight in the hands of Russian and Polish Jews'; while Mr Simmons, a native of Spitalfields and a dress-trimming maker, substantiated the change with underlying hostility. 'I know a street, when I was a boy there was not a Jew . . . and now it is completely full of them.' Which street? Those of Spitalfields were remnants of decayed respectability, infested with cheap lodging-houses and abodes of criminals and prostitutes. The incidence of Jewish immigration meant the ousting of brothels and disorderly houses, much to the chagrin of their occupants. Such was the case of the then infamous Flower

42. Wilkins, *The Alien Invasion*, p.20.

and Dean Street, which in 1902 temporarily accommodated the American writer Jack London, who was exploring unsalubrious sites for his East End investigations for *The People of the Abyss.* Earlier Amadeus, correspondent for the *Tower Hamlets Independent* (4 February, 1882) described it as a street

> well known to most persons in the East End, at all counts by the reputation it bears as the harbour of refuge of people of a certain class . . . made up of tramps, beggars, dock and other casual labourers . . . Others are evidently of a criminal type and class, and not a few are known to have been convicted for various crimes . . . it being useless for the police to follow beyond a certain point, even when they happen to appear on the scene as the houses communicate with one another and a man pursued can run in and out like a rabbit in a warren . . . It was unsafe for police to venture in alone . . . One had his skull recently cracked with an iron crowbar; another on reaching a certain point in the street at a late hour in the night was threatened by a man standing on a kerbstone, who held a large stone in his hand and said, 'If you come a step further, I'll knock your brains out with the stone!'

Near by, and parallel to it, ran Hanbury Street, which reached its peak of inglorious fame on 8 September, 1888, with the discovery of the Jack the Ripper murder of prostitute 'Dark' Annie Chapman in the rear of number twenty-nine. By 1907, the Rev. W.H. Davies, then Rector of Spitalfields, could report a change for the better.[43] A Rothschild social investment had led to the demolition of the rabbit warrens in Flower and Dean Street, and neighbouring Thrawl Street, which were replaced by functional, high-rising, Charlotte de Rothschild dwellings. Also, Jews had moved into those houses where certain rooms had been used for vice. Initially they would occupy one room, and persist in staying, notwithstanding the insults and provocations by the bordello operators. Eventually the Jew would take over a second room, and, in the long run, tough Jewish puritanism proved formidable against its more permissive antagonist. The *demi-monde* could see no profit or pleasure in remaining, and eventually took off to more lucrative areas.

Yet, paradoxically, the Jews themselves were not free from

43. LCC Report on Accommodation and Attendance, 1907. Minute 9768.

the 'social evil'. Immigration provided limitless opportunities for the white slave trafficker. The initial centre of operations was the Pale, where *HaMelitz*[44] reports

> empty and dissolute men and also evil women who go about — from town to town and across the countryside . . . and deceive Jewish maidens with slippery tongue into leaving their native land and going under their guidance to distant parts, saying that there they will find good pay for their work in business firms.

Presentable young men, hired for the purpose of undertaking marriage with suitable young women, would soon 'take them by boat to India or Brazil or Argentina or to other American countries and sell them to houses of prostitution'. England did not escape the traffic. Here, young men were employed to pick up lonely girls embarking at the dockside and inveigle them to a place of refuge, which soon revealed itself as a brothel. Within the ghetto the single girl, living alone, provided a permanent challenge to the seducer-cum-*procureur*. Virginity being regarded as sacrosanct before marriage, the fallen women could find no redemption but to sink deeper into the morass of prostitution. By 1898 the extent of the danger was recognised when a letter signed jointly by seven leading European rabbis was sent to eastern Europe exhorting the rabbinate there to warn prospective immigrants, particularly girls, to be wary of strange men who presented themselves as suitors. We have seen that the Jews' Temporary Shelter was already fully alive to the problem in the late 1880s by their close liaison with the Hebrew Ladies' Protective Society, whose agents watched carefully at the points of disembarkation for unaccompanied girls. Yet the persistence of the evil manifested itself in the exposure of the 1909 Conference of the Jewish Association for the Protection of Girls and Women, when they reported (of the years 1903 to 1909) 222 'cases of girls who have taken to immoral lives and who, in many cases, have eventually disappeared from the country' and 198 'people and houses suspected of being concerned in the Traffic'. However, most of the victims were designated for 'service' abroad, and only a couple of

44. *HaMelitz* XXXVIII, 67 (27 March-9 April, 1898).

streets constituted public evidence of a brothel quarter in the East End.

With recurring pogroms, expulsions and the ceaseless struggle for existence in Eastern Europe, so did the area of Jewish settlement extend its boundaries eastward along Stepney, following the general line of the two main thoroughfares.[45] By 1911, there were 106,082 'Russians and Poles' recorded in the current census, to which must be added a further 20,000 Jews emanating from the eastern borderlands. The majority were funnelled into the East End. At first there appeared few signs of adverse reaction to the newcomers. But for those Londoners who faced the expanding ghetto, their growing fear and distaste for the bizarre invaders would be appropriately utilised: by demagogues seizing on the traditional scapegoat, politicians on the make, or trade union leaders (albeit ill-informed and prejudiced) who viewed their coming as a threat to the livelihood of their members. In the land of the open door, powerful exclusionist forces were already mobilising.

45. The Whitechapel and Commercial Roads with their connecting streets, courts and alleyways.

3. Briton and Alien

They [the Jews] cherished thrift, sobriety and industry. He almost wished that they were all Jews in his parish. He thought New Road should be called Jew Road — and a very good road it was.

> Speech by the Rev. D. Ross at meeting at St. George's Vestry, East London, protesting against the persecution of the Jews in Russia reported in the *Tower Hamlet Independent*, 18 March, 1882.

We must prevent them [the aliens] from growing into a body at once more noxious and more disliked than they are at present.

Mr Burns and Mr Tillett and Mr Mann could raise a *Judenherze* tomorrow if they like to do. It is for the prudent statesman to cut away the ground under their feet.

> S.H. Jeyes, in *The Destitute Alien in Great Britain*, edited by Arnold White (1892).

Be it Russian or Pole, Lithuanian or Jew
I care not but take it for granted,
That the island of Britain can readily do
With the notice: 'No Alien Wanted'.

> 'Will Workman' in *The People*
> (February 1909).

In Britain the general attitude towards Jews underwent some transformation during the course of the nineteenth century. There was an overall sense of ambiguity in notions which could accommodate fear and distate with envy and respect. Sir Walter Scott, commenting on the Jew, Isaac of York,[1] reveals the symptoms of his time.

The obstinacy and avarice of the Jews, being thus in a measure placed in opposition to the fanaticism and tyranny of those under whom they lived, seemed to increase in proportion to the persecution with which they visited . . . On these terms they lived; and

1. *Ivanhoe*, 1819.

their character, influenced accordingly, was watchful, suspicious and timid — yet obstinate, uncomplying and skilful in evading the dangers to which they were exposed.

His romantic contemporary Byron was more true to form in his vilification of the Jew as symbolising unprincipled rapacity, and wielding unlimited power:

> But let us not to own the truth refuse,
> Was ever Christian land so rich in Jews?
> Those parted with their teeth to good King John,
> And now, Ye Kings! they kindly draw your own.
> All States, all things, all sovereigns they control,
> And waft a loan from 'Indies to the Pole'.
>
> (*The Age of Bronze*)

But the poet was no dispassionate judge expressing a balanced verdict against a public enemy. He proceeds to expose to the reader the source of his own prejudices — the excessive demands of a spendthrift and dissolute youth:

> In my younger days they lent me cash that way
> Which I found very troublesome to pay.

Coleridge struck an ambivalent pose — respect for ancient Hebrew lore but contempt for the modern Jew. 'The two images farthest removed from each other which can be comprehended under one term are, I think, Isaiah — "Hear, O heavens, and give ear, O earth!" — and Levi of Hollywell Street — "Old clothes!" — both of them Jews, you'll observe, *Immane quantum discrepant!*'[2] There was no attempt at rational explanation which might vindicate the community under attack. In line with his fellows, he refused to concern himself with historical and social forces outside the Jews' control, which forced on them the traditional economic role of 'peddlers and fiddlers' and, for the majority, the realities of poverty and degradation. Dickens's Fagin was the inevitable *reductio ad absurdum* of the distorted image which prevailed

2. *Table Talk*, 14 August, 1833. He went on to suggest that 'the Jews of the lower orders are the very lowest of mankind; they have not a principle of honesty in them; to grasp and be getting money for ever is their single and exclusive occupation'.

among all classes. Charles Lamb had some respect for the pariah, but was all for keeping him apart, on the precept that centuries of injury, contempt and hate on one side (the Gentile) cloaked revenge, dissimulation and hate on the other, affecting the blood of the children. He confessed that he was not in favour of approximation between Jew and Gentile, which was becoming fashionable, affirming that the 'spirit of the synagogue is essentially separative'.[3]

Yet the demand for easing restrictions on Jews was mooted early and projected on the political scene. Robert Grant, MP for Inverness, proposed the admission of Jews to the House of Commons. It was carried on the first reading by a majority of eighteen, but lost on the second by sixty-three. In an article in the *Edinburgh Review* (January, 1831), Macaulay openly espoused the cause of Jewish 'liberation', demolishing old shibboleths, and pointedly rejected the widespread accusation of their 'lack of patriotism by living morally and politically in communion with their brethren who are scattered all over the world'. There followed continual petitioning by socially established Jews for political equality; and their case was championed by Lord John Russell, who annually introduced his bill to bring Jews with the right qualifications within the pale of the Constitution.

But animosity to the prescription of granting full citizen's rights to the Jews persisted. Among the Jewish professionals, up to 1828, only twelve Jewish brokers were allowed to practise their calling in the City of London. Even converts were excluded. No Jews could own a shop or retail goods there until 1832. For the race tainted with the 'crime of Calvary', even in freer England, the road to full emancipation would be long and hard. Young Gladstone was still opposing admission of Dissenters to Universities and Jews to Parliament in the same year (1833) when Jews were first allowed to practise at the Bar. The legal erosion of disabilities was sustained particularly in favour of the financial and professional minority. In 1845 the offices of Alderman and Lord Mayor were open to Jews. The next year a Parliamentary Act legislated for them to hold land, and Jewish schools and

3. Essay, 'Imperfect Sympathies'.

synagogues were placed on the same footing as those of Dissenters. This was paralleled by the repeal of Queen Anne's statute, which encouraged conversion, and the abolition of the anachronistic *De Judaismo* prescribing special dress for Jews. By 1847 Gladstone 'astonished his father as well as a great host of his political supporters by voting in favour of the removal of Jewish disabilities'.[4] The politician explained that his change of tactics was dictated by the principles of justice and logic.

Certainly the steady acquisition of civil rights focused the absurdity of denying Jews political equality, although prejudice and fanaticism continued to act as a brake. Baron de Rothschild was returned five times for the City of London — yet he was still denied a vote. Religious obscurantism could be no better exemplified than in the case of Alderman Salomons, elected MP for Greenwich in 1851. He took his seat in the Commons, but on repeating the oath he omitted the words 'in the true faith of a Christian'. He was promptly fined £500 and expelled from the House. The farce could not endure for long. In 1858 came the Act allowing Jews to omit the oath, thus granting them free entry into Parliament. The 1870 Factories Act enacted further religious tolerance in permitting Jews to labour on Sundays, provided they observed Saturday closures. In 1871 the University Test Acts enabled Jews to graduate without violating their religious principles. By the 1870s established Anglo-Jewry had experienced the legal demolition of prejudice and bigotry. It would appear that, after centuries of discrimination, they could measure themselves in parity against the citizens of their adopted country. They had been poised, too long, on the brink of acceptance. At the point of fulfilment came the warning signals — as their Russian co-religionists responded dramatically to the accelerated pace of Tsarist persecution.

Already in the 1870s a marked increase in alien Jews was a source of fear and embarrassment to Anglo-Jewry. In March 1871 its mouthpiece — the *Jewish Chronicle* — perceived with obvious relief 'the very pleasing fact that there is a very material decrease in the number of poor foreign Jewish

4. John Morley, *Life of Gladstone*, London, 1903, vol. 1, pp.106, 375.

immigrants, and a very material increase in the poor Jews who have left this country to seek subsistence elsewhere' during the past year. The threat of a swarm of distinctive, peculiarly clad, Yiddish-speaking paupers descending on Britain weighed heavily not only on the socially eminent but also on the recently settled German and Dutch immigrants. The one feared social retrogression through being identified with such unpalatable co-religionists; the other feared for his newly-found acceptance and occupation, both threatened by the newcomer. The Board of Guardians had adopted the Poor Law formula of restricting the possibilities of cash relief by imposing a residential qualification of six months before any applicant could be considered. It was tough luck on the poor 'greener' who had nowhere else to turn. The unspoken assumption was that starvation was a rational deterrent. But such inhumanity would focus the alien issue still further to the detriment of the good name of the Jewish community, founded on the tradition of mutual aid. Ultimately, for their own interest, Anglo-Jewry would have to formulate a more positive help programme.

The dilemma posed, attitudes fluctuated between a kind of patronising hospitality and cold neglect. One way of averting the increase in unwanted guests was to invest in propaganda in the European and Russian press to dissuade Jews from leaving. Another was to encourage them to go forward to America. Those who persisted in settling must be quickly indoctrinated with the English language and way of life. The modes of the *stetl* were discouraged, Yiddish was to be eradicated. These were a permanent concern to the Establishment — secular and religious. The latter is noted by the *Jewish Chronicle* (12 January, 1877) with an impertinent comment on 'Foreign Immigrants'. 'A correspondent who signs his communication "A Jewish Minister" writes to us urging that greater efforts be made to raise the *moral tone* of Foreign Jewish immigrants. He writes at some length desiring that this subject should receive the attention of the Jewish clergy.' The reaction of the *Jewish Chronicle* reflected accurately the response of Anglo-Jewry from the first impact of the pogroms. Soon after the assassination of Alexander II (1 March, 1881) it warned of the dangers accruing to western

Jews from increased persecution of their Russian brethren.[5]

> In Western Europe one is apt to forget that the centre of gravity of Judaism is in Russia . . . Any improvement in the intellectual condition of the Russian Jews may have ultimate influence on the Jews throughout the world. And, on the other hand, any deterioration in their conditions is sure to throw a further burden on the benevolence of their Western brethren.

With the outbreak, concern with the 'burden' as much as the victims soon manifested itself. On 27 May, 1881, the *Jewish Chronicle* reported a conference of the Council of the Anglo-Jewish Association called on 22 May, 1881, to organise a protest meeting at the Mansion House against Russian persecution. Owing to the 'cordial reception' given by the Tsar to a private Jewish delegation in Russia, it was judged inexpedient to hold a public meeting here. Instead, a collection of funds was undertaken to 'alleviate the distress of sufferers by the outrages', to which the chairman Baron Henry de Worms contributed £100. Such views were reinforced by the credibility shown towards the Tsar's 'good intentions' by the English rabbinate at the same time. On 18 May, 1881 at the German Synagogue, New Broad Street, ninety Jews were assembled 'at the invitation of the Russian Emperor to take the oath of allegiance to his Imperial Majesty'. In his sermon, Rabbi Dr Herman Adler comforted his audience with the proposition that 'his Imperial Majesty viewed these outrages and excesses with detestation, and that his Imperial Government were doing all in their power to quell and repress these unhappy disturbances'. But other thoughts of his Imperial Majesty were invoked by the Rabbi when he 'regretted to see that some Russian Jews had been guilty of forging the notes of the Russian Government. Such a proceeding was a violation of the law "Thou shalt not steal".'[6] Was the victim part cause of his own persecution? The theme was developed further. On 10 June, the *Jewish Chronicle* editorial, commenting on the recent expulsion of Jews from Kiev, suggested:

5. *Jewish Chronicle*, 25 March, 1881. The editorial refers to Nihilism as 'the patriotism of dynamite' in which a number of Jews were involved.
6. Ibid., 20 May, 1881

The only protective measures which seem possible are political liberation by the Czar or intellectual progress by their own efforts. The former appears hopeless; the latter remedy lies within their reach. *The pressing need for Russian Jews at the present moment is the renunciation of their exclusive attitude and their assimilation to their fellow citizens.*

An extraordinary deduction — since it was, ultimately, the autocrat who had the power to decide and any such expectation from the All-Highest was wishful thinking. By 29 July the *Jewish Chronicle* had got the message. The victim was no longer to blame — in Russia.

The Russian intolerance against the Jews is, practically speaking, the root of all evil in Judaism throughout the world . . . The intolerance of the government finds its counterpart in the superstition of the subjects, and the narrow and rigid ultra-orthodoxy of the Polish Jews is mainly an outcome of the intolerance of his superiors . . . By open protest and secret entreaty every means must be taken for the future to bring the Czar and his advisors to a sense of their duty towards the Russian Jews.

But with the victims now encamped on its own doorstep the paper voiced its fears for Anglo-Jewry. Here the immigrants could constitute a danger:

Our fair fame is bound up with theirs; the outside world is not capable of making minute discrimination between Jew and Jew, and forms its opinion of Jews in general as much, *if not more*, from them than from the Anglicised portion of the Community.

They retain all the habits of their former home and display no desire to assimilate with the people among whom they dwell. They appear altogether to forget that in accepting the hospitality of England, they owe a reciprocal duty of becoming Englishmen. As it is, they join a *Hebra*, mix only with their fellow countrymen, and do in England as the Poles do.

It looked to 'the process of transformation from Poles to Englishmen' as a salutary one:[7]

Let us aid by all the means in our power to hasten this consummation. By improving their dwellings, attracting them to our synagogues, breaking down their isolation in all directions and

7. Ibid., 12 August, 1881, editorial 'Our Foreign Poor'.

educating their children in an English fashion, we can do much to change our foreign poor into brethren, who shall not only be Jews but English Jews.

And this policy was tortuously pursued during the long years of immigrant intervention. It was constantly subjected to buffetings derived from shifts in Establishment policy in response to the ebb and flow of 'anti-alien' sentiment.[8]

The first reaction of British non-Jews to the incoming victims of the pogroms was one of universal sympathy. Their concern evoked a climax of protest in January, 1882. Charles Reade, voicing the Christian conscience, wrote to the *Daily Telegraph* (21 January, 1881) calling on England to dissociate itself 'from the crime of those picture-worshipping idolators and cowardly murderers by public disavowal and prayerful humiliation, since the monsters call themselves Christians'. On 14 January, Lord Shaftesbury in *The Times* had already condemned the outbreaks as 'connived at by the (Russian) government officials and executed by the multitude (Poles included, to their everlasting shame) such as, perhaps, has never been known since the destruction of Jerusalem'. The poet Algernon Swinburne joined the chorus in the *Daily Telegraph* (25 January, 1882):

> O Son of Man by lying tongues adored
> By murderous hand of slaves with feet red shod
> In carnage deep that ever Christian trod.

And the great Tenniel, in his cartoon in *Punch* entitled 'A cry from Christendom', symbolised Christian horror at Russian

8. A reasonable discussion of the positive and negative policies pursued by Anglo-Jewry can be seen in Gartner, *The Jewish Immigrant in England (1870-1914)*, section 'Native Jewry and Immigration', pp.49-56. One is forced to agree with the immigrant historian, A.R. Rollin, in his deduction that 'the victims of the Russian pogroms were not treated with the sympathy and compassion they deserved', (*Transactions of the Jewish Historical Society of England*, vol. XXI, p.211), which is verified by personal evidence of many survivors. The insensitivity of the *Jewish Chronicle* is again exemplified in the editorial of 6 January, 1882, reiterating after a terrible year, that 'we must restrict the advantages of emigration to the able-bodied and skilled workman' by promising aid only 'to certain ages and definite occupations'. The rest, presumably should be left to the mercy of the *pogroms!*

barbarism; the effect apparently enhanced by such melo-
dramatic versifying as:

> But the horrible rage of brute hordes by the slack hand of Power let
> slip
> The cold Mephistopheles smile on Authority's cynical lip —
> These Christendom fearlessly brands;
> Tells Emperor, Prince or dull Peasant 'tis playing a ruffian part . . .

Again, on 21 January, signatories to a letter to the Lord
Mayor of London urging him to call a public meeting to
afford 'public expression of opinion respecting the persecution which the Jews of Russia have recently and for some
time past suffered' included such eminents as John Morley,
Benjamin Jowett, Matthew Arnold and Charles Darwin.

There is little evidence to suggest that there was any
dramatic change of mood as the pace of immigration
heightened during the early 1880s. The *Lancet* report of
1884 was a warning signal and was recognised as such by the
organs of Anglo-Jewry. The overtones of patronisation and
distaste were there. It was to be expected that conflict
between local habitants and immigrants would arise as a
result of their mutually exclusive styles and cultures. A
climate of fear and suspicion would be sustained by the
incidence of job competition in a period of depression. The
earliest official outburst against aliens is observed in the *Pall
Mall Gazette* (February, 1886) which referred to 'A *Juden-
hetz* brewing in East London', deduced from a letter it had
received warning its readers that 'the foreign Jews of no
nationality whatever are becoming a pest and a menace to the
poor native-born East Ender' in that 'fifteen or twenty
thousand Jewish refugees of the lowest type . . . have a
greater responsibility for the distress which prevails (in the
East End) than probably all other causes put together.'[9] No
more restrained accusation or muffled innuendo. The problem was out in the open. Anglo-Jews quickly caught on to
the political implications. N.S. Joseph of the Jewish Board of
Guardians was first to jump on the restrictionist band-waggon
urging controls. Since the US Aliens Act and Bismarck's

9. *Jewish Chronicle*, 26 February, 1886.

expulsions of Poles from Prussia, 'What can happen, but an inundation?' The ball had now entered the political arena. On 10 March, 1887, in the House of Commons, Captain Colomb, Conservative MP for Tower Hamlets, Bow and Bromley, set the tone for a generation of restrictionists:[10]

> What great states of the world other than Great Britain permit the immigration of destitute aliens without restriction; and whether Her Majesty's Government is prevented by any Treaty obligations for making such regulations as shall put a stop to the free importation of destitute aliens into the United Kingdom.

By May 1887 the hunt was on. The *St James's Gazette* joined in the fray with a series of articles entitled 'Jewish Pauperism' which reached a crescendo of vituperation when it defined the immigrants as 'a colony of 30,000 or 40,000 steeped to the lips in every form of physical and moral degradation' and whose 'vast majority . . . are nihilists and anarchists of the worst type'. The pack soon found a leader. In the 19 May issue of *The Times* appeared a letter by the jingoist author Arnold White, deploring 'foreign paupers . . . replacing English workers and driving to despair men, women and children of our blood'. The official 'euphemism' voiced by Mr Henry G. Calcraft that 'a great deal of inconvenience is felt in certain districts of the East End' was met by the angry rejoinder, 'Not many of your readers would gather from the use of the word inconvenience the sombre faith of famine, shame and despair.' White offered himself as champion for the cause of free-born Englishmen dispossessed by the aliens:

> The question is one which the inarticulate portion of the community feel with intensity and bitterness. If the House of Commons will order a real inquiry into the facts, I for one will undertake to prove the reality of the evil, the urgency of the situation, and the feasibility of effective prevention.

Unemployment was a major pressure gauge for anti-alienism. By December, 1887 (following a peak year of unemployment), Bennett Burleigh wrote: 'Since 1883, during each recurring winter in London and other large towns, people have become

10. *Hansard* 3SH (311) 1724, 10 March, 1887.

familiarised with what is known as the "unemployed agitation". Is it a genuinely political agitation? My answer is: Quite as much so as any political movement.'[11] Those years had also highlighted the growing numbers of Jewish immigrants. Thus a ready-made scapegoat was available. 1887 was the year of opportunity both for political demagogues flying the anti-alien kite and the new social reformer. The East End borough of Tower Hamlets provided a focus, although it would be fair to say that commentaries in that area reflected a growing mood outside. On 19 April, 1887 the first recorded public meeting was held for the ratepayers of Mile End to petition for the exclusion of destitute aliens. It took the form of a debate with the motion put by Conservative MPs Captain Colomb, Howard Vincent and Lords Charles Beresford and Brabazon, and opposed by Jewish communal leaders led by Samuel Montagu, MP. The chairman was the ubiquitous Arnold White. The result was a compromise — a demand for a government enquiry.[12] But the great patriot White would not let go. On 14 July, writing *en route* for South Africa in the mail steamer *Athenian*, he directed (under the stirring title 'England for the English!') a second broadside through *The Times*: 'Will you permit me to fire a parting shot at the pauper foreigner? He is successfully colonising Great Britain under the nose of H.M. Government.' With what danger? Certainly to the employment of Britishers, especially the 'poor English girls who are struck the hardest by these famished aliens'.[13] He demanded a Parliamentary Commission on Immigration. But he was voicing attitudes already adopted by the government.[14] By 10 February, 1888, the appointment of a Select Committee of Inquiry had been agreed upon.

The government seemed to have been easily persuaded; not so the new school of social researchers headed by Charles Booth. But they too, helped overemphasise the alien issue as 'social reform became a dominant concern in English

11. Article 'The Unemployed', *Contemporary Review*, December 1887.
12. Reported in the *Jewish Chronicle*, 22 April, 1887.
13. Published in *The Times*, 23 July, 1887.
14. That legislation was under consideration was stated by the First Lord of the Treasury, W.H. Smith. (*Hansard* 3SH (520) 490, 12 July, 1887.)

politics'. In 1887 appeared Booth's first group study, *Conditions and Occupations of the People of Tower Hamlets 1886-1887*. Much scope is given to an 'objective' study of the alien contingent. Yet the report is not free of patronising sentiments or current prejudices. Certain descriptions of the Jews are neither elevated or detached:[15]

> Some (foreign Jews) may add nihilism and the bitterest kind of socialistic theories to very filthy habits . . . They seem capable of improvement, and so far have improved. It may take them 'several years to get washed' but if we compare the newcomers with those of the same race who have been settled here some time, the change is very marked.

The filth attributed to the Jews, as though it were their own peculiar import, is extraordinary, to say the least. Compared with their immediate neighbours they were paragons of cleanliness. For, in accordance with religious custom, to which most of the newcomers paid more than formal regard, weekly bathing and change of clothes were incumbent on every practising Jew on the eve of Sabbath. In addition their women were subjected to the compulsory ritual bath (*mikvah*). Further questionable observations on the Jews according to Booth appear elsewhere.[16]

Lower-class responses to Jewish infiltration were communicated to the upper social echelons and vice versa. Most of them created pictures of the immigrant in the image of their own prejudices. In the East End there is ample evidence of a build-up of both anti-alien and anti-Semitic sentiments with little subtlety of distinction. The ever-watchful Arnold White had mobilised his zealots for the fray: priests, publicans, clerks, stallholders and *lumpen* with one voice warned of increasing economic and social dangers accruing to their British brothers if the alien flood was not stemmed. Between the years 1888 and 1895 'we find the aliens becoming an important political and partisan problem, via private members' Bills, Government pledges and Liberal

15. Booth, *Conditions and Occupations of the People of the Tower Hamlets 1886-1887*, p.48.
16. See pp.80-2 below.

opposition and via trade union and Trade Union Congress resolution'.[17]

Although the ruling party appeared to have succumbed easily to the persuasions of the exclusionists, the outcome of the report proved ambivalent.[18] Its conclusions revealed both a setback and a promise for the agitators. The Committee expressed no urgent need for legislation but resurrected some antiquated clauses from an Act of William IV[19] to quantify immigration: by the compilation of statistics based on the compulsory reporting by masters of ships entering port of the number of aliens on board. The ultimate figures produced were invalid since they did not exclude immigrants in transit, and thus unwittingly provided fuel for the alarmists.

By 1888 prejudice had broken surface. Political agitators were already mouthing rhetoric derived from the lowest common denominator — the irrational hatred festering in the mind of the slum-dweller. The Whitechapel murders of that year provided the setting for a minor outbreak of Judophobia. After the third 'Ripper' murder a local editor observed under the heading 'A Riot Against the Jews':[20]

> On Saturday in several quarters of East London the crowds who assembled in the streets began to assume a very threatening attitude towards the Hebrew population of the District. It was repeatedly asserted that no Englishman could have perpetrated such a horrible crime as that of Hanbury Street, and that it must have been done by a JEW — and forthwith the crowds began to threaten and abuse such of the unfortunate Hebrews as they found in the streets. Happily the presence of a large number of police . . . prevented a riot actually taking place.

The Committee had been fact-finding during a year of relatively low unemployment and immigration. The following year was different. The aftermath of mass expulsions from Moscow and Kiev and a rising rate of unemployment re-dramatised the issue via a vociferous outburst of anti-alien propaganda. Arnold White got his reinforcements in print. In

17. John A. Garrard, *The English and Immigration 1880-1910*, 1971, p.27.
18. August 1889.
19. 6 William IV, c. x1, s.2.
20. *East London Observer*, 15 September, 1888.

September, 1890 W.H. Wilkins demanded the formation of 'a society for the protection of British workmen' from 'the hordes of destitute Jews'.[21] Agitation against the 'destitute aliens' grew in volume and intensity between 1891 and 1895, although the influx declined.[22] By then the hard core of anti-Semitism had formed. An 'Associating for Preventing the Immigration of Destitute Aliens' was set up in 1891 under the auspices of the Earl of Dunraven and Arnold White, with Wilkins as Secretary. On 24 July it held its first meeting. It advertised speakers who, significently, were drawn from a wide spectrum of society, including Conservative MPs and trade union leaders. 1892 was a peak year of propaganda and registered the first large-scale entry of the alien problem into active politics.

Conservative politicians were now astir. A caucus of back-benchers,[23] acting as a pressure group, hustled the Conservative government into commitment to an Aliens Bill as an election gambit. Written support came from two expected sources.[24] They constituted an amalgam of exclusionist polemics. Early racist overtones are detected — a promise of the more sophisticated theories diffused by Houston Stewart Chamberlain. In Arnold White's symposium, a Montague Crackanthorpe accused the incoming Jews of exposing 'our working class' to the dangers of 'ruinous competition'. 'The Polish Jew drives the British Workman out of the Labour market just as *base* currency drives a *pure* currency out of existence.'[25] Another contributor, the Rev. G.S. Reaney, presumably a local priest, commented on the 'moral aspect' of the case against immigrants when applied to the East End:

> Into that area of helplessness we permit to pass every day a dirty, alien and yet more helpless inflow of humanity . . . bringing with it poverty, ignorance and the vices common to the deeper depths of continental cities.

21. *National Review*, September 1890.
22. From 7,000 in 1891 to 3,000 and below after 1892.
23. The most vociferous were Howard Vincent (MP for Sheffield Central), Captain Colomb (Tower Hamlets Bow), and J. Lowther (Kent, Thanet).
24. *The Destitute Alien in Great Britain*, essays edited by Arnold White, London, 1892; and Wilkins, *The Alien Invasion*.
25. White, *The Destitute Alien in Great Britain*, p.59.

He voiced his parishioners' sentiments with obvious sympathy:

> When visiting the poor when times were bad I often heard the weary complaint, 'It's them Jews'. Time after time I heard that lament. Many men and women, struggling to keep a home over their heads, but driven out of work by the foreigner, who could 'live on less', and would take less, and work longer, have said to me, 'What's the use? The Jews are coming by thousands, and there will be nothing left.'

And his observations were tainted with his parishioners' naive conceptions and myths on Jews in general:

> Their alien looks, habits and language combined with their remarkable fecundity, tenacity and money getting gift, make them a ceaseless weight upon the poor amongst whom they live . . . truth compels the sentiment, that wherever the foreigner comes in any numbers, the neighbourhood in which he settles speedily drops in tone, in character and in morals . . . Their very virtues seem prolific of evil, when like some seed blown by the wind, they fall and fructify on English soil.[26]

Only the effect of a new exodus could bring relief 'when thousands of the race that spoiled the Egyptians journeyed down the broad streets that lead to the docks of Poplar'. Only then was this Christian gentlemen convinced 'that in thousands of hearts of London's poor the thought would kindle like a new-born hope, "We shall have a chance now" '.

Commenting on 'Foreign Pauper Immigration', one S.H. Jeyes adds to the volume of diatribes.[27] To him the aliens were a deposit of outcasts shot on out by the continent. 'They are sifted here by natural selection and we keep the refuse.' He called on his readers to follow the working men, the strongest advocates of restriction. He defined their prejudices by enumerating the vices attributed to the immigrant:

> They submit without grumbling to the petty tyrannies of the overseer and the mean exactions of the sweater; they join no Trade Union; many of them do not speak English and they mix very little

26. Ibid., pp.87-92.
27. Ibid., pp.174-191.

with Englishmen; they marry and give in marriage amongst their own people; in their virtues as in their vices, they are a race apart. Under no circumstance would they be popular here; but since they succeed, if not in taking the bread out of the English mouths, at least in reducing the margin of wages which might be spent on beer and gin, they are naturally and not quite unfairly detested.

In reducing the rate of wages they 'therefore strengthen the spirit of discontent and disorder . . . which in time may pollute the ancient constitutional liberalism of England with the visionary violence of Continental Socialism.' W.H. Wilkins went further and accused them of swelling 'the secret socialistic or foreign revolutionary societies', which 'have papers of their own circulated among themselves, written in Yiddish, breathing the vilest of political sentiments – Nihilism of the most outrageous description.'[28]

The impetus towards restrictionism brought together strange bedfellows: Conservatives and Imperialists on the one hand and radicals and trade-union leaders on the other. A popular cry for the vote-catchers had arrived.[29] Trade unions, by definition, were forced into ambivalent postures, for instance exclusion to protect their members, but later inclusion by attempts to organise the Jewish worker. The reaction of dockers' leader Ben Tillett typified attitudes at the grass roots; though, at times, it was tempered by the philosophical demands of the brotherhood of the working class, notwithstanding race or creed.[30] The earliest, less savoury manifestation of Tillett's anti-alienism was observed by Beatrice Webb at a dock labourers' meeting at the Tabernacle Hall, Barking Road, in Canning Town.[31]

Secretary Tillett opened the proceedings. A light haired, little man with the face of a religious enthusiast; might have been a revivalist. Honest undoubtedly, but ignorant and unwise. He ranted against White Slavery, subcontract and irregular hours.

28. Wilkins, *The Alien Invasion*, pp.47-8.

29. See 'Jewish Immigration in British Party Politics in the 1890s', a paper presented by I. Finestein, QC to the Jewish Historical Society of England at a joint conference of Anglo-American Jewish Historians, 12 July, 1970.

30. Garrard, *The English and Immigration, 1880-1910*, Chapter 9.

31. Diary of Beatrice Potter (Webb), 1 December, 1887, in *My Apprenticeship*, p.307.

The bulky form of a local worthy, XY, makes its way to the platform.

> No one knew him except the secretary. He took the seat nearest to me, and asked the chairman to give him the resolution to look at. Then in a stage whisper to the Secretary, 'I will give you twenty pounds but don't let my name appear. I don't want it to be known. Of course *you* will support me about foreign immigration.'

The inference is there, although Beatrice Webb does not record Tillett's acceptance of what appeared to her a political bribe. Wilkins listed forty-three unions who, by 1888, had condemned unrestricted immigration; prominent among these was the Dockers' Union.[32] Tillett, in his own autobiographical commentaries, *Memories and Reflections* (1931), appears to have conveniently forgotten his early antipathies. In *The Dock Labourers' Bitter Cry* (published 1889) he had voiced the sentiments of his largely Irish dock labourers by his polemics:

> The influx of continental pauperism aggravates and multiplies the number of ills which press so heavily on us . . . Foreigners come to London in large numbers, herd together in habitations unfit for beasts, the sweating system allowing the more grasping and shrewd a life of comparative ease in superintending the work.

By 1931 his 'memories' did not appear to serve him well. Musing on his experiences as a young seaman, he recalls his reaction to the sight of Cossacks beating up Jews.

> In the market place at Riga I had seen crouching Jews, poor souls, with bent figures, beaten, cursed and kicked. *From that moment I felt it to be part of my ambition to assist every refugee and maltreated person it was possible for me to assist.* [!!]

He 'reflects' back to July, 1887, when the common sight of 'No Irish Need Apply' aroused his indignation, at the very

---

32. Other unions who condemned unrestricted immigration according to Wilkins included the ASE, Amalgamated Society of Locomotive Engineers and Firemen, Amalgamated Society of Carpenters and Joiners, Miners' Association (Durham), United Operative Plumbers' Association of Great Britain and Ireland, Progressive Union of Cabinet Makers, The Shoemakers' Association and the Master Tailors' Association (Liverpool).

time that he himself was indulging in anti-immigrant tirades. His memory is more succinct of the meeting at the Tabernacle Hall (Beatrice Webb had just published her own account in *My Apprenticeship*), when he chose to remember her as 'our rather aristocratically prejudiced visitor; she was young, clever, much petted by the intellectuals of the older generation, undoubtedly sincere, anxious to help, but somewhat condescending'. Perhaps it would be more charitable to Tillett to suggest that his confrontation with the stranger could be summed up by his own welcoming words to some new immigrants arriving at the dockside, 'Yes, you are our brothers and we will do our duty by you. *But we wish you had not come*';[33] and not those he chose to indulge in, in old age, to a joint meeting of representatives of women's labour organisations and workers for Moral Rearmament:[34]

> Years ago, I believed that when we began to get an international sense of things, learned to look beyond our own borders, fraternised with workers of other lands . . . regardless of race, colour and creed, that we would be making a bold step towards universal peace and goodwill.

It would appear that, to most trade unionists, the alien Jew meant sweating. Wilkins, in enlisting evidence from them, cites a letter sent to him by the secretary of the National Society of Amalgamated Brass Workers (10 June, 1891), calling for state regulation of immigration, with the hope that Wilkins's 'efforts will bring about such restrictions as will put an end to an evil which has been the means of providing a surplus labour market to become a ready prey to the sweaters', thus subscribing to the myth that all Jews aspired to entrepreneurship. Trade-union leader John Hodge, presiding over a session of the twenty-fifth Trade Union Congress at Glasgow (September, 1892), deplored the 'enormous immigration of destitute aliens' who 'take work at any price' such that 'the tailoring and kindred trades have been practically ruined'. It was during this session that a final

33. Cited in C. Russell and H.S. Lewis, *The Jew in London*, London, 1900, p.13.
34. Speech in National Trade Union Club, 5 February, 1940.

resolution was passed calling for government legislation to halt the entry of pauper aliens.

Was the immediate identification of Jew with sweating justified? Did he deliberately perpetuate the 'system'? One scrutinises the balance-sheet of argument. J.A. Garrard[35] suggests that 'the causal connection . . . was not without a certain amount of validity. Immigrant trades were generally sweated trades.' In spite of terrible conditions in the small workrooms and outhouses, even if he could obtain a job in a factory he would inevitably return to his workshop; and conversely he would be found to quit his job when and where factorisation took place. This and the drive for master's status, perpetuated by the facility with which small, independent concerns could come into existence, helped to delay, in their area, the build-up of a factory system.

The validity of such evidence can be debated. What opportunities were there for the mobility of Jewish labour? How many Gentile employers, in non-immigrant trades, would be prepared to employ alien Jews who, as previously cited, were generally unpopular in a period of economic stress and job competition? Each was forced back on his own. 'Britons first' was the normal response of masters and trade unionists. Where could the greener turn for work, but to the insatiable demands of a self-generating, cut-throat industry dominated by his kith and kin? At least there he could find some promise (albeit illusory) of job stability; and security among his fellow Yiddish-speaking expatriates, sharing a common religious and cultural experience, and above all, the bond of past persecution and imminent want. As a stranger within the gates, his isolation and, therefore, work choice were as much externally imposed as self-inflicted.

But sweating had existed long before Jewish immigrants and would have sustained itself without them. Their impact was marginal. Beatrice Webb had studied the problem at first hand and thought it through. She observed that, although the Jews monopolised the coat trades and the boot-finishing process in the East End, they were virtually strangers to the

35. *The English and Immigration*, p.159.

manufacture of vests and trousers nationally.[36]

> If the investigator surveyed all the industries in which the evil conditions of sweating prevailed the Jewish workers were found to be but a fraction of the whole body of workers, and also, to a large extent, as a non-competing group, confined to the manufacture of certain commodities, which had not been produced in the locality before. In short, if every foreign Jew resident in England had been sent back to his birthplace, the bulk of the sweated workers would not have been affected, whether for better or for worse.

She went on to deny that the sub-contractor, middle-man or wholesaler were any of them alone responsible for sweating. Asked by a member of the Select Committee of the House of Lords on the Sweating System how she would define it,[37] her reply was: 'An enquiry into the Sweating System is practically an enquiry into all labour employed in manufacture *which has escaped the Factory Act and Trade Unions.*' Later, in a paper read at the twenty-fourth Annual Congress of the Co-operative Society held at Rochdale (June, 1892), she went further:

> The sweater is, in fact, the whole nation. The mass of struggling men and women whose sufferings have lately been laid bare are oppressed and defrauded in every relation of life: by the man who sells or gives out the material on which they labour; by the shopkeeper who sells them provisions on credit, or forces them under the truck system; by the landlord who exacts, in return for the four walls of a bedroom, or for the unpaved or undrained back yard, the double rent of workshop and dwelling; and lastly by every man, woman and child who consumes the product of their labour.

The common features present where sweating was extensive were certainly 'small masters in hidden workshops' or 'workers in their own dwellings'. Such phenomena were not only confined to East End Jews.

Yet the would-be detached observer still reveals the limitations innate in a Victorian 'bourgeois' upbringing, when she makes her inconsistent and, sometimes, prejudicial

---

36. Beatrice Webb, *My Apprenticeship*, p.331.
37. Question 3248 — Report from the Select Committee of the House of Lords on the Sweating System (1888-9).

pronouncements on Jews. Earlier,[38] she had argued that the character of Jewish compulsive entrepreneurship was not that of a bloodsucker or agent of the rich to suppress the poor. 'Given a quantity of ignorant, poverty-stricken, unskilled men, scattered in their wretched homes in the purlieus of a crowded city, what other plan could bring them to work at all?' Yet, later, the old Adam is evoked. These ignorant paupers are transformed into a more erudite species, with such intellectual propensities which make for skill in outwitting the Gentile in the struggle for the main goal — material success; and the 'scientific' approach is marred by conventional myths and presumptions. Together with Sidney Webb, she essays a more sophisticated analysis of the social and economic motivations sustaining the immigrant in 'The Jews of East London'.[39] Together they recall Booth's prognosis that, although these Jews are 'placed in the midst of the very refuse of our civilisation', they always 'as a mass shift upwards'.

Why? The Webbs explain that even the poorest Jews had inherited, through the medium of their religion,[40] a trained intellect; that the absence of class distinction in the Judaic theocracy provided a striking equality between co-religionists and that a common, though narrow, level of intellectual training equipped Jews with a strong memory-power for sustained reasoning and elaborate calculation. Thus in East London one saw a race of brain workers confronting a class of (inferior?) manual labourers.

Such 'striking equality' between co-religionists was a figment of the imagination. Conflicts in trades were as sharp and bitter between master and men as elsewhere.[41] As we have noted, social stratification between the new immigrant and home-born Jew was self-evident; as well as that sense of

'38. *Conditions and Occupations of the People of the Tower Hamlets 1886-7*, p.49.

39. Beatrice and Sidney Webb, *Problems of Modern Industry*, Chapter 11.

40. The Talmud is invested with the properties of 'a training ground for his [the Jew's] intellectual and emotional faculties ... the key to all the varied perplexities and manifold troubles of his daily existence'. Since the Talmud is 'emphatically a *Corpus Juris*' and 'Divine Law', Gentile laws, according to the Webbs, are to be evaded, or obeyed by the Jews, as expediency allows.

41. See especially Chapters 6, 7 and 11 below.

caste division based on territorial origin, for instance Litvak, Galician, Ukrainian, etc. As for the dubious qualities of 'reasoning' and 'calculation' attributed specifically to these Jews, this may equally be suspect as hyperbole, rather than accepted as a conclusion derived from empirical observation. Even a Jewish conspiracy thesis is evoked! 'He [the Polish Jew] suffers oppression and bears ridicule with imperturbable good humour; in the face of insult and abuse he remains silent. For why resent when your object is to overcome? Why bluster and fight *when you may manipulate and control in secret*?' The 'scientific method' which would place the Jew under a microscope revealed a specimen who was 'deficient in that highest and latest development of human sentiment — social morality': one who

> seems to justify by his existence those strange assumptions which figures for man in the political economy of Ricardo — an always enlightened selfishness, seeking employment or profit with an absolute mobility of body and mind, without preference, without interests outside the struggle for the existence and welfare of the individual and the family. We see these assumptions verified in the Jewish inhabitants of Whitechapel.[42]

If such was an 'objective' assessment by would-be sympathisers, one would be forced to concur with the earlier warnings of the editor of the *Poilishe Yidl* that 'the Englishman has no liking for the Jew'![43] A closer examination of the sub-culture of the ghetto, with its peculiar life-style and language, over a longer period, would have modified the deductions arrived at by the Webbs.

Such intellectual extravaganza could provide confirmation for those laymen who prejudged the issue. Sweating and 'craftsman-entrepreneurship' had long pre-dated immigration as a feature of English economic life. To the growing class of skilled labour — a self-conscious élite — unrestricted entry of unskilled aliens constituted a security risk. Such fears accord with Edward Thompson's explanation that 'where a skill was involved, the artisan was as much concerned with maintaining his status against the unskilled man, as he was in bringing

42. *Problems of Modern Industry*, pp.43-5.
43. *Poilishe Yidl*, editorial, no.12, 10 October, 1884.

pressure upon the employers'.[44] Hence the displacement of labour charges brought against the immigrant, for example one by a Mr Goodman, one-time Executive Member of Liverpool Operative Tailors' Society, who in evidence to the Sweating Committee warned that unrestricted alien labour would oust native labour in the large cities; another by a Mr J. Murfin, who called for a 'simple test of efficiency' as a requisite for entry under an Aliens Bill,[45] while Ben Tillett attributed the debasement of skills and increase in cut-throat competition in the docks largely to an invasion of new men 'ousted from their own trade by the foreigners'.

Numerous charges were made of the aliens' malpractices as competitors. Bakers suggested that their Jewish counterparts baked on Sunday, not because of religious conviction (as many, it was claimed, opened on Saturdays too!) but for the purpose of monopolising local trade. Their 'great object' was to 'supply Christians with bread . . . It is well known that the Jew supplies five times as much bread to the Christian as [to] his co-religionist.' So complained John Jenkins, secretary of the Amalgamated Union of Operative Bakers and Confectioners, to a Brixton meeting.[46] Gentile greengrocers accused Jews of depressing their business on the same grounds as stallholders, either by stealing their location or through Jews buying only from Jews. Certainly Jewish butchers and poultry dealers would have cornered the local Jewish market, since they alone supplied 'kosher' meat, but all fishmongers would have profited, since fish was the staple food of immigrants. There is therefore no record of animosity from local fish distributors or big stores, such as Venables or Gardiners, which benefited from the expansion of sales derived from Jewish custom!

The trade unionists' crime of blacklegging — actual or potential — was attributed to the alien, whose acceptance of lower living standards incurred the risk of depressed wages through unfair price competition. Strikes made the immi-

---

44. E.P. Thompson, *The Making of the English Working Class*, London, 1964, p.244.

45. Cited in the Royal Commission, vol. 11, p.512.

46. Report in *Jewish Chronicle*, 16 July, 1897. The Union in the same year took out a number of summonses against bakers operating on Sundays.

grant more vulnerable to the accusation, and there is a little evidence of this, significantly, in the bootmaking trade, which according to the Lords' Commission Report (1889), was one 'which attracts the largest number of "greeners" '.[47] By 1894 the numbers were diminishing as pressure towards factory production increased. In 1891 1560 'Russian and Polish' males and thirty-one females were employed in the boot and shoe trades in East London. By 1911, when factorisation was almost complete, the total numbers engaged were 1,936 males and seventy-four females. Yet there was no diminution in the cry of Jews capturing the trade, their destroying the system of apprenticeship and flooding shops with such 'cheap and nasty stuff that destroys the market and injures us'. Complainants to the Select Committee on Immigration (1889) went so far as to accuse the aliens, not only of depressing the boot trade in London through unfair competition, but in so doing of inflicting harm on the centres of production outside, such as Northampton, Leicester, etc. But how could a minority, which barely totalled 10,000 at its peak, have such a damaging effect on a labour force numbering 224,059, 248,789, and 251,143 in 1881, 1891, and 1901 respectively?[48] In fact the boot and shoe trades had suffered a steady deterioration in numbers up to 1881. They subsequently rose steadily to recover finally the 1861 total in 1901; and this notwithstanding the influx of aliens and the introduction of machinery with its labour-saving devices. Thus the two widely publicised charges by British bootmakers (the first before the TUC in 1894, the second before the Royal Commission in 1902) that the Jews were ousting native labour had no foundation in fact.

Tailoring, according to the exclusionists, evidenced the worst effects of alien intrusion. With sweating came the illusion of Jews displacing native labour. The reverse was

47. Evidence of this can be deduced from press reports. A case of strike-breaking appears in *Reynolds News*, 18 November, 1894, when a non-unionist, Eleazar Cohen, a bootlaster, was involved as plaintiff in a case of intimidation during a strike at an East London boot factory. He was threatened with a knife by a striker while blacklegging.

48. Fiscal Blue Book (1903), cd. 1761, p.362. Statistics from table giving numbers of workers in England and Wales through censuses taken every decade.

1. 'Jewish immigrants just landed'. From G. R. Simms, *Living in London*, London, 1902, vol. 1, p. 49.

2. A Jewish tailor's workshop before 1914.

3. Winthrop Street, typical of nineteenth-century Whitechapel; recently demolished.

4. Aron Lieberman.

true. The immigrants continued the tradition of transferring manufactures from the Continent to Britain. The new Jewish clothing trade steadily eroded the import of German garments. This is verified from diverse sources. By 1898 a City manufacturing house could report:[49]

> In the year 1885 demand for ladies' tailor made jackets came into vogue and to meet the demand for our British and Colonial trade we were compelled to import large quantities of these garments from Germany . . . We tried to produce these garments in our own factories, but without success, our women workers were unable to manipulate the hand irons used by the tailors, and we could not get them to do the work. As the fashion became more pronounced, large orders went abroad, and in 1888, £150,000 was sent to Germany in payment of these accounts. In 1887 we decided to introduce foreign Jewish tailors and their special methods into a factory we had recently built, with satisfactory results. Their work has been excellent. British material has been used instead of German, and a large part of the money sent formerly to Berlin had been distributed amongst British manufacturers and in wages.

Booth in his *Life and Labour* . . . had already declared that 'the ready-made clothing trade is not an invasion on the employment of the English tailor but an industrial discovery'. It made for overall expansion and greater, not less, employment for British workers — especially women, who even began replacing alien workers.[50] By 1901 there were 259,292 registered in the clothing trade of which 122,046 were women, nearly half the labour force. Of the 24,850 aliens registered, only 4,895 were women! Myths die hard. After careful deliberation the reality would be assessed and presented in the Aliens Commission Report of 1903, paragraph 129.

49. Letter reported in the *Jewish Chronicle*, 22 April, 1898, from Hitchcock, Williams and Co. of St Paul's to J.A. Dyche — alien artisan and writer. A contributor to the German periodical *Neue Zeit*, no.3 of 1893 was already explaining that 'the cause of the diminution of the mantle trade in Germany is the transference of the trade to England by Russian and Polish Jews'.

50. In 1881 the tailoring trade consisted of 107,668 males and 52,980 females. By 1901 it registered 137,246 males and 122,046 females, a dramatic rise in the percentage of females coincidental with, and to some extent accruing from, the immigrant intervention.

> The development of the three main industries — tailoring, cabinet-making and shoemaking — in which the aliens engage has undoubtedly been beneficial in various ways; it has increased the demand for, and the manufacture of, not only goods made in this country (which were formerly imported from abroad) but of the materials used in them, this indirectly giving employment to native workers.

Those presupposed to listen, listened. For the prejudiced and ill-informed, the realities were of no consequence. The drive towards an Aliens Bill had begun.

Although the volume of immigration declined after 1892, the intensity of agitation continued. The TUC repeated its resolution against the admission of 'pauper aliens' in 1894 and 1895. It was again carried, but this time against strong opposition. (Jewish trade unionists were also mobilising.) On the political level a Parliamentary Immigration Committee of Conservative MPs had been constituted (March 1894) and was collecting funds 'to enable the movement to be placed fairly before the public'. The campaign appeared to herald its first success with the attempt of Lord Salisbury to introduce, as a private member, an Aliens Bill (July, 1894), aimed at excluding destitute aliens and anarchists, who were currently terrorising Continental governments. It scraped a second reading but finally received short shrift, thanks to the personal determination of the Chief Whip of a Liberal Government. Lord Rosebery's arguments, that Jews cared for their own poor, prevailed, although he added that he did not rule out the possibility of legislative restriction, if and when foreign persecution resulted in a further inflow of paupers 'tending to degrade and impoverish — our industrial population'. The more persistent Conservatives would not let him forget it. In the General Election campaign of 1895 the issue featured prominently in their election programme. Joseph Chamberlain had already publicised his adoption of alien legislation as part of Unionist policy[51] and confirmed it at a major election speech at Walsall the following year. Included in the pack of Conservative exclusionists were the Jews Harry

51. In a speech at Bradford reported in the *Jewish Chronicle*, 6 June, 1894. In the later speech the editor accused Chamberlain of trying to make electoral capital out of the immigrants (*Jewish Chronicle*, July 1895).

Simon Samuel, MP for Limehouse and Council member of the West London Synagogue, who openly declared for 'the absolute prohibition of alien pauper immigration', and Harry Marks, MP for St George's-in-the-East, who was strongly condemned by the *Jewish Chronicle* for his scurrilous attacks on pauper aliens.[52] When it came to the crunch, political ambition overrode any feelings of concern for their less fortunate co-religionists.

The paper's view, however, that agitation 'has served its only purpose', that is vote-catching, proved invalid. The TUC persisted in formulating its anti-alien resolutions that year, and a deputation met the new Conservative President of the Board of Trade, C.T. Ritchie, to advocate fulfilment of his electoral pledge. He was a sympathetic listener. He had business connections in the East End and had been involved in local political activity for over twenty years. He was considered a Tory reformer, having taken a strong stand on restriction in his election address at Croydon (although *Hansard* reveals that on 24 March, 1892, as President of the Local Government Board, he had opposed legislation on immigration, informing an anti-alienist MP that his figures on the subject were 'misleading'!). Now 'in his scheme of things, the exclusion of destitute aliens was a natural reform'.[53] It was not surprising, therefore, that the Queen's Speech of 1896 included a Bill to restrict entry. Yet it was never introduced. Successive government ministers persisted in 'bearing in mind their pledges' but 'the constant difficulty of legislation' was a repeated excuse for postponing the issue.

The rationale for prevarication was complex. It could be argued that public distaste (as expressed in press and Parliament) for anti-Semitism in the form of pogroms and the current exposures of the Dreyfus case was influential in postponing laws against immigrants who were predominantly Jews. In localities such as the East End, where the problem bit deeply, anti-alienist sentiment spread outward and upward. It is difficult to estimate the extent of this. Even the

---

52. *Jewish Chronicle*, 26 July, 1895.
53. See Finestein, 'Jewish Immigration in British Party Politics'.

most virulent working-class antagonists presented a superficial obeisance to the norms of tolerance and brotherhood
which offset the possibility of a continental *Judenherze.*
There is little evidence that electoral behaviour in general was
strongly affected by the alien question. In the areas of
concentration this might have had a marginal effect on voting
habits. Later, the Mile End by-election (January, 1905)
focused the issue. In a period of large-scale unemployment
and during the peak of anti-alien agitation prior to the Aliens
Bill, whose major proponent, Spencer Charrington, had been
the borough's own MP, his successor's 'safe' majority fell
from 1,160 to 78.[54] The Aliens Bill passed. But in the
General Election that same year its prime instigator's
majority fell from 1,065 to 637![55]

The reality was that, in the last five years of the century,
there were far more imposing problems and vulnerable areas
elsewhere. Experiments in social reform were by that time
superseded by the immediacies of the Irish question and
imperial expansion. The struggle for South Africa was
pending. Much earlier, the *Jewish Chronicle* (3 April, 1892)
had associated the rejection of an Aliens Bill from Conservative policy with the government's warning to Kruger of the
evils of subjecting his own British immigrants to anti-alien
legislation. With Joseph Chamberlain at the Colonial Office,
passions were diverted towards the overseas foreigner as the
boundaries of British rule widened. It was anticipated,
erroneously, that the cessation of large-scale pogroms
heralded an improvement in the lot of Russian Jews, which in
turn would reduce immigration. This appeared to be borne
out by the Board of Trade Report on Emigration and
Immigration (May, 1896), which purported to show that by
balancing the figures for 1895 the number of aliens had
actually decreased by thirty-two. Yet agitation against the
home alien was rekindled sporadically. In January 1897 a
Private Member's Bill was introduced into the Commons,

54. 1900 election, Spencer Charrington (C.) 2,440, Goddard-Clarke (L.)
1,280. In 1905 by-election, H. Lawson (C.) 2,138, Straus (L.) 2,060.
55. 1900 election (Borough of Stepney), Evans-Gordon (C.) 2,783, H.
Steadman (L.) 1,718. In 1906 election, Evans-Gordon (C.) 2,490, D. Stokes (L.)
1,853.

followed by a demand from Howard Vincent (9 February)
that the Government fulfil its pledges on restriction. Successive Private Member's Bills were introduced in 1898 — one
into the House of Lords in May, the other into the Commons
in July. They received no more than vague promises as
government ministers pleaded pressure of more urgent
business. Such was the decline of interest that Labouchère
could contemptuously deride the fears of anti-alienists in an
article, 'The Colonisation and Exploitation of England', in
the journal *Truth*.[56] Yet there was no let-up from the
restrictionists. Again, on 4 August 1899, Vincent demanded
of Ritchie that he honour his pledge, but was again fobbed
off. The following year, although agitation had reached a new
crescendo, an 'Old Londoner', when warning his fellow-
countrymen of the 'presence in their midst of these foreign
Jews', could lament the fact that 'there was a time when
Englishmen could be aroused, but now they appear to accept
everything as inevitable'.[57] But the observation of J. Have-
lock Wilson, restrictionist leader of the Seamen's Union, that
'workmen throughout the country are generally in favour of
some legislation on the subject', was probably more perceptive.

By 1900 the alien question was again to the fore. The
previous year, thousands of persecuted Rumanian Jews
marched across Europe, of whom 2,903 found their way to
Britain. The Jewish Board of Deputies, roused to the danger
of unilateral evidence, was already competing with the Board
of Trade in compiling statistical data on immigrants. New
opportunities were afforded for MPs operating on the
anti-alien ticket as the volume of unemployment rose. In the
East End constituencies restrictionist candidates made full
play with this in their general election addresses.[58] One of
the most vociferous was T. Dewar, Unionist nominee for St

56. Reproduced in the *Jewish Chronicle*, 31 December, 1897.
57. Letter in *East London Observer*, 29 September, 1900.
58. East London anti-alienist MPs included:
        Thomas Dewar — St George's
        H. Forde-Ridley — Bethnal Green S.W.
        Claude Hay — Shoreditch (Hoxton)
        Harry S. Samuel — Limehouse
        Major W. Evans-Gordon — Stepney.

George's-in-the-East, who was officially sponsored by Sir Francis Montefiore and Lord Rothschild, and defeated his Liberal opponent – the Jew B.S. Straus. Rothschild also supported the Stepney Unionist candidate, Major W. Evans-Gordon, later prime mover of the Aliens Bill, and founding father of the first quasi-Fascist organisation in Britain – the British Brothers' League. The *Jewish Chronicle* had continuously pressed home its emphasis on the Jew as an Englishman first, and derided 'the absurdity of the myth about Judaic sympathies in politics'. It had earlier deluded itself with the proposition 'that Jews have become so thoroughly English that they regard their responsibility as voters entirely as Englishmen' (26 November, 1885). But with the imminent threat of exclusion, the view that 'politics might impinge upon Jewish interests' prevailed. It was a case of the tail wagging the dog as a united community pressurised its leaders into unqualified support for those opposed to the Aliens Bill.

As for that miserable subject of all this heated controversy, it would appear that little had changed. A century before, a commentator had remarked on the immigrant Jew: 'These poor people seem the butt, at which all sections and persuasions level their contempt.' Morris Winchevsky, a newcomer with high literary sensitivity, voiced the sentiments of his people towards Anglo-Jewry. 'They are ashamed of us; not as one is ashamed of poor relations, but as one is shamed by a leper, an outcast, a black sheep . . . and their charity always has a flavour of riddance payment.'[59] Of the attitudes of local workers the editor of the *Poilishe Yidl* expresses his own trepidation:[60]

But although the Jews have freedom of entry, rights etc., do the English like the Jews? The answer is No!

Go any Sabbath afternoon to Whitechapel and stand for a few moments in a doorway near where some English workers lounge with their pipes in their mouths, and you will hear, every time a Jew passes by, the loving call 'Bloody Jew!' Is this a token of love?

At the same time in Brick Lane you will often see dolled up Jewish women, girls with golden rings on their fingers sitting outside

59. M. Winchevsky, *Erinerungen* (Memoirs), New York, 1927.
60. *Poilishe Yidl*, no.11, 3 October, 1884.

in the street. Look in the eyes of the passing Englishmen and can't you discern the look — which is already half indicative of a pogrom?

When you seek to rent a house you will find many who will ask you if you are a Jew. If you answer 'Yes' you will not get the house . . .

If you look for a house and the agent informs you, 'Our Society does not undertake to find houses for Jews'. What do you call that?

When the *Standard* talks of 'Jews — and Christian gentlemen'; when the *Pall Mall Gazette* prints the words 'It is a swindle which passes for a Jew project'; when the *Referee* gets angry at a Jew who owns the winning horse . . .

Jews dwell on this. A pogrom in Brick Lane, in the crossroads of Commercial Road can be a more bloody and terrible affair than one in the Baltic.

This may have been an exaggeration, but by no means as irrational as Professor Gartner suggests. It is but a short step from verbal to physical assault, as the aborted 'Ripper' riots confirm. The British Brothers' League registered the possibility of crowd violence. Thirty years later the Fascist attacks in Stepney would prove the reality.

The *Poilishe Yidl* was the first Yiddish Socialist journal published, and the editors tried to free it from the dilettantism of the folksy press — not always with success. They diagnosed the symptoms of Jew hatred and claimed it was derived from two sources: from the nature of the English temperament and from the aberrations of the Jews themselves.

The English dislike the Jews for three reasons. First they are an insular folk and have less love for the stranger than others. Secondly they are a sullen people and suspect foreigners who are unwelcome guests. Thirdly the Englishmen has no love for the Jew . . .

But the editor calls upon the Jews to be honest with themselves:

Jews are mixed up in business enterprises and bankruptcies with much discredit. Many, to our shame, soon took to getting rich quick in England . . . The most scandalous English newspaper, which is written to popularise dissolute behaviour and demoralises young people, is issued weekly by a Jew. At the Stock Exchange, which the British worker quite rightly calls the 'Gambling Den' there you can, perhaps, find twenty when the Jews constitute but a fraction of the population. Among the assistants one finds dealers in gold sovereigns who seek to accumulate gold and get even richer — these, to our misfortune, are also Jews. In tailoring we get the sweaters; restaurants and dining rooms where they play cards and cause grief to youngsters — these are of Jewish patronage!

Underlying the self-criticism is that assumptions against Jews *in toto* are accepted as self-evident truths; although the editor detects the major source of Judophobia — a minority of establishment Jews.

This the Englishman sees, and we ask ourselves, 'Isn't this enough for him to hate us?' The worst trouble is that those guilty are our élite . . . They are the leaders, the gentlemen; they are ashamed of their own kind and they speak English.[61]

The views expressed by the *Poilishe Yidl* were symptomatic of the emotive reactions of immigrants to their new environment — sentiments which would endure well beyond our time-span. They sought freedom and found it within the limits of old restrictions, some derived from their own cultural peculiarities, others imposed from without. They were still, though with less physical danger, confined within the bounds of the ghetto. Nostalgia for their Russian and Polish homelands (the *heim*) persisted among a people in self-confessed exile (*goles*). The spiritual walls of the *stetl* remained firm. But exits were there, bolted, albeit loosely, on both sides.

Initially the immigrant was defenceless, readily identifiable, always available as the easy target. He was soon jolted into awareness of his alienation, as press, politician and local anti-Semite sporadically embarked on the anti-alien rampage. It was quickly brought home to him if he tried to break outside the job ring and apply to a Gentile concern. His escape was short-lived. Yiddish, as a bar to communication, was part of the score. More so was the blatant hostility shown to him outside the bounds, where to employ an immigrant was tantamount to a betrayal of the English working man. The Jew was an imposition, who must at least be contained. Forced back on his own, he suffered the dreary

61. Ibid., no.12, 10 October, 1884.

ugliness of slum life, the unremitting struggle for bread,
poised tenuously on the margin of existence. The ghetto
dreamer consoled himself by the conviction that materially
he could haul himself to the top. Only man-made obstacles
stood in the way. For the majority such expectations proved
chimerical: alienated from English workers more from design
than choice, and subjected to the calumnies from co-
religionists, as well as those mouthing ideals of universal
brotherhood, they fell back on the realities voiced by Hillel.
'If I am not for myself, who will be for me? But if I am only
for myself, what am I? And if not now, when?' The cry for
bread and the right of life was barely heard in those grand
palaces of worship where pedantic functionaries uttered stern
warnings of the vengeance of the Lord, against the evil
Socialists who transgressed against 'the laws of God and
Man . . . given on Mount Sinai'.

But God appeared either indifferent or incapable of meeting
the demand for daily bread. Unrequited want decreed that the
Socialists got a hearing too. They assumed the role of fighting
advocates for their people in the daily struggle against
exploitation and prejudice. From a changing pattern of radical
élites there emerged a social movement of extraordinary
dynamism, whose impact was to extend well beyond the
frontiers of London's East End.

Part Two
Radical Response

4. Aron Lieberman: Socialist Prophet

The poverty and alienation of the ghetto Jews of London provided fertile soil for the activities of a group of radical intelligentsia who sought refuge from the Tsarist police. In the East End they found their 'landsmen' exploited by their own masters, despised and rejected by the Gentile workers. They had no political or economic organisation to protect them. The struggle, under the leadership of this élite, to form both, poses one of the most fascinating, yet neglected, chapters in British labour history.[1]

The earliest record of a Jewish workers' organisation was a union of Lithuanian Tailors founded in Whitechapel in 1872. Its leader, Lewis Smith, was a refugee who had participated in the Polish insurrection of 1863, fled to France and there fought with the Communards. He arrived in London in 1872 and made his way to the East End. Here his political acumen led him to believe that only by unionisation could the workers defend their living standards against the masters. The organisation was shortlived: seventy-two workers joined, but in a few weeks the group disintegrated.[2] But Smith had set the pattern for the voluntaristic involvement of a politically educated élite in the social and economic struggles of Jewish workmen. The same year he left for America, where he became a prominent labour leader. London had become a training centre for Jewish socialists, the majority of whom went on to the States to assume top leadership in the radical movements which were developing there. The freedom in London for effecting agitation and propaganda meant a base

1. For problems facing the social historian in this area see Chimen Abramsky's article, 'The Jewish Labour Movement: some historiographical problems' in *Soviet Jewish Affairs*, no. 1, June 1971.
2. An account of the union is given by Isaac Bookman at the 6th session of the Hebrew Socialist Union recorded in the minutes of 24 June, 1876.

for the accumulation of political experience and literature that could be fed back into Russia. In this context the East End ghetto provided a catalytic function. In Whitechapel the first separate (though non-separatist) Jewish Socialist organisation came into being. Its founding father was Aron Lieberman.

Lieberman was born in 1849[3] at Louny in the Grodno district of Russia, and subjected in his formative years to a strict religious orthodoxy and the subculture of the *stetl*. Little is known of his youth, except that he entered the Petersburg Institute of Technology and dropped out. He was already socially motivated in his teens when he responded emotionally to the sufferings of both Jews and peasants during the tragic aftermath of the Polish insurrection (1863). By 1870 he was ensconced in Vilna, where he was employed in the administrative branch of the Dvigatel Insurance Society. It was here that he discovered and joined a revolutionary circle based on the rabbinical seminary he had previously quit.

A minimum of Jews was allowed into high schools or universities. Jewish culture turned inwards, virtually isolating itself from the main stream of Russian language and life. The young barely gleaned a basic knowledge of Russian or Polish, and the *stetl* steadfastly perpetuated Yiddish as the lingua franca and Hebrew for religious ritual as compulsory norms. Many of the privileged few who entered universities became revolutionaries, especially in the 1870s, when they participated in the 'go to the people' movement. They underplayed the drive for Jewish liberation *per se*, relegating it to a minor programme in their total objective – the overthrow of the autocracy. Rejecting their Jewish heritage they went to the people, the Russian *moujiks*, in an attempt to identify themselves socially with the peasantry. They failed. Few had the foresight of going to the Jewish masses of the Pale. For the radical *intelligent* eschewed religion as

3. The date of birth given varies. Boris Sapir in article, 'Lieberman et le Socialisme Russe', *International Review of Social History*, 1938, vol.3, pp.25-88, gives 1849. So does Rocker, *The London Years*, 1956, p.112. Kalman Marmor (ed. *Letters of Aron Lieberman*, YIVO, 1951) suggests 1842 or 1844, but 1849 is probably correct.

obscurantism maintained by the rigidity of superstitious ritual and rabbis who acted as a brake on anti-Tsarist activity. Jewish tradition was associated with the physical and mental degradation of the ghetto; and Yiddish was despised as the jargon of slaves, while Hebrew was elevated to the proper form of communication between Jews. Vladmir Jochelson, Lieberman's comrade in Vilna, postulated their view:[4]

> We had broken away and become estranged from the culture of the Russian Jews of that period; we had a negative attitude to the bourgeois and orthodox sections, whom we had left when we became acquainted with the new teachings. As for the Jewish working masses, we believed that the liberation of the Russian nation would also liberate all the other nationalities in Russia. I must admit that the treatment of the Jewish world in Russian literature had impressed us with the idea that the Jews were not a nation, but a parasite class. This was the view put forward even by progressive Russian writers.

The seminaries, founded under the auspices of Nicholas I to supervise and control the religious élite, turned out atheists and social revolutionaries. They went into the hinterland or in exile, where they joined the multifarious organisations bent on destroying the régime. In Vilna, the 'Jerusalem of Lithuania', the famous theological seminary became a hot-bed of socialist militants. The Director and teachers tried desperately to cover it up, but a student informer notified the police. As a result the seminaries of both Vilna and Jitomir were closed down. Lieberman topped the list of men wanted by the Russian police. He had been inducted into the Vilna circle by Aron Zundelevich[5] who had become leader since the departure into exile of its founder Arkadi Finklestein (1872). Close touch with kindred groups in Petersburg and Moscow was maintained. Two of the liaison officers were women: Rosalie Idelson and Anna Epstein. The former was to marry Smirnov, joint founder of Lavrovist periodical *Vperyod*, and the latter Dmitri Klements, a leading terrorist in Narodnaya Volya. It was through Rosa Idelson's friend Dr Leo Ginsburg that Lieberman was introduced to

4. In 'Dalekoe prochloe', *Byloe*, no.13, Leningrad, 1918.
5. See pp.123, 125, 126 and 130 below, on Zundelevich's involvement with Lieberman.

Lavrov, and later recommended for employment on his journal.

The doyen of young intellectual radicals was Peter Lavrov. But there were conflicting pulls on their ideology-making — from the peasant Anarchism of Bakunin to the Jacobin-Communism of Tkachev. Unlike the other two, Lavrov conceived the movement as self-determined from below, and not to be artificially evoked from above. Yet he persisted in the formation of an élitist group to foment agitation and propaganda. At the outbreak of insurrection they would place themselves at the head and direct the masses towards the overthrow of the present system and supervise its replacement by the new. In Zurich he founded *Vperyod* (1872) with Valerian Smirnov as sub-editor and party organiser. In 1874 the press was transferred to London, where the journal was issued bi-monthly, together with other popular and revolutionary literature. These were smuggled into Russia and played an influential role in the political education of the Vilna circle — in itself subscribing to no particularist creed. Lieberman's activism reflected the wide-ranging sources from which they drew their individual motivation. Paradoxically this drew him back to his own people. Jochelson made note of this and remarked on his personal concern for spreading Socialist propoganda amongst the Jews:

> He (Lieberman) had a command of several European languages, and he was an orator. He was thoroughly conversant with the Talmud, and he had a great love of Hebrew literature. He was a talented Yiddish publicist. He was a freethinker, but he was no less occupied in our circle with questions of national conscience with regard to the Jewish people. He worked in our group to get Socialist literature published in the Yiddish language.

Opportunities afforded him by his job allowed him to travel extensively through the Pale. In the districts of Kovno, Vilna and Grodno he observed at first hand the social conditions of his folk. He recorded carefully the poverty and exploitation suffered by the workers engaged in the tobacco, paper and textile manufactories. He studied rural society and relation-ships between ethnic groups. His commentaries on these experiences were later reproduced in his column 'From Bialystock'. He had already conceived the view that each national group had certain qualities derived from its own cultural and historical experience, of which the Socialist movement must take account, if it was to find sympathetic contact with all peoples. Later he would indulge in contradictory postulations which appeared to militate against national self-consciousness. But, in the main, his concept of Jewish autogestion prevailed.[6]

His attacks on Vilna's rabbinical Establishment for associating themselves with Tsarist authority were reciprocated by action from the rabbis, who continued to fulminate against the Socialists from the pulpit. On 12 July, 1875 the Tsarist police moved in on the Vilna circle. Lieberman, together with his comrades, fled to Germany, where he linked up with a Jewish student *émigré* group in Berlin, but not for long. Ginsburg, acting as intermediary, wrote to the editor of *Vperyod* (August, 1875) asking them to engage Lieberman. 'He is an honest man. He wishes to edit some revolutionary material in the Jewish language. He has great capability for this type of work . . .'

So Lieberman, together with his Vilna comrade Wainer, made his way to London, arriving sometime during the first fortnight of August, 1875. Here he would observe and react to the abrasive side effects of mature capitalist industrialisation on his 'landsmen'. Meanwhile he was received and put to work immediately by the editors of *Vperyod*. His first article appeared in issue no. 16 dated 1 September, and by his second article he had received his first cash payment of one pounds sixteen shillings and sevenpence. He undertook to learn composing for future clandestine work in Russia and spent several hours a day practising on the machine type. It was understood that this job was short-term, so he sought new employment with a rabbi as teacher in a Jewish school. He was rejected on the basis of his lack of knowledge of

6. He stated in one of his letters that he was an internationalist who 'knows only men and classes — no more!' See Marmor, *Letters of Aron Lieberman*. In no.14 Lieberman writes to Smirnov: 'I hate Judaism, just as I hate all other Nationalities . . . I am an internationalist. I love only the oppressed masses, otherwise I would not take the name of Socialist.'

English, but was promised an alternative post on the *Daily Telegraph*. This was not forthcoming, but by the end of December the same rabbi offered him the profitable task of translating from the Russian a paper on the Polish insurrection submitted by a Jewish government spy. Lieberman indignantly refused. By January, prospects of a permanency with *Vperyod* were confirmed. From 1 December, 1875 he had already been accepted into the communal household of Lavrov and Smirnov at no. 3 Tollington Park, North London. In Petersburg, Mark Natanson had formed his revolutionary Union, one of whose obligations was to forward articles on the Russian situation to *Vperyod*. Union directors abroad, consisting of Smirnov, Linev and Goldenberg, were agreed upon Lieberman undertaking five functions: as compositor, writer, designer, editor-in-charge of the press and *future editor of a Jewish journal*. He had soon mastered the technical side of his craft. He designed the covers of popular brochures edited by *Vperyod*, and in the Smirnov archives are to be found sketches of Marx and Smirnov drawn by Lieberman.

It was Smirnov who encouraged and guided Lieberman in his literary ventures. Yet old habits die hard. It was difficult for Smirnov, a Russian professional, to regard himself other than a patron to the semi-intellectualised plebeian Jew, while he himself deferred to the Russian aristocrat, Lavrov. Although Smirnov treated Lieberman with a certain reserve, his compassionate nature overruled other considerations. He cared for Lieberman during any illness, and acted out the role of sympathetic consultant to whom the latter poured out his worries and neuroses. Lavrov regarded the young Jew's style and habits with distaste, but this did not deter him from employing an able colleague. Lieberman might well have suffered the chill of isolation in the new land had not the new year brought in his old Jewish comrade Goldenberg from Geneva (18 January, 1876). Two other members of the printing staff offered their friendship: Linev, typesetter and machine expert, and the extraordinary Georgian aristocrat, Tcherkesov, who later associated himself with Rocker and his Libertarian *Arbeter Fraint* group in the East End.

It was soon clear to the editors that Lieberman's interests

were directed towards the Jewish question for the purpose of propagating Socialism amongst the Jews. Added to the lessons derived from his formative experience amongst the Jews of the Pale was the emotional impact of Whitechapel. Not unnaturally he was drawn to that area. In an unsigned article in *Vperyod*, later elaborated in no. 3 of his journal *HaEmet*, he observed the condition of his poor kinsfolk 'come to seek a better life'. He noted the concentration in certain trades:

> The Jews, already numbering 55,000, mostly tailors (about 12,000), hatmakers, bagmakers, carpenters and watchmakers . . . also work in sugar factories, metal shops and tobacco factories.

He was appalled by the milieu, where there seemed no hope of redemption.

> In the narrow, crooked streets of Whitechapel, in the smelly and dirty holes and corners of the workshops working twelve to fourteen hours a day for a paltry starvation wage . . . here have the Jewish workers of Poland, Russia, Germany, Austria . . . found their better life?

There is no over-dramatisation in his picture of the *chazar mark*.

> A thick stream of people covers the length of the road for about half a mile. Almost all are young men; all foreigners from distant lands, most from Russia and Poland. Their faces pale as death and their eyes deeply sunken. Hunger and poverty have robbed them of their youth and given them the appearance of old men.

Lieberman tramped the streets of East London and soaked himself in the atmosphere of the ghetto. Encouraged by Lavrov and Smirnov, he was resolved to set up a permanent dual-purpose organisation: to spread Socialism and unionise the Jewish workers at the same time.

On 20 May, 1876, at his friend Leib Wainer's home in 40 Gun Street, a one-storeyed house in the heart of Spitalfields which still stands, ten men met to form 'Agudah Hasozial-

istim Chaverim' — the first Hebrew Socialist Union.[7] Five of
them were tailors; of the rest one was a hatmaker, another a
cabinetmaker. All shared a politicised background from the
homeland. Lieberman was appointed secretary by common
accord and undertook to draw up the statutes of the union,
which he completed in classical Hebrew and Yiddish. It was
submitted to the second meeting on 27 May 1876 and, after
agreed modifications, was accepted by the members. The
minute book (*Pinkes*), which still exists,[8] is prefaced by
Lieberman's programme. It manifestly proclaims his adherence to the European Socialist tradition:

> The system, everywhere, is no more than oppression and injustice;
> the capitalists, the rulers and their satellites, have usurped all men's
> rights for their own profit and through the power of money have
> made workers their slaves. As long as there is private ownership,
> economic misery will not cease. As long as men are divided into
> nations and classes, there will be no peace between them. And as
> long as the clergy hold dominion over their emotions, there will be
> religious strife.
>
> Redemption for all mankind can only be attained by a universal
> political, social and economic upheaval which will destroy the *status
> quo*, and replace it with a society based on Socialist principles,
> which will end injustice with the domination of capital, together
> with parasitism and the system of 'mine' and 'thine'. That all peoples
> should have equal rights and rid themselves of religion; to retain only
> one's own free will by ending superstition for the peace of mankind.
> While we Jews are a part of humanity, we cannot achieve personal
> liberation except through that of all men.
>
> The emancipation of all mankind from oppression and slavery can
> only be brought about by the workers themselves, in their united
> efforts to wage war against their exploiters; first to destroy the
> existing order and then to replace it by workers' control, justice,
> freedom and the brotherhood of man.
>
> And as the workers of Europe and America have already joined
> together in various organisations to rouse the dispossessed and
> dedicate themselves to revolution for the victory of workers'

7. The first members appended their names, forming a *minyan* of 10!

A.S. Lieberman	Isaac Stone
Leib Wainer	Eliezer Goldenberg
A. Goldstein	Salman Jacob
I. Rosenthal	N. Levenkind
Hirsh (George) Sapir	Jacob Alexander

8. At YIVO New York, included by E. Tcherikover in his 'Beginnings of the
Jewish Socialist Movement', *YIVO Historische Schriften*, I, Vilna, 1929, pp.512-94.

Socialism, so we Jewish sons bind ourselves to this noble alliance and to this end we have created a Jewish Socialist Union.

This our comrades understand to be true and correct, the supreme arbiter of their relationship with each other and other people, notwithstanding colour, race or creed, and undertake to accept the following:

(1) The Union's aim to spread Socialism among the Jews as well as non-Jews; to support organisations recognised by it and to unite all workers in the fight against their oppressors.

(2) The Union's undertaking, in brotherly fashion, to unite with workers organisations from other nations.

(3) Any worker can join the Union on the recommendation of two members.

(4) All members are equal; all must pay a weekly subscription of 2*d.* a week or 8*d.* a month.

(5) Meetings will be held every Saturday evening. Each meeting will elect its President and resolutions will be passed by vocal majority.

(6) A secretary and treasurer will be elected for six months, but can be replaced before then.

(7) Any member whose behaviour does not accord with these statutes will be expelled. [9]

Lieberman was elected secretary, and Isr Moritz Rosenthal treasurer. Lieberman volunteered to print the statutes of the Union at his own expense. Lazar Goldenberg presided over the first meeting, but henceforth, on libertarian principles, the chair was to be rotated amongst members. Inflated rhetoric and tautology make up the document. But such language was indicative of the highly emotional Yiddish style which carried conviction among its recipients.

Twenty-six meetings were held between 20 May and 28 December, reaching a maximum caucus membership of forty. The minutes reveal considerable information on the thinking and action of the group and recall the clash of wills, the subtle and open recriminations accruing from doctrinal antagonisms. During the second meeting an argument rose over the question of admission of small masters and travellers — such as trousers peddlers. The motion put was unresolved, referred back for discussion and reintroduced

9. Translated from the Yiddish by W.J. Fishman.

during the sixth meeting (24 June). Four recommended the admission of clerks, small travellers, glaziers and small masters. It was conceded that glaziers and small travellers had similar characteristics – both could be divided into three classes. First, those who were weekly primed, namely dealers for a seller operating on a weekly basis. Secondly, those defined as discount travellers, that is working for a percentage of sales (generally five per cent or a shilling in the pound). Thirdly self-employed travellers who worked exclusively for their own account. It was agreed to accept clerks and piece-workers but not masters or travellers. It was no mean conclusion. The principle was fundamental to the existence of such a Union. Because of peripheral changes from worker to master and vice versa, it was necessary to define the group in terms of wage labourers alone. Members were enjoined (27 May) to keep a personal notebook recording information on local wages and hours, together with their own views on worker-master relationships. Such records would be available at every meeting, so that all comrades would be kept up to date with a detailed picture of conditions within the local industry. One example was afforded by Isaac Stone, who reported at the next meeting (3 June) his own master's tactics in 'robbing' the workers. The previous Friday evening workers were allowed off early on the eve of Sabbath, under mutual agreement that they would work an additional two hours' overtime on return to compensate for time lost. Stone related how he was consequently overloaded with work which took him four-and-a-half hours to complete, but for which he received only two hours' pay. A similar case was presented by Rosenthal, who rendered a poignant account of the exploitation of 'greeners' in workshops.

The Union purported to assume the roles of educator and propagandist for Socialism. There is a sense of *naïveté* in an early proposal calling on members to agitate among the militant Irish in order to build up an all-Workmen's Society. (The local Irish were notoriously anti-immigrant.) It was then felt more practical to call an open public meeting to sound out the possibilities of creating such a society. Efforts at educational mutual aid proved more fruitful. At the fourth meeting (10 June) Goldenberg discoursed on the workers' movement in Switzerland, stressing the relationship between political parties and those international Socialist parties whose representatives participated in the International Working Men's Congress of 1866 at Geneva. He analysed the progress of the Congress, explaining the diversity in ideologies underlying the dissensions between Mazzinists, Jacobins and the like. Sapir appropriately remarked on the prominent part Jews had played in the Socialist movement, which, while not directly with the masses, was yet always as the vanguard. On 17 June guest speaker Kaufman gave a learned commentary on the French philosophers of the eighteenth century as the precursors of the French Revolution of 1789. The secretary noted simply: 'He explained that the writers Voltaire and Rousseau and the Encyclopaedists began the struggle against the aristocracy, religion and royalty, and that the Great Revolution had proclaimed the rights and freedom of mankind.'[10] On 2 July, Lieberman himself discoursed on the plight of the Jews in Russia and the deliberations of the International, and added an appraisal of contemporary workers' movements. The following week Sapir spoke to the meeting on 'the life and death of Bakunin on 1 July this year. How much his Russian revolutionary spirit had earned him a place in the Socialist fold — not only in Russia but in the whole of Europe.'[11] The Union purported to discard Jewish parochialism but the dilemma remained: whether to work for Socialist unity through a broader workers' organisation or to build up initially a *Jewish* socialist party working in liaison with its non-Jewish counterparts.

This duality in goals underlay Lieberman's own vacillations, but would explain his dissent from Sapir's more global view in subsequent debates. At the ninth meeting Lieberman took his stand on the primacy of his Jewish identity against Sapir's dogmatic anti-religious assimilation-

10. Minutes of the 5th meeting of the HSU held at 77 Leman St, E.1. (17 June, 1876).

11. Minutes of the 8th meeting of the HSU held at 77 Leman St, E.1. (8 July, 1876).

ism. The minutes of 22 July, 1876 report:[12]

> Finally the Secretary (Lieberman) brought up the question of the next meeting. Next Saturday night would be the Ninth of Ab. Might it not be better to transfer the meeting to another day?
>
> Citizen Sapir contended that this day was no concern to us Socialists. We have discarded the old traditions, and, therefore, we should not put off our meeting because of this day. All we know is our cause, which is at the same time the cause of humanity as a whole, and that is all.
>
> The Secretary replied that meanwhile the Ninth of Ab had the same significance for Jewish Socialists as for all other co-racials. So long as the Social revolution has not taken place, political liberty was of great importance to every nation. This day, the Ninth of Ab, was the day when we lost our independence, and for that our people mourns till now, more than eighteen hundred years. It should have so much significance for us that we should shift the meeting to another day.
>
> The meeting voted on the question and decided to hold the next meeting on Sunday night, 10th of Ab, 30 July, 1876.

Why was Lieberman at this stage so persistent in his emphasis on Socialist propaganda geared to quasi-Nationalist ends? And why directed towards the Jewish labouring poor? Partly because of his own cognisance of the alienation of the Jewish intellectuals from their compatriots. Earlier he wrote: 'As for the means of agitation amongst Jews, one cannot draw one's inspiration from the socialist ideas belonging to the youth of higher education alienated from the Jewish world. The majority among them have become strangers to their own people'.[13] He had observed, not without personal anguish, the false caricaturing of his people as parasites and exploiters. He disdained the unitary view: that of one Jewish folk bound by a common religion and culture. Instead he affirmed social divisions amongst Jews as amongst other peoples. 'We [the popular Jewish masses] do not . . . place hope on persons such as kings or rich Jews of the same stamp, whose interests are diametrically opposed to those of the people. The people

12. Lieberman was not the first secularist to identify 9th Ab as a day for national mourning. In 1862, Moses Hess 'the Red Rabbi' had been 'deeply moved' by the family rituals on that day. Lieberman transformed an emotive response into practical action.

13. *Vperyod*, no.27, pp.83-4, 1876.

only have hope in the social revolution'.[14] In the *stetl* the wealthy operators and the priests ruled. When the time came, being Jews would not save them from the retribution of their own poor.

The injustice of native anti-Semitism, carried over into the bigoted assumptions of the radical intelligentsia, was not lost on either Lieberman or Lavrov. The latter, as editor of *Vperyod*, was the recipient of correspondence which confirmed this, and Russo-Jewish Socialists were not unfamiliar with the anti-Semitic tirades of the Bakuninists and social revolutionaries. No. 5 of the Anarchist review *Worker* (May 1875) included the fashionable calumnies in an article, 'The account of a man who has lived long', when a Jewish clerk is exposed as a police informer; a role, it is pointed out, particularly suited to the Jewish ethos. 'He is a Yid, by race, and it is inherent in him to make money through pawn-broking. One recognises this as the soul of a Sheenie.' Lavrov was uncompromising in his rejection of such prejudice.

> Those who permit themselves to insult *en masse* 'Germans' or 'Yids' and deny the possibility of a serious workers' movement in the heart of such and such a race, those who stifle enthusiasm in affirming that their compatriots *alone* are capable of making the social revolution, reveal that they have not worked hard enough to acquire the most elementary notion of the workers' question.[15]

Hence with the publication of the statutes of the Hebrew Socialist Union in no. 37 of *Vperyod*, his *alter ego* Smirnov appended both a warning and a plea to the Jewish workers:

> Comrades! You will have to surmount, in your action, handicaps perhaps far greater than those with which we have to grapple, we, your brothers in the cause, and in humanity . . . the insults, the calumny, the outrages, the filth with which they will cover you more . . . than they would attempt against socialists of other nationalities. All power to your energy, and may your persistence grow with the difficulties you will have to meet and surmount.

14. *Vperyod*, no.16, p.505.
15. P. Lavrov, *Gosoudarstrenny element v boudoutchem obchtchestve*, p.167. London, 1876.

Such fears were confirmed, in response to this and such articles as 'In Vilno', etc. attributed to Lieberman. While thousands of dedicated young Jewish *intelligent*, facing worse hazards than their Gentile comrades, had 'gone to the people' in the ranks of Zemlya y Volya, the Ukraine Socialist leader Serge Podolinsky protested against the Judophilia assumed by the editors of *Vperyod* with the premise that

> in my view *Judophobia* is as indispensable to all Russian Socialism as hatred of the bourgeoisie. With some nearly insignificant exceptions, which are hardly worth considering, I contest the existence, and even the possibility of existence in Russia (not only in the Ukraine) of Yid Socialists, absolutely sincere in their way of life, which the Socialist must be.[16]

Evidence suggests that such rejection of Jewish participation in the Russian movement was not underestimated, not least by Lieberman. Pressed by both Lavrov and Smirnov, he wrote and delivered his 'Call to Jewish Youth' — the first Jewish Socialist manifesto in Hebrew. It was reproduced in full in no. 38 of *Vperyod* (July 18, 1876) and, in pamphlet form, smuggled into the Pale. It reflected a change in Lieberman's pronouncements on the usefulness of the Jewish *intelligent*. In biblical style, he urged them to relinquish their privileged status in order to pursue the unfulfilled duty of propagating Socialism amongst their own folk. Young leaders were enjoined to mobilise the Jewish poor against their own exploiters — the minority bourgeoisie and rabbinate. Lieberman fulminated against the wealthy Jew in the language of the prophets:

> We have had to pay for your sins! The race hatred, the religious hatred, with all their terrors, have fallen mostly upon us. You kindled the fire that devours us. We have you to thank that the name of Israel became a curse. The entire Jewish people, suffering and astray, must suffer more than all other peoples because of your greed. It is your fault that we have been exposed to calumny. International speculators, who have dragged our names through the mud, you do not belong to us.

16. In letter to Smirnov, 19 June, 1876.

The call was in tune with those circulated by the Russians among their own student youth. But its message was exclusively for the Jews, who are urged to join in the struggle for social liberation, side by side with other nations.

> Private property leads to class war, and places personal interest above the interests of society. Governments established on the principle of Nationality incite one nation against another causing war. Those who think they can profit this way range themselves between the friends of the people and their enemies. Your future does not lie in the old commandments of the past, which have long lost their moral value. Emancipate yourselves from the lust for power which is fundamental to privilege. Stop praying to gold and might! Away with the cult of the past! Ally yourselves with the people and its true friends! All nations are preparing for battle. The proletariat is uniting to shake off the yoke of capital and tyranny. Oppressed humanity is organising to regain its rights and liberties. The Social Revolution has raised its banner, and calls you to the community of labour, of labour production and social wealth, the free fraternity of the workers of all lands, the removal of all rule by force and of everything that is opposed to the demands of justice. IT IS TIME FOR THE WORKING MASSES OF THE JEWISH PEOPLE TO JOIN IN THIS GREAT WORK. Human brotherhood knows no division according to nations and races; it knows only useful workers and harmful exploiters. Against these the working people must fight. You have to thank for your education this despised people, that has had to pay with its suffering and its blood for your privileges.

Lieberman ended with the traditional appeal of Zemlya y Volya:

> Go to the people, and suffer with it. Inspire the one, and strengthen the other in the great fight against the lords of the world, against the oppressors and exploiters of creative labour!

The call founds its way into the ghetto towns of the Pale and re-oriented a host of young Jewish intellectuals towards the task of working among their own folk, as a prerequisite for emancipation. In Ber Borochov's estimate,[17] this appeal and the formation of the Hebrew Socialist Union in London qualifies Lieberman as the founding father of Jewish Social-ism; the progenitor of the 'Bund', and, in the long term, 'Paole Zion' — Socialist Zionism.

17. See *Nationalism and the Class Struggle*, pp.169-73.

Meanwhile the Anglo-Jewish establishment, sensitive to their recently acquired acceptance as bona fide citizens, responded to the dangers accruing from these foreign 'Nihilists'. Led by the Chief Rabbi, Dr Adler, and the master tailors, a campaign was opened up against them. On 23 June, 1876, the *Jewish Chronicle* published a warning against a paper, 'Mischievous in its tendency', circulating among the Russian and Polish workers in the East End:

> The paper purports to contain the rules of the 'Hebrew Socialist Union' — a body which possesses no existence whatever, except in the imagination of the insane originator, who is striving to create such a body. We forbear publishing extracts from the paper as they would tend to mislead. Such puerile tracts are not likely to have the slightest influence on the least informed of our brethren. Indeed we more than suspect that they emanate from the enemies of the Jews, and were put into circulation in order to injure them. In any case, those in whose hands such tracts fall should not assist in their circulation, but strive to discover their authors, with a view to their exposure.

The Socialists took up the challenge. At their eighth meeting (8 July) it was agreed to organise a mass meeting to expose exploitative conditions and agitate for the formation of labour organisations amongst Jews. A printed handbill, which survives, was explicit on this, and warned of the open hostility of English workers against them because of their lack of trade union consciousness:

> It is known that working men find themselves everywhere in distressing conditions . . . But however difficult life may be for all workers, it is worse for the Jewish worker, especially here in London, where the Jew has to work harder and longer and yet receives less wages than the non-Jew. Why is this? Because the Jewish workers are not as united as the others. Here in England the Trades Unions consisting of thousands of workers' societies in different occupations are closely banded together to protect themselves against the employers. But among the Jews there is no unity and the masters can do what they please. Thus we not only suffer from disunity but also as a result draw upon us the dislike and hostility of the English workers who accuse us of harming their interests.

For the *Jewish Chronicle*, reporting on Communism

among the Jews in Vilna (7 July), the threat was ominous. Allies would have to be found to combat the enemy from within. Why not among the immigrant clergy, who wielded spiritual power over their *chevras*? The popular Maggid of Slutsk, Zvi Hirsch Dainow, voiced his timely condemnation of Lieberman and the Union in a letter, zealously summarised in the *Jewish Chronicle*'s column, 'Party Socialism' (11 August, 1876):

> We are happy to learn from a letter addressed by the Russian Maggid to the *Habazaleth*, that the circular proceeded from one individual, of Jewish parentage, a member of the communist committee, which has its seat in our metropolis, but that the Jewish body coming from Russia are quite free from this taint. At the same time the Maggid warns the Jews in Russia that if they should receive any circulars of the sort from London, to hand them over forthwith to the authorities, and to be assured that there exists no communistic Jewish body in London. The Maggid further believes that the late arrests among the Jews of Wilna have been a consequence of the transmission of circulars of this sort from London, the individuals to whom they have been addressed having been suspected of communistic tendencies by the police. The Maggid writes in bitter and strong language against this individual, whom he knows personally and whom he charged with vagabondage, dishonesty and avowed transgressions of the law of God and man, especially the laws given on Mount Sinai.

The next week Lieberman alleged that Dainow had planted a spy in their midst. (He actually revealed himself as N. Berlin.) Others thundered against the Union from the pulpits in Whitechapel. Some found to be members were sacked by their masters, others yielded to economic pressure and quit. But at their meeting-place at 8 Leman Street, the majority held fast and persisted in their deliberations for a public meeting. The minutes convey a high level of debate. At the twelfth meeting (5 August), the humour and irony of the speakers and the breadth of subjects in discussion are manifest. A proposal of Bookman's that masters should be denied entry to the meeting brought a rejoinder from Lieberman 'that this could not be made effective, as English law proffers the right on everyone to attend an open meeting, even if it is of a special kind. We should not attempt anything we cannot enforce.' A resolution by Sapir to charge an entrance fee for guests was also disposed of firmly by Lieberman. 'We must show the world that *we* work for an ideal, whilst others worry about the cost to the individual. Perhaps later, when we achieve Anarchy, we can unanimously vote for charging entrance fees.' Goldenberg spoke of French workers chosen as delegates to the International Socialist Congress at Philadelphia. They wanted to publish the resolutions and distribute them internationally and called upon individual working-class organisations to contribute towards the cost. He proposed that their Union should send five shillings but, after discussion, the meeting raised the sum to twelve.

The public meeting registed the high-water-mark of Union activity. Accounts of its preparation make quaint but moving reading. Here was a small group of dedicated workers, 'natural' intellectuals, committed to guide their kinsfolk towards self-liberation. There is the sadness of inevitable failure in their naïve optimism and rhetorical postures. 'Thus we have organised an open meeting with the hope of attracting handworkers to get together and discuss how to improve the lot of our Jewish workers and to create an organisation of *all* handworkers . . .' It stands *in memoriam* to a noble piece of local social action hitherto obscured from those primarily concerned with the wider historical record. As we read the terse notes, the picture builds up of the heady days preceding the grand performance. On 18 August, two thousand handbills were taken out by members, who were allocated areas of distribution along the Whitechapel and Commercial Roads. Saturday was the day for *spazieren* (strolling) along the thoroughfares and the workers would be out in droves. At first, many refused the hand-outs, believing they were missionary texts. Some Jewish workers, imbibing at a local pub, caught on and proceeded to take over the distribution among their own friends. Master tailors who were inadvertently approached, became angry 'and spoke threateningly against the workers' organisations — revealing to all the division between boss and worker'.

The great day, 26 August, came. The chronicler, Lieberman, recorded the details.[18] The location, advertised as

18. See Minutes and Account of Public Meeting, Hebrew Socialist Union, 26 August, 1876.

Zetland Hall, 51 Mansell Street, Goodman's Fields, was a small, shabby hall with wooden bench seating, unadorned to the point of severity. At 8.45 p.m. a packed meeting opened under the chairmanship of Goldenberg. Honoured guests were introduced: Charles Goddard, representative of the London Trade Unions and executive committee member of the Journeyman Bookbinders' Society and Peter Lavrov, editor of *Vperyod*, representing the London International Workers' Educational Union. The chairman began proceedings by stating the object of the meeting and defining, in his own terms, the meaning of Socialism. The Jewish Socialist Union had taken the steps to call the meeting in order to enlighten the Jewish workers on how to alleviate their hardship. Its end aim, Socialism, meant the emancipation of the working class from the oppression of Capitalism. I. Stone (tailor) followed with a vivid picture of the struggles of the Jewish immigrant and related them to those of his English counterpart. 'Through the division of labour has the worker become the smallest and cheapest part of the machine.' He ended: 'The unity of Israel has become a great lie since the underlying class struggle exists also amongst Jews ... Therefore Jewish workers must unite among themselves against the other spurious unity — that with the masters!'[19] Moishe Rosenthal (tailor) spoke of the development of his trade in Russia and London. He explained how Capital had, step by step, squeezed out the poor worker to replace him by the machine. He told the story of tailoring in London, and finally exhorted the Jewish workers to unite in the only way they could against the domination of Capital — by Socialist organisation. Louis Wainer (carpenter) next rendered an account of class struggles in history; his emphasis being on the economic causes motivating the French Revolution, 'with Capital seeking to achieve supremacy'. The proletariat responded by organising themselves to do battle against the usurper, particularly in England. Thence, Wainer sketched the development of trade unions from 1851 to the present day. Hirsch Sapir, in German, added his views on the development of the fight for 'the normal working day'. He explained that

19. Later to recall his own observations on this and the subsequent meeting in articles in the *Poilishe Yidl*, no.4, 15 August, 1884 and no.5, 22 August, 1884.

in mediaeval times, the struggle was for the twelve-hour day. Since 1802, Parliament in London had legislated five acts for the working day: from sixteen hours in 1802, fifteen in 1833 down to ten hours in 1848. He pleaded for the formation of trade unions among the Jews, in order to implement and defend the ten-hour day.

The deliberations were proceeding smoothly until Lieberman rose to speak. It would have been expedient to continue warily at this juncture. But this was, for him, temperamentally impossible. His arrogant demeanour and caustic wit would inevitably provoke antagonism. He began by passionately evoking the oppressive condition of Jewish workers as compared with other folk. He proceeded to fulminate against the Jewish financial aristocracy as the greatest misfortune which befell the Jews till then — especially in eastern Europe. As long as they predominated, so would the Jew remain in bondage. The brotherhood of man could only be achieved under Socialism. He went on to expose the local rabbinate, whom he accused of exercising a malign influence, and attacked their imposition of a marriage fee of three pounds ten shillings, which even the poorest members of the synagogue were forced to pay.[20] In their own hands the workers had the democratic weapons with which to govern themselves. With their own efforts they could build a workers' republic free from 'authoritarian' masters!

At this point, a man sprang on to the platform shouting that the speaker had insulted the Chief Rabbi. Chaos ensued. With difficulty order was restored as the next speaker, Charles Goddard, mounted the platform. It was a momentary respite. He was an unfortunate choice, since he spoke English to an uncomprehending audience. It gave the opponents of the platform their opportunity. They set up the clamour that the Socialists were obviously missionaries. Fights broke out between factions but ended as quickly as they began. A young learner tailor, Yitzchok Goldstein, jumped on the table and appealed to the audience not to be diverted from

20. Lieberman's criticism seemed to have had the desired effect. The United Synagogue Executive later reduced the marriage fee to 10s.6d. 'with complete remission of fees where necessary'. (United Synagogue Executive minutes 16 July, 1877.)

5. Gun Street, Spitalfields; at no. 40, the first meeting of the Hebrew Socialist Union took place on 20 May 1876.

6. Minutes of the meeting on 20 May 1876 when the Hebrew Socialist Union was formed.

ב״ה האלט איווער פֿאַרזאַמלונג:

פּוּבְּלִיק־מִיטִינְג
פֿיר אידישע ארבייטער.

עס איז בעקאנט, אז דיא ארבייטער בעפינדען זיך אומעטום
און איין מדינדיגע לאגע און זיער שווער קומט זיי אן צו פערדיענען
זיער שטיקל ברויט. אבער ווא שווער עס איז אויך דער לעבען פון
אללע ארבייטער, ווען דער אידישע ארבייטער ווייס מעהר פֿאַרשוואַרצט
אלס אללע איבריגע, און בפרט נאך הייר אין לאנדאן. דער איד מוז
מעהר שטונדען ארבייטען אין בעקומט ווענינער מעצאהלט אלס דער קריסט.

און וואָרום איז דאס אזוי? ווייל דיא אידישע ארבייטער זיינען
ניט אזוי פעראיינינט אנטער זיך ווא דיא אנדערע, דיא קריסטליכע
ארבייטער זיינען פעראיינינט צוא געזעללשאפטען. הייר אין ענגלאנד איז
דא דיא טראדעס יוניאנס, איין פעראיין פון מיהענדע ארבייטער
בעזעללשאפטען פון מערשידענע פראפעסיאנען, וואס זייא האלטען זיך
אללע מעסט צוזאממען און לאזען זיך ניט אינטערדריקקען פון זיערע
מאבריקאנטען און מייסטער; אבער ביא אינזערע אידישע ארבייטער איז
ניטא קיין אחדות, דעריבער קענען דיא מייסטער אונז דריקקען ווא זייא
וויללען. פון אונזער אונאיינינקייט ליידען מיר אלליין און לאדען נאך אויף
זיך דעם האסס פון דיא ענגלישע ארבייטער וואס בעשולדיגען אונז, אז
דורך דעם וואס מיר ארבייטען מעהר צייט און כ׳ז ווענינער לאזען מזהרען
מיר זייא אויך אין שאדען.

דאַרום רופען מיר צוזאממען איינע אפּשענטליכע מערזאממלונג צו
לאדען חאמפליהבט דאצו אין יעדען אידישען האנדווערקס־
געזעלל, אום צוזאממען ראטהע צוא האלטען ווא צוא פערבעסערען דיא
לאגע פון אונזערע אידישע ארבייטער און צוא בילדען אין געזעללשאפט
פון אללערליי האנדווערקער. מיר האפפען, אז יעדער ארבייטער, וואס זיין
אייגענעס אנטערעססע איז איהם מדיער, וועט נעהמען אנטהייל אן דעם
מיטינג. — אייניגע מיטגליעדער פון אונזער מעראיין וועלן האלטען רעדען
איבער דיא ארבייטער־אַנטערעסטען אין יעדעם ארבייטער וועט שטיין פריי
אויסצושפּרעכען זיין מיינונג אפענטליך אין דער פערזאממלונג.

דער מיטינג וועט זיך אין אנ׳ליים ד׳ אלול ה׳ תרל״ו—
(26 אוינוסט 1876) שבת צוא נאכט אום אכט אודר אזר אין
צעטלאנד האלל, 51 מאנסעל סטריט, נאדמאנ׳ס פיעלדס z. (ביא
אלי׳ וויוטמעו).

אגד׳ חסציאליסטיס העברעים.

A PUBLIC MEETING
OF JEWISH WORKING MEN,
WILL BE HELD AT
ZETLAND HALL, 51, MANSELL ST., GOODMAN'S FIELDS, E.,
On Saturday August 26, 1876, at 8 o'clock in the Evening.

ערשטער געדרוקטער אויפרוף צו יידישע ארבעטער, לאָנדאָן, 8 אויגוסט 1876

(ארכיוו פֿון „בונד", בערלין)

(אָריגינאל־גרויס)

7. Handbill for the first Jewish Socialist public meeting,
held on 26 August 1876.

their main task — the formation of a union. A request to be heard was finally granted to a member of the audience, a Mr Tone, described as a traveller and one-time tailor. He told of his own sufferings in a sweat shop: of rheumatism, acquired by continuous standing and working on trousers, racking his limbs, while the master scoffed at his 'malingering'. 'When a horse falls, you replace it. So they do a worker.' He implored them not to delay in forming a union; not to believe the masters' libel that the Socialists were missionaries. He knew the Socialist Union well, although, as a traveller, he was debarred by its rules from joining.

The meeting ended at eleven p.m. in a wave of enthusiasm. Eighty signatures were appended to a document undertaking to support the formation of a tailors' union. A chairman's appeal for a second meeting was passed unanimously. It would be held at 8 Leman Street, the Socialist Union's meeting-hall, the following Saturday night. Shouting 'Down with the masters!' the audience dispersed. The first Jewish Socialist endeavour had proved a success. But not for long. A determined opposition, bent on its destruction, had also been set in motion.

Their action was recalled eight years later by I. Stone in the *Poilishe Yidl.* [2] [1]

> The masters became frightened and sought plans to stop the Socialists. They found them. They ran to the Anglo-Jewish editors, to get them to warn the workers to have nothing to do with the bespectacled *Litvaks* [i.e. Lieberman & Co.] as they indulged in regicide and were missionaries displaying a cross on the forehead. They approached the Rabbi and appealed to him to send Synagogue officials to listen to the Litvaks' speeches. Their request was granted.

The second meeting, officially a closed one, was to be infiltrated by anti-Socialists. It took place at the Leman Street Hall on 3 September. The secretary noted in his minutes that a hundred people were present, the majority workers with a noticeable sprinkling of 'bourgeois' intruders. Stone refers to them as 'the holy Jews — masters gathered on one side with synagogue wardens on the other'. The

21. *Poilishe Yidl*, no.5, article, 'Jewish Workers in London'.

chairman, Goldenberg, advised on the purpose of that meeting. 'The workers must strive for a shortened working day, for all-round defence, and the formation of a workers' information bureau. They did not need others to bear their load.' He then called on Lieberman. According to Stone:

> Then a small *Litvak* wearing glasses got up to speak. The audience was quiet. The *Litvak* adjusted his spectacles and began to harangue with a sharp tongue, with words that struck like spears in the hearts of the listeners. The orator ended by expostulating, 'It is even too costly for a poor man to marry in London!' Hardly had he got the last words out when a storm broke.

According to the minutes, opposition shouts rang out that the Socialists were no more than missionaries, 'whereupon the speaker hurled back bitter accusations against the clergy and Anglo-Jewry.' This 'enraged a *shamus* (the Rev. A.L. Green) sent by Dr Adler, who had crept into the meeting with a couple of "bourgeois". They sprang on the platform. Green, with the aid of another, pushed aside the speaker and attempted to address the audience.' At this point, Stone recalled,

> everybody started fighting; *cupals*, glasses, hats and sticks flew. These men of God did not stand idly by! It was indeed a *shamus* who attacked the bespectacled one [Lieberman]. So those around went for him and beat him up from head to toe. 'No', cried the *shamus*, cowering beneath the blows, 'I am the *shamus*. Have pity on the *shamus*!' 'Beat him, brothers!' cried the crowd in unison. During the mêlée [Leiberman] was rendered black and blue as people beat the hell out of each other. Bodies were pulled out like casualties from the field of battle. Then the police arrived . . .

According to the minutes 'the bourgeoisie had got their way. This time the workers left. Many begged the Union not to be deterred by this.' Seventeen persons had already signed on to form a trade union.

The *Jewish Chronicle* was adept in exploiting the successful disturbance against the Socialists, by identifying their recent activity as missionary tactics. It reported on 8 September:

ANOTHER CONVERSIONIST TRICK. To what straits the conversionist hirelings are reduced to in order to make a pretence of earning their hire is evident from the tricks they now resort to in order to attract a few ignorant Jews to listen to their unavailing attempts to lure them from adherence to the ancestral faith. Another trick has come to our knowledge. A publican in Duncan Street, Whitechapel, was induced to let a room on the pretence that a meeting of Jewish tailors was to be held for the purpose of protesting against the long hours which they work. Invitations to the meeting were also issued to this effect. The decoy was successful so far that some Jewish tailors were attracted to the meeting but when they discovered the trick which had been played them they unmistakeably showed their sense of the trick. A scene of great uproar ensued and those who addressed the 'meeting' were assaulted. The aid of the police had to be called in to quell the disturbance. Seeing that these conversionist agents by their miserable tactics invited from the deluded Jews who they trap to their 'meeting' a breach of the peace we should think that the law could be enforced which prevents such meetings or at any rate punishes those who convene them.

It was beating the right drum. Tcherikover, who gauged the consequences correctly, commented that the 'accusation was a good weapon. It worked strongly on the psychology of the masses.'[22] Apostasy, to them, was tantamount to eternal damnation as well as the prospect of excommunication here and now!

The 'greeners' were well warned, if not already experienced in the ways of the missionaries. For the first time they found themselves exposed to an organised army of proselytising agents, ensconced in the immigrant quarter.[23] On Sabbath evenings they held open-air services, the speakers orating in broken German, to attract the appropriate audience. They instituted a 'travellers' home' for poor Jews in which Bible classes were interspersed with courses in English. Philip Kranz insisted that many Jewish workers in London in the 1870s and 1880s certainly derived a knowledge of English by attending missionary classes.[24] Christian charity (as well as

22. Tcherikover, *The Beginning of the Jewish Socialist Movement*, cols 503 ff.

23. Old Mission houses still existed until recently, e.g. in Old Montague Street, Fournier Street (corner Wilkes Street), Philpot Street, and one apparently uninhabited near Booth House in the Whitechapel Road.

24. Article, 'Missionary Organisations in England' in *Voschod*, no.11, 1884 by I. Rombro (P. Kranz).

missionary zeal) decreed that they welcome destitute immigrants, provide them with food and money and 'thereby draw them into proselytisation'. Kranz blamed the English Jews: 'The main task for which their "emigrant society" was conceived was to help Jews emigrate *from* England.'

Lieberman, as late as the twenty-fifth meeting,[25] was still puzzled: 'Why do the Jews go in hundreds to hear the missionaries preach?' Rosenthal enlightened him: 'The missionaries offer them practical help.' As immigration increased, so did the number of missionaries. Tcherikover reckoned that they had over a hundred settlements in London during the 1870s, operating under the jurisdiction of two great Missionary Societies – the 'British' and 'London'. One specialist group concentrated specifically on the homeless, among whom the newly-arrived 'greener' or the workless, unable to afford lodgings, proved fair game. Winchevsky later complained (1879): 'The "conversion business" was bleeding us. Many of the youngsters who had nothing to eat, let themselves be taken in by the missionaries.'[26] The reality was otherwise. For all the missionaries' outlay in energy and expenditure, there was poor return in terms of numbers. During 1881-2, the peak year of Jewish immigration, the London Missionary Society recorded a total conversion of eighteen adults and thirty-one children. The cost of each conversion was estimated at £2,000 – an expensive exercise. Winchevsky wrote that each proselyte cost the missions up to fifteen thousand dollars! It was truly a conversion business – and apostasy, for the convert, could be made profitable. A needy, and enterprising, immigrant would undergo a series of 'conversions' as he wandered from one mission to another, accruing clothes, money and free board and lodgings on the way. Notwithstanding threats and warnings from the rabbinate against attending, missionary medical clinics offering 'service to the ill and ailing with a most ineffective proselytising effort' were popular, and used widely by the Jewish poor. 'Thousands of Jews annually attended such places as the Mildmay clinic and remained unpersuaded by

25. Minutes of the Hebrew Socialist Union, 11 November, 1876.
26. Winchevsky, *Erinerungen*, vol. I, pp.166-7.

the missionary lectures and hymn-singing which they heard while waiting.'[27] Coupling the Socialists with conversionism paid off. There were no compensatory advantages in proclaiming oneself a Socialist. On the contrary it could mean the sack and exclusion from the community.

This was reflected in the deliberations of the newly formed Tailors' Union. It was clear that they would have no truck with their Socialist progenitors. Lieberman was the *bête noire*. He was deemed responsible for the arrests in Vilna (1875 and 1876), and the new executive felt that 'here in London, workers' conditions could worsen through Socialist intrigues and political meddling'.[28] A picaresque tale of the rise and fall of the tailors' organisation is recounted, in retrospect, by its Socialist participant Isaac Stone. It is marked by that fusion of wit and irony which adorns Yiddish speech.[29]

> The workers organised. They printed huge posters announcing a people's meeting. The first met in a synagogue, with an audience representative of the Jewish community, such as cantors, *maggids* and *dayanim*. It was a full audience. Speeches followed — each speaker outdoing the other with due reference to biblical analogies . . .
> After the oratory a collection was held and money thrown in from all sides. Letters were sent to Rothschild, Sir Moses Montefiore, Montagu etc. Every rich man had underwritten the Union. A *shochet* was elected president, a *doyen* treasurer, a *maggid* secretary — and all three were one! Cantors and shamuses became committee men. Sermons never failed them. For the workers they prayed for castles in the air. And would you believe it? At one stroke the whole set-up went up in a puff of smoke and vanished heavenwards. There was no more Union. The cash book was stolen; the money flew away to *Eretz Yisroel*. Now the *dayanim* and cantors reverted to normal. So did the workers — still as oppressed and enslaved as ever!

Tcherikover presents a more sober assessment. At its inception

27. Quoted by Gartner, *The Jewish Immigrant in England*, p.165, from Report on Medical Relief of the Jewish Poor, 10 June, 1891, in Jewish Board of Guardians, Minute Letter Book, p.39.
28. Report to Hebrew Socialist Union at 16th Meeting, undated October 1876, which included the tailors' attack on Lieberman.
29. *Poilishe Yidl*, nos. 5 and 6, dated 22 and 29 August, 1884. Articles 'Jewish Workers in London'.

Lieberman had nervously proclaimed: 'This evening will be recalled some day in Jewish history, as it will have great influence on the Jewish nation.' But this did not happen. Divorcing itself from the Socialists, and without leadership, the Union proved ephemeral. Its immigrant ranks remained ill-informed, ill-led and helpless. Truly 300 workers joined, but it functioned for only three months, then collapsed. £80 had been collected when the treasurer absconded with the funds to America.

As for the other unionising ventures undertaken by the Socialists, 'worse happened. The plan to form a slipper-makers' union remained on paper.' Tcherikover goes on to suggest that, in future, there was little possibility of trade union organisation among London Jews, even in the long term. He quotes T. Rothstein,[30] an old Socialist activist who lived in London over a long period, who wrote:

> Not being a proletarian at home (i.e. Russia) and seeing the potentialities of becoming a master ... the Jewish worker in England could never identify himself with the proletarian psychology. Thus he could not establish either a secure organisation or a professional body, through which the English Trade Unions had gathered their strength. The Jewish professional unions rose up and burst, like air bubbles in water ... the Jewish worker in England is still the petit-bourgeois fortune-seeker!

This was a misinterpretation of the facts; certainly in the context of defining the Jewish workers' role and motivation during the latter years prior to 1914.

After the public meeting the Socialist Union began to deteriorate. Lieberman was a main source of conflict. Rejection by the Tailors' Union prompted Sapir to demand a change of identity and programme together with the establishment of a permanent venue, since 'without a building we cannot maintain propaganda'.[31] Lieberman opposed him and thereby brought to a head the personal animosity between them. Sapir replied that 'nothing went well when Lieberman's suggestions were put into practice' so that 'Lieberman

30. Minutes of the second closed meeting of the Hebrew Socialist Union dated 16 September, 1876.

31. Article 'The Jewish Socialist Movement in England' in *Volkszeitung*, no.137, 1906, by T. Rothstein. The author was first a Bundist, then a Leninist and later a Soviet candidate for the Ambassadorship in England.

had brought nothing but harm to the Union'.[32] Majority opinion was ranged against him. Rosenthal aligned himself with Sapir: 'We Socialists are hated in town since that public meeting to which Lieberman brought such disaster.' Stone added his piece: 'Lieberman was selfish and arrogant.' Even his own followers were critical. Wainer was forced to concede that 'even if the accusations against him were incorrect, it was the wish of every member that Lieberman must go!' Thus the founder of the Union became the scapegoat for its failures. It was not wholly undeserved. There were other factors which led to his quick departure from both the Union and London.

Not the least were his own personality defects. Sapir observes that 'many things about Lieberman became repulsive to Smirnov'.[33] It was never an easy relationship. The cool, self-disciplined doctor reacted sharply against Lieberman's *bonhomie*, which he regarded as puerile. 'He could not excuse . . . other character traits of Lieberman, especially his tendency to posture.' After his short trip to Berlin in June 1876, Lieberman showed Smirnov a photo taken with Zundelevich, where he is about to draw a revolver. Smirnov commented: 'Masquerade and comedy. Otherwise he was very embarrassed about it . . . because he knew perfectly well that I am a realistic revolutionary and that all this childishness seems ridiculous to me and annoys me.'[34] His persistent tactlessness lost him any sympathy or help he had come to expect from Smirnov. In May, 1876, prior to his German visit, Lieberman had promised to translate certain *Vperyod* articles for the benefit of the Danish Social Democrats. He failed to deliver, and Smirnov, who bore editorial responsibility for such functions, was furious. 'He (Lieberman) only knows how to correspond with Jews', complained Smirnov.[35] Lieberman unwittingly provoked him further by his correspondence with the Russian Jacobin, Petr Tkachev, over an article on Vilna published in his organ *Nabat*.

32. Minutes of Hebrew Socialist Union meetings 19 and 20 (4 and 17 October, 1876).
33. Sapir, 'Lieberman et le Socialisme Russe'.
34. Letter to Rosa Idelson, 18 June, 1876.
35. Letter to Rosa Idelson, 11 June, 1876.

Smirnov fumed at Lieberman's 'stupidity'. He felt that Tkachev, who had broken with Lavrov back in 1874, would interpret such overtures as a tentative change of direction on the part of *Vperyod* in order to resume relations with him. Jacobinism was anathema to Lavrov. By the end of June, Smirnov's alienation was complete. He was also quite ill and no longer able to control his feelings towards real or imaginary recalcitrants. In October, after strong pressure from his comrades, he went abroad first to Heidelberg, then to Montreux, where Rosa Idelson assumed care of him. Lieberman had become an extra burden on a journal now facing liquidation. The closure of the Lavrovist headquarters in Paris in November meant the end of the bi-weekly *Vperyod*. Lavrov resigned and with him went Lieberman's job as typesetter and lithographer. The blow coincided with growing opposition towards him in the Socialist Union. His last notes as secretary record meetings between the executive committee and representatives of the sleevemakers for 2 and 9 December. The minutes of 28 December, the last report of the Union's activity, bear the illegible signature of a new secretary, for Lieberman had quit London abruptly on the 19th.

His departure spelt *finis* to the organisation. The ill-informed majority and his own followers had, in the end, denied him to their cost. Sapir's views on a permanent building and new hope from the 'German' school were carried. His rigid adherence to the primacy of *international* Socialism, with its concomitant rejection of a Jewish identity, destroyed the Union's viability. In defaulting on Lieberman's programme, the remaining members brought to an end the first experiment in *Jewish* socialist organisation. In the contemporary setting, Lieberman's proud declaration had been valid: 'London, or England, is the *only* place, where we Socialists can operate openly ... To Jewish Socialists in other lands, our Union is an example.'

Lieberman, in Europe, was resolved to fulfil his other ambition — the production of a Jewish Socialist journal, which had been sponsored by both Lavrov and Smirnov. The latter had been prime mover on this project, and had earmarked Lieberman as editor. Natanson, founder-leader of the Petersburg 'Union', had appeared in London (January-February, 1876) and expressed interest in such an innovation. Smirnov, with the support of Zundelevich, who promised a monthly subsidy of forty roubles,[36] followed this up with a letter to the leaders of the Russian 'Union' requesting a loan of seven hundred roubles for two years to cover costs.[37] Smirnov felt it incumbent on the Russian party to underwrite the venture. The money was not forthcoming. *Vperyod* had no funds and the 'Union' showed little concern for instituting a Yiddish journal. In April, 1876, the Lavrovists quit the 'Union'. Lieberman persisted in his belief that the 'Union' would provide credit, together with the Berlin Jewish students, with whom he had been associated since his period of transit between Vilna and London. To stir things up he revisited the Berlin group (May 23-18 June, 1876) and received generous promises. But nothing transpired from that quarter either. Yet Lieberman still held to the belief that financial aid was imminent. By December, 1876, the accumulation of frustration and defeat in London prompted him to reassess possibilities on the continent.

Leipzig, headquarters of the SPD, warranted his consideration as a base, since a press would be available there to produce the long-delayed Jewish journal. He conceived a plan of distribution inside Russia through a supply line linking a ring of cities, namely Kiev, Kherson, Odessa, Kremenchug and Jitomir; and mapped out two points of entry along the Austro-Russian border, through which clandestine literature could be smuggled.[38] He chose to act as an independent operator, but non-co-operation from a Lavrovist leader and Smirnov's warning of the greater risks involved in time of war (the Russo-Turkish conflict) persuaded him to stay put, initially in Berlin. Here Lieberman threw himself into feverish activity. He organised a Jewish Socialist conference amongst the local student *émigrés*, to whom he tried to interpret the mood and direction of the revolutionary movement inside

---

36. Letter from Zundelevich to Smirnov, 17 February, 1876.
37. The letter dated 22 February, 1876 was jointly signed by Goldenberg, Linev, Smirnov, Lieberman and Zundelevich.
38. Letters to Smirnov, in Marmor, *Letters of Aron Lieberman.*

Russia. The long-promised biography of Stenka Razin appeared in the SPD *New World* and his lengthier *Ideals of Mankind* was finally completed. His attempt to accumulate funds for his journal was backed by Johann Most, SPD representative in the Reichstag, and currently editor of the *Berlin Free Press*.

From his letters to Smirnov, first from Berlin and later Vienna, we gauge some evidence of his role in the Russian liberation movement: his liaison with the revolutionary workers in Petersburg (1876-7) and his articles in *Vperyod* on the defence of the accused in the 'trial of the 50' (February, 1877) with photographs including, for example, that of Jessie Helfmann. He informs the reader of his clandestine aid, which entails the supply of printing presses and accessories to the issue of proclamations and other radical propaganda. He reminds 'Moshel' (Zundelevich) to hide Mark Natanson's printing press in Petersburg, at the same time encouraging the federation of home tailors' circles. He renders a dramatic account of the Nihilist writer, Ivan Pisarev, at the 'Square of our Lady of Kazan' demonstration (16 December, 1876), together with relevant commentary on the spread of Jewish revolutionary proclamations in Poltava and Kiev.

The 'Berlin Section', and Lieberman's adherence to it, needs reappraisal, both in the light of subsequent Jewish Socialist history and in its effectiveness as an arm of underground Russia. The second is easier to evaluate. To the Russian movement the young 'Berliners' brought 'a relay of communication between illegal circles and emigration. The transport of publications, organisation of illegal transit of militants across the border, a place of welcome for Russian refugees — the student youth of Berlin occupied themselves with all that.'[39] They also acted as a friendly bridge between Russian and German socialists by feeding information to the SPD press on up-to-date Russian revolutionary activity. Lieberman turned up in Vienna, probably at the beginning of March, 1877. He informed Smirnov[40] that his initial project

39. Sapir, 'Lieberman et le Socialisme Russe', pp.51-2.

40. Letter to Smirnov, 6 March, 1877, no.20 in Marmor, *Letters of Aron Lieberman*. Lieberman informed Smirnov that he had arrived several days before to set up the first page of a pre-planned book on Jewish heroes.

consisted of Yiddish translations of a popular Russian
revolutionary brochure and copies of his own stories. At last
the Jewish journal was born with sufficient funds to sustain it
for four months. On 25 March he had completed his first
outline of *HaEmet* in Hebrew. Smirnov was both astonished
and indignant. He recalled Lieberman's own words in
London: 'Hebrew is unintelligible to the majority of people
[i.e. Jews] and is only accessible to . . . small number of
cultivated hypocrites!' This volte-face was no doubt brought
about by his experience in London. His letters from Vienna
reveal that Lieberman welcomed the opportunity to get back
at the 'Jewish Socialist Party' of London, whom he refers to
as *Zhids*, the Russian derogatory term for bourgeois Jews. He
withheld from them all information of his existence and
activities, requesting Smirnov to mention the proposed
HaEmet only to his Vilna comrades, while 'without argument
the others should be kept absolutely ignorant of this, without
deceiving Rosenthal'!

His letters also provide a wealth of evidence on *HaEmet*
and the problems which beset him. Printing materials were
expensive and so was the cost of living. He continued to
suffer poor health and begged Smirnov, as a doctor, to advise
him on remedial measures for a persistent cough, since he
could not afford the luxury of a Viennese medico. He
repeated his promise to print and distribute 'forbidden
Yiddish pamphlets' and gave notice that, when the time came
'to move quickly', he would quit Vienna and settled in either
Leipzig, Berlin or London. A passport bearing the pseudonym 'Arthur Freeman' was requested from his Russian
comrades. This was the indictable offence which led to his
arrest.

Smirnov's replies were rarely without criticism. He was
particularly censorious of *HaEmet* appearing in Hebrew, and
also questioned its political alignment, which 'appeared to
characterise the journal as National Liberal'. Lieberman
defended his stand on the premise that he was 'willing to
have his head cut off, if a person *versed in Hebrew* [a knock
at Smirnov] could not recognise his approach as anything but
Socialist'. In turn he repeatedly complained of the unfriendly
attitudes adopted by Russian contacts, attributing it to the

false information passed on by treacherous Jewish comrades.

Only three numbers were issued between May and September, 1877, but they were rich in socio-political observations on contemporary European Jewry. The essays vary in content from a social novel, poems and book reviews to informed articles on the 'Jewish Question', 'The Jews in London' and 'The Social Status of the Jews in Hungary'. The main contributor — the head and heart of the journal — was, of course, Lieberman. *HaEmet* was smuggled into the Pale and proved such a success that a second edition of the first issue followed. Its popularity seemed assured, when Lieberman was suddenly arrested, initially on a technical oversight. He had failed to produce press copies for the Austrian censor. He was seized in February 1878 and according to the police report, was charged on three counts: belonging to a secret society, using a false US passport, and assuming another person's name. He was summarily imprisoned for ten months, after which a Viennese tribunal acquitted him[41] on the first charge, but condemned him to another month's solitary confinement on the other two. After completing his sentence he was forced to undergo a further month's detention, when the Prussian government demanded his extradition under the new anti-Socialist laws. The Austrian Foreign Minister officially refused to hand him over, but he was in fact delivered up to the Germans by being forcibly expelled across the Bavarian border. He was promptly arrested by German police at Munich (18 January, 1879) and transported to Berlin.

The Berlin group had already been rounded up. The Prussian authorities were never really aware of its operational functions. A report from the Police-President of Berlin (1.9.1878) referred to two divisions among the Russian Social Revolutionary organisation: one labelled the Greater, the other the Small Russian party. Both were controlled by a Professor Lavrov from Paris, who associated with Communards and Carl Hirsch, German Social Democrat. Under Lavrov was Professor Dragomanov, who held brief over the Berlin section. On 26 April, 1879, Lieberman and two

41. 10 November, 1877.

medical students — M. Aronson[42] and G. Gurevich — were tried at a Berlin court. Lieberman was sentenced to eight months' imprisonment, taking into account the two months' detention, and served his time in the Plötzensee. Released on 26 November, he was expelled via Hamburg to England. His two years' stay in goal was a traumatic experience from which he never fully recovered.

He returned, almost destitute, to his old haunts in Whitechapel. He found cheap lodgings at 21 Elder Street, Spitalfields, from which he ventured forth daily to stomp the alleys of East London, 'seeking work as photographer, lithographer, teacher or shoe-shine!'[43] The Jewish Socialist Union had long since gone. Most of the old comrades had transferred to a new organisation — the Third Section of the Communist Workers' Educational Union. Hopefully he renewed his acquaintance with Johann Most, who, since 1879, had been publishing his *Freiheit* in England. At Most's request, Lieberman contributed several articles on the Russian movement, and he was frequently invited to address the predominantly German First Section of the Communist Workers' Educational Union, at its headquarters in the West End.[44] He made a last, short-lived attempt to organise a Jewish Working Men's Benefit and Educational Society, and drew up its statutes with a firm reference that members 'must be addressed in their own tongue'.[45]

Such few, albeit pleasant, diversions could not assuage his deep concern with political events in the homeland which, together with other relevant problems, brought on mental depression. Readjustment to freedom is always painful in itself, added to which were the nagging fears preoccupying a workless foreigner, alone in a Whitechapel slum, endlessly foraging for bread. His ex-comrade Wainer, who welcomed him back, no longer spoke the same language. (Perhaps he

---

42. Brother-in-law of 'revisionist' Edward Bernstein. The latter commented on the proceedings in his *Die Geschichte der Berliner Arbeiterbewegung*, Zweiter Act, Berlin, 1907, p.34. This was, of course, the famous Nihilist Trial of 1879.

43. Letter to Smirnov, under the name Arthur Freeman, 5 January, 1880.

44. The *Republican*, April 1880, reports of a meeting held at the Rose Street Club, off Charing Cross Road, to commemorate the revolution of 1848 and the Commune, in which Johann Most and Aron Lieberman were the prime speakers.

45. The manuscript is in the Winchevsky collection in the YIVO archives.

had already taken the road to *embourgeoisement* which eventually led to his ownership of a profitable cabinet manufactory!) The *Vperyod* group was gone, and his two closest collaborators abroad, Zundelevich and Zuckerman, had been seized by the Russian police. A split in the ranks of the *Narodniki* added to his ideological confusion. A 'Black Partition' faction (which included Plekhanov) remained faithful to the concept of an immediate social and economic transformation engendered by a spontaneous uprising of the masses; while the opposing group, Narodnaya Volya, was pledged to attain political advancement by means of terror and regicide, with no formal adherence to Socialism. Lieberman sensed the futility in continuing agitation solely among Jews. But he was reluctant to join a conspiratorial minority whose principal aim was a Liberal constitution. A crisis in ideology was complicated by his feeling of remorse. He was under the illusion that he was twice guilty, through negligence, of providing information against comrades on trial.

At the time of his arrest in Vienna, incriminating letters from his Berlin contacts had been found on him, and the Prussian police used them as material evidence. Lieberman viewed his own carelessness as the cause of betrayal. Later, on hearing that Zundelevich had been arrested in Russia, he informed Most, who published it in *Freiheit*. The result was a diatribe from *Vperyod*, who demanded the name of the informant. For Zundelevich, the most wanted man in police files, had been arrested under a false name. *Freiheit's* action might have disclosed his true identity. This subsequently preyed on Lieberman's mind.

Renewed political activism could purge his conscience and provide him with a *leitmotif*. Although dubious of violent means, he offered his services to Narodnaya Volya. The opinion of a leading terrorist, Leo Hartmann, was decisive. He was considered unsuitable, and turned down. A morbid love affair drove him towards a tragic finale. Yet the last act conceded a measure of hope for the resurgence of Jewish Socialism.

In 1879, Lieberman befriended a young compatriot, Morris Winchevsky, who had participated in underground activity in Königsberg. The latter lodged with the Harrises —

Jewish *restaurateurs* in the East End. Here Lieberman was introduced to Winchevsky's sister-in-law, Rachel, an exotic though overblown young lady, married to a nondescript husband. Lieberman was attracted to her but, true to her Orthodox commitments, she refused to respond. (Rachel also knew that Lieberman had left a wife and children back in Vilna.) Her own husband set off for New York, leaving her behind. Paradoxically, she was reluctant to go, but repelled by Lieberman's advances, she was driven to join her husband. Lieberman followed, but was again rejected. In despair, he shot himself in a cheap lodging-house in Syracuse (18 November, 1880).

One discerns that Lieberman's contradictory assertions on agitprop among Jews stem from his own psychological quirks. Certain consistencies, however, do appear in his correspondence. To the end he is concerned with Jews operating as a separate entity within the global struggle for social liberation. He never subscribed to factionalism or petty dissensions arising from divergences in ideology. With Liebknecht he defended the cause of uniting both Internationals — Marxist and Bakuninist, which brought on his head the wrath of the Lavrovist leadership. He persisted in his 'attachment to the idea of general solidarity amongst Socialists of all kinds', without which, in his view, one could not be a true Socialist; and deplored such parochialism where one was forced 'to stand with one party and one person'.

The eclecticism by which he formulated his own brand of Socialism, is conceived in his letters to Smirnov (November, 1876). Lieberman saw himself as 'a binder of peoples' via a federation of all Socialist groups and, while seeking a *modus vivendi* with the leaders of the English working class, was still primarily concerned with creating a Jewish trade union. It is difficult to determine what kind of society Lieberman ultimately envisaged. Evidence suggests that he veered closer to Anarchism than to any other creed. He had shaped his course according to Smirnov's rejection of an élitist seizure of power. 'We don't need substitutes for the people — only organisation of workers in all lands.'[46] But he was quick to

46. Smirnov, *Vperyod*, March 1874.

recognise (and here he was much more perceptive than Marx) that each national group had a unique quality inherited from its own cultural and historical experience, of which the Socialist movement must take account, if it is to gain sympathetic contact with all people. In *Vperyod* he quotes the Jewish experience as an example:

> The community has always been the basis of our whole existence. The revolution itself created our tradition. The community was the basis of our legislation, which in unmistakable words forbade the sale of land, and in the sense of equality and brotherhood required a redistribution of the soil every seven years. Our most ancient social system is anarchy; our true federation over the entire earth – the International. The great prophets of our time, Marx, Lassalle and others, based themselves on the spirit of our people, and thus attained inner ripeness.

There is no substitution for revolution from below, that is the spontaneous insurrection of the masses. In a letter to his comrade Zuckerman, he urges him to build up his imagery on this theme in the poem 'Corn or Bread. Bread or Dead!'[47]

> All cry, 'Why is this different from all days?'. And it brings forth a mighty shout from all throats, 'Corn or Bread. Bread or Dead!' They run out in the open, bound together, solid as a rock, all interlocked – not by privilege or religion, be it Jew, Russian, Pole, Lithuanian, or even stranger, German or French. One to the other 'Give me your hand'.
> There they assemble – the people. They unsheath their swords, the blades bright and sparkling, sharpened and polished. The Generals say 'Why have you come together – worker to worker? Do you mean to free *yourselves* from your rulers?'

The class battle is joined and ends with the inexorable triumph of the poor and hungry.

Lieberman's polemics were marked by a rabid anti-clericalism. In his youth he had nourished the hope that the power of the rabbi could be utilised for the political and social amelioration of his flock. In an early letter to Reb Shmuel

---

47. Letter no.4, To a Jewish Typographer, August 23, 1875, in Marmor, *Letters of Aron Lieberman*, pp.34-7.

Joseph Fine[48] he suggests that he warn the people of the danger of accepting government promises at their face value. The Jews must be made aware of their dignity, and divest themselves of the habits of slaves.

> And how quickly in the past have they bent their backs to the iron yoke. Have they forgotten that they are men and not cows in the field? They have no confidence in themselves when faced with a glimmer of . . . hope.

He begs Reb Shmuel to assume the role of political mentor, too:

> You are the Rabbi! You are the guide of all the children of your people. God made you a shepherd, to tell Jacob the right thing. Therefore, come! Speak out!

Lieberman was quickly disillusioned. Soon he was attacking the rabbinate for engendering spiritual stagnation among the Jewish masses. He accused theologians of denying the message of the ancient prophets: that instead of labouring for a spiritual and physical regeneration of their people, the reverse was true. Priests endorsed the social enslavement of the Jew. This was brought home to Lieberman during his activity with the Vilna underground, when the rabbis preached in the synagogues against the Socialists in order to ingratiate themselves with the Tsarist authorities. In *Vperyod* he exposed them as government agents. 'During his first sermon (1 July, 1875), the seventy-six-year-old Vilna Maggid, Reb Elijah Landy, reading from a paper sent to him by the secret police, exhorted the Jews to report their own children or relatives.'[49] Later Lieberman added:[50]

> In his second sermon, held in the Vilna synagogue, the last day of *Pesach* [4 April, 1876], the same individual warned the older folks to watch their children, so that they should not befriend those who express terrible ideas 'against God and his anointed'.

48. Letter no.1. Written in Bialystock, 23 March, 1866. Reb Fine was Inspector of all Hebrew training establishments in Vilna district, and editor of the Hebrew weekly *HaCarmel*.
49. *Vperyod*, 1 October, 1875.
50. Article 'Correspondence from Vilna', in *Vperyod*, 15 June, 1876.

He did not then remind anyone about reporting or eavesdropping. For in them was mirrored the image, terrible to behold, of a downtrodden, tortured mass.

After him came a short speech by the Kazioner Rabbi, Shaftl Kliatchko. He did attempt to denounce his people. He *knew* that he, and all his ilk, were regarded by the people as the mouthpiece of the government. Therefore he only referred to revolutionary propaganda and suggested, in the words of Police-General Losiev, and army General Balandorf, that 'Freedom lay in the existence of Tsardom'.

In London, as we have seen, he continued his attacks on the Jewish priesthood with disastrous results, for it was incumbent on Lieberman, as on others who upheld the sanctity of the French revolutionary tradition, to parade his implacable hostility to God's 'cowled advocates'.

The labours of Lieberman and his comrades to create a Jewish Socialist movement in Whitechapel may have been unsuccessful — in the short term. They were pioneers working on hard soil, but their seeds would eventually bear fruit. Henceforth East London was never without some radical group dedicated to the fulfilment of Lieberman's dream.[51] Moreover the prophet had left a disciple — Morris Winchevsky. It was he who supplemented organisation with effective propaganda and, in the process, presented the Jewish world with its first Yiddish Socialist journal.

---

51. In a novel, *Der Tahapuchot* (The Confused Generation), J.A. Trivaush portrays Lieberman as the hero Frank. The author reveals Frank's inner contradictions, as a Nihilist spurning antiquity, anti-Nationalist, yet a committed Hebraist and lover of his Jewish folk.

5. Apostles and Agitators

Our Jewish comrades are not only Socialist propagandists. They are energetically occupied in organising trade societies to combat the sweating system, raise the rate of wages to subsistence level, hold out a helping hand to friendless immigrants, who ignorant of English and English wage rates are helpless victims of the sweater and his agents, and to communicate the real state of affairs in the London labour market to their brethren abroad.

Freedom, 8 May, 1888

Against the background of the great Russo-Jewish exodus, the upward curve of immigration registered an increase of approximately 30,000 alien Jews between the years 1881 and 1891.[1] We have already noted how the uncomplaining tolerance of the hosts diminished as numbers grew and the demands for housing, work and bread on the Jewish sub-economy increased. Within the ghetto job competition was intensified by the pressure of ever larger numbers on limited trades. Transmigration was a negligible factor in easing the situation. Both handicapped efforts to create a unified work force under the auspices of a political or union-based organisation.

Unionisation provides another story. Symptoms of radicalism revived as the 'greeners' poured in after 1881. This paralleled the earliest warning of an 'alien problem', which underlined the Report of the *Lancet* Special Sanitary Commission of 3 May, 1884.[2] Two months before, a factory Inspector, Mr Lakeman, had commented publicly in East

1. According to Census Return of Aliens in England and Wales under the categories of Russians, Russian-Poles and Roumanians:
    1881   14,559   (including approx. 2,000 Christians)
    1891   45,808   (including approx. 3,500 Christians)
2. See above, pp.50-2.

London on the evasion of the factory acts by Jewish master tailors.[3] 'The Factory Laws have socially raised every trade which has been subjected to them, and have given independence to workers in every case, save the one degraded and wretched trade of East London tailoring!' The *Jewish Chronicle*, sensitive to any public criticism involving Jews, quickly responded by proposing remedies which could be applied by the Jewish Board of Guardians. Its observations were perceptive enough to note (with implied criticism) the tailors' inability to organise themselves collectively as a means of bettering their conditions. The Board therefore should set up a committee to investigate wages and hours of labour and impress its recommendations on the masters.[4]

> The functions of the Board include the prevention of pauperism as well as its relief. The Jewish workmen are well known to be amongst the least inclined to organise for the purpose of aiding each other in obtaining better wages. In the tailoring, boot and cigar trades, the proportion of Jewish society is extremely small [?], and there are few trades where the wages range lower than in these. The Board of Guardians could also greatly assist in bringing them to improve hygienic conditions under which they employ their hands. Some of these factories are veritable hotbeds of disease.

The *Jewish Chronicle* re-emphasised its plea after the publication of the *Lancet* report with the additional rider that 'the evils from which this section [tailoring] of the industrial class is suffering, in so far as they are susceptible of remedy, are to be cured by the pressure of public opinion acting upon the unscrupulous masters, and by combination among the work people themselves'.[5]

The immediate result was a combination of masters. On 18 May, at The Yorkminster pub hall in Philpot Street, Whitechapel, a meeting of the Mutual Tailors' Association took place. It was presided over by Mr Mark Moses,[6] and the

3. Speaking on the state of East End tailoring at a meeting of the local branch of the Amalgamated Society of Tailors at the Skinners' School, Bishopsgate, 11 March, 1884.

4. *Jewish Chronicle*, 21 March, 1884, 'Notes of the Week'.

5. *Jewish Chronicle*, 16 May, 1884.

6. Mark Moses was a leading clothing contractor and later emerged as the master tailors' spokesman in the 1889 tailors' strike. He was the father of the popular Jewish club leader and social worker, the late Miriam Moses JP.

Jewish Chronicle reported that nearly four hundred master tailors attended. What started out as a panic meeting to refute 'the many charges made against them' evolved into a debating forum to put forward ideas on protecting the individual master against unfair competition. There were complaints of poaching on each other's territory by enticing workers away with offers of higher pay. Moses recommended the issue of a written form of discharge to any employee who quitted, and that no employer should hire anyone without its possession. There were tentative proposals for the reform of the industry which could benefit all. A Mr Samuel Danziger seconded the formation of a new association (the Master Tailors' League proposed by the President) on the premise that it should implement 'good hours, good shops and good wages', thus ameliorating conditions for both masters and men. A sensitive nerve was pricked when Mr Simon Ansell called on those who presumed to be masters to provide reasonable accommodation and hours of labour. Many of them were better off if they remained journeymen. The low state of the trade could be attributed to excessive competition. He recalled instances where garments were produced for one and threepence and even ninepence each and where workshops struggled to exist from year to year. Underlying every discussion was the reality: that the *raison d'être* of any masters' association was its power to control poaching and price-cutting between members. Above all was the unspoken assumption of the common threat posed by the workers. The previous year (16 July, 1883) a meeting of Jewish tailors had succeeded in resuscitating a Tailors' Union, who had established for the first time an association with their English counterparts.

In spite of the *Jewish Chronicle*'s lamentations over the fact that Jewish workmen seemed chronically incapable of organising themselves collectively, it was in the interests of the Anglo-Jewish Establishment that, where such unions were created, they should remain under its control. The Lieberman group was a warning. A union's image must be kept respectable, free of such dangerous Socialist influences, which might focus unwanted attention on Jews. Unions would be better constructed along the lines of self-help — as

Friendly Societies covering sick and death benefits and the like. Such limited functions would serve the interests of the entrepreneur. They would render the unions impotent by directing them away from their true purpose as the workers' bargaining power in times of dispute. With comic irony Isaac Stone recalls this and other diversionary tactics, consciously or unconsciously performed by infiltrators into the would-be union of 1879:[7]

> Workers' meetings were no longer called. All those who wanted to form a Jewish Union had to canvas individuals one by one – till it became a union of the élite. It sought to give full benefits for sickness and doctors fees. The outcome was that the workers obtained a masonic building with attached library containing many books. Teachers were present so that workers could learn to read and write English and Yiddish . . . The Union's image was respectable. In a couple of months the workers were fed up with all their books, and could barely pay their subscriptions. During those months they had learned more reading and writing than their teachers. The Union became a heavy burden on them. They quit one by one until there was no more Union!

Two years later a Jewish Tailor's Machinist Society was actually founded by the millionaire MP Samuel Montagu. It demanded a twelve-hour day (including breaks for lunch and tea), but strictly prohibited the strike as a weapon in negotiations. 'They had no funds to disburse as benefits; they had no indigenous leadership; and they depended on wealthy patrons.'[8] By 1884 the message had been received by a large body of immigrant workers that they must control their own destiny. What was needed was a press in the *mame loshen* and agitation in the interests of their own kind. One man provided both. He was Morris Winchevsky.

Winchevsky (*né* L. Benzion Novochovitch) was born in 1856 at Yanova, near Kovno in Lithuania. At thirteen he entered the Vilna seminary and underwent the usual conversion from piety to radical atheism. He responded to Lieberman's 'Call to the Jewish Youth', left Russia in 1877

---

7. *Poilishe Yidl*, no.6., dated 29 August, 1884, article 'The Jewish Worker in London', by I. Stone.

8. Gartner, *The Jewish Immigrant in England (1870-1914)*, p.118.

and settled in Königsberg, where he gained employment as bookkeeper in the local branch of a Kovno merchant banker, Feinberg. Here a publisher, Rodkinson (uncle of the future editor of the *Arbeter Fraint*, A. Frumkin), commissioned him to write for his Hebrew periodical *Asefet Chachomim* (Assembly of the Wise). When Lieberman was arrested, Rodkinson publicised his paper as successor to *HaEmet*, from which he stole many of its ideas and techniques, and exploited Winchevsky mercilessly. During the round-up preceding the Nihilist trials, Winchevsky was arrested too but, thanks to the intervention of his banker patron, who bribed the authorities to release him, he was free to leave Germany. He made his way to London via Paris. Here he met up with members of the defunct Hebrew Socialist Union, and later, on Lieberman's release from prison, befriended and helped him during his last months in London.

Winchevsky first lodged in Whitechapel with a student friend Margolis, who was subsidised by the Jewish Educational Aid Society. Its secretary, the humane Rev. Albert Löwy, noticed during a visit to Margolis a book on Socialism with erudite criticisms pencilled in alongside various paragraphs. He asked to meet the scribbler and was shocked to find him (Winchevsky) in a state of abject poverty. Löwy undertook to introduce him to the City banker Seligman, who offered Winchevsky a job as bookkeeper, which he accepted under the name of Leopold Benedikt. Winchevsky was the pseudonym he adopted as a political expedient. It would conceal his true identity, on the premise that his employer would not take too kindly to such extraneous activity.

Five years in Whitechapel strengthened his affirmation as a radical. He was convinced that Jewish workers needed a newspaper which would undertake certain obligations. It would be printed in Yiddish — the language of the masses. It must meet the urgent need for radical propaganda which, although not exclusively Socialist, would introduce the reader to 'the principles of Socialism'. Winchevsky eschewed religion, but would not be averse to drawing on Biblical or Talmudic analogies with which every Jew was familiar, to illustrate his arguments. He was shrewd enough to learn from the failure of the Hebrew Socialist Union, that over-zealous indulgence in anti-religious sentiment was counter-productive. It offended the majority of workers, in whom orthodoxy was inculcated from birth. In their reckoning, atheism and even apostasy was equated with Socialism. By treading warily one could counteract this. The plan was to present an all-embracing picture of immigrant life to which the reader could respond sympathetically with political indoctrination more subtly applied.

On 25 July, 1884, under the sponsorship of Winchevsky and his friend E. Rabbinowitz, appeared the *Poilishe Yidl* — the first Socialist newspaper in Yiddish. The address of its publishing office was given as 137 Commercial Street, E.1., located in the then centre of immigrant settlement. The editorial explained its functions in down-to-earth terms. It proposed a three-sided approach to the reader: as a man, as a Jew, and as a worker. Its major objectives were also threefold: 'To instruct and support our brothers who know little or nothing of other languages; to help 'greeners' who have recently arrived and are seeking work; to give its men and women readers some insight into world affairs'.[7] Sixteen issues appeared, and Winchevsky's distinctive style may be discerned throughout, with its regular alternating sweep from pathos to bitter irony in the traditional patois of the *stetl*. He and his co-writers present the reader with a many-sided picture of immigrant life in the 1880s. Features included local, national and world news with political analysis and commentary; correspondence from the other great Jewish centre in Leeds and weekly dramatic criticism of the *spiel* at the Yiddish theatre. But above all was a didactic appraisal of the harsh conditions suffered by Jews, with practical suggestions for their amelioration.

The *Poilishe Yidl* turned its attention continually on the Jewish workers' vice — gambling. In the opening issue it reports a hilarious scene of Jews engaged on their weekly ritual:[9]

> Leeds workers and small masters, as soon as they are paid . . . run straight to the pubs and bet on horses. The main centre for these

9. *Poilishe Yidl*, no.1., 25 July, 1884. 'Correspondent in Leeds'.

pursuits is Swan Street — the Leeds workers' main rendezvous. Here 6 to 1 is offered for 'Tsaddick' which Charles Ward will ride; 3 to 1 elsewhere, whilst another shouts and makes hand signals. Cries of 'Little Dog!' and 'Cleopatra!' for the winners. Everyone has a *Sporting Chronicle* in his hand to learn whether he can retrieve from the horse the week's wages he has laid out on bets, counts with his fingers and questions and talks in English like a born Russian. In short the Jewish workers hand over the money and the Christian bookmakers take it gladly. Everybody is happy. Everyone thinks he has backed a winner ... The day speeds on. Holy Sabbath has arrived. The bookmakers and Jewish workers are still there in Swan Street. The pub is there; beer, rum, brandy and whiskey, all there. 'Lechayim' to 'John Jones', 'lechayim' to 'Tsaddick', 'lechayim' to all good horses. The clock strikes 4 p.m., a quarter of an hour to go and the telegraph will bring luck to the happy crew. The fifteen minutes are up — the telegraph is here. Everyone leaps up, runs, cries, 'Well!' 'Where!' 'What!' Noses are buried in papers. Suddenly one shouts out a pair of words and the whole company lowers their noses and murmurs, 'An outsider!'

... And he who was lucky enough to hit the jackpot is the bookmaker — a welsher, as the local saying goes, that is a swindler, who will not pay up. And you cannot force him to as betting is illegal. Thus is everyone's miserable wage squandered away.

A poem by Ben Ez (that is Winchevsky) strikes a more solemn note on the evils resulting from card-playing. In 'A Character Sketch of Jewish Life In London'[10] he tells of a young mother with a sick child, living in a small, dirty room, anxiously awaiting the return of her husband, whom, she hopes will bring home money to buy food. The girl coughs incessantly. She waits in vain. For he is

> In another room,
> Dirty and small,
> In a fine house,
> Full of Jews.
> Wages and silver watch gone,
> Whilst sitting by a table
> Both lost in cards.

Gambling, therefore, is no recipe for the easy life. But here the worker has some control over his own destiny and can reject such indulgences.

10. Ibid., no.4., 15 August, 1884.

In job opportunities he has no such choice. He is a prisoner of his environment where alternatives are scarce. The *Poilishe Yidl* confronts us with the quality of life endured by contributors, who are personally involved at the work-bench. It casts a jaundiced eye on the masters, those *weile Jungen* (wide boys) who feed on innocent Jews, equipped only with their trade craft and no one to advise or help them. The bosses sit on the backs of workers but the paper warns: 'Ride for a time but don't take liberties with the horse!'

The *Poilishe Yidl* mirrored the lives and fortunes of its clientele, and probed into those areas of experience with which every immigrant was familiar. The reader could readily identify himself in such articles as 'The Woeful Tale of the Greener in London'.[11]

> We must ask the question, 'Is the "greener" here worse off than the dispossessed Jews in Russia?' — a question which we believe is most pertinent for all London Jews who have not yet forgotten. They are a pitiful sight. See the many hundreds walking abroad all night (it is illegal to sit down), with swollen lips for they may not have eaten or drunk for three days and are barely clad. Nobody cares.
>
> After being robbed and beaten in Russia the poor Jew comes to London without a kopek, and if one of the hundreds still has a couple of roubles this will be shared between the Christian who takes him off the boat and the one who looks after his belongings whilst the poor 'greener' tries to find his family or *landsleit*. He must even bargain with four old shirts, which even the poorest in Russia wouldn't handle, to hold the bit of ground allowed to him for an hour. When he finds his *landsman* he is confronted with an immediate 'Sholem Alechem!', followed by warnings on backbreaking labour and the admonition, 'Why have you come here? What will you do? . . . You will be unable to take the hunger!' He is not even offered a drink of water, and departs with an aching heart, thinking to himself, 'What do I do now? Hang or drown myself?' Midst these thoughts he is struck on the head with a stone. Full of pain, he looks to see where it came from, and observes the blackguard taking aim again. So he continues day and night with bruised lips . . . helpless.

Hungry and desperate he is succoured by a strange figure who accosts him and offers help:

> Sometimes a certain person meets him in the street, inquires about

11. Ibid., no.2, 1 August, 1884.

his means, then gives him a shilling and an address, whence he could call for aid. The poor one recognises him as a missionary, and is reluctant to go. But first, he thinks that one cannot be so rude to such a benefactor who is one's saviour for the night; and second, what else can one do other than to continue counting stones in the street?

So he succumbs to the inducement. The 'greener' who after all these adversities has managed to hold on to some money, or has found *landsleit* in Whitechapel, congratulates himself on his good fortune — but not for long.

Some close friends, after hard efforts, get him a job as learner machiner, presser, furrier's blocker and the like. Then comes the crunch . . . A pound or two must be paid for learning the trade. Four to six weeks is spent as free labour. During this time he learns to make the fire, clean the stove, act as tea or water carrier and must wheel the work away on a barrow. His time spent in trouble and suffering, is all taken up for love. Reduced to a weakened state, the Russian craftsman soon breaks down, choked by the English fog.

Any hope accruing from the possibilities of a first pay packet is quickly dispelled.

Then the master tells him, 'You haven't understood the work and still don't know it. But I'll have mercy on you and pay you four shillings a week.' He must be satisfied with that. For he knows that he has been taken for a ride and will not argue, since the master can get another 'greener' plus another two pounds on top. He has certainly worked diligently and on the eve of Sabbath he gets his first reward — four shillings — and a second. The master informs him that he does not need him any more because it is very slack. Thus is he beset with new troubles. No money, no prospects. He is sunk.

Almost every 'greener' suffered those visitations of Job, which the chronicler faithfully records. In turn he fixes his eye on the lodgings scene, on another predator who feeds on the misfortunes of the desperate hand.[12]

The landlady (lodging missus) is looking forward to the lucky day when he will begin to earn and then she knows that she will receive his income for half a year. She had obtained a large golden ring from

12. Ibid., no.7, 5 September, 1884.

a traveller, and promised to pay with the 'greener's' wages. What terrible trouble here, as we listen to her groans and pleas. But the ring returns to the traveller, and she remains with the 'greener's' old shirts. In anger, she gives him notice to quit. Perhaps she means a week's notice. No fear! That very night he has nowhere to lay his head.

. . . A few pieces of dirty washing left. Anything else is hidden with the loyal pawnbroker. For all he has now is in trust with the landlady. Perhaps some day he will redeem his washing.

The sense of pathos is reinforced in a poem by Winchevsky, who has suffered with the victim:[13]

> Have you seen a young man
> Hungry and dirty
> Passing here, and seeking
> All through the long night
> A small place —
> A door, a hole in the pavement
> Where he can lie down and rest?
> It is so cold and wet . . .

An earthy image of Jewish tailoring life is conveyed in the mood and language of the hands themselves. The curse of the local trade is the insecurity derived from the ebb and flow of seasonal demand.[14]

Two seasons befall the London tailors — busy time (full employment) and slack (hunger) . . .

. . . Slack time the tailor must undergo twice a year. Both are a plague; perhaps busy time is worse.

So when you come to London, on Sabbath take a stroll to the well known . . . *chazar mark* and you will see masters (you can distinguish them by their fat bellies!) scuttling about like a plague of mice between the poverty stricken workers [calling] , 'Jack, are you a machiner? John! I need a presser! Jim! I need a hand!' This is how they address the workers — not as a whole man, but by his hand, foot etc . . . Eventually you will discern a belly grab an arm just as a wolf seizes a lamb. As for those unfortunates who are left without a master, they gaze with baleful eyes which could consume belly and hands together. They are upset because they must remain here with their impoverished families, without work for the week.

13. Ibid., no.8, 12 September, 1884, 'The Sad Tale of the Greener in London'.
14. Ibid., no.9, 19 September, 1884, 'Busy and Slack in London'.

As for the fortunate ones, they are next observed in the confines of the sweat shop, trapped in an endless round of production.[15]

> It is already ten a.m. and the lambs are wondering since they have been working since seven a.m., when they can get something in their mouths. The machiner sews, but eats at the same time. But he is an angel who can perform two good deeds at once. (The rest are ordinary mortals who can only perform one at a time.) . . . He gives a turn on the handle, then a bite on the bread — a turn — a bite. The master's wife is very helpful. She brings each one a cup of coffee, or something resembling it, which must be drunk as you work, instead of the English way, granted by the boss, which allows half an hour off for breakfast. But our Jewish tailors use their brains and work out that half an hour off in the morning and evening adds up to one hour, and that costs money . . . To avoid the men losing the first half an hour, in which time one garment could be made, the good wife brings the coffee round for breakfast, and almost forces a cup into each worker's mouth, just as you stick grass down a horse's throat before he runs, in order to save time.

The whole shabby scene of exploitation and sharp practice instigated by the boss follows, exposed by a raconteur who has evidently been on the receiving end:

> But the coffee, or muddy water concoction, remains near each person, until it is either cold, poured away or filled with fag ends, since there is not time to drink. The master stands over his coats shouting, 'That's enough! Look sharp! What's all this then — A coffee house? A restaurant? On *Shabbas* you'll have plenty of time to drink coffee — not now! Quick — that's enough!'
> That's the picture of a tailor's breakfast in the busy season.
> The men work on without a pause like horses, until ten or eleven at night. How much more is there? The machiner looks at the clock and is amazed. Instead of the small hand standing at XI it stands at IX and the master is putting more work beside him which will last another three hours. 'That's the lot,' cries the master. 'The clock shows nine o'clock only and the work must be finished.'
> The good wife, of course, now brings up tea and almost pours it down the birds' throats. 'Only work, children!'

It is the inevitable results of overwork which are the more telling. The writer invites us to view the full damage wrought

15. Ibid., no.10, 26 September, 1884, 'Busy Time in the Workshop'.

by the busy season as we observe 'these same people carting home bottles of medicine from various hospitals. One has already lost a lung, another his heart, another a pair of feet.'

Slack time is, marginally, less hazardous, as the workers face only one danger — hunger. The noise of machines is muted in the dark attics. 'The master sits in his office and fares well on a lump of meat and a loving wife.' Only one man is doing a roaring trade now. It is 'Peter' with the three brass balls.

> We watch a housewife carrying, rolled up in her pinafore, a bundle containing a pair of trousers, a petticoat, a child's garments etc. The 'Peter' is a good chap. He examines each article to see whether it is still of any value. But more than that, as a good friend, he enquires about the lady's working husband as to whether he still has a shirt on his back. 'How much do you want for this?' asks the 'Peter'. 'Three shillings,' replies the poor wife, in tears. 'Ho-Ho,' laughs the 'Peter', and there is something to laugh about. It was as though one has taken the last bit of hole in one's skin and offered it for a piece of bread. 'Three shillings!' cries the 'Peter' and he grumbles a bit. Then out of friendship and kindness he shouts, 'Won't you take a shilling for these?' 'What can I do?' replies the woman. 'Give me the shilling. My children are crying for food. My man is hungry, and I can't even spit out my soul!'[16]

But she does not get the whole shilling. The pawnbroker pulls out a heap of coins and counts the pennies on the counter, totalling eleven and a half in all. He casually retains a half-penny for himself. The woman does not seem to notice, for she has already snatched up the money and rushed out to buy bread for her children. Outside there is the spectacle of hundreds of unemployed tailors milling about, shabby and collarless, trembling with cold.

> As hungry as wolves they run from one coffee house to the other, perhaps to meet an acquaintance who will treat them to a cup of coffee to wet their dry tongues.

The gay wantonness of youth is crushed by the harsh realities of want.

---

16. Ibid., no.11, 3 October, 1884, 'Workers Slack — "Peter" busy'.

These young men had, at one time, sweated in their ovens, that is, during busy time . . . Then they could clang two pennies in their pocket. They laughed at the whole world and no body of men was more carefree. They haunted the music halls with no thought for the future. To-day, these same people walk about with gaping wounds.

In the last resort, the hungry can turn to the 'committees', *ad hoc* centres set up by Anglo-Jewry to dispense charity. According to Isaac Stone, they were not all engendered by compassion, and their acts of benevolence were scarcely free from insensitive patronising. Such was the legend, that any prospective supplicant expected a painful and humiliating confrontation.

We have already indicated that the *Poilishe Yidl* held a watching brief on rising anti-Semitism.[17] It proclaimed its own sympathy with an honest English critic who blamed the Jews themselves for their cowardly submission to the masters. It chides its readers: 'What good is talk when Jewish workers are complaisant and smug and nothing perturbs them? . . . What one cannot or is afraid to do alone, can be done by a host — by a united workers' party!' What worries the editor is that the Jews help sustain the poison of anti-Semitism by the misdeeds and follies they perpetrate in their own trade. In the same issue[18] it prints in full a warning letter from a correspondent.

Listening at a meeting near the 'Dublin Castle' in the Mile End Waste, one speaker told how Jews had broken a strike of coat finishers. Jews took the work out of the shops to finish the work at home, and did well out of it . . . 'The Jew,' he continued, 'is always the enemy of the Christian and is never thankful to the land that grants him freedom. How should a Christian country deal with such enemies of humanity? Through an anti-Jewish Society succeeding in England, and exporting the Jews to Palestine, as he is no use to Europe.'

Not one voice was raised against all this anti-Semitic rhetoric.

We think that every Jew can recognise how far the Jews are detested. We can see with both eyes and hear the attitude of the English press and people towards the lost Jew.

It is no laughing matter. The Jews must be vigilant, or they will regret it.

17. See above, Chapter 3, pp.90-2.
18. *Poilishe Yidl*, no.13, 17 October, 1884.

The theme is pursued by the editorial in the following
issue.[19] Although Jews were over-sensitive to slights or
imaginary slights, they had a right to be indignant over the
current play, *Moss Joel*, at the Drury Lane theatre. The title
role is portrayed as

> an arsonist, a thief, a dealer in counterfeit notes, a swindler . . . a
> destroyer of hundreds of people – a combination of all these . . .
> and a boor to boot. Is such a character possible? Is there a Jew with
> such evil qualities, without one redeeming feature, that on being
> caught can only say, 'I don't want to die. I am too prosperous!'?
>
> Is such a Jew possible that he can show no remorse, when,
> through him, a boat has been sunk with all aboard?
>
> And there is Moss Joel, on stage every night, in the largest
> auditorium in London, giving pleasure to thousands, who leave
> thinking, 'That's quite a Jew!'
>
> It is interesting to note that the crime of placing a time bomb on
> a ship to obtain insurance was based on a real character involved in
> the case of a boat explosion in Germany. The man, who certainly
> existed, to mankind's shame, was called Thomas; and this Thomas
> was neither an English Jew or a German!

The slightest evidence of anti-Jewish sentiment is reported. In
the last copy[20] two instances are cited. The first concerned
the *Daily News*, which, in a congratulatory note to Moses
Montefiore on becoming a centenarian, gibed at the Jews'
unwillingness to settle in Palestine, since they 'prefer to stay
in Europe, where they are sitting on gold!'. The editor
remarked that 'the writer is, perhaps, casting no aspersions,
but maybe he has never been to those quarters, where one
can see four or more Jewish families crowded into a small
house, children without shoes in October, and hungry
workers all the year round'. The second was the oft-repeated
complaint of exploitative conditions imposed by Jewish
master tailors, this time in Leeds. 'The outcome is that
everywhere we hear the English tailors remark, "The Jews
have spoiled the trade"; and the result – thousands of
enemies.'

The *Poilishe Yidl* illuminated other facets of ghetto life.

19. Ibid., no.14, 24 October, 1884, editorial 'Week to Week'. Correspondence
from Leeds.
20. Ibid., no.15, 31 October, 1884.

8. 21 Elder Street, Spitalfields, where Lieberman spent his last months in London.

9. Christ Church Hall, Hanbury Street, where the great strike meetings of the 1880s and 1890s were held.

We learn of the performances of the Yiddish theatre group run by the popular young actor — director Jacob Adler, who operated a drama school at 9 Raven Row, off Sidney Street. He was continually advertising for young men and women trainees, and regular criticism of the group's performances appeared in the paper. Productions based on Biblical episodes included *Shulamith* and *Bar Kochba*, written by the Yiddish playwright, Goldfaden. The Adlers — Jacob and Sarah — laid the foundation of a Yiddish theatre, which continued to flourish here, long after the pioneer troupe had moved on to greater triumphs in New York.[2 1]

Editorial policy also aimed to enlighten its readers on national and international affairs. The Franchise Bill sponsored by Joseph Chamberlain was critically assessed and the Liberals dismissed as 'people who are neither fish nor fowl, who are afraid to take the final step', namely the abolition of the House of Lords. There was regular coverage of the conditions of Jews in Central and Eastern Europe against the background of national politics. A personal account of the life of a Cantonist gives the lie to the belief in a unitary Jewish folk within the *stetl*. The rich, whose money has brought them freedom from conscription, are caricatured 'with havana cigars jutting from their mouths, playing cards after a full meal, and fulminating in unison against those young men who run away from conscription as a disgrace to the Jews!' The *Poilishe Yidl* encouraged immigrants to seek tuition in Yiddish and English. Replying to this plea from the editor, the Jewish Tailors' Union, located at the Brown Bear, Leman Street, wrote to inform readers that classes were already held by a Society of the Union. 'Our Secretary, Isaac Stone and also Mr Lewis Lyons offer their time and knowledge to undertake the task of teaching gratis.' It

21. One of the last announcements printed in the *Poilishe Yidl*, no.13, 31 October, 1884, was 'The opening of the Russian Hebrew Workmen's Club and Institute, 10 Houndsditch, E.C.' in which 'Mr Adler and Co . . . will entertain members three times weekly, Saturday night, Sunday and Monday'. Enrolment of members was limited to 200. There was a supporting advertisement by Adler stating that he was no longer resident at 63 Lambert Street (where his group played at the Jewish club) but had moved to the above address where 'the Jewish Workers' Club will be the most attractive and enjoyable spot for the Jewish workers of the East End'.

hammered away ceaselessly at its demands for the formation of unions. The final issue advertised a meeting called by the Builders' Union at 11 Weaver St, Brick Lane, to enrol more workers. And it added a broader commentary on the Jewish world outside. There are two promising reports on agricultural colonies in the USA — at Painters Wood, near Bismarck in the Dakotas, and Vinland in New Jersey,[22] in contrast to the ever-pessimistic accounts of the Jewish condition in Central and Eastern Europe.

One of the by-products was the first exercise in Jewish Socialist pamphleteering, which even found its way into the non-Jewish radical press. *Justice* (10 January, 1885) commented favourably on a letter received from a Not Rothschild, informing the editor of the progress of Socialism among the Jews, and enclosing a pamphlet, written in Yiddish by Winchevsky, in which a Socialist's creed is presented as a parody of Maimonides' *Thirteen Articles of Faith.*[23] The catechism embraces four fundamental precepts:

> I believe, with perfect faith, that whoever profits by the labour of his fellow man without doing anything for him in return is a willing plunderer.
>
> I believe, with perfect faith, that 'the poor shall never cease in the land' until each man shall work for the community as much as he can and the community shall provide each man with his needs.
>
> I believe, with perfect faith, that women will remain the slaves of men, or their playthings, as long as they will depend upon the will of others instead of enjoying the fruits of their own labour.
>
> I believe, with perfect faith, that labour and handicraft will be despised by all, as long as the working man will labour to satisfy the appetites of the idlers.

But the editor of the English paper was somewhat premature when he chose then to deduce that 'the success of the

---

22. *Poilishe Yidl*, no.12, 10 October, 1884.

23. The pamphlet, first devised in 1879, was published in London in 1885, as *Yehi or eyre unterhaltung iber di farkerte velt* (Let there be light or a topsy-turvy world), and reprinted in *Mahzor in tfila Zaka*, Leeds, 1903, pp.60-3. Based on an imaginary conversation between two workers philosophising on the condition of the world, it was supposed to have had a considerable impact in spreading Socialist ideas among Jews in England and the USA.

movement amongst the Jews in East London has already been quite remarkable. Thousands of them, we speak without any exaggeration whatever, have already taken up with the doctrines of Socialism in a greater or less degree.' Twenty years later, this comment would be more valid.

On 31 October, 1884, a special announcement informed its readers that 'because of difficulties in selling in Russia under the present name', it was to be changed to *Zukunft* (The Future)[24] with effect from 16 November. The reality was the fundamental split in ideology between the editors. Winchevsky, as a committed Socialist, resented the intrusion of advertisements, religious and commercial, by Rabbinowitz. The latter was withdrawing to a nationalistic, even parochial stand, and the split came when he accepted an advertisement from the local Liberal Jewish candidate, Samuel Montagu. Winchevsky opposed this final surrender to the 'bourgeois *mores*'. The partnership ended abruptly. Winchevsky left to found an open, but non-partisan, Socialist paper, the *Arbeter Fraint* (Worker's Friend), which first appeared as a monthly on 15 July, 1885. There was no going back after the *Poilishe Yidl*. It had initiated a tabloid for Jewish self-observation and criticism, as well as providing a sounding-board for the few working-class intellectuals dedicated to bringing social consciousness to their comrades.

The *Arbeter Fraint* extended the dimensional possibilities of its predecessor, and gathered around it a formidable array of youthful talent. There was a growing supply of Yiddish *intelligent* among the recent immigrants. Its expression of non-alignment, that it was 'originally open to all radicals . . . social democrats, collectivists, communists and anarchists'[25] brought in the support of Socialist groups, whose differences were not yet irreconcilable. There were certain features it maintained throughout a long and chequered existence. It stressed a global view of Socialism, yet betrayed the paradox of the outcast Jew in the diaspora. Winchevsky's writings exemplify this. He intellectualised revolution as the weapon

24. The *Zukunft* lasted till 4 January, 1889. Its policy was concentrated on local Jewish affairs, and the possibilities of the return to Palestine; it ended up as rabidly anti-Socialist.
25. *Arbeter Fraint*, no.1, 15 July, 1885, editorial.

to end all anachronisms, yet remained a *heimische Yidl* ('a homely Jew') emotionally committed, in language and life, to his own Jewish poor. Hence the continuation of their mother tongue, Yiddish, as the language of propaganda. Yet the *Arbeter Fraint* persisted in denigrating the ancient faith. Holy days, religious offices and services, were parodied mercilessly. The Bible itself was quoted against the holy ones as evidence for the validity of atheism; and Jewish nationalism *per se* was rejected as a danger to Socialist cosmopolitanism.[26]

One of the young lions, appointed editor on Winchevsky's recommendation, was Philip Kranz.[27] He was born Jacob Rombro in a *stetl* in Podolia, left Russia during the pogroms of 1881, and arrived in London by way of Paris, where he spent some time as a student. Encouraged by Winchevsky, he submitted his first article on the Russian persecutions to the *Poilishe Yidl*. The new press was set up at 282 City Road, and the editorial address given as 29a Fort St, Brushfield St, in the heart of Lieberman's old territory in Spitalfields. The first editorial sounded the call for a united front of all Socialist denominations against the capitalist system. This was not too difficult to accept, as the Jewish anarchists emerging at this time were also indoctrinated with the idea of economic materialism. In the short term co-operation proved possible. Differences would arise later when drawing practical conclusions from the Marxist conception of history.

Kranz and his close collaborators accepted the Lassallian doctrine of the iron law of wages. They attacked 'Economism' as an inept function of trade unionists, on the premise that there could never be any improvement for

26. The question of Yiddish was raised at the First Congress of the Second International in Paris (1889). Lavrov apologised for its use by the *Arbeter Fraint* with the excuse that 'the Jewish Socialists assure the Congress, that although they are compelled to use the sole language which the Jewish workers understand, they are indeed distant from the notion of national separatism and participate in the Socialist workers' movement wherever they may be'. (*Protokoll des Internationalen Arbeiter – Congresses zu Paris, 14-20 Juli, 1889*, Nuremberg, 1890, p.35.)

27. Born 1858, died 1922. His initial lack of Yiddish was rectified under Winchevsky's tuition. He remained editor until May 1889, when as a Social Democrat he broke with the Anarchists and departed for the USA. Here he carried on his Socialist activities as editor of the New York *Arbeter Zeitung*. (See Zalman Reisen's *Leksikon für der Yiddishe Literatur un Presse*, Warsaw, 1914.)

workers in capitalist society, since wage rises attained by collective bargaining lead to price increases, which, in turn, offset real gain. After a brief fluctuation, workers' conditions inevitably revert to the same low level. The old campaigner, Isaac Stone, was back in business warning of the dangers of mere trade union consciousness. In an article in the first issue he discarded trade unions as 'of little use to the workers. Their effect is actually harmful, since they divert them from the right path of Socialism!' Kranz reinforced this dictum in the next issue, arguing that the bourgeois system never allows the worker to earn more 'than he must needs have to buy the bare necessities — no more and no less than is required to keep him from starving'. It might appear that such opinions were not conducive to inspiring workers to unionise. Belief in the imminence of the social revolution by the *intelligent* partly explains their unwillingness to be involved in side issues. Nevertheless the realities of the sweatshop brought home the urgency for industrial action, and the *Arbeter Fraint* was forced to concede to necessity.

In a climate of want and abuse, the propaganda made itself felt. The Jewish outcasts had found a voice of their own, and with it the renewed signs of an independent Jewish Labour movement. Radical organisations allied themselves and grew with the journal. In 1884 a Society of Jewish Socialists had inaugurated an International Workers' Educational Club, and its founders became patrons of the *Arbeter Fraint*. In February, 1885, the club took over premises at 40 Berner Street, a narrow slum thoroughfare off Commercial Road, and reconstituted itself the International Workingmen's Educational Association. It offered a base for radical and trade union movements in the East and West End. Mot, who later became a member, described its setting and activity:[28]

It was an old wooden two storey building . . . The Club was a spacious room with a capacity of over 200 people and contained a stage. Here were performed by amateurs, mostly in Russian language, plays by well known Russian revolutionists — Chaikovsky, Volchovsky, Stepniak . . .
Invariably, on Saturday or Sunday, there was a truly international

28. Eyges, *Beyond the Horizon*, pp.79-83.

gathering of Russian, Jewish, British, French, Italian, Czech, Polish and other radicals . . .

Quite often the renowned radical poet, William Morris, was seen there reading his splendid verses . . . Like Faneuil Hall in Boston, Berner Street Club was the 'Cradle of Liberty' for the workers' emancipation from economic slavery.

In June, 1886, the Club took over control of the *Arbeter Fraint*. As a monthly, it could no longer meet the growing demands of subscribers and contributors. The collection of a voluntary fund by enthusiasts enabled it to appear as a weekly in July 1886. It marked a dramatic change in the tone of the paper. An earlier stilted dogmatism was replaced by the more popular vernacular and the circulation soared. The result was twofold. It helped to stimulate the drive towards unionisation both in London and the provinces. Small trade unions under workers' leadership sprang into existence in the major tailoring and shoemaking trades as well as among the smaller cigarette, cabinet and stick making industries. In Leeds the Jewish Socialists responded by forming a Workers' Educational Union, which generated the largest and strongest trade union in the clothing industry. Willing or not, Socialist and trade union forces were merging into a common front and moving in the same direction. Socialist societies proliferated in Glasgow, Liverpool and overseas in Paris, where a group of immigrant activists were involved in radical agitation. All owed their inception to the teachings of the *Arbeter Fraint*.

Secondly, the club and its paper provided a rendezvous for displaced intellectuals from abroad. A group of bright young immigrant writers found their niche in Berner Street. In December, 1887, a regular contributor was discovered in Antwerp — Benjamin Feigenbaum — master of anti-religious satire. He was born in Warsaw in 1860, the son of a Chassid, and went through the process of conversion to atheism after the normal youthful exposure to rigid orthodoxy. In 1884 he emigrated to Belgium, where he later came across the *Arbeter Fraint*. He offered contributions on the development of Socialist movements in various European countries, which were published. He was obsessed with debunking religion. He aimed at replacing orthodoxy by exposing its rites to ridicule, yet employed the device of Biblical interpretation to qualify the rationale of Socialism. Kranz prevailed on him to come to London, and he arrived early in 1888 at an appropriate time. Events had prepared the ground for an anti-religious campaign. Clerical and lay leaders of Anglo-Jewry had viewed the *Arbeter Fraint*'s propaganda as a danger to the Jews' standing in the community. They set out to destroy it. One attempt was to bribe the printer, but he was a Socialist sympathiser. The back page of each issue carried the appeal in heavy type: 'Workers, do your duty. Spread the *Arbeter Fraint!*' The compositor was more amenable to easy money. When no. 26 appeared it bore the legend: 'Workers, do your duty. *Destroy* the *Arbeter Fraint!*' The pay-off enabled the culprit to remove himself promptly to the USA. The next step was to get at the printer again, and he finally succumbed. On 6 May, 1887, without any warning, the *Arbeter Fraint* ceased publication. Not until 29 July could the group procure an alternative press to print a leaflet explaining how and why the paper had been stopped.

The result was a new lease of life. It reappeared on 5 August. Few Jewish printers could dare stand out against the pressures of the community leaders. When its readers learned of the means employed to gag free expression, they rallied to its aid. Volunteer groups were formed and funds poured in from sources ranging from East London to East Side, New York. The Club acquired its own printing machine and the *Arbeter Fraint* an independent press. With Feigenbaum at the helm it opened full blast against Orthodoxy. A spate of liturgical satires shocked the majority of practising Jews. The Passover *Seder* was ridiculed[29] and the lamentations on the 9th Ab transformed into 'Lamentations for the Worker', where the desert homes of the exiles were portrayed favourably against the slum habitations of their descendants in the East End. The holiest Day of Atonement (Yom Kippur) came under special attack. Declamatory passages such as, 'the Lord reigns . . . and reigns for ever' were represented as, 'Mammon reigns . . . will reign but *not* for ever'. The same day the first

29. Published as *A New Version of the Passover Haggadah* by the Workers' Friend Printing Office, 1888.

public ball was held as a gesture of contempt for ancient superstitions.[30] Such acts of blasphemy were counter-productive. They gave offence to those still tied to the chains of faith — the very people they wished to recruit. Jews would not take kindly to such tactics from within, at a time of growing agitation against aliens, whose dangers were brought to their own doorstep with the incidence of the 'Ripper' disturbances. Nevertheless Feigenbaum proved an asset to the movement. He was a clever and popular speaker, whose political ideas, in speech and print, influenced a wider circle of workers. His pamphlet *Where Does Man Come From?* was one of the most successful works of propaganda during that period.

Socialist attacks on the leaders of Anglo-Jewry reached a peak in the late 1880s. The Chief Rabbi Adler was a natural target, since his activities against the Hebrew Socialist Union were not forgotten. He was particularly concerned with the rapid anglicisation of the immigrants as a means of eroding the 'alien' question. As long as the newcomer persisted in his foreign speech and uncouth manners, anti-Semitism would be sustained, and the English Jew implicated by association. One of the traditional purveyors of Yiddish language and culture was the Yiddish theatre. In January, 1886, David Smith, a butcher of Dorset Street, patron of Jacob Adler's company, financed the acquisition of new premises at no. 3 Princes Street (now Princelet Street) off Brick Lane. From current hearsay, there was a rumour that the Chief Rabbi had attempted to rid London of Adler's troupe by offering them money to emigrate to the States, which they had refused. A subsequent tragedy caused them to reverse their decision. During the evening of 18 January, 1887, a benefit performance of a popular operetta, *The Gypsy*, was being given to a full audience of five hundred. At about eleven p.m., at the height of the performance, there came a cry of 'Fire!' and a panic-stricken audience stampeded towards the single exit. There was no fire. But within a few minutes seventeen people were crushed to death. A few weeks later (March, 1887) Adler and his group left for New York with rabbinical aid.

30. *Arbeter Fraint*, 21 September, 1888.

The culprit was never found. But the poison of suspicion against local enemies remained.[31] Socialist agitation against the Chief Rabbi was renewed after his negative response to an appeal that he join with the Anglican and Catholic Primates in condemning workshop conditions revealed by John Burnett in his 'Report on the Sweating System in the East End of London'. He dismissed the report as an exaggeration, which brought the rejoinder from the *Arbeter Fraint* that he was a self-confessed ally of the sweaters. The accusation was enhanced by his rejection of a call by Jewish strikers in Leeds to help them redeem their jobs. He would do so only if the masters invited him too. His arrogance and apparently callous indifference to the workers' sufferings continued to provide the *Arbeter Fraint* with a ready-made target for its anti-religious propaganda.

Their other *bête noire* was Sir Samuel Montagu, Liberal MP for Whitechapel, who regarded the Socialists as serious rivals for control over the immigrants.[32] He was suspected of buying off the two printers whose absconding had brought the paper to a temporary halt. On resuming publication, the editor accused both Montagu and F. Mocatta of harassing or bribing printers to stop them publishing Socialist literature.[33] After his role in the 1889 strike, Montagu was seriously convinced that the Socialists constituted the gravest threat to Judaism, when 'the influence of a few Atheists over Jewish working men can no longer be ignored'. He viewed the consolidation of the *hebras* as a force to be employed against them. Hence his support for the Federation of Synagogues was partly to encourage them 'to take the lead in combating this most serious evil'. The *Arbeter Fraint* and its acolytes answered in kind. The paper inaugurated a non-stop verbal assault on religion and its institutions. Mot recaptures one incident which took place, appropriately, on Yom Kippur evening. He had been persuaded to attend the Socialist mass meeting and ball instead of the synagogue.[34]

31. See article by A. Rollin in the *Jewish Chronicle* 15 June, 1962.
32. He was financial sponsor of the Jewish Working Men's Club, the Federation of Synagogues, conservative trade unions, and self-proclaimed arbiter in trade disputes.
33. *Arbeter Fraint*, 29 March, 5 and 12 August, 1887.
34. Eyges, *Beyond the Horizon*, pp.77-8.

The large Christ Church Hall in Hanbury Street was nearly filled to capacity when they arrived, and still more men and women kept coming. Finally the meeting was opened by the chairman. After him came two speakers on 'The Absurdity of Religion'. Then Feigenbaum was introduced as the principal speaker of the evening, on the subject 'Is There a God?'.

He was of medium height with broad shoulders and gesticulated as he spoke. He started out by saying that every religion was an absurdity and that the notion of God was impossible. He explained in detail that in the name of religion charlatans took advantage of the weakness of men and women. He became more eloquent as he spoke. 'What is God?' he exclaimed. 'It is an abstract word, coined to designate the hidden forces of Nature, while the belief in God is but a mechanical habit of childhood, a prejudice handed down from father to children.'

He spoke for nearly an hour, extemporaneously, freely quoting from scripture, science and history. Mot listened intensely, obsessed with a feeling of enthusiasm and fear. Suddenly the speaker stopped. He took out his watch from his pocket, placed it on a small table in front of him, paused for a moment and with a dramatic gesture shouted: 'If there is a God and if he is Almighty as the clergy claims he is, I give him just two minutes' time to kill me on the spot, so that he may prove his existence!' The challenge created a tense silence in the hall. Mot felt a shiver running through his body, fearing that something might happen to the speaker. The two minutes finally elapsed. The speaker in his dramatic pose exclaimed: 'See! There is no God!' A thunder of applause echoed through the hall. In the meantime the music struck up the Marseillaise, the national hymn of the French Republic, at that time the revolutionary hymn throughout Europe. Then the Yom Kippur ball was announced and the meeting was over. Mot had been converted to free thought.

At first the club offered a stereotyped programme of activity. Saturday nights were set aside for the delivery of papers on socio-economic themes, followed by discussions. Sundays were devoted to social and cultural activities such as plays, concerts and dances. On Tuesdays there would be lectures in English on literary and political topics, while on Wednesday and Thursday evenings tutorial classes in English were offered to members. In one sense it was an early experiment in adult education within limited terms of reference. The conglomeration of individual Socialists soon began to crystallise out into a hard core of self-styled Anarchists. The Haymarket Affair in Chicago resulting in the 'judicial martydom' of the five Anarchists (November, 1887) captured the imagination and sympathy of most Berner Streeters, and subsequently increased the orientation towards the Libertarian group. Earlier, the fifth issue of *Arbeter Fraint* had contained an article by J. Jaffe, 'What is Anarchism?'. Jaffe, who was then writing from Paris, came to London in 1887 and was invited to join the editorial board. His inclusion provided a fillip to Anarchist influence, which was reinforced by four talented young writers: Harry Kaplansky and Simon Freeman in London and S. Yanovsky and Michael Cohn from the USA. Later the two Yiddish Libertarian poets David Edelstadt and Joseph Bovshover also sent contributions. It meant that the journal was attracting an international Jewish audience. By 1888 the Anarchists were emerging as the largest and most active element, and had formed themselves into a distinctive group — the Knights of Labour. One of their aims was to reverse the tide which had been removing the most gifted of their comrades to America. Thus when one of their members, Rutenberg, went across, he was delegated the task of persuading S. Yanovsky to come to London and assume control of the *Arbeter Fraint*.

Contradictory approaches towards social action persisted throughout 1888. In one of many instances union meetings of local carpenters and boot finishers are advertised, while in the following issue there is the distinct Libertarian flavour in an editorial attack: 'On Workers' Union — towards What?'[35] 'Central committees strive for weak and useless aims . . . Only the overthrow of the capitalist system on the principles of freedom, equality and justice is valid. All else is cold comfort — a waste of time!' Yet in the 'notices' one observes that 'the publishing office of the *Arbeter Fraint* will gladly exchange its paper with *all* Socialist Periodicals', and that it had already received a number of copies from abroad including *Autonomie, El Socialismo, Freiheit*, New York Jewish *Volkszeitung*, and *Le Socialiste Parole*. Against the current demand for a Parliamentary Commission on sweating, it gives notice of a meeting to be held locally on 4 February,

35. *Arbeter Fraint*, 13 January, 1888.

under the chairmanship of lawyer Thomas, who was arguing the case for parliamentary discussion and legislation. This was dismissed by the *Arbeter Fraint* on the premise that any hope of effective improvement through an Act of Parliament was illusory. 'The East End worker, above all the Jewish worker, would achieve less through such a Bill, than the preceding Factory Acts!'[36]

The inbuilt malstructures of the sweated trades perpetuated the upsurges of discontent, which by now were represented by a voice and a party. Even the Chief Rabbi had come to terms with the obvious, which forced him into a series of contradictory postures. Addressing the parents at the Old Castle Street Board School's prize distribution (18 April, 1888), Dr Adler made some dutiful comments:[37]

> Much has been heard of the 'Sweating System' and its attendant evils. The result of the education received at the Old Castle Street School would be that these evils would be reduced to a minimum, and *in Heaven's own time*, would be easily removed. They were taught a Divine discontent with their lot, not that discontent which sought relief in Socialism, but the remedy which taught that every man depended for his lot upon his individual efforts.

Less than a month later (12 May), in a sermon heavy with cant and breast-beating, his congregation was exposed to an oration which smacked somewhat of Socialist heresy:[38]

> What is to be done to remedy these various evils?
> It hurts me to the quick when I hear how the manufacturers take advantage of the stress of competition that exists between middleman and middleman to beat down prices lower and lower. I am bitterly grieved when I hear the names of certain manufacturers mentioned, who, either themselves or through their managers use every pretext and subterfuge in order to cut down payment for work, treating those who are in their power with insults and contempt.

The exploiter is warned: 'What mean ye that crush my people

36. Ibid., 20 January, 1888.
37. *Jewish Chronicle*, 20 April, 1888.
38. Sermon at the Great Synagogue reported in the *Jewish Chronicle*, 18 May, 1888.

and grind the faces of the poor?' But, as though that were too one-sided, both employer and worker are exhorted: 'Obey the precepts of your God, keep the laws of the land!'

The young lions of the Left continued to offer a different recipe. Throughout that long, hard year their mouthpiece expanded its polemical thrusts against both the *sheine Leit* of Anglo-Jewry and the British establishment. By December, the *Arbeter Fraint* was rejoicing that from the New Year its size would be increased to eight pages. 'The young child in spite of the assaults of its enemies – the swindling, conspiratorial great Jewish moneygrubbers – has grown into a sharp, strong man!' It increasingly set its readers' problems against the background of current social discontent. A detailed report is presented of a delegation of workless Londoners come to plead for positive aid from the Lord Mayor. He attempted to side-track the issue by offering to help the six delegates alone to find work.

> They replied that they were not here to beg for themselves but for *all* their comrades ... Seeing the lack of intention, they suggested that they would return and inform the workers that, instead of work, the Lord Mayor had offered them stones. The Mayor strongly denied this and promised to see what he could do.

The *Arbeter Fraint* comments drily that it knows what 'doing something' means to the workers.[39] The theme of the struggle for equality is unceasing. 'Only man distorts what is ordained by nature.'

> Nature gives the right
> To everyone – not too much, just sufficient.
> She does not understand weakness or might
> Poverty, strength or wealth.[40]

A recent inquiry into the 'old' slavery – Africa style – had evoked a universal outcry. It was a red herring to divert the minds of the 'new' serfs from their own cruel environment.

> The difference is that the old slave had to be nourished and, to an

---

39. *Arbeter Fraint*, 14 December, 1888.
40. Ibid., 14 December, 1888. Poem 'The Free Nature', by S. Freeman.

extent, cared for to preserve his capacity for labour. Today's [wage] slave need not be bought. They [the employers] need no longer fear whether he gets ill or dies. There are plenty of replacements drifting round the streets.

It conceives of other political diversions to confuse the masses. A columnist attacked Gladstone for a recent address at the Limehouse Town Hall (16 December), where he bemused his audience with Lord Hartington's speech on Ireland and the glory of Home Rule. What relevance has the 'old bourgeois' and the complex Irish Question to the East End, where a hungry people desperately cry out for work? And the commentator sadly reflects on the uninformed workers shouting 'Bravo' to a man who does nothing for them except perpetuate their role as the exploited.[41]

With Feigenbaum as a major contributor, religion was elevated to the prime target. Seizing on an accusation in the *Church Times* that Jack the Ripper was a Russian Anarchist (one victim was found at the entrance of the Berner Street club), he replied, 'Such homage from the Holy Spirit! What the almighty watchdog, Charles Warren, could not discover — the Whitechapel murderer — the Holy Ghost has revealed!' He followed this with a savage diatribe against religious belief, which supposedly 'thrives on murderers, exploiters and the perpetual ignorance and subservience of the masses'. It was 'no instigator of morality. Most law breakers are brought up in the faith and remain law breakers. Where can we find a God's servant who has ever frightened the ruling class against that shedding of blood which permeates the good book itself?'[42]

The radical conclave girded its loins for a full-scale operation, which would bring the Jewish labourers out on the streets in direct action. The *Arbeter Fraint*'s last editorial of the old year sounded ominous. While Parliament talked of Inquiries into Sweating, 'the workers must realise once and for all that *they alone* can free themselves from all burdens, that is through social revolution'. The Jewish worker was no longer slow to respond to the disease of social unrest which struck the following year.

41. Ibid., 21 December, 1888.
42. Ibid., 21 December, 1888. Article, 'Frank and free', by B. Feigenbaum.

6. 1889

I hate your superstition, workingmen,
I loathe your blindness and stupidity . . .

But when I contemplate your ceaseless toil,
Your quiet activity and sunless life,
Your works of splendour, and gigantic strength,
I bow my head in reverence to you.

'To the Toilers' by Joseph Bovshover
(Yiddish radical poet)

At the same time other workers quite outside the dock industry
took advantage of the agitation to demand better conditions for
themselves. Coal porters and carmen, printers' labourers, iron
workers and their helpers, tin-plate workers . . . tailors . . . ceased
work, and like Oliver Twist, asked for more.

Freedom (October 1889)

It was a cold hard winter in 1888-9. Men roamed the shabby
thoroughfares of Stepney looking for work — native and
immigrant alike sharing the realities of hunger and want.
There was 'never glad confident morning again in the outlook
of the world' observed R.C.K. Ensor. 'It is symptomatic that
the word unemployed used as a noun is first recorded by the
Oxford English Dictionary from the year 1882; the word
unemployment from 1888!'[1] Episodic disorders had broken
out during the preceding three years. The authorities were
alarmed at a growing militancy exemplified in the meetings
and marches of the unemployed, now organised and led by
the Social Democratic Federation,[2] and which culminated in

1. R.C.K. Ensor, *England 1870-1914*, Oxford, 1936, pp.111-12.
2. On 7 February, 1886, police intervention at a Trafalgar Square meeting led
to a mass outbreak of window smashing at Pall Mall and the subsequent
prosecution of the leaders H.M. Hyndman, John Burns, Jack Williams and H.H.
Champion. They were acquitted. On 21 February a grand march of 50,000 to
Trafalgar Square ended with a clash with the police.

the affair of Bloody Sunday (13 November, 1887). Jewish radicals had marched and participated in the great demonstrations and although the activist groups 'were not united in a great inclusive organisation' (Kautsky) there were vigorous derivatives. A weekly journal, *The Link*, edited by Herbert Burrows and Annie Besant, was born out of the confrontations at Trafalgar Square. One of its articles exposing the conditions of the match girls at Bryant and May's factory in Bow sparked off the (successful) strike of July 1888, which set a precedent whose possibilities were not lost on the Jewish radical leadership in the East End.

The *Arbeter Fraint* sniffed the air and stepped up its agitation. In the first issue of the new year, the section 'Unions and Meetings' reported a packed meeting at the club the previous Saturday, the audience no doubt drawn by the popular speaker Feigenbaum. He commenced his delivery by emphasising that the real boundaries dividing people were not national but class barriers. He went on:[3]

> In *this* world we can build a Garden of Eden . . . it was unnecessary to hope for a Heaven to come or a land of Israel where the same troubles prevail . . . The true mother of us all, the earth, has enough milk in her breast not only for your own children, but for three times the amount of people who exist. Statistics reveal this. The fault lies in the institutionalised robbery of capitalist society.

Finally he explained in detail how that robbery was effected and its injustices perpetuated. He reiterated that its replacement could only be resolved by social revolution.

The political climate, coupled with the belated recognition by hungry workers that direct action was a palatable necessity, brought the radical caucus at Berner Street their moments of opportunity. The first was provided by their old enemy — the Chief Rabbi. A 'courteous request' from the committee of Jewish unemployed that he deliver a Sabbath sermon on sweating and unemployment was turned down with the excuse that sweating was better than hunger, and if sweating meant overwork, then both he and his (rich) congregants were equally victims. He argued against the

3. *Arbeter Fraint*, 4-11 January, 1889.

demand for a legislated eight-hour day, on the old *laissez-faire* proposition that state intervention could never influence real conditions of labour. The Socialists 'who woke up their worst passions' for no purpose must be rejected.[4] The *Arbeter Fraint* responded in kind. The Chief Rabbi was put on the spot. The journal had already published a handbill announcing Dr Adler *would* preach a Sabbath sermon on 16 March on the very subject of sweating. It now recalled his own words to the Sweating Committee, inferring that he could not renege on his own evidence. In the same issue[5] it enjoined all workers to participate in 'a synagogue parade'. A procession would mobilise on that very Sabbath at Berner Street and march to the Great Synagogue 'to demand work, bread and the eight-hour day'.

> Brother workers,
> Our enemies, detractors and holy satraps want to convince you that riots will result during the procession so that you should not join us — your well known dedicated friends. In reply we say that there will be no riots and disorder. As we do not intend to protest against the police, so they will not interfere with us.
> Come in your masses, workers — come with us to the Great Synagogue to show the world our plight and that we will no longer be slaves to the sweaters.
>
> In the name of the workers' committee
> Lewis Lyons and Philip Kranz.

The next morning, 16 March, a happening took place in the East End, 'quite unparalleled in the history of the Jews in London', sorrowfully records the *Jewish Chronicle*. The number who eventually marched was debated,[6] although it must have been in the region of 2,000 at least. The *East London Advertiser*, not unduly sympathetic to immigrants, gives us perhaps the best, though colourful, report of the incident. Under the title 'A Hebrew Hubbub in Whitechapel'[7] the editorial began its commentary: 'The Hebrews are a

---

4. *Jewish Chronicle* 22 February, 1889.
5. *Arbeter Fraint*, 15 March, 1889.
6. The *Jewish Chronicle* estimated 300-400 to underplay the situation; the *Arbeter Fraint*, 2,000-3,000; the *East London Advertiser* reckoned on 'below 2 or 3 thousand'.
7. *East London Advertiser*, 23 March, 1889.

peaceful and industrious folk, but on the principle that even a worm will turn, we have been treated to a Hebrew demonstration.' A huge crowd gathered in Berner Street at about twelve-thirty p.m. and marched off

> headed by a German brass band and a repulsive looking black and white banner, bearing the words 'JEWISH UNEMPLOYED AND SWEATERS' VICTIMS'. They proceeded to Duke Street. A more abject and miserable set of men it would have been impossible to have seen anywhere. Ill-clad, dirty, unwashed, haggard and ragged, they looked in the bright sunlight, a picture of abject misery . . . The traffic was stopped, notwithstanding that it was just the busiest day in the haymarket. A liberal estimate would give the numbers at below two to three thousand. Arriving at the synagogue the leaders, Messrs Burrows, Lyons, Kranz and Feigenbaum, discovered the delegate Chief Rabbi was not in attendance.

His substitute, the Rev. L. Meisels, after overtly associating Socialists with conversionism in his sermon, opened up against the crowd parading outside:

> Are they, perhaps, the first, or the only people on earth who are not doing well, who seek work and cannot get it, who find it hard to maintain themselves, their wives and children? Can we, is it possible for anyone to go through life without tasting of its bitter as well of its sweet?

With this cold comfort for the poor, he could afford to denigrate the Jewish protestors. *The Times* reported a 'strong force of [fifty] city police under Mr Superintendent Foster' who blocked the path of the would-be invaders. An alternative meeting at Mitre Square being disallowed,

> the processionists . . . went to the Mile End Waste, where addresses were delivered by the leaders, and a resolution was passed condemning the action of Dr Adler 'for refusing to comply with the courteous request of the Committee of the Jewish unemployed to preach a sermon at the Great Synagogue having special reference to our position and prospects', protesting against the labour sweating indulged in by certain members of the Jewish community, complaining of the indifference of the rich Jews, and calling upon the work people 'not to depend upon the rich classes but to organise in a strong body for the abolition of the capitalist ruling class'.[8]

8. *The Times*, 18 March, 1889.

The day was not yet over and the best (or worst according to one's light) was yet to come. Riots and discomfitures followed. After the dispersal of the crowd at the Waste, many made their way to Berner Street, 'where in anticipation of a disturbance, the police were present in strong force'. Such prophetic insight on their part was rewarded by a fight which suddenly broke out at the entrance of the Berner Street Club. 'The police felt bound in the interests of the public peace to make some arrests.' In the subsequent mêlée three club members were seized: Lewis Diemslietz, an unlicensed hawker of 40 Berner Street; Samuel Freedman, cap blocker of 31 Weaver Street, Spitalfields, and Isaac Kozelrodske, machinist of 40 Old Ford Road, Bethnal Green. Presumably all three had gone berserk. A witness at Thames Police Court (18 March) reported that

> between two and three o'clock on Saturday afternoon he was walking down Berner Street. He saw some boys and girls knocking at the doors of the Socialist Club. Suddenly some twenty or thirty men, armed with sticks, rushed out of the club, and attacked everyone indiscriminately. Freedman said, 'I will do for someone tonight and don't care if I get twelve months for it!' The witness was then struck in the mouth and about the body.

This accorded with police evidence which spoke of 'a crowd of 200 gathering outside the Berner Street Club ... Diemslietz and Freedman came out with their coats off followed by thirty other persons. A free fight then began through the Socialists attacking the people outside ... The Socialists acted more like a lot of wild beasts than human beings!' The defendants pleaded that a crowd attacked the club with stones and Diemslietz claimed that a policeman (P.C. Frost) had assaulted him.[9] This tallied with an opposing report presented by *Freedom* (March 1889).

> After the proceedings (i.e. mass meeting) were over, Mr Monro,[10] scenting Socialism, not to say Anarchy, beneath the audacity of the wage slaves, sent some of his men to break, without any sort of pretext, into the Berner Street Working Men's Club. The representatives of law and order broke windows, tore down pictures and

9. *East London Advertiser*, 23 March, 1889.
10. Chief Commissioner of Police.

posters and fell with their fists and batons upon a few of our comrades who happened to be there. One, wife of the steward, they threw down and kicked, others they beat until the blood streamed, three were dragged to the station, again beaten and then charged with assaulting the police.

The prisoners were remanded by the magistrate, a Mr Saunders,[11] for trial at the sessions. But during the day application for summonses was made out against a police inspector and a constable by a barrister, Mr W.M. Thompson. Protest groups were organised on the Left, including one by the generally unsympathetic SDF, and a legal aid fund was set up by the Socialist League under the treasurership of the British Anarchist, Frank Kitz. A moving appeal, hand-written by a Berner Streeter, the copies reproduced on a 'jelly', has come down to us (Plate 12).

> Sir,
>   We ask assistance of your branch to obtain funds for the defence of the members of the International Working Men's Club, 40 Berner Street.
>   On 16 March the Police invaded the Club, ill-treated the members and arrested several on the charge of assaulting the Police. These men are now sent for trial. We earnestly appeal to all who believe that wrong should not triumph, to assist us. The wealthy Jews and sweaters, both Jews and Gentiles, wish to see these men in prison and their club destroyed. Her Majesty's Government by Police brutality and legal injustice are aiding the sweaters.
>   We are poor men. Will you help us?
>   Defence Committee
> All subscriptions should be sent to F. Kitz, Treasurer, 13 Farringdon Rd, E.C.

Although one of the arrested was subsequently sentenced to three months' imprisonment, the Jewish radicals had succeeded in widening interest and involvement in the Jewish

11. It was the same Mr Saunders who sentenced the labour leader Lewis Lyons at Thames Police Court to two months' hard labour for kicking a policeman at a Dod Street, Limehouse meeting on 21 August, 1885. Owing to Lyons's brilliant cross-examination of the policeman concerned, the sentence was quashed at the Middlesex Sessions. At the same hearing, William Morris was set upon and arrested for disturbance at Court. 'That the same magistrate promptly dismissed the charge against Morris is no fault of the police. It was the fault of the prisoner being in "a respectable position" of Society' (*Commonweal*, October 1885).

workers' cause. This would pay dividends, when the great tailoring strike broke out later that year. On the other hand, their anti-religious obsessions persisted in alienating the simple and orthodox, which added to the difficulties of mobilising the majority under the Socialist flag in direct trade union activity. The Social Democratic faction in the club recognised this and toned down their views while the Anarchists remained adamant – a posture which inevitably helped to split the membership.

The ephemeral nature of trade unionism among immigrant Jewish workers has been noted.[12] But by the spring, united militant action could no longer pass them by. As a postscript to the match girls' strike, the East End was pin-pointed as a pioneering centre for development of the new unionism. Between March and June, thanks to the leadership of Will Thorne and Eleanor Marx, ninety per cent of all gas workers were organised. By July, a strike threat by this mass force gained the new organisation a victory *without* strike action: the eight-hour day and an extra shilling per hour. A victory parade for the new unionism was symbolised by the march of the 12,000 from the Embankment to Hyde Park on the 28 July. The despised unskilled were mobilising for the fray. Within a fortnight the great dock strike had begun.

Throughout August the struggle of the dockers continued to crescendo, a crisis point being reached when the strike committee called for an all-London general strike to strengthen their action. There had already been a response to the current ferment by a strike of 154 Jewish cap makers resulting from the employers' refusal to re-employ previous strike leaders. They were joined by a group of 200 men from a firm of government contractors, and workers in associated shops in Leman Street and Brick Lane stopped work. The Jewish labour leaders seized their moment of opportunity. They anticipated the dockers' request and took appropriate

12. A succinct analysis of the reasons for this is given by Gartner, *The Jewish Immigrant in England (1870-1914)*, p.119. Added to these were the counter-influences for really effective trade unionism by such anti-strike stalwarts as the clergy, Montagu and the Anglo-Jewish Establishment and, for the most part, the *Jewish Chronicle*. The fragmented nature of trade unionism within the tailoring trade seemed endemic in London, not in Leeds where extensive factorisation had already taken place.

action. Under the jurisdiction of the three tailoring unions still functioning (of which the Jewish branch of the AST was the strongest), a public meeting was called for 26 August, 1889, when a resolution for a general strike was adopted. A tailors' strike committee of seventeen was quickly elected and convened under the leadership of Charles Mowbray, John Turner (English Anarchists) with the real direction invested in the hands of Lewis Lyons (chairman) and Woolf Wess (secretary). The resulting manifesto was a declaration of intent in tune with the current demands of militant Labour.[13]

TO TAILORS AND TAILORESSES
Great Strike of London Tailors and Sweaters' Victims

Fellow Workers — You are well aware that a Commission of Lords have been appointed to enquire into the evils of the sweating system in the tailoring trade. The revelations made before the Commission by witnesses engaged in the tailoring trade are a disgrace to a civilised country. The sweaters' victims had hoped that this Commission would have come to some satisfactory conclusion as to an alteration in the condition of the sweated tailors. Finding they have just put off their deliberations until next session, we have decided to take immediate action.

It is too long for us to wait until next session, because the hardships inflicted on us by the sweater are unbearable. We have, therefore, decided to join in *the general demand for increased comfort and shorter hours of labour*. Our hours at present being in an average from fourteen to eighteen per day, in unhealthy and dirty dens, we demand:-

1. That the hours be reduced to twelve, with an interval of one hour for dinner and half an hour for tea.
2. All meals to be had off the premises.
3. Government contractors to pay wages at trade union rates.
4. Government contractors and sweaters not to give work home at night after working hours.

We now appeal for the support of all tailors to join us and thus enable us to successfully enforce our demands, which are reasonable. Tailors and tailoresses support in joining this General Strike.

We appeal to all tailors, machinists, pressers, basters, etc to meet

---

13. *Commonweal*, dated 7 September, 1889, printed the Manifesto and reported that on Monday 2 September 'some 5,000 men and women turned out against the long hours of labour'. The leaders listed 'have assisted in bringing the Jews up to the scratch of Unionism'.

The *Arbeter Fraint* reported on the action from 30 August, 1889, with a special edition as a strike extra.

en masse on Thursday, Friday and Saturday morning at ten o'clock (outside the Bells) Goulston Street, Whitechapel, E.

Piece workers finish up, week workers give notice at once. All work to cease on Saturday afternoon, when the strike will be declared.

(Sgd) Strike Committee
W. Wess. Secretary

Tailors Strike Committee Room,
'White Hart', Greenfield St,
Commercial Rd, E.
Aug. 27th 1889.

Posters in Yiddish and English appeared on street walls; a special edition of the *Arbeter Fraint* urged its readers to back the action and strike fever, carried by word of mouth, spread from workshop to workshop. But the driving force lay in the leadership of those two remarkable men: Lewis Lyons and Woolf Wess. Processions with bands and banners were mobilised and daily marches to the now traditional parade ground of dissent — Victoria Park — took place, where, from the platform comradely encouragement was given by such guest speakers as the docker leaders Tom Mann, John Burns and Ben Tillett. From the first walk out on 2 September to the third week of the strike over 6,000 hands had quit work and 120 workshops were known to lie idle. The press reported this first mass venture of striking immigrants in London with interest, and, in East London, with some sympathy. Local cover was sustained in detail. A contemporary picture of strike headquarters was given by the *East London Observer*[14] with a favourable, though somewhat patronising appreciation of the Secretary, Woolf Wess.

The strike of the East London tailors bids fair to make 'The White Hart' public house in Greenfield St, Whitechapel, almost as famous as 'The Wades Arms' which formed the headquarters of the Strike Committee during the dockers' agitation.

In an upstairs room are the headquarters of the Strike Committee who are bossing affairs for the tailors. Or rather to speak correctly, there are two rooms — a long compartment with forms and benches all round to serve the purposes of a big meeting of the Committee,

14. *East London Observer*, 21 September, 1889. Report on 'Interview with the Secretary' on 19 September.

and a smaller room littered with papers and posters of every description sacred to the presence of William Wess, who is acting as Secretary, and to unusually confident palavers.

Whatever may be said of the other members or officers the Strike Committee have evidently got hold of a very able and capable Secretary. Although a foreigner . . . Wess is remarkably intelligent and even well educated man and speedily put the reporter in possession of all the facts of the case.

Perhaps a superficial observation, but the reporter had caught a glimpse of the strength of character in a young man who emerged as another of the pioneers of the Jewish Labour movement in Britain. For he was one of the few immigrant radicals who were equally at home in both Jewish and Gentile Socialist and Anarchist circles. His early mastering of the English language enabled him to function as a permanent liaison officer between the two, throughout the rest of a long and active political career.[15]

Wess went on to explain the circuitous tactics employed by the masters, who had organised themselves into the Master Tailors' Protective and Improvement Association under the chairmanship of the ubiquitous Mark Moses;[16] how they refused to recognise the strike committee when formed so as 'to keep us in almost daily hopes of a settlement being arrived at and so prevent us from appealing to the public for funds and causing our men to resume work from sheer starvation'. To counteract this 'we have made arrangements with several provision dealers to give us credit for two or three hundred pounds' worth of goods and, tomorrow, to 'commence the work of relief by distributing tickets for provisions and also appealing to the public for funds'. Under such leadership the strike committee was learning to match cunning with cunning.

A joint meeting had been called for employers and workers

15. He was born in Vilkomir near Kovno in 1861 and died in London in May 1946. He was the son of a Chassidic master baker and at the age of twelve apprenticed to a shoemaker. To avoid military service, he was smuggled out of Russia about 1881 and came to London. Up to the advent of Rocker he provided continuity in the Jewish Labour leadership and was equally involved as liaison 'officer' and propagandist with the English Socialist League.

16. 300 master tailors gathered at the Jewish Working Men's Club on 10 September. They proposed change to an hourly wage rate which, in effect, would tie their employees to the old hours in order to obtain the same pay.

and representatives of the London District Committee of the AST, whose deliberations had lasted throughout the night of Thursday 12 September. Tentative agreement was reached on the following terms:

1. That the hours be reduced to twelve per day with an interval of one hour for dinner and half-hour for tea.
2. All meals to be had off the premises.
3. Only four hours' overtime may be worked in a week.
4. Not more than two hours' overtime be worked on any one day.
5. The first two hours' overtime to be worked at the ordinary rate, the second two hours at time and a half.

The settlement was to be confirmed the following day after a meeting of the strikers had approved the terms. But the next (Friday) afternoon there was no ratification by the masters, while a rumour that the strike was off was spread by them to confuse the rank and file. Wess viewed the terms as disastrous, and revealed to the reporter that the masters had issued posters falsely declaring the strike over, thus inducing a number to return to work, in order to force 'our' consent to work by the hour.

> The effect would be this. If we consented to be engaged by the hour, we might go to the shops at eight o'clock in the morning only to be told that there was no work for some hours, and then, when we came back, those of us who have families to support would be compelled to work till perhaps twelve o'clock at night in order that we might be able to earn sufficient for the day . . . that condition would counteract the very thing for which we are fighting — a uniform ten-and-a-half hour day.

Wess was confident, if the workers stuck it out, of victory when

> it will be our great object to get every tailor and presser and machinist into one of the three societies — either the Machinists, the Pressers or the Jewish branch of the AST. We shall *then* have a Union which it will be impossible for the employers to resist.

No mean feat if realisable. But such optimism, as he and his successors, would discover, would remain a pipe dream. Nevertheless effective counter-measures were taken. A printed handbill was issued and distributed by the strike committee denying agreement, with the accusation that the masters had broken their word by refusing to pledge the terms agreed on at joint conference. 'We, therefore, declare that *The Strike Still Continues*!' An appeal for financial aid was sent to other unions including the AST, compositors, cigar makers, boot and shoe operatives and dockers, with rewarding results.[17] A favourable response was received from established Anglo-Jewry. Lord Rothschild sent a cheque for seventy-three pounds and even the *Jewish Chronicle* offered its sympathy with reservations. 'The worm has turned at last ... An appreciable improvement in the material condition of the foreign tailors of the East End would do much'; nevertheless there was danger in the 'questionable policy on the part of the poor foreigners to give an exaggerated idea of their numbers by parading through London, and thus excite further prejudice against their entire body, especially when they place themselves under the leadership of men conspicuously associated with Socialistic movements.'[18]

It was probably the last threat that brought Samuel Montagu into the fray as self-styled mediator. On 20 September, he wrote to both the strike committee and the Masters' Association offering his services, while a letter was despatched by Lord Rothschild for the same purpose. On the 25th, Lewis Lyons informed his committee[19] that Montague had seen Mark Moses at noon that day and the latter had agreed to waive the 'hours' question. Montagu was to speak at a masters' meeting on Saturday the 28th, and had suggested that the strikers in turn call a meeting the following Sunday or Monday at the Jewish Working Men's Club, when he would report on the masters' proposals. The MP had left a cheque for ten guineas in aid of strike funds, and promised more if the strike continued. As to the relief of strikers, substantial help had been received as a result of their appeal such that Wess could inform the reporter: 'Hitherto, we have been giving tickets to married men valued at two shillings and to unmarried men at a shilling but owing to the Jewish

17. See Appendix 2, 'Balance Sheet of the Great Strike of East London Tailors'.
18. *Jewish Chronicle*, 6 September, 1889.
19. *East London Observer*, Special report 28 September, 1889.

Holidays we have had to increase those allowances.'
Questioned on future action, Lyons replied that he would
await the outcome of the masters' decision on hours. 'Next
Monday night we are going to hold a great meeting at the
Jewish Working Men's Club, to which we intend to invite
Lord Rothschild, Mr Montagu MP, Mr Tom Mann, the Bishop
of Bedford and others.' The masters could be in no further
doubt that they were facing an able and determined
leadership for the first time.

The Grand Mogul of Anglo-Jewry would not be left out of
it. The *East London Advertiser*[20] reported on a deputation
consisting of Messrs Wess, Fricke, and Leek calling on Lord
Rothschild in response to his offer to act as mediator. They
were received by a Mr Ornstein, secretary to the Council of
the United Synagogues, authorised to act for his master. The
deputation pointed out the need for funds so that

> when the masters or middlemen saw that the workers were being
> assisted in their agitation and were not starving in the streets, their
> demands would be conceded ... If the present agitation achieved its
> object it would do more than better the condition of the garment
> workers who had to work fifteen or sixteen hours a day.

They went on to demonstrate the arguments of their British
colleagues (as well as a reluctant sop to current anti-alien
sentiment shared by some of the upper echelons of Anglo-
Jewry!). Success

> would compel workers to join the Trade Unions and thus directly
> prohibit the immigration of unskilled labourers, for none but fairly
> skilled men would have a chance of entering these unions, and the
> congested labour market of the Continent would have to find fresh
> outlets than the sweated districts of East London.

No reliance could be placed on Moses's spoken agreement
on the hours question. The Masters' Association must ratify
agreements on their official form. The strike committee
rejected arbitration (also on the premise that the radicals
might, as they eventually did, lose control in negotiations)

20. *East London Advertiser*, 28 September, 1889.

since the men had already offered maximum concessions. Lord Rothschild could help by subscribing to the strike fund and using his powerful influence on the masters to accede to the abandonment of the hours system, with the ten-and-a-half hour day to be binding on both masters and men. A confident deputation spoke with authority, and was received as such by Ornstein, who promised to pass on their request to Rothschild.

Much to the discomfort of the local masters, their men's cause, like the dockers', was being exposed to the nation at large, and was bringing practical support from yesterday's unfriendly, if not hostile, witnesses. On Thursday morning, 26 September, Miller of the dock strike committee had handed over one hundred pounds to Fricke, treasurer of the tailors' relief fund, at the White Hart. On Sunday the 29th, a large demonstration was held at Hyde Park, where the immigrants found themselves joined by a host of enthusiastic supporters from the ranks of the West End tailors and leading members of the Socialist League and the SDF. Urgent correspondence, including telegraphs, passed between both City banking houses and the White Hart. Scenting victory, the strikers' committee demanded one hundred pounds as a guarantee of the masters' good faith. Montagu provided the sum. Recognising the political dangers accruing from delay, he extended his services to the men and on Monday 30 September, he accepted an invitation to speak to a crowded meeting of the strikers, under the chairmanship of Lewis Lyons, at the Working Men's Club in Great Alie Street. The following Wednesday he addressed the masters, who met to consider the workers' proposals at the Hanbury Street Hall. The result was common accord on the principle of submitting the dispute to arbitration only. But this would take time and neither party wished to prolong the issue. Compromise was urged on the masters, who finally agreed 'to all the five clauses of the previous settlement of 12 September, plus an additional clause (six) *that the hour system be not introduced*' while the strike committee undertook that no wage claims would be made upon employers for the following twelve months. Committee delegates of both parties signed the agreement, witnessed by Montagu on 3 October. The strike leaders proclaimed their victory in a printed manifesto on the same day, with an order for the men to resume work on 6 October.

The *Arbeter Fraint* barely concealed its anger at the intervention of Montagu, who had outflanked the radical leadership in determining the terms of settlement. With irreverent irony it poured scorn on 'Reb Shmuel's', that is Montagu's, intentions.[21]

Bravo! Welcome comrade Montagu!

Brothers. Do you know of a bank that will lend us, the *Arbeter Fraint*, a few thousand pounds on trust? Someone whom we can pay, we have. We expect tomorrow morning a few thousand pounds from our comrade Samuel Montagu, as a first contribution to his and our organ, the *Arbeter Fraint*. You laugh? Yes, he has openly declared himself a Socialist by being seen with the Strike Committee on Sabbath night at the Jewish Working Men's Club. We were overjoyed — not so much with his person, that is never a pleasant sight — but with the pounds we expect from him for propaganda. Also we imposed on Montagu the task of presenting at our club a foreword on the theme 'The Jewish Bankers and the Social Revolution!' Moreover, as the Strike Committee burst out laughing when Montagu declared himself a Socialist, he replied that he meant thereby that he was for free enterprise. Doesn't he know what Socialism means?

Further suspicions of his intention were conveyed by questioning Montagu's introduction of the passage that 'heads of the present strike should not be allowed to intervene in future disputes'.

How far this will be of any use to the worker, we will wait and see. But what is certain, Reb Shmuel is the architect of this, and the main thing is that his one hundred pounds was thrown down the drain.

Yet, perhaps as consolation, a self-congratulatory note creeps in, on the part played by the Socialists in rousing the workers' political consciousness, which expressed itself in strike action.

21. *Arbeter Fraint*, 4 October, 1889.

Whence comes this militancy? Only we can give the right answer.
Socialism has penetrated your hearts ... Not your orthodoxy or
godliness ... This is it. The holy teachers of Socialism have long
cried to you, 'You are also human beings and you have the equal
right of all men to follow a human existence'. . . . You began to feel
your strength, which *we* made you aware of. You began to draw
together your divided strength, and unanimously undertook to put
aside problems of the next world to concentrate on workers'
problems in this. You have made the first step towards Socialism.

The workers must beware of the Montagus and Rothschilds
('who come to you because they are afraid of losing you
completely' and, too late, 'as emissaries to bring you back to
God!'). By their action against the sweaters, they had won the
sympathy and support of the English workers ('You will now
cease to feel strangers in a foreign land, and the great English
working-class mass will accept you as brothers in their
midst'). What sad optimism. More realistic support would
come from New York, where the Knights of Liberty group
and the Jewish section of the Socialist Workers' Party were
advertising in the same issue a monster ball and raffle to be
held in the East Side Clarendon Hall on 26 October, in aid of
the *Arbeter Fraint.*

While crowing over their success, the Socialist organ
echoed the workers' distrust of the masters fulfilling their
part of the bargain. In its 'Notebook' column, it complained
that even the strikers' victory was claimed by the capitalists,
when 'fat belly stuck his nose in, and affected the pretence
that it was thanks to them that the strikers won'. The main
target remained Montagu. It balanced up certain addenda he
had prescribed in the terms of settlement, against his
comment that the peace 'treaty' was 'the happiest day of his
life': namely that fourteen days' notice must be given before
a strike was contemplated and the workers must collect their
own strike funds (inferring that they could expect no further
financial help from the neutral bankers). Suspicion remained
paramount as the strikers returned to work on the following
Monday (7 October). The *Arbeter Fraint* maintained its task
as watchdog.

Many masters wanted to continue the long hours. The Strike

Committee therefore sat for another week to keep a watching brief. We helped to form a vigilance committee of workers, in which masters could also participate, in order to carry out inspections to prevent any master breaking his contract.

Blacklegging, hinted at during the strike, was now revealed as a serious breach in the workers' ranks, although the scabs' misdeeds would now rebound against them.

The masters, who employed scab labour, will, of course, not cease to work long hours. This chokes the scabs, now spurned by their fellow workers and needing to strike. But who will help them? Let them learn, these nothings, that they should, in future, be loyal to their brothers!

But it must have choked the editorial too, in exposing a strike deficit of sixty pounds which the strike committee attempted to meet by sending a deputation to Montagu and Rothschild to underwrite it.[22]

The radicals, however, remained jubilant. In the final count, the participation of immigrants in successful strike action registered a tremendous advance. 'It is true that all these victories mean a minor amelioration in the economic burdens of the working masses. But the workers are learning unity in action, and are moving step by step towards their self-realisation as a class.' It would appear from the evidence that the current strike proved a spur to unionisation. Co-operation with the masters, according to the *Arbeter Fraint*, was simply not on. Workers could only advance their interests by unilateral action. This was stressed by its representative speaker, M. Weinberg, at two consecutive meetings.[23] At the first he warned against the so-called co-operation between Capital and Labour. 'The aim of the workers' movement is quite different. Co-operation is only one means whereby workers' conditions could be affected, but it would be more helpful for the workers to organise

22. *Arbeter Fraint*, 11 October, 1889.
23. The first was at a public meeting of the Mantle Makers' Co-operative Association at Toynbee Hall, on Saturday 19 October, 1889. The second was at a preliminary meeting of the Carpenters' Co-operative Workshop on Sunday 20 October. Both were reported in the *Arbeter Fraint*, 25 October, 1889.

themselves, [thereby] achieving class consciousness.' At the second, Weinberg spoke against the inclusion of masters at a proposed Carpenters' Co-operative, observing that the discussion on this evidenced overwhelming opposition from the workers themselves.

The expansion of nascent organisations and the proliferation of new unions appeared to validate the radicals' case. One notes in the 'Unions' Calendar' that, from the number of meetings advertised, it suggests that craft organisations had more than doubled since the tailors' dispute.[24] The small Stick Makers' Union reported growth to 100 members (25 October), since its formation only seven weeks before, such that its English counterpart now sought a joint meeting with them on 28 October to discuss common approaches to unionism and co-operation. The leaders called on all members to attend so that 'from all sides we will clasp hands and bind ourselves together'. Steps towards inter-union co-operation followed quickly. On 27 October came a pioneer attempt to form a Jewish Workers' Central Committee. The *Arbeter Fraint* records that an assembly of

> delegates from various Jewish workers' unions met at Berner Street club to found a central committee of united workers' trades, *a creation born out of the great tailors' strike in the East End*. A resolution was passed, that, on reflection, most Jewish workers were unacquainted with the English language, which would hinder union with their English brothers. The meeting, therefore, found need instead for the creation of a Jewish Central Committee.

In the same issue appeared a detailed coverage of all local union activities for the first time.

The ding-dong battle between the *Arbeter Fraint* and its enemies continued unabated. It explained that current lateness of delivery was due to the constant need for publication elsewhere. A major cause was 'our rich friend (we will not deem to name him here!) who talks round the many Whitechapel printers, who would take on the printing of the *Arbeter Fraint*, to call it off'. It was, therefore, vital for the

---

24. Five union meetings were advertised on 25 August, thirteen in the October 25 issue of the *Arbeter Fraint*.

10. Morris Winchevsky, Yiddish poet and pioneer Jewish socialist.

11. Woolf Wess.

Sir We ask the assistance of your Body to obtain funds for the Defence of the members of the International Working Men's Club 40 Berner St on 16th when the Police invaded the Club ill-treated the members and arrested several on the charge of assaulting the Police. These men are now sent for trial. We earnestly appeal to all who believe that wrong should not triumph to assist us the Wealthy Jew and Socialists both Jews and Gentiles wish to see these men in prison and their Club destroyed. Her Majesty's Government by Police brutality and Legal injustice are aiding the Socialists. We are poor Men will you help us

Defence Committee

all subscriptions should be sent to F. Kitz Treasurer 13 Farringdon Rd EC

12. Appeal for aid by anarchists arrested during the Berner Street riot, 16 March 1889. See p. 168 for transcription.

journal to own its own press. A Christmas lottery would be run based on the support of London and US comrades. 'With so much strength we can surely collect the fifty pounds needed to pay for the best rapid press with the newest system.' On its flanks, the 'new Amazon', Lady Rothschild, had joined the attack; her weapon the formation of a social club in the East End 'in which the workers' problems will be undertaken in correct Rothschild terms, i.e. from the bourgeois standpoint, not the Socialist one, as enunciated by the Berner Streeters.'[25] A new triumvirate was astir. The Chief Rabbi and Montagu were extending anti-Socialist forces. A letter had been sent by the latter to the Federation of Jewish Synagogues,[26] warning them:

> We can no longer be ignored . . . the whole Jewish Kehilla were on their feet against our growing strength. The fear-stricken Federation convene special meetings to discuss plans for forming a fighting committee against us. They think that the battle will endure not less than three years. Religion and 'goldsack' have united against us. The finance minister of the Jewish Kehilla, Reb Shmuel . . . has already donated the necessary funds, 900 sovereigns, and the Jewish ghost conveyors have contributed — their prayers. A suitable battle commander (at an annual salary of three hundred pounds) is needed. He is to be a *maggid*.

Other reports added derision to their contempt for clerical functions. Two 'free' marriages (that is without religious sanction) were reported. Editorial congratulation followed speeches by *Arbeter Fraint* representatives on both occasions, who encouraged such examples which 'will render a sharp

25. *Arbeter Fraint*, 16 November, 1889.
26. See Joseph E. Blank, *Minutes of the Federation of Synagogues — A 25 Years Review* (London, 1912), pp.20-2. Montagu, the Acting President of the Board, wrote on 6 November, 1889:

> My experience gained during the recent strike convinces me that the influence of a few Atheists over Jewish Working Men *can no longer be ignored*. I therefore appeal with confidence to the Federation of Synagogues, comprising so large a number of observant Jews, to take the lead in combating this most serious evil.

On 30 January, 1890 a Dr M. Lerner of Wurzheim was elected to the post of Maggid. Blank reveals that the Federation by 1912 was acting wittingly or unwittingly as a counter-'radical' force (see para. 2, p.8).

blow on the nose to the moralists of Back Church Lane and greater amelioration [in the lot] of struggling Jewish brides to be'.[27]

There were no holds barred in the attack on the 'Kehilla'. As the Federation sought a candidate for the post of *maggid*, the *Arbeter Fraint* responded by issuing in bold print on their front page for two consecutive weeks a mock-satirical advertisement, 'Maggid for the London Jewish Kehilla'. The successful applicant must follow eleven precepts, which must be reflected in his sermons and Talmudic discourses, so 'as to convince us (true or false) that the workers *are* rich, satisfied and happy, and if not, have no right to be, since God has decreed it . . . from the Rothschilds will be born the Messiah . . . ' and that 'the Federation of Synagogues is not a Socialist Union'. No wonder the Federation girded its loins to do 'battle against the Berner Streeters and rescue the workers from their great atheistic influence'; which the radicals gaily countered by voicing the morality of atheism which 'frees the human spirit and strengthens one's self-awareness in the striving for truth, so much more effective than the belief in God in bringing us to a common human morality'.[28] The Chief Rabbi continued to share the brunt of their diatribes. Philip Kranz chided him for refusing to continue a written discussion on Socialism, and 'kindly' invited him to resume the debate at a public meeting to be held at the Dramatic Club, 3 Princes Street, on the following Friday (Sabbath) evening, 27 December.

As the year drew to its close the balance sheet of radical voluntarism seemed promising. The *Arbeter Fraint* was now recognised by all Jewish unions in operation as their official organ. The success of other strikes, such as in Manchester, with parallel aims, would appear to justify Gallop's commentary ('such resolution, such eagerness to organise, such steadfastness in battle . . . as have been exhibited during the endless series of bloodless workers' struggles of the past year — such has not yet been seen or experienced by mankind')[29] — and, locally, the expectations for a radical

27. *Arbeter Fraint*, 23 November, 1889.
28. Ibid., 6 December, 1889.
29. Ibid., 3 January, 1890.

greening of Whitechapel. But it was more the wish than the reality. Attempts at unity with their Gentile comrades — a vital necessity to maintain long-term efficacy — proved as elusive as ever: a situation apparently 'unavoidable, because customs, habits and modes of work and, unfortunately, often language stood in the way'.[30] Advantages gained in the strike settlement were ephemeral. *Commonweal* (7 December), under the column 'Labour Struggle', was already exposing the 'discontent among the men concerning the way in which the masters are breaking the agreement by which the strike was concluded; a renewal of the conflict seems by no means improbable'. Lewis Lyons, at a crowded meeting of East End tailors at Christ Church Hall, Hanbury Street on 18 January, confirmed that 'two weeks had not passed from the signing of the agreement before some of the masters had broken it, and now the majority of them appeared to follow their example'. The meeting was urged to consider means of enforcing the agreement 'if necessary by a general strike throughout London and the Provinces'.[31]

Yet the year of militancy registered other positive achievements. From the growth of individual unions came the recognition of the necessity for collective action as a more effective strike force. After a series of meetings at Berner Street 'the desirability having for some time been felt among the organised Jewish workers of the East End to federate under one head' led to the call for a mass rally. At three p.m. on Saturday 28 December at the Great Assembly Hall, Mile End, 4000 Jewish workers attended a meeting under

the auspices of the Hebrew Cabinet Makers' Society, Stick and Cane Dressers' Union, International Furriers' Society, Tailor Machinist Union, Tailors and Pressers' Union, Amalgamated Lasters' Society, United Cap Makers' Society and International Journeymen Boot Finishers' Society[32] with the object to get the agreement of the members of these unions to the proposed amalgamation . . . The

30. According to Ben Cooper, Secretary of the Cigar Makers' Union, when advising, as late as 1901, a separate Jewish Trades Council acting in alliance with the London Trades Council.

31. *Commonweal*, 25 January, 1890.

32. According to the report in the *Arbeter Fraint* 17 January, 1890 (Column *Social Movements*) there were delegates from 30 unions present.

following resolution was put by comrade Wess (secretary *pro tem.*) of the newly formed federation: 'That this mass meeting of East London workers, recognising the great benefits that can be derived from a combination of all existing unions, hereby inaugurates the *Federation of East London Labour Unions* and pledges itself to do its utmost to support and strengthen it.'[33]

Countervailing forces, new and old, would prevail to nullify short-term gains. Seasonal oscillations in trade, busy and slack, perpetuated cut-throat job competition. In addition the new year would bring a further influx of pauper immigrants, driven by a fresh spate of oppressive laws and outrages in Russia. This, in turn, meant little respite for an over-congested labour market. Factional disputes were simmering within the radical leadership: between Socialist and Anarchist, believer and atheist, the tolerant and the inflexible. Perhaps a more sober evaluation was made by the 'Mad Philosopher' (Winchevsky) in his final commentary on the dying year — 'the hundredth anniversary of the Great French Revolution'. 'What I wished for from that year will, I hope, be seen by my grandson: a free mankind — uplifted, satisfied, fulfilled.' Events in the New Year would justify his scepticism.[34]

33. *Commonweal*, 4 January, 1890.
34. *Arbeter Fraint*, 27 December, 1889.

7. Fragmentation

The tide of local militancy did not subside at once.[1] Direct action had come to stay, notwithstanding the inbuilt limitations peculiar to the Jewish immigrant and the exigencies of his trade. But there was never enough money in the kitty to carry through a long-term dispute. Blacklegging (notably in tailoring) was difficult to detect and counteract while local industry was infested with multiple workshops, many of which were hidden in out-of-the-way alleys or *ad hoc* hutments in back gardens. Settlements, agreed upon in writing, had no institutional machinery to enforce them.

There was no going back to those raw days when bread spelt submission to the dictates of the master. Consciousness of power to determine their own fate had marginally penetrated to workers in other trades. (The mushrooming of unions in minor crafts in 1889 exemplified this.) On 8 February, *Commonweal* publicised the 'Strike of Stick Makers in the East End', in order to mobilise general support against the London sweating employers, and to back the local craftsmen involved. A cool, informed article displayed the urgency of their cause.

> It seems that these two sweaters [i.e. employers Strauss and Metz] have seen what effect the union would ultimately have upon the robbery of labour, that cost what it would, they would use every effort to smash the organisation. The finishers can earn at the utmost an average wage of twelve shillings per week of 15 and 18 hours per day, with a reduction of fourpence to sixpence for the use of gas according to wages earned, one penny for cleaning the shop, and one penny interest in the shilling is charged on all money lent during the week. Filers and benders can earn from twenty shillings

1. Here I disagree with my colleague Professor Gartner, *The Jewish Immigrant in England (1870-1914)*, p.126, since two reasonably successful strikes were to follow in 1890 from the events of 1889, which had created a precedent for collective action.

to twenty-five shillings per week, with the reductions at the above rate. Notwithstanding the sweating wages paid, Metz of 20 Worship St., and Strauss of Playhouse Yard, Golden Lane, insist upon a reduction of 45 per cent on these miserable wages, which will render impossible for the employees an opportunity of bare existence.

The employer Strauss not only contemptuously ignored a written demand to receive a deputation of workers, but also sent the men's written suggestion to the International Society of Stick Makers, stating that he would have nothing to do with 'that damned Union!'. *Commonweal*, gauging a lack of outside support, deplored 'the present indifferent attitude of the Trade Unions of London' when it might become 'the most effective means of retarding the movement itself'. Its appeal 'to all workers of whatever nationality, to aid the stick makers against tyranny of the most brutal kind ever adopted against workers' organisation' did not fall on deaf ears. The ensuing number[2] reported that, at a strikers' assembly held at Banner Street Hall, St Luke's (5 February), Tom Mann and Ben Tillett promised to speak at a future meeting. In this case it was evident that both individual craftsman and union had derived from the experience of others in 1889 the pressing need for collective strength in terms of numbers and the accumulation of funds. At the next meeting (12 February) held in the same hall, the committee reported that membership had increased by 350 since the strike began, and that, although it was a young society, ten shillings a week had already been paid to strikers. A tale was told of one master ratting on his own kind. This stick maker who held a large stock 'could obtain no sale for them . . . Since the strike he has obtained that sale and is even supporting the Union. This should teach the workers how to make use of "master blackleg" as master makes use of "workman blackleg".' The following day, 13 February, the strike ended with a decisive victory for the men 'who received an advance instead of suffering a reduction. They have thereby practically learnt the advantages of combination.'[3]

2. *Commonweal*, 15 February, 1890.
3. S.P. in *Commonweal*, 22 February, 1890.

It would appear so. The tailors, reacting to the breaking of the 1889 agreements by the masters, had met and unanimously resolved on strike action for 1 March. The same week also saw a large meeting of last riveters and shoe finishers in the boot trade at Shoreditch Town Hall with 'the men set in their demands last autumn calling on them [the masters] to provide them with workshops, so as to prevent the sweating that accompanies the present system of working at home'.[4] Yet both *Commonweal* and the *Arbeter Fraint* had reservations on the pragmatic economism which motivated the workers. The former voiced its trepidation on the general thrust of the agitation, of which the Jewish movement was one example:

> Everywhere the hope was expressed that this movement would not be like the labour agitations of the past, that its essential character would be Socialistic . . . If the present movement is to aim at nothing higher than a paltry amelioration of the condition of the working class while the good trade continues, at nothing more than a mere modification of the tyranny and oppression under which the workers groan, then the movement will become only a farce, a failure . . . [5]

The *Arbeter Fraint, vis-à-vis* its own people, was even more pessimistic. It made play on the lack of funds and leadership (thereby revealing its own internal ideological conflicts in which the main antagonists were strike leaders – actual or potential) and deplored the negation of Socialism in current appeals to priests and royalty.

Sceptical though they might now be towards 'economism', when the following great strike broke out, the Jewish radicals threw themselves into the fray with gusto. In March 10,000 men in the boot trade came out after 'unavailing negotiations'. The masters agreed to provide workshop accommodation on their own premises (as the first step towards the elimination of out-work competition demanded by the men) on condition that the men submitted the question of wages to arbitration. This the workers refused. Evidence could be

4. *Commonweal*, 1 March, 1890.
5. Ibid., 5 April, 1890.

produced by the masters from lower-paid country districts to challenge the validity of their present low rates. The men's action brought immediate success. On the following Monday, 1,700 Jewish workmen, urged by the *Arbeter Fraint,* joined in, and 97 out of 400 masters, including those controlling the first-class firms, had given in. 'It is only the sweating Jewish firms that are now resisting,' complained *Commonweal.*[6] They had resorted to

> some cunning ruses, being slippery and eel-like in their nature. They have sent work to Ipswich, but the union has stopped that little game by sending certain instructions to the local branch of the union. Another enterprising person sent work out in biscuit tins, but the pickets were alert and sent it back again.

The new traditional mass demonstration played its part in highlighting the strikers' case. On Thursday 3 April, a huge parade led by a brass band marched from the East to the West End, through Ludgate Circus and Fleet Street, completely blocking the traffic *en route*. The following Sunday another mile-long procession converged on Victoria Park, where it was announced that 192 masters had given way.

Anti-Jewish sentiment manifested itself among the strikers, not only due to the obstructionist attitudes of Jewish masters. At the height of the dispute, a special meeting was called by Jewish strikers at the Christ Church Hall, Hanbury Street, to protest at the incidence of English 'comrades' refusing to work in certain shops employing Jews. Yet it was at the White Hart pub, of Jewish tailors' fame, that the Boot Makers' Strike Committee met, deliberated, issued its manifesto and a plea for help from the International Union of Journeyman Boot Finishers.[7] The strikers were learning new strategy. They publicised a threat to leave London *en*

6. Ibid., 12 April, 1890.

7. *People's Press,* 19 April, 1890. The meeting took place on 10 April. The accusation was so serious that Horobin, Treasurer of the National Union, attended to disclaim such action and 'bore testimony that the Jews have acted most loyally'.

In the same issue, the strike committee's plea for aid is published. 'We have decided to strike and not to resume work until the manufacturers will take us to work indoors, where we shall at least be able to work not more than twelve hours per day.'

masse, which could deprive the masters in the capital of the best workmen. Other unions responded to their appeal. The London Trades Council issued a call for financial aid from other trades. By 19 April, *Commonweal* could inform its readers that 215 out of the 400 masters had now acceeded to the workers' terms. The large minority still insisted that the men should, in future wage disputes, submit their claim to a court of arbitration. This was again rejected. The workers had tested their own strength and proved the advantages of freedom of action. Splitting tactics on the part of Jewish employers also proved abortive.[8]

On 26 April *Commonweal* noted the end of the strike 'as far as the orthodox Trade Unions are concerned'. But the terms were indefinite. The manufacturers would open workshops at the earliest possible date. Matters relating to classification and all other questions, except a direct reduction of wages, would be referred to arbitration. A uniform statement of wages was to be prepared immediately for all shops except the first and second houses. At the same time an arbitration committee was formed of seven masters and seven men to discuss the time to be taken by the employers to provide workshops. Agreement was to be enforced by a neutral third party elected by the joint conciliation board. It was a pioneering effort at institutionalised arbitration. The Jewish representatives opposed the arrangement. They accused the sweaters of agreeing to such terms so as to tide the busy season over and 'after Whitsuntide they will have the men at their mercy and then break their word'. (Their suspicions arose from the experience of their tailoring comrades in the 1889 strike, when, after the sweaters had got the men back to work, they broke every clause in the agreement.) 'The men, therefore, refuse to return to work unless workshops are provided *at once*.' But a week later the Jews had been forced back into line; and the masters had conceded an advance of threepence per dozen pairs of boots.

In this case the major objective of the strike would be realised in the long term, that is the elimination of sweated

8. *Commonweal*, 19 April, 1890: 'Some of the Jew employers have offered ten shillings and a pound to men to take work home and thus break the ranks of the strikers, but in not a single instance have they been successful.'

outwork. The Board of Trade report on Alien Immigration[9] suggested that the small masters had also seen the light when their association opted to join the National Union. Many relinquished their status to apply for workmen's jobs in the new factories. The change was not always amenable, when, as Jews, they 'were teased and annoyed beyond endurance' such that considerable numbers reverted to their role as 'chamber masters'. By 1894, between seventy-five and a hundred shops still operated on the old system. But it was already a dying concern. 'Greeners' no longer provided a steady stream of recruits to domestic outwork, and immigrant Jews who persisted 'formed a decreasing minority of the total immigrant labour force'.[10]

With tailoring the old order would remain intact. Following the boot makers, union leaders pressed for conditions mutually agreed on in 1889. A strike committee of the London Tailors and Pressers' Union, located at 20 Booth Street, Spitalfields, issued a fact-finding circular to all members to evaluate current malpractice, and called on them to endorse strike action for 4 May.[11] This was a tactical move, following as it did the final report of the Lords Sweating Commission which had received widespread publicity. The strike leaders insisted on the masters formally signing a document embodying previous terms. This time the masters responded immediately. In the 17 May issue, *Commonweal* wrote that during the preceding week

> eighty-two masters have already surrendered. Sweaters resolved at a general meeting that they should join hands with the men against their common oppressor — the shopkeeper. They have decided to open negotiations with the men to boycott the shops which will not pay sufficient for the keeping of proper hours.

By 18 May the strike was over. The masters signed an agreement to the set terms. Only union men would be employed, and they would 'combine with the workers to

---

9. *Reports on the Volume and Effects of Recent Immigration from Eastern Europe into the U.K.* C.7406, 1894, pp.76-7.

10. See Gartner, *The Jewish Immigrant in England (1870-1914)*, pp.79-80.

11. *People's Press*, 10 May, 1890, gives details of the questionnaire issued to each worker. 'Compulsion' was the common answer to long hours.

bring pressure to bear on the shopkeepers by refusing to work for any firm that will not pay the union prices. A committee of masters and men has been formed to arrange details of united action.' For the men victory was an illusion. It would not even provide short-term respite. In the same issue of *Commonweal*[12] its correspondent, gloomily but correctly, predicted 'Another Trade Depression Coming'. In Russia new blows were struck against Jews with their expulsion from Moscow and Kiev and the tightening up of old decrees.[13] This meant a fresh influx of refugees into England and locally a further inflation of the labour market. For the tailors, economism alone would become a perennial and futile gesture. The masters knew that they held the whip hand. There was no dearth of greeners in the years to come.

The radical leaders were already succumbing to the wear of constant frustration. Stationed in the forward echelon of the tailors' dispute, they viewed with scepticism the familiar inbuilt hindrances to a successful operation: confusion in aims, the intervention of the old *bête* Montagu, and the response of wives and sweethearts to hunger. The masters played on the last to force the men back. A meeting of women was sponsored at 20 Booth Street on 13 May in which Yanovsky, eloquently supported by Wess and Kahan, persuaded them 'to back their men to the end'.[14] When the strike ended on a note of rapport between the two sides, the editor warned that 'friendship between wolf and sheep is an illusion and bodes little good for the worker'. Ultimately more serious was the factional rift which began to manifest itself openly at this time.

Ideological differences between Social Democrats, Anarchists and non-aligned groups had lain beneath the surface ready to erupt. In a series of articles in the *Arbeter Fraint* (February-July, 1890) M. Baranov had tried to explain impartially to its readers the fundamental theories of the two protagonists ending on the note: 'I personally find the

---

12. 24 May, 1890.
13. A postscript to the persecution of 1890 was that 7,000 new immigrants entered England in 1891. (Estimate of Board of Trade report of 1894.)
14. *Arbeter Fraint*, 16 May, 1890.

absolute truth in neither of these two socialist ideas, which battle with each other to-day.' Within the club, conflict was reflected in the pages of the *Arbeter Fraint*, where open debate and hard criticism between contributing colleagues began to appear. In issue of 23 May, Yanovsky came out strongly against Feigenbaum on his article 'Thinkers and Rabbis'.[15] In the correspondence column the following week, H. Kaplansky complained of the disruptive behaviour of Social Democrats at a recent Knights of Freedom (Anarchist) meeting which provoked the editor to remark that the animosity which the two sides had recently 'assumed . . . can bring no good to the movement, only shame'. The split paralleled that in the ranks of their nearest British colleagues, the Socialist League, which reached a crisis with the publication of Morris's article 'Where are we now?' in *Commonweal* on 15 November.[16] Attempts at papering up the cracks were contrived. Paradoxically, what was conceived to represent the high-water mark of radical strength at a time of growing disunity, was an emotive joint celebration of the club's fifth anniversary. A moving description is given by Harold Kaplansky in an article 'Our Holy Day: The Fifth Anniversary of the International Working

15. Ibid., 23 May, 1890, fully reports the end of the strike after joint conference on 20 May under the chairmanship of Mark Moses. A working committee of three workers and three masters was elected to arbitrate when a dispute was pending in future. A General Strike of both masters and men was threatened if the shopkeepers refused to meet union prices.

16. Morris's theme appeared to deprecate violence in the form of ill-timed riots and revolts advocated in the writings of some of his colleagues, and appealed instead for Socialist action in the form of an educative programme. It aroused open dissension in the ranks and split the leadership. On 29 November, 1890 the weekly issue was suspended and so were notices of meetings of the Berner Street group. A monthly issue of *Commonweal* appeared with a change of venue from 24 Queen Street, W.C. to 273 Hackney Road. In February 1891 a correspondent A. Coulon wrote, 'every friend of Liberty is pleased to see the 'Weal move towards Anarchy'. In March 1891 a notice appeared by Frank Kitz stating that he had no further connection with the London Socialist League. It is interesting to note that anarchist S. Yanovsky had also just taken over the editorship of the *Arbeter Fraint* on 20 February, 1891. Thus both English and Jewish groups were moving in the same direction, namely becoming predominantly Anarchist. For in May 1891 *Commonweal* returned to a weekly issue and changed its sub-title to *A Revolutionary Journal of Anarchist-Communists*. The dual change is reflected in a common platform being shared in an April meeting on the Mile End Waste by Yanovsky and Mowbray.

Men's Club, 8 June, 1890', in which Kahan, Feigenbaum, Winchevsky and Yanovsky spoke jointly for the Berner Street Jewish group.[17]

> It was an imposing, joyful and instructive day — a historical day. The great hall, colourfully decorated and illuminated, fully packed with workers in their holiday suits, with wives and children. Joy was reflected in everyone's countenance — real joy. At half-past five, after tea was over, when today's Chairman, our beloved Comrade William Morris gave the signal for speeches to begin, everybody sat with quiet concentration to await the deliberations.
>
> William Morris opened the meeting with a brief but informative speech, and those who understood gave him prolonged applause. He praised the club for its endless dedication and observed that the English comrades could take an example from it. The Jewish immigrants had not come to England for fun, but were driven here by despotism and discrimination, with the tragic experience of leaving their home land and arriving here with the hope of finding a quieter and humane life. Instead they found the terrible sweating system. New troubles began for them, and they sank into further depths of despair until the International Working Men's Club brought renewed hope to the hearts of Jewish workers — the holy message of Socialism.

Kahan enumerated the successes due to the club, notably 'the fears it had inculcated in the Jewish goldsacks and kindred swindlers'. Its outstanding features were the international implications of its activities.

> When the Club was created, the Jewish workers, not only in England but throughout the world, were asleep, and had no idea of workers' unions or organisation. Now we find [Jewish] unions in all the great cities of England, not to mention the thousands of Jewish workers' societies in other lands, especially in America, who should all thank their existence . . . to our club and its organ the *Arbeter Fraint*.

Feigenbaum followed this self-congratulatory piece on a different note. He brought to the surface the underlying antagonisms, by closing his address with a plea to members 'to cast aside partisan feeling . . . to assume that fraternity . . . by which we brought about such happy and successful results during the last five years'.

17. *Arbeter Fraint*, 13 June, 1890.

After a spirited intercession by Stepniak came the man who, more than any other Jew, symbolised for his audience the root yearnings of the immigrant poor, and the nobility of the Socialist cause.

> The chairman announced that our beloved friend Morris Winchevsky, the well-known Jewish poet, would read his last two poems to my brothers of the *Arbeter Fraint* numbers 15 and 23, and the whole audience rose as one man and greeted him with tumultuous applause. Then after two minutes a dramatic silence, whilst the quiet trembling voice of the poet brought tears to the eyes of those who understood.

An interval collection was announced by Morris. His daughter May and Stepniak went round with the plates 'whilst the choir of the Hammersmith branch of the Socialist League rendered Morris's lyric "Down among the Dead Men" '. The sum realised was two pounds six shillings and fivepence with an additional ten pounds contributed by the 'recent Nihilists in Paris'. The recess over, the doyen of international anarchism, Kropotkin, rose to speak. He had just returned from a propaganda tour of the provinces which confirmed that 'Berner Street is the tenth Jewish Socialist group in England but the organisations in Manchester, Leeds, etc. had to give thanks to the energetic dedication of *our* club . . . and that the *Arbeter Fraint* and all *our* pamphlets were widely read at home' (i.e. Russia). Yanovsky, the last speaker, summarised the significance of the commemoration, stressing the link with the growth of radical agitation in the USA during the previous five years. The reading of telegrams and a mass chorus of the 'Marseillaise' heralded the finale — at least of the speech-making. Then 'the tables were withdrawn and the hall prepared for a concert and dance. The festivities went on throughout half the night.' It was their brief gesture of glowing abandon in the slum ghetto, the gaiety echoing as far distant as those misnomers Providence and Christian streets. The chronicler, obviously made of more serious stuff, could only recall that, after the ball, 'all dispersed with the knowledge that unity is strength, that only in brotherhood could there be satisfaction'!

The festival was inconsequential to the factionalism and

fragmentation which was eroding both leadership and rank and file in Berner Street. Only a week later the *Arbeter Fraint* was complaining that 'other than Social Democrats and Anarchists the Jewish socialist movement has a third party – Synagogue Socialists. They talk of Socialism and revolution but marriage must be celebrated in a synagogue. For this one day they reveal themselves as false hypocrites.' Doctrinal disputes had entered the correspondence columns. The same week a letter from Yanovsky refuted Kranz's[18] proposition that, as workers' conditions got more depressed, it hastened the possibility of revolution. The old trade union *genosse* Lewis Lyons was pilloried. His attempt to perpetuate a combined organisation of small master tailors' and workers' unions, on the premise that only by such united action could economic improvement for all members of the trade be effected, brought on his head the scorn of the *Arbeter Fraint*.[19]

> The *Arbeter Fraint* is, for Mr Lyons, a bone in the throat. The *Arbeter Fraint* is too free, too generous. It stands too firmly for the principle of workers' interest. This is a bad omen for such people who regard the working masses as so many little fishes in the water.
> One of these . . . is Mr Lewis Lyons!

The *Arbeter Fraint* accused his advocacy of 'union' with the masters as 'playing' with the workers:

> But instead of giving an explanation, at an opportunity presented to him by the editor of the *Arbeter Fraint*, he chose to . . . boycott the *Arbeter Fraint*.
> This is foolish, Mr Lewis Lyons . . . we would like to ask you a further question . . . How much do you hope to make from the masters and the goldsacks for boycotting the only Jewish paper which stands in the vanguard of workers' interests in London?

Yet in denouncing the 'two previous secretaries of the Jewish working men's procession to Dukes Place Shool', the paper exposed its own dilemma. 'One [i.e. Lyons] would destroy

18. Kranz had resigned his editorship the year previously and had departed for the USA, where he became involved in the *Worker's Times*.
19. *Arbeter Fraint*, 27 June, 1890.

the *Arbeter Fraint*; the other, Comrade Kranz, suggests in his *Worker's Times* (No. 15) that the *Arbeter Fraint* will, in the near future, have to clarify its unclear programme. *It must either become Social Democrat or Anarchist!*'[20]

There would soon be little doubt of the outcome of the conflict. Even Baranov, who claimed to belong to neither camp, ended up his series on a note of sympathy for the anarchists. ('Socialists do not change, only they have not forgotten their belief in humanity, in man's progress . . . And of the socialists, the anarchists believe more than anyone else in human beings.') During the second half of 1890 there is ample evidence that the Anarchists were gaining the upper hand. On 18 July, at an important meeting called for all members 'to whom the *Arbeter Fraint* is dear', the editor Gallop, commenting on a third party, the Social-Revolutionaries, that had recently come into existence, appealed for unity at the top to fight the common enemy.

> We do not sit on both stools, but perhaps on a shaky stool. We can do with the help of both social-democrats and anarchists. We tell ourselves not to go hand in hand with either one or the other . . . As long as it is unnecessary to quarrel about the fall of the still living bear, we say, Fools! First shoot the bear!

He repeated this the following week[21] in the context of rejecting nascent Zionism. 'There is only one enemy you must fight . . . till you destroy him. Your enemy is CAPITAL'. By 29 August his appeal had changed to a desperate plea[22] for the recognition of the rectitude of all Socialists as 'part of one and the same large Socialist Party, in which theory and practice is merely parcelled out between the various groups'.

20. *Arbeter Fraint*, 4 July. Yanovsky, in an article 'What They Say About Us Socialists', explains and defends the Libertarian slant on the family, private enterprise, the class struggle and the necessity for revolution. The *A.F.* 11 July includes an editorial by P.D. Nieuwenhaus and publicises a lecture on 'Anarchism' by W. Wess for 8 August. A conference of the Anti-Parliamentary Socialist Organisation of 3 August is also reported, which included delegates from the Berner Street Club and the 'Knights of Freedom'. On 15 August appeared an anti-Parliamentary editorial by S. Freeman. These pointed the direction in which the *Arbeter Fraint* was moving.

21. *Arbeter Fraint*, 18 July, 1890.

22. Article 'Is Unity not Possible?', by K. Gallop, *Arbeter Fraint*, 29 August.

A spurious unity could be maintained as the current series of brutal acts against the Jews in Russia brought a fresh stream of refugees into London. Supported by *Commonweal*, the *Arbeter Fraint* called on the Jewish workers in London to support a mass meeting 'organised by the London International Workers' Educational Club, for Saturday 1 November, 1890 in the great Assembly Hall, Mile End ... to protest against the persecution of your brothers in Russia'. A platform was to be shared by an impressive group of speakers including Kropotkin, Morris, Cunningham-Grahame MP, Edward and Eleanor Marx Aveling.[23] On the Thursday before the meeting was due, Charrington, proprietor of the hall, withdrew his permission for its use, apparently at the instigation of Dr Adler and Samuel Montagu. This forced the demonstration to take place outside on the open Waste, since, due to the short notice 'difficulties were found in hiring alternative sites'. The *Arbeter Fraint* wrote accusingly: 'Dr Adler, your religious con-man and Samuel Montagu ... bourgeois swindler went to Mr Charrington, and by cunning intrigue, persuaded him to withdraw his promise to let the hall.' The outdoor meeting, however, attracted a massive audience. Eleanor Marx Aveling[24] joined her husband on the platform to support 'a strong resolution censoring the heads of the Anglo-Jewish community for procuring the boycott of the meeting which was carried unanimously'.[25]

It was the intervention of S. Yanovsky (1864-1939) which precipitated factional divisions. In the final dissolution, it was he who ensured that the Anarchist group would remain with the greatest numbers and influence, although the Berner Street club would be destroyed in the process. His biographer, Abba Gordin, wrote that from his earliest years he was 'gifted with a sense of humour, eloquence ... strength of character and, above all, a sharp pen'.[26] Rocker declared that

23. *Arbeter Fraint*, 31 October, 1890.
24. Eleanor was already concerned with a sympathetic appraisal of her own Jewish roots. In a letter to Woolf Wess, dated 21 October, 1890, she wrote, 'I shall be very glad to speak at the Meeting on November 1st, *the more glad, that my father was a Jew*'.
25. *Arbeter Fraint*, 7 November, 1890; *Freedom*, December 1890, reports that Wess got twenty pounds from Charrington for breach of contract.
26. Abba Gordin, *S. Yanovsky: his Life, Struggles and Achievements*, Los Angeles, 1958, p.11.

his arrival in London in March, 1890 'opened a new epoch in the Jewish labour movement'.[27] After a childhood in Russia (Pinsk), in which he was a (fortunate) recipient of both a Jewish and Russian education, he came under the influence of the revolutionary *intelligent*. He was drawn to the Libertarian ideology after digesting the works of the masters Proudhon and Bakunin and, in 1885, crossed the border with a false passport, en route for the USA via the old German transit points, Königsburg and Hamburg. In New York he joined the Anarchist group which, in 1889, produced *Wahrheit*; this was the first Anarchist journal in Yiddish and helped establish his reputation as a journalist activist. (After twenty issues the paper was reconstituted as the *Freie Arbeter Stimme*, which is still published in New York.) It was at the instigation of the recent immigrant from London, Rutenberg, that Yanovsky was prevailed upon to assume the editorship of the *Arbeter Fraint* from Gallop, who was ill and presumably willing to resign. Fares were provided for both Yanovsky and his wife, but on arrival in London (March, 1890), Gallop's assumed withdrawal did not take place; he refused to relinquish his post on the pretext that his health had improved. Yanovsky was forced to seek work as a capmaker in a Whitechapel sweat shop, and for nearly a year lived on the margin of subsistence. Gordin claims that Yanovsky had blinkers over his eyes in that he retained an inflexible belief in the moral superiority of the working man, although he himself must have observed the fortunate employee 'even acting swinishly towards a fellow worker seeking a job, to sit by a machine and earn a living. The worker, already employed, looks down on the unfortunate lumpen, or job seeker.'[28]

At first he earned sixpence a day and it was impossible to exist. A comrade taught him stick making. Here his confidence in the humanity of the working man was confirmed when, in one workshop, he was welcomed by the hands, who had discovered that he had been brought over from New

27. Rocker, *The London Years*, p.128. Both Rocker's and Gordin's appraisals were those of a sympathetic partisan. Both Sam Dreen and Aron Rollin remember him as rigid and aggressive in his attitude to supporters and opponents alike.
28. Gordin, *S. Yanovsky* p.145.

York to be appointed editor of the *Arbeter Fraint*. It was a harrowing experience. 'The first two days were spent in sandpapering sticks, but I rubbed more skin off my hands than [wood] off the sticks ... My palms became open wounds.' Those who had invited him felt that he ought to be found more pertinent and amenable employment. After all, they had been responsible for inviting him over on what transpired to be false pretences. Advertisements were placed in the *Arbeter Fraint*[29] offering private lessons in Russian by Yanovsky, a language in current demand by British firms and government officials. Unfortunately there was little response. The difficulty was 'that students of Russian were found among the rich, the élite of the business world ... so how could a hated immigrant, a ghetto dweller of Whitechapel, gain an entrée there?'[30] To ensure him a regular income, it was finally decided to collect a weekly subscription from the more affluent comrades, in order to pay him a pound a week for an indefinite period, while he undertook to produce a propaganda brochure, 'What do the Anarchists Want?' as an extra to his journalistic commitments. Within a week he had produced a twenty-two page pamphlet, which, however short, was received as 'the most fully comprehensive exposition of Anarcho-Communism in Yiddish ... It has since been translated into German, French and Dutch among other languages.'[31]

Superb journalist and polemicist that he was, with an aggressive dynamism to boot, his presence was not conducive to good personal relationships. In rigidly defining the terms of his party line, he accelerated the split between Anarchists and the rest, although, by the end of 1890, the former already constituted the majority in Berner Street. In the natural course of events, the current Social-Democrat editor, Gallop, after enduring prolonged criticism, was manoeuvred into resigning. Yanovsky replaced him by popular vote (20 February, 1891). In the short, very short, term the *Arbeter Fraint* overtly continued its non-partisan policy. On 10 April,

29. *Arbeter Fraint*, 13 June, 1890. Advertisement: S. Janowsky, 108 Brady St Buildings, Block E. Lessons in English, German and Russian.
30. Gordin, *S. Yanovsky*, p.146.
31. Ibid., pp.147-8.

Yanovsky disclosed the official switch over to Libertarian direction after the Anarchists won, by a bare majority of 23-21, at a special meeting called to decide control of the paper. It was not long before the fractious new editor drove off the residual Social Democrats. The universally respected Winchevsky (who was also related to Gallop) disliked Yanovsky, denigrated his talents as a writer, and also quit. On 1 May appeared a new radical journal *Die Freie Welt* (The Free World), with contributions from the breakaway leaders Baranov, Feigenbaum, K. Liberman and Gallop under the ideological direction of the now veteran Winchevsky.

Changes and fluctuations in the affairs of otherwise un-newsworthy local immigrant politics did not escape the watchful eye of the ultra-conservative *Anti-Jacobin*, which registered alarm at the appearance of a new Yiddish socialist paper.[32]

> Six years ago there was not a single 'Jüdish' organ in existence that preached communism; now there are three, printing, it is said, between 12,000 and 13,000 copies each on an average. Three years ago there was but a single Anarchist organisation amongst the foreigners of East London, that which had its headquarters in Berner Street, Commercial Road. Now there are three more: 'The Knights of Freedom' with a club in Hanbury St; the 'Verein' meeting at a house in High St, Whitechapel and the association known as the 'Proletariat' in Wood St . . . It may be mentioned too, that there is an anarchist club composed exclusively of women in Berner St. It is clear, therefore, that the Jüdish press of East London may reckon the support of a rapidly growing clientele.

The *Anti-Jacobin* was engaging in one of its usual over-imaginative extravaganzas. There was no justification for its last forecast. By 26 July, 1891 the *Arbeter Fraint* was complaining that its London sales had dropped to 200, of which many were unpaid; while the *Freie Welt*'s average circulation per issue was 509, of which most were sales in the USA. Although the departure of the Socialists brought financial difficulties to the *Arbeter Fraint*, this gave no corresponding boost to the income of its new rival. Both shared a limited paying clientele, although the capacity for

32. Article 'Judish Journalism' in *Anti-Jacobin*, 16 May, 1891.

free readership was greater, owing to editorial policy of exhorting its buyers to 'pass the paper on'. In fact the *Arbeter Fraint* continued to print advertisements for the *Freie Welt* as the mouthpiece of the International Socialist Proletarian Union until August 1891,[33] when 'Jacques', for the editorial board, in a 'necessary declaration', warned of the prospect of a 'cold war' between the two, while disclaiming responsibility for the irregular publication of the *Freie Welt*, which was printed on the same press 'at cost price — without profit'. With Yanovsky at the helm, there would be no compromising Libertarian 'principles', and therefore less possibility of change in the mode of propaganda in order to attract more readers. 'The greater part of the immigrants, who remained bound to traditional orthodoxy, were repulsed by the militant atheism of the *Arbeter Fraint*, and were too painfully involved in the struggle for existence to care about (political) ideology.'[34] Nor could any future reliance be placed on American demand, when in New York a new non-partisan paper was produced with the conscious aim of preserving a united workers' movement.

Under Yanovsky, the *Arbeter Fraint* quickly developed a cohesive Anarchist programme; his main concern being to strengthen local unions and weld them into effective fighting units against attacks on the workers' standards. Rocker claimed that the paper 'gained by no longer having to keep a united front on questions about which there were disagreements': for instance the so-called 'iron law of wages', espoused by Social-Democrat Philip Kranz, 'which did little to encourage Trade Unions'.[35] During Yanovsky's editorship there would be no concert or compromise with the masters, while he urged the unions to constitute themselves as revolutionary organisations. He focused his polemics on 'corrupt' union officials ('I punctured the puffed up pretences of Baranov') and it was inevitable that Lewis Lyons should become the chief target.

Lyons had already fallen from grace by his championship

33. *Arbeter Fraint*, no.33 of 1891.
34. Gordin, S. *Yanovsky*, p.163.
35. Rocker, *The London Years*, p.129.

of a combined workers' and small masters' union. His argument, which had some degree of validity, was that both were victims of the wholesaler (the real sweater, who determined cost of production right down the line), and therefore a united front could force him to pay a reasonable price per finished garment. But, in an industry based on small domestic concerns, where the work situation institutionalised conflict between master and hand, united action for mutual benefit was impossible. A now almost perennial strike of East End tailors, led by Lyons, which lasted from 31 May to 26 June, 1891,[36] occasioned a bitter attack by Yanovsky. In 'Notice Book',[37] Lyons was accused of pocketing union funds without the members' sanction. He 'used a letter from the Trades Council to solicit help from other unions to settle debts accrued by the Tailors' Union in the recent strike, in which he managed to collect twenty-one pounds by touring the workshops. Several committee members were given twenty-eight shillings apiece!' Yanovsky appealed to the tailors. 'How long will you allow yourselves and your union to come to such shame, by letting this man lead you by the nose? ... Do you want a union which will be strong enough to press your interests? Then get rid of Lyons.' The attack was sustained in the following issue's correspondence column by Harris Hiller who, in a piece of cutting irony, confirmed Lyon's 'guilt' in milking the workers and splitting the union through strife and argument. The pillorying of Lewis Lyons did little to help mend the fractured labour movement. On the contrary it perpetuated the split between the two major factions (Lyons had committed himself to the Social-Democrats). He was too charismatic a figure to be cast down so easily. Five months would endure before he would be taken seriously to task. Not until the 28 November was a full meeting of East End tailors at the Working Lads' Institute called upon 'to condemn the action of Lewis Lyons, whose recent conduct has been so bad that the Tailors, Machinists, and Pressers' Union has been broken into what seems

36. For informed details of the 1891 tailors' strike see *The Times*, 25 and 29 May, 1, 2, 3 June and for the outcome, 26 June.
37. *Arbeter Fraint*, 10 July, 1891.

hopeless sections of dissatisfied and disgusted workmen'.[38] *Commonweal*, reasoning with some degree of objectivity, probed deeper into divisive causes. 'It is a pity that the Jewish workmen of East London are trammelled so much by their religion, jealousy and suspicion as to render it almost an impossible task to organise themselves.' John Burns had promised to do it. After that whimsical threat, partisanship will out. 'We would suggest that Yanovsky, Wess and other Yiddish-speaking comrades [i.e. Anarchists] should not leave the work entirely in his hands . . .' In the same issue, under a triumphant caption, 'Exit Lewis Lyons', it recorded that on 5 December, a resolution was carried by an overwhelming majority under the chairmanship of John Burns at the Kay Street Radical Club, in which the meeting condemned Lyons for his 'action . . . in connection with the management of the affairs of the International Tailors, Machiners and Pressers' Union, which, in our opinion, has tended to do great harm to the Labour cause and places no confidence in him as a leader'.

With or without their confidence, Lyons remained unchallenged as militant leader of the Jewish Unemployment Committee, and whether they liked it or not, many a rank and file 'Anarchist' marched behind him on future *journées*. Rocker may have been unfair in dismissing him as an opportunist.[39] During the harsh winter of 1892, he led a deputation, representing nine local Jewish unions, to the Chief Rabbi to supplicate his aid. *The Times* (15 November, 1892) gave a clear account of the confrontation. Lyons informed him that

from our statistics at least 10,000 men, skilled and unskilled, were on the verge of starvation. He thought that they might not know such distress if they had the franchise and could so secure proper representation in parliament. They found employers working men 18 and 20 hours a day and cutting down prices, and they wanted the Chief Rabbi to use his influence to put an end to the state of things. They believed the employers would listen to him as the head of the Jewish people. He also asked that a weekly labour sermon should be allowed to be preached in one of the synagogues. The Chief Rabbi in

38. *Commonweal*, 12 December, 1891, 'East End Tailors'.
39. Rocker, *The London Years*, p.130.

reply calling the deputation 'fellow working men' said he called them such because he also had to toil from morning until night, and he probably had to work harder than any of those whom they represented!

The Chief Rabbi continued tactlessly to suggest that the figure quoted of 10,000 unemployed was greatly exaggerated, and although he sympathised with the Committee, he strongly advised them to call off a proposed barefoot march, which would only endanger their health and expose them to public ridicule. 'In that room words had been used, which certainly sounded like threats. No good would be effected by menaces or the preaching of doctrines of Anarchism and Nihilism.' They could instead utilise the Jewish welfare and charitable institutions. It was outside his jurisdiction to denounce Jewish employers publicly, or allow laymen to do so from his pulpit. Finally 'he earnestly hoped that when the depression of trade passed away, their troubles would also pass away'. With such cold comfort he dismissed the deputation, who withdrew muttering. The *Jewish Chronicle* supported the Chief Rabbi's firmness with the homily 'that whatever efforts are made by the working classes to improve their condition ought to be made on a purely unsectarian basis. Special interference by Jews for Jews cannot be too strongly deprecated.'

This only made Lyons more persistent. With Adler well in his sights, he followed up the meeting with a demand that a conference of Jewish ministers and trade-union leaders be convened to discuss jointly the problem of unemployment. The rabbinate refused. Lyons responded by summoning a mass meeting at Tower Hill, where, in an emotive speech, he accused the bourgeois Jews of contemptuously ignoring their poor co-religionists, who at that very time, he claimed, were being forced to sell their children for bread. The demonstration achieved widespread news coverage — but little else. The only reaction from their more fortunate brethren was a fresh outburst of recriminations; and some anti-alienists used it as an opportunity to beat the exclusionist drum. Maverick without a party, yet Lyons remained a pernicious thorn in the flesh of the Establishment throughout the 1890s. On 19

January, 1894[40] he mustered a committee of unemployed who invaded the Jewish Board of Guardians to demand instant relief. It was refused. A few days later[41] he spurred on a large group of unemployed to enter the Great Synagogue, Duke's Place and seek audience with the long-suffering Chief Rabbi. There were two 'invasions', one on the 24th, which went off peacefully, a second at the Sabbath service on the 26th when 500 to 600 unemployed entered the building. Over a hundred attempted a 'sit-in' and were forced to disperse by police armed with truncheons. The *Evening News*, among other dailies, waxed indignant at the antics of this 'mob of foreigners' in creating a riot.

> It is a natural result of our previous humane treatment of the Jewish immigrant . . . It is bad enough to have these people coming over to undersell our workers, but it will be a little beyond endurance if they begin to riot in the streets because we fail to find employment for them.[42]

Protests and demonstrations continued throughout the rest of January, proving more of an irritant to the police, who had to extend their duties. A series of joint conferences, that is confrontations, with the Board of Guardians were a waste of time, since the latter claimed that its terms of reference did not include providing work; but the *Jewish Chronicle* (2 February) contributed more than its solemn musings on the necessity for a more scientific approach to industrial problems. Sensitive to the dangers of Jewish immigrants on the rampage, it issued sharp warnings to both the wealthy and the clergy. 'Too prominent display on the part of the Jewish unemployed will necessarily give volume to the antagonistic voices' (i.e. anti-alienism as a subterfuge for anti-Semitism) and 'many, far too many, wealthy persons fail utterly to appreciate their duty to the poor'. It took the clergy to task, inferring that the poor associated atheism with the struggle for bread. 'Why should the working classes be allowed to regard irreligion as the necessary qualification for leadership in labour and social questions?' To counteract this,

40. *Jewish Chronicle*, reports dated 19 and 26 January, 1894.
41. Ibid., reports dated 26 January and 2 February, 1894.
42. *Evening News*, 24 January, 1894.

the clergy 'must be willing to make many personal sacrifices to render it clear that they have no want of sympathy with the trials of the working classes'.

The *Jewish Chronicle* need not have been over-perturbed. It would remain an uneven struggle with the cards stacked on the side of established authority. During the decade 1891-1901 an additional influx of almost 50,000 East European Jews[43] kept the immigrant at the mercy of an overcrowded labour market and helped reinforce the defence of religious orthodoxy against the onslaughts of the radical atheists. On the other hand, the core of radicalism survived to operate a second take-off at the close of the century, thanks to the dogged persistence of the Anarchist group. Paradoxically they were sustained by their own separatist flavour, while the Social-Democratic factions veered towards the policy of Jewish absorption into the host working class, the ultimate surrender of the Jewish identity which few immigrants were prepared to accept. The *Freie Welt* reasoned[44] that the end aim of Social-Democratic propaganda was:

(a) Through lectures, addresses and writings to educate the Jewish working masses and to bring them as far as possible to the spiritual level of the advanced working classes in the lands in which they live.

(b) To organise the Jewish workers and to make them capable, as fellow class members of the native working classes, of taking part in the class struggle of the land in which they live.

Many immigrants would read into such implication of their inferiority, which could only be improved by integration, a call to Jewish self-immolation. This could account for the ephemerality of the *Freie Welt*'s self-proclaimed successor in 1892 — the *Vekker* (Awakener) — which lasted less than a year. Its appeal ('Discard your Asiatic customs . . . Cast away your wild tongue and learn the language of the land in which you live . . . better yet, where possible enter English

---

43. From census return of aliens in 1891 and 1901; e.g. total no. of aliens under categories Russian, Russian Poles and Rumanians in 1891 was 198,113; in 1901 it was 247,758. These were almost all Jews. One can exclude estimates of Christian Poles: 3,500 in 1891, 3,200 in 1901.

44. Published in *Freie Welt*, II.5, November, 1892.

unions!')[45] would hardly endear it to the Jewish workers
currently exposed to calumnies flavoured with the same
sentiments emanating from both anti-alienists and trade
union officials. By 1894, 'as Jewish Socialism (i.e. Social-
Democracy) petered out in London, and progressed in
America, its leaders followed the movement.'[46] Kranz had
departed in 1890, Feigenbaum in 1891, whilst Baranov
followed later sometime in 1893 or 1894. Gallop had
succumbed to consumption in 1892. The veteran Winchevsky
finally quit for New York in 1894 after the failure of the
Vekker, where he assumed leadership of the anti-de Leon
movement and participated in the foundation of the famous
Forwärts in 1897. The pattern was now set. Emigration to
the USA would continue to deprive London of a Jewish
Socialist élite who had served their political apprenticeships
in the Whitechapel ghetto.

Thanks to Yanovsky's firm leadership, the *Arbeter Fraint*
caucus retained its strength and coherence in the face of less
favourable conditions. With the indefatigable Wess at his side,
he extended his operations outside London, stomping the
country, sharing platforms at times with Louise Michel and
leading British anarchists,[47] but always keeping a tight brief
on the *Arbeter Fraint*, which was rarely without an article
written in his distinctive style. He adopted the role of
watchdog, sniffing out corruption or double-dealing by
trade-union officials or rival radicals. Through a letter from
L. Glassman to the *Arbeter Fraint* (11 December, 1891), he
helped expose the Moishe Rosenberg scandal. Rosenberg,

45. See B.Ruderman, 'The Jewish Socialist Movement in England', in *Freie Arbeter Shtimme*, 25 September, 1925.
46. Gartner, *The Jewish Immigrant in England (1870-1914)*, p.135.
47. See *Commonweal* (April 1891) — Yanovsky spoke at the South Place Institute, 18 March at a meeting commemorating the twentieth anniversary of the Commune; (May 1891), he shared a platform in the Mile End Waste with Mowbray, Mainwaring, etc. at a mass meeting surrounded by a 'guard of honour' of twenty-five mounted police and dozens of foot constables; (20 June, 1891), at Hyde Park, 14 June, he spoke on the foreign problem. Editorial commented 'I am sure what he said will not be forgotten if ever an attempt is made to fan into flame any anti-foreign feeling'. The same month Yanovsky was booked to speak at an open air meeting at Norwich.
On 11 November he joined Kropotkin, Louise Michel, Malatesta and Wess on the platform at a Chicago Martyrs memorial meeting at the South Place Institute.

secretary of the East London branch of the Bootmakers'
Union, was suspected of having pocketed fifty-five pounds of
branch funds. The editorial claimed that, having checked the
last balance sheet, they supported the accusation. As a result,
Yanovsky said, 'I was threatened . . . that I would be done in
in some dark alleyway'. Undeterred, he appeared at the branch
meeting and, notwithstanding the efforts of the secretary and
his acolytes to prevent him from speaking, he publicly
repeated the charge. This time he was lucky. He managed to
depart safe and sound. A few months later he paid dearly for
pursuing what he regarded his acts of duty. On Wednesday 15
October, 1892, at nine p.m., while returning from a final
check on the current issue of his paper, he was attacked from
behind, and felled to the ground with an iron bar. He was
discovered bleeding and unconscious and carried to the
London Hospital, where doctors confirmed that wearing his
thick cloth cap had saved his life. Yet, even while confined to
bed for a week, he continued to work on the proofs of the
Arbeter Fraint so that publication would be on time.[48] In
the same issue he published a statement repudiating the
rumour that he was dead – a piece of wishful thinking not
only on the part of his enemies.

While he continued to remain at daggers drawn with the
Social Democrats, his relationships with his own group were,
at times, little better. He dominated the group and its organ
with an abrasive authoritarianism, such that Kropotkin was
called in on at least one occasion to caution him. It meant
that however devoted he was to the paper, as long as he
remained editor public relations and therefore sales would
decline. The advent of the Walsall Trials (April, 1892)
paralleled that of the infamous propagandist-by-the-deed
Ravachol in Paris.[49] Thanks to the press, public indignation
was aroused to full pitch against continental terrorists, and
the London police were moved to take a more serious view of

48. See Gordin, *S. Yanovsky*, p.172. A less accurate version of the assault is
given by Rocker, *The London Years*, p.130.
49. François-Claudius Ravachol was an extreme exponent of terrorism and
initiated a series of brutal murders in France in 1892 in aid of his own 'personal
needs' and that of 'the Anarchist cause'. He was executed on 11 July, 1892.
Posthumously his name produced the verb *ravacholiser* – 'to blow up'.

alien politicals. One of those accused in the Walsall affair was the English Anarchist Mowbray, whose wife had died four hours before his arrest. The generosity, but characteristic lack of foresight, of Yanovsky and his group, is shown by the advance publicity that 'the members of the International Working Men's Club, 40 Berner Street, Commercial Road have decided to take in hand the funeral and to look after his family' and that the 'funeral will take place on Saturday from the Berner Street Club at 3.30'.[50] Reporting on 'Mrs Mowbray's Funeral' one week later, *Commonweal* estimated that since 1887 'no such sight has been in East London as that which was witnessed last Saturday afternoon. Long before the time named for the procession to start large crowds of people lined Commercial Road and literally packed Berner Street from end to end.' Such action would endear the Berner Streeters even less in the eyes of the law and John Laws in the *Pall Mall Gazette* made full play on this gesture of alien impertinence. On 23 July a public meeting was called to debate the subject 'Ravachol or Carnegie' (the latter had recently contributed a £1000 gift to found the Aberdeen Library) in which 'a most enthusiastic audience ... cheered any allusion to Ravachol's struggles against society'! Such public postures boded ill for the future of both the club and the *Arbeter Fraint*.

Both were clearly on the downward descent. In August the *Arbeter Fraint* was appealing for support for a concert and ball to be held in the club on the 28 August 'in aid of the fund for the enlargement of the *Arbeter Fraint*'.[51] Enlargement? On 28 August *Commonweal*, another casualty on the way and finally ensconced at Berner Street, presaged the fate of both. 'Unless more funds are forthcoming we shall not be able to publish next week. Donations to the Printing Fund should be forwarded to *Commonweal* office, 40 Berner St ...' The last issue in the British Museum bears the note 'suspended for a time — message brought by bearer of this copy 6.9.1892'. The *Arbeter Fraint* had already suffered a break in publication (22 January to 8 April), re-emerging

50. *Commonweal*, 23 April, 1892.
51. *Arbeter Fraint*, 26 August, 1892.

with a new sub-title 'Anarchist-Communist Organ' to face the
prospect of crisis after crisis. The August tea-party, with
platform support from Louise Michel and Mowbray, proved a
notable success and a short term respite from unending
financial difficulties. An unexpected blow fell from another
quarter in November 1892. On the 18th the editor gave sudden
warning of a special general purposes meeting to be held that
same evening, in which all members were instructed to attend
to discuss the urgent question of alternative premises. On the
25th, under the bold headlines 'MOVED! MOVED!', came the
notice declaring the end of the Berner Street Club. ('This week
has the *Arbeter Fraint* and the press moved from 40 Berner
Street to 77 Aldgate Avenue, Block 12, Aldgate, E.C.') It was
followed by the explanation:

> The truth is that we had no idea about moving, until a County
> Council Inspector warned us that the club was very old, that it was
> too dangerous to stay here any longer, and that we must expect a
> notice to quit any day. Rather than wait for that notice we thought
> it better to get out and are now seeking a new club.

It needed no wide stretch of the imagination to suspect that
police and Jewish anti-Anarchist pressure, together with the
paper's critical lack of funds, were as much behind the move
as the dictates of an official from the local authority.

Henceforth the ex-denizens of Berner Street constituted
themselves a section of the London International Working
Men's Association with the Aldgate address as their venue.
Future business meetings of the *Arbeter Fraint* were to be
held in the Sugar Loaf public house in Hanbury Street, in a
large hall behind the bar, where it was hazardous to get
through to their meeting while 'there were always several
drunks there, men and women who used foul language and
became abusive when they saw a foreigner'. Thanks again to
Yanovsky, the troop held fast. There might no longer be a
fixed headquarters, but the battle for the minds of the
immigrant workers continued to be fought in print and in the
streets. In their intellectual expeditions into common
areas with the Social-Democrats, the Anarchists led the field.
The quality of their anti-religious criticism had reached a far
more sophisticated standard in that it was 'grounded in

positivism, Darwinian thought, and contemporary research in comparative religion and folklore'.[52] Its effect, however, was unrewarding. It proved a counter-productive weapon, yet Yanovsky persisted in following through his rabid anti-clericalism to the end. He emphasised his attacks on the twin bastions of Jewish traditional worship — Rosh Hashana and Yom Kippur. Of these he wrote:

> It is not the Supreme God who determines the kind of year you should have. It is a different God, an earthly one and his name is Mammon . . . He writes down that before the year is over . . . there will be widows and orphans swollen with hunger, cast out, barefoot and naked into the cold, dark streets . . . that hundreds will endure living suffocation in their black holes . . . As long as he (the God Mammon) exists he will be almighty. One must be rid of him completely . . . This is the one wish, the one hope of the anarchists . . . The time is not far off, when no one will have another write down how he should live, when he alone, a man with will and understanding, will underwrite his own destiny.
>
> All Jews who are honest and can still think for themselves will avoid the synagogue like the plague. Instead of going there they will worship *Kol Nidre* in the Berner Street Club where the reader will be S. Yanovsky at eight o'clock in the evening.

The worst criticism was levelled against the Yom Kippur ritual in the synagogue, which he regarded as a prime example of the sanctioning of class distinction: 'the rich overdressed and overfed in seats set aside for the *sheine leit*', while the poor 'pressed together by the door, hungry and ill-clad with no prospects of a sumptious fast-breaking meal to return to'.[53] Yom Kippur balls were already an annual feature of Anarchist activity,[54] but it proved bad tactics in trying to woo the immigrant to their cause. Religion was ingrained in the cultural experience of the *stetl*, and an inalienable part of his identity as a Jew. Lenin would point the moral which lay in expediency: 'The unity of that genuine revolutionary struggle of the oppressed class to set

52. Gartner, *The Jewish Immigrant in England (1870-1914)*, p.136.
53. Quoted in Gordin, *S. Yanovsky*, pp.216-22 and *Arbeter Fraint*, nos 32 and 33, 1893.
54. For descriptions of these 'blasphemous' meetings see Eyges, *Beyond the Horizon*, pp.76-8; article 'The Day of Atonement and Freethinkers' in the *Westminster Gazette*, 11 October, 1894 and below, pp.259-61.

up a heaven on earth is more important to us than a unity in proletarian opinion about the imaginary paradise in the sky.' Yanovsky would never learn, but outside this area he remained a master of agitprop. He was a convincing orator and a superb organiser of demonstrations, at the end of which he invariably shared the platform with the movement's international greats. On Friday 17 March 1893, he spoke with Louise Michel and Peter Kropotkin at the South Place Institute to commemorate the anniversary of the Commune. The third international May Day pending, he was resolved that Jewish workers would march for the first time as a separate contingent. In the *Arbeter Fraint* (22 April, 1893) he issued a 'Manifesto of 1st May to all Jewish Workers', declaring the day 'the holiest and dearest for the workers of the world' and enjoining the Jews to set an example as a vanguard of revolutionism and to confirm that role on May Day. The call succeeded. He feared that, at the most, 150 would sacrifice one day's work to join the march. Instead, 'over 800 marched through the streets of the Jewish quarter on to Hyde Park . . . And we must declare that, for the first time, the anarchists achieved a rich and enthusiastic success.' Throughout 1894 he continued to be involved in most major 'happenings' in the London scene. On 19 March he again represented the Jewish workers on the platform at the annual celebration of the Commune held at the Club and Institute Union, Clerkenwell Road. In April *Freedom* reported: 'Mowbray and Yanovsky have been very busy lately in attending scores of meetings in the East End, both Trade Union and unemployed, at which they have done a remarkable amount of good.' Later, aided by his loyal *genosse* Wess, who here played the more active role, he participated in the formation of a Jewish Co-operative Bakery at Brushfield St, Spitalfields and in the extension of premises and functions for the so-called headquarters of the International Tailors, Machinists and Pressers' Union (30 September, 1894).[55]

55. For a full report on the formation of the Co-operative Bakery, see article on Bakers' Co-operative in the *Westminster Gazette*, 18 September, 1894, and for its activities, the *Jewish World*, 5 October, 1894. The latter also commented briefly on the opening ceremony of the headquarters of the International Tailors,

WILLIAM MORRIS.

13. William Morris, a frequent orator at the Berner Street club.

14. Rudolf Rocker during the London years.

15. Rocker and the 'gentle' anarchists. Rocker is in the middle, the young Sam Dreen at the right end of the back row.

But internal and external pressures were forcing him to reappraise his future both in London and in England. Pernicious attacks levelled against him within the group reached a climax, due partly to his persistent inflexibility, and partly to a conflict of views over the rationale of 'propaganda by the deed'. Yanovsky attacked terrorism as a danger to the movement, both in the *Arbeter Fraint* and at open meetings, against its supporters – the younger activists. The result was a split in the ranks which led to his withdrawal from the editorship. Other events accelerated his departure. The Federation of Synagogues was strengthening its forces against him. In 1894, *vice* Dr Lerner, they elected a formidable opponent to radical atheism – the saintly and charismatic Yiddish preacher the Kamenitzer Maggid, Chaim Zundel Maccoby (1856-1914). A proponent of Choverei Zion, he countered the godless Socialists by fervent religious sermons from the pulpit of the Chevras after his arrival in January 1890. Zangwill eulogised him in a poem; Selig Brodetsky, as a youth, recalled that 'he moved the women and often the men to tears', while, at one of his addresses in the Great Synagogue, the *Jewish Chronicle* noted: 'So immense was the crowd that admission had to be refused to thousands of people. A force of twenty policemen was required to regulate the throng.' His self-imposed poverty and acts of kindness and concern for the poor enhanced his popularity against that of the Anarchists, who were not in a position to practise overt acts of charity. It was Montagu who grasped his potentiality as a counter force to the atheists, and successfully sponsored his appointment to the Federation. Other visiting *maggids*, such as Zvi Hirsch Maliansky (1856-1943), preached to receptive workers' audiences. For Anarchists to overcome such opposition proved the labour of Sisyphus. There is also evidence that Yanovsky was undergoing marital difficulties, which the gentle and tactful Wess, as mediator, helped to reconcile.[56] By the end of 1894 he felt tired and dispirited. An approach by old comrades in the

---

Machinists and Pressers' Union in the same issue. Wess's involvement in the Bakers' Co-operative is recorded in his diary 8-9 September, 1894.

56. Wess's role as mediator in a family quarrel can be detected from entries in his diary from 11 to 14 September, 1894.

States to take over the editorship of the *Freie Arbeter Stimme* (Free Workers' Voice) was timely. He accepted, and in January 1895 returned to New York, leaving behind a splintered, though still vital, group. Kaplan, who took over the editorship of the *Arbeter Fraint*, was a powerful street-corner orator, but lacked the literary qualities required to maintain the high standard set by his predecessors. The first long gap in publication took place between 27 July, 1894 and 19 April, 1895.

Meanwhile the *Arbeter Fraint* group, with no fixed abode, wandered from one meeting-place to another. In October 1894 their press was located at the top of a tumble-down building, 'half workshop, half warehouse', in a narrow by-way, Charlotte Street, at the Commercial Road end of New Road. Smaller off-shoots made their own rendezvous in *ad hoc* rooms in unsalubrious back alleys such as London Terrace (between Morgan and Umberstone Streets) and Greenfield Street, with common weekly meetings held first at the King's Head in Fieldgate Street (closed in 1894), then permanently at the Sugar Loaf in Hanbury Street.[57] 'It was an intellectual élite who met every week in this common public house.' So wrote Rudolf Rocker, who first made their acquaintance in 1895. His fortuitous arrival there would, in the long term, result in a movement which would project East London on the international scene, while contributing the most fascinating chapter in the story of Libertarian Socialism.

57. See Appendix 1, 'The Haunts of the East-End Anarchist', in the *Evening Standard*, Tuesday, 2 October, 1894. A colourful but mainly authentic description of the locale and 'rituals' of the *genosse* is given.

8. A Question of Survival

By the mid-1890s the quality of immigrant life became even harsher than that appraised in Winchevsky's *Poilishe Yidl* the decade before. Anti-alienism was being resuscitated in various forms. In the General Election of 1895, Joseph Chamberlain and his fellow Unionists led the Conservative Party to adopt alien restriction as part of its social policy, with Chamberlain himself as the most effective spokesman. He had the active support of Sir Charles Howard Vincent, then chairman of the National Union of Conservative Associations. Both demanded restriction, partly as an immediate palliative for current social ills, but mainly to accord with their protectionism. Pressure against entry continued spasmodically throughout the second half of the nineties from the promised Bill in the Queen's speech of 1896, to the General Election of 1900. That year the anti-alien trumpetings reached a crescendo, notably in the East End, where the strongest blasts were sounded by the Unionist candidate for St George's-in-the-East, Thomas Dewar, and the Conservative candidate for Stepney, Major W. Evans-Gordon.

With the end of the trade boom in 1892, urban discontent was reflected in a series of industrial stoppages and rising unemployment. It was fair opportunity for the restrictionists. Charles Williams, Secretary of the Central Unemployed Organisation Committee, actually appealed by letter (7 November, 1893) to the Chief Rabbi to use his influence to stop pauper immigration, and 'as head of the Jewish Faith to bring pressure upon the government to induce them to place restrictions upon this nefarious traffic'. In reply, Dr Adler assured his correspondent that he shared his fears, and that Anglo-Jewish leaders were responding accordingly by using 'every possible influence to prevent immigrants coming over here from Russia and Poland, by representing to the Jewish

authorities in those countries the overcrowded state of the
labour market here, and the great distress that prevails in
consequence'.[1] The TUC had already highlighted the issue by
a resolution condemning the landing of pauper aliens
(September, 1892), repeated in 1894 and 1895, with an
interim debate favouring prohibition in 1893. Although a
permanent trade recovery after 1895 stilled further TUC
protest at the national level, in the East End unionist
animosity towards the immigrant remained unchanged.

A major contributory cause of hostility was a chronic
housing shortage. Demolition of slums to make way for new
accommodation or railway termini at the centre stimulated
an exodus of both artisan and casual labour to peripheral
districts. Overcrowding was rife since a time lag invariably
persisted before rebuilding could meet the demands for
alternative homes for the poor.

> But in certain of these districts, notably in those where housing was
> being sacrificed to the extension of workshops and small factories
> like parts of St Luke's Shoreditch, and Whitechapel, overcrowding
> was doubly intensified, since new centres of employment attracted
> additional labour into the area to compete for a diminishing amount
> of house room.[2]

There lay the rub. The greater the influx of immigrants, the
greater the propensity towards overcrowding with its concomitant aberrations. Between 1880 and 1900 the highest
percentage increase in rents in London is recorded in Stepney
(33%), and to this must be added the local afflictions of
premiums and key money. Within this area the most
extensive demolitions took place between 1891 and 1901,
when homes decreased from 7,277 to 5,735 during those
years of the maximum inflow of aliens. While the population
of Whitechapel increased slowly from 75,552 in 1871 to
78,768 in 1901, the proportion of foreigners rose dramatically in the ghetto area, such that overcrowding remained

1. See *The Times*, 13 November, 1893.
2. An excellent account and analysis of the social results of housing policy in
London concerning the labouring and casual poor is given in Gareth Stedman-
Jones, *Outcast London*, Oxford, 1971, part IV, pp.159-235.

endemic.[3] It was this factor that, according to some,[4] accounted for the enormous divergence of rent rises between the East End and the rest of inner London; and it would endear the immigrant even less to the local labouring poor, unwilling or unable to move out, or to those recently enrolled in the growing army of casuals. Internally, according to Winchevsky, in retrospect, 'the tragic social-democratic/anarchist civil war wreaked havoc in the unions, the only area in which we could have achieved anything of significance among the Jewish workers'.[5] Anti-immigrant tirades by the trade union leaders confirmed the bankruptcy of the anti-'Jewish separatist' view. Palliatives might not accord with Anarchist principles, but for practical everyday living, they needed to be fought for.[6] It was against this background that the Anarchist survivors struggled to maintain their operations.

Thus it was for the *Arbeter Fraint*. It was almost a weekly fight to exist, and its revival under the editorship of I. Kaplan proved unpromising. He was replaced on 11 October, 1895 by the old stalwart W. Wess, who personally undertook all aspects of production in his own little flat at 42 Cressy Houses, Redmans Road. He kept the paper afloat. It publicised the weekly meetings of the group, now permanently ensconced in the Sugar Loaf every Sunday. The first advertised lecture by the young German *genosse* Rudolf Rocker at the pub appears for 8 November, 1895: the subject, 'The significance of Karl Marx and Lassalle in the Worker's Movement'. His success was evidenced by a second invitation to complete the theme on 29 November, and yet a third on the following 3 January to analyse the current debates between Anarchists and Social Democrats. However small the group, its self-sacrificial dedication and dynamism was infectious. It caught the imagination of a new, younger coterie of 'greeners' from both sexes. On 10 January, L. Baron

3. Board of Trade, *British and Foreign Trade and Industrial Conditions*, PP 1905, p.39.
4. See Stedman-Jones, *Outcast London*, pp.325-6.
5. M. Winchevsky, *Gesamelte Verk*, p.307.
6. Argued in retrospect by B. Ruderman in one of his series of articles on 'The Jewish Socialist movement in England', in *Freie Arbeter Stimme*, 10 July, 1925.

joined Wess as co-editor. On 7 February, the paper was sponsoring support for a lecture by Kropotkin at the large Working Lads' Institute, 137 Whitechapel Road, and on 28th a public meeting for Jewish and Gentile workers at the Imperial Hall, Redmans Road, to debate the question 'Why should the Anarchists oppose the forthcoming International Congress?' with Kaplan and Wess as the main speakers. A weekly drive for funds was sustained by the labour of a group of young enthusiasts. In the 17 April (1896) issue we note among the list of collectors, the names of Millie Witkop, L. Sabelinsky and Fanny Weinberg. Three weeks later (8 May) the overburdened Wess obtained timely relief with the acceptance of joint editorship by a newcomer to the group — Abraham Frumkin.

The Jewish Libertarian movement was never short of selfless devotees, and perhaps the most attractive and dedicated of them all was Frumkin. He was born in Jerusalem in 1872, where his father was a communal leader, an eminent Hebraist, and publisher of the weekly journal *Havezeleth*. After an early career in journalism he spent a year (1891) in Jaffa teaching Arabic at the Belkind School, and thence, with the promise of a stipend, went off to study law at Constantinople. Finding that there was no money forthcoming, he took off to the *goldene medina* — the USA — arriving there in 1893. It was in New York among the Jewish *chaverim* that he was first exposed, then won over, to the Anarchist ideology. With proselytising zeal he returned the following year to Constantinople to make converts, and convinced the generous bourgeois couple Moses and Nastia Shapiro. Thenceforth their home became a rendezvous, discussion centre and temporary shelter for young revolutionists. In turn Shapiro introduced Frumkin to the *Arbeter Fraint*; for Shapiro embarked on a study mission to Western Europe in 1895, came to London, met Wess and began sending back copies of the paper to the Constantinople group. The result was that Frumkin offered himself as a contributor, forwarding articles and reports to Wess. They proved a boon to the hard-pressed editor, who had till then, been forced to write most of the weekly material himself.

In April 1896 Frumkin came to London and went straight

to Wess, whom he found 'pale with sunken cheeks, strained forehead, sleepless and worn out'. According to Frumkin, Wess regarded his coming as a godsend since

> he had to write up the notices, but also had to set up the front page and finalise the issue as he was without editor or typesetter.
> Poor man! He couldn't do everything. But he was forced to produce a theoretical article on the second page, complete the first with notices and news, make out the letter casts, and personally fill up any vacant space as well as reading and correcting manuscripts!

Wess introduced the newcomer to the two major centres of Anarchist activity, which the chronicler records:[7]

> We came to Romford Street, a small dark street, where the composing room of the *Arbeter Fraint* was located in a great loft to which we had to climb through an opening. I left the typesetter [i.e. Wess] at his work. He was busy all day till late at night for he had to complete all sides himself, carry them to the printer, make up the packages for the post, then proceed to the Sugar Loaf to attend the weekly lecture, which he never missed.
> The Sugar Loaf was then the centre of the Jewish Anarchist movement in London ... The weekly meetings held on Friday nights bore an international character. Lectures were delivered not only in Yiddish, but also in English, German and Russian. Often would come the great critics of Marxism — W. Tcherkesov, the Englishman John Turner, and, from time to time, our own Rudolf Rocker, who then lodged with his fellow Germans in the West End, and could not realise the role he would play in the Jewish workers' movement. Most of the lectures were given by I. Kaplan, who could hold and rouse his audience. Others were delivered by W. Wess, H. Sachs, S. Freeman, I. Friedenthal and a couple of weak orators.

Frumkin conveys a picture of the group as a whole, as well as its individuals, with a sensitivity devoid of false sentiment. 'I have since worked with many groups in London, Paris and New York, but never did I find any other that laboured with such willingness and dedication.' They could barely scrape a living; yet not one would hesitate to sacrifice his last penny for the movement or its paper. Within the intellectual caucus there was a diversity of views, derived from individual

7. A. Frumkin, *The Springtime of Jewish Socialism*, New York, 1940 (in Yiddish), pp.65-6.

temperament and ideological interpretation. Discussions often became heated, particularly between such two self-acknowledged depositors of wisdom as the able dialectician Kaplan and emotional rebel Baron. Debate and argument was encouraged as a catalytic function, without, apparently affecting the harmony of the group. It was the new recruits who provided the muscle, if not the brains,

> younger comrades who never missed a meeting. They were Millie Witkop and her sister Polly; Sara Krein, who, the same year, became my loyal, devoted life's comrade ... Marie Grossberg (afterwards Mrs Sabelinsky), and Fanny Weinberg, who later married Anarchist Morris Jeger.[8] They remained silent in discussion but the most active in doing-organising, working or collecting funds for the *Arbeter Fraint.*

Through Frumkin's eyes, and pen, we are left with a moving sketch of those unsung heroes of any labour movement:

> the little cobbler Rubinstein, with twinkling black eyes, who used to come running straight from work to wait until the paper was ready, so that he could help to take it over to the various booksellers. He couldn't wait to take off, and should there be a hold-up by the printer, he would prance about as though he had lost his head ... Kerkelovich, who would never have the satisfaction of being able to read the *Arbeter Fraint*, for which he was ready to go through fire and water ... and Tapler, Kerkelovich's twin brother, who for years and years distributed the paper and performed the hardest physical labour ... I remember well the good-natured Kerkelovich running around in rain and fog, from meeting to meeting, to sell the *Arbeter Fraint.* He used to beg people to read him what was written in the paper ... the poorest of poor comrades who would give his last sixpence to the movement. It fills one's heart with warmth and love to recall such sacrifice.

Such was the legacy, in terms of human commitment, that Rocker inherited. The editor accepted the task of unremitting labour, with no guarantee of a weekly income. Wess had received twenty-two shillings a week, given there was sufficient money left in the kitty, that is, if any credit could

8. See below, p.239. Morris Jeger first offered Rocker the editorship of a Yiddish journal.

be extracted from the balance of sales and expenses. The week's printing began with a presumed capital input of twelve pounds. After the third week Frumkin found there were insufficient funds for the next production. Every Monday there was the loaded question, 'How can we obtain formes from the printers?' Without them, the following number would be forfeit. Printers never gave credit.

Shapiro, who had preceded his friend, collaborated with Frumkin in opening a separate printing press, where both the European classics and radical literature were translated (mainly by Frumkin) and published in Yiddish.[9] Here Frumkin worked three days a week, which enabled him to function as editor of the *Arbeter Fraint*. He made little change in the layout: the notice-book appeared on the front page, a theoretical treatise on the second, and, at the end, the 'Correspondence' containing news of workers' movements at home and abroad. Reproductions of French Anarchist features (especially those of Faure and Sorel) were predominant, since Frumkin thought little of such English Anarchist tracts as existed. The system of production remained fragmented. Frumkin assembled the incoming material at his home, to which articles were carried or sent by post. Proofs were finally corrected at the loft in Romford Street, which even lacked a table with the right dimensions. In spite of these appalling conditions, the *Arbeter Fraint* appeared weekly, on time.

Frumkin transmits to us a fascinating tableau of the recreational life of the immigrant *chaverim*, temporarily released from the sweat shops. He lodged with the Shapiros in Leyton, then a 'pleasant, airy neighbourhood with trees and fields'. Shapiro opened his home to the comrades every Sunday. After tea the whole company would walk to Epping Forest, singing revolutionary songs *en route,* and settle in some quiet glade to discuss some pertinent topic such as 'Should an Anarchist keep a bank book?'. Shapiro was horrified to learn that one of the group had a savings account. It was incomprehensible to him that an 'anarchist

---

9. The *Arbeter Fraint* press reproduced a number of these in its permanent premises at 163 Jubilee Street after 1906.

could accumulate savings whilst others were in need'. For Shapiro was another of those men of rare generosity of spirit that pervaded the *Arbeter Fraint* group. He had little money but was prone to produce his 'banquets' at the drop of a hat, that is brown herring, black bread and baked apples, especially for some less fortunate *chaverim* who might be visiting. Anyway, his total cash assets were always displayed on a sheet on the commode — at the disposal of anyone in need, be it friend or guest.

Frumkin recalls one Sunday in June of that year when Kropotkin, accompanied by his wife and daughter Sasha, joined the weekly guests at the Shapiros. They ate outside in the mild sunshine, and Shapiro, in the seventh heaven at having such a distinguished guest, begged the doyen's opinion on Anarchists holding a bank book. The reply to the question posed tells as much of the character of Kropotkin as it does of his questioner:[10]

> Kropotkin could not take the question seriously. Which Anarchist then had money in the bank? At that time, he was himself receiving an honorarium every three weeks for his contributions to the *Nineteenth Century*, but this would immediately be spent on bread, milk and meat. When the money was used up he lived on tick until the next emolument arrived. Sometimes there was not a shilling in the house, and he recounted the incident concerning Stepniak, who had come from Hammersmith to Bromley to visit him. Stepniak discovered that he needed half a crown for the return ticket but there was not a penny in the house and Mrs Kropotkin ran round and borrowed the money from neighbours.

The difficulties confronting Frumkin as editor were as overwhelming as those of his predecessor. On 3 July Wess opted out to participate in the English Anarchist movement, and there were no more articles from him. Those received from other regulars such as Kaplan, Sachs or Jeger needed to be revised or rewritten, since their literary capabilities were poor. Temporary relief arrived from new overseas contributors and helped fill space in the journal. One of these, Dr Ben Zion, wrote from Constantinople under the pseudonym 'the small man', in a style distinguished by its sharp, critical

10. Frumkin, *The Springtime of Jewish Socialism*, p.74.

erudition with an ironic wit in the Yiddish idiom. During his youth in Odessa, he got himself into debt by sponsoring unsuccessful plays for the Yiddish theatre. These were later purloined by American producers, who claimed them as their own, and profitably adapted them for Yiddish opera. For a short period he became a Christian, assumed the role of missionary, but promptly relinquished both when he saw the light at Frumkin's Libertarian circle in Constantinople. He lived in penury, but continued to compose and forward articles of a socio-political character for a series, 'Excerpts from the Story of Nature', which gained a high popular rating.

America provided a new crop of writers of whom the most gifted was M. Katz. Frumkin had previously collaborated with him in the joint editorship of the *Freie Gesellschaft*. His style effectively combined sophisticated elegance with a deep emotionalism. Others included the younger L. Robotnik and A.L. Wolfson, the latter contributing a number of revolutionary poems which would be widely recited on both sides of the Atlantic. Problems of Jewish life in the USA were presented by Robotnik and Albert Levine. It would appear that the *Arbeter Fraint* was recapturing the high standards it had achieved before the factional split in 1892.

Frumkin was found wanting on two counts: he was neither a business manager nor a platform orator. For short periods these defects were overcome with the help of Kaminetzky and Kaplan, who in turn shared the editorship with him. On 20 November, 1896, the paper informed its readers that it had moved to 1 Chance Street, an even dingier locale in Bethnal Green, to the home of D. Isakovitz. In the same issue, the editor made a rhetorical plea: 'What are you doing to haul the *Arbeter Fraint* up onto its feet? . . . The answer must be very little!' and the paper went out of circulation until the new year. On 1 January, 1897 it reappeared, limped on for a few months, and then finally ceased on 26 March.

But the movement went on. Thanks to Frumkin and the inner circle, the Libertarian identity was preserved. Individually, or in smaller groups, the 'comrades' proceeded to activate trade union consciousness within and without the immigrant unions. They provided the strongest militants in what had almost become an annual event — a tailors' strike in September, 1896. The Sugar Loaf meetings continued to flourish. Before its suspension the paper had advertised a lecture for Saturday evening, 23 January, at the Christ Church Hall, as the third great public meeting to be held, with Kaplan orating on 'What do the Anarchists want?' On 9 January, a concert and ball held in aid of the Bookmakers' Union revealed the existence of an *Arbeter Fraint* Singers' Union![11] Certain events, however, were creating a less favourable climate in which Anarchists could legally operate. After Ravachol a series of outrages directed police attention towards the local breed, particularly to those who were propagandising among the unemployed and casual labourers. In 1894 came the Polti and Ferana case, judged an Anarchist plot to blow up the Stock Exchange, and Bourdin's bungled attempt to destroy the Greenwich Observatory. The evidence was circumstantial. The worst outrage to date attributed to Anarchists occurred in April 1897, when an explosion in a London Underground train caused one death and a number of wounded.[12] The other Socialist groups were only too anxious to dissociate themselves from the Anarchists, as Frumkin noted, when at the 1896 International Socialist Congress, the majority voted to allow them to be present, but rejected their claim as *bona fide* delegates to participate in debate.[13] It would be difficult to convince the lay immigrant that a flirtation with the Anarchists did not constitute a threat to their newly won security. After all, rarely did those Anarchists, who privately rejected propaganda by the deed, publicly disavow it, since, in their rationale, it might be justified as the only means left to combat oppressive authority. Sporadic assaults, even riots (such as that in Cornwall Street)[14] brought home the recurrent danger of a *Judenheze* as more and more streets succumbed to alien

11. *Arbeter Fraint*, 8 January, 1897.

12. See *The Rise of Scotland Yard*, by ex-Detective Douglas E. Browne, pp.232-5, although much of what he records must be treated with caution. *The Times* (16 April, 1897) made its appropriate comments in an article, 'Anarchists in London'.

13. Frumkin, *The Springtime of Jewish Socialism*, pp.86-97. Chapter 'An Unforgettable Week'.

14. See B. Gainer, *The Alien Invasion*, London, 1972, pp.56-9.

overcrowding. By 1898, but for their militant incursions into strike action, the Anarchists and their ideology remained a pernicious irrelevance to immigrant aspirations as a whole.

It was not surprising, therefore, that the *Arbeter Fraint* was fighting a losing battle for survival. After the last crisis, Frumkin gave up. Shapiro had returned to Constantinople and left him his small press, on which he began to publish an alternative paper, the *Propagandist*, acting as writer, type-setter, and printer. It appeared irregularly: each issue dependent on sufficient income accruing to meet costs. After eleven numbers it ceased. Attempts to launch two new papers at Liverpool and Leeds proved equally abortive. Reduced to dire poverty, Frumkin departed for Paris in June 1898. There seemed little hope for the revival of the *Arbeter Fraint*. Wess, now permanently involved with the English 'Freedom' group, refused to undertake the burden a second time. Eighteen months later it reappeared under new management: a fortuitous act of salvation for both the paper and the Jewish labour movement. On 19 October 1898, the new *Arbeter Fraint* was reborn under the editorship of a German gentile — Rudolf Rocker.

Part Three
The Ascendancy of Rudolf Rocker

... an astonishing phenomenon in Jewish life, born a Roman Catholic, who for sixty years devoted his life to the Jewish working class and to Yiddish language and literature.

Solo Linder

9. An Anarchist Missionary to the Jews

'It is the unsuccessful revolutionaries who have been the chief victims of those historians who are only interested in success.'[1] Recent investigations suggest a change in direction: that the study of failure can often be as instructive and rewarding as the study of success. For how can one define failure — as a finality — in the historical process? Men and ideologies, hitherto rejected as making negligible contributions to a course of events, have been rehabilitated and subjected to more serious reappraisal. It may be that the radical *événements* of the 1960s, with all their diversity, have forced the issue: when the quaint prognostications of Kropotkin and Tolstoy are no longer quaint, or the activist stratagems of Bakunin or Blanqui seem to proffer a new vision and relevance. A more profitable application could be found for such 'smaller' fry than their recent discovery by Academia as subjects for PhD theses. In this context the work of Rocker, as teacher, philosopher and labour organiser of the immigrant poor in East London, would be demonstrably pertinent.

Rocker was born in Mainz (25 March, 1873), the son of a *notenstecher* (typographer). The city was the birthplace of Johan Gutenberg, who set up his first printing press there, and had already established a healthy tradition of resistance to oppression, while currently opposed to Prussian expansionism. Rocker recalls a popular folk-rhyme chanted in his youth:

> You are crazy, my child!
> To be off to Berlin
> Where the lunatics live.

1. James Joll, *The Anarchists*, London, 1964. Introduction.

But the Rhineland fell under the hegemony of Prussia in the 1870s and the Rockers were in the forefront of the opposition to an alien authoritarianism. Orphaned at the age of ten, Rudolf came under the temporary charge of his grandmother, and then entered an orphanage. He had already absorbed the free, inquiring spirit of his environment, which was reinforced by the influence of an uncle, Rudolf Nauman, a radical intellectual, who inculcated in the boy a love of learning. He responded to the harsh discipline of the Catholic orphanage by frequently absconding, and was spared a forcible transfer to a reform school by the timely arrival of a more liberal-minded administrator who, recognising that the young offender had creative talent, offered him the opportunity of being apprenticed to a bookbinder: a craft which notoriously attracted a race of wandering revolutionists.

Between the years 1886 and 1891, a bleak period, when, for the most part, the Socialists were forced underground, Rocker was inducted into a Social-Democratic group by his uncle. He accepted such doctrines of the party which underlined its international and revolutionary commitments, but was soon disillusioned with its bureaucratic intolerance of dissent. His wide-ranging interests, especially in the language and culture of other peoples, kept him free from the disease of chauvinism which was infecting many of the older rank and file. It was, therefore, not surprising, that after the SDP was restored to legality (June, 1890), he joined the young oppositionists (*Jüngen*) who were subsequently expelled from the party in October, 1891.

Meanwhile his European education was extended by his travels on foot as a *handwerksbursche* (journeyman) throughout Germany, Austria, Switzerland, Italy, France and Spain. It also reinforced his belief that individual freedom, in all its aspects, was the ultimate test of the good society. Hence he was drawn to the Libertarianism of Johann Most and became involved in the smuggling of clandestine propaganda into Germany. Rocker explains his motivation:

> The underground activity had a peculiar attraction for me as a young man and appealed strongly to my romantic imagination. It also early developed in me a profound aversion for the brutal suppression of ideas and personal convictions.

In 1893, the police caught on to his activities and he saved himself by a precipitate flight across the border. It was Rocker's entry into *goles* (exile) which would last for twenty-five years.

His first personal experience of Jews and Jewish radicals came in spring 1893, while strolling round the Parisian boulevards with a friend, Liederle, who asked him if he would like to attend a Jewish Anarchist meeting. *Jewish* Anarchists! Identification in religious terms seemed, to Rocker, a travesty of the meaning of Anarchism. He had scarcely known Jews in Mainz. Religious hatred, which did exist, was between Protestant and Catholic. In his youth some local anti-Semitism had been sparked off by the writings in the town paper of a fanatical Protestant pastor, Linker, although there was a wider movement in Hesse, where the Jews had been forced into their traditional role of middlemen, notably in the sale of livestock. They had become the subject of hatred by poor peasants, who regarded them as an instrument of exploitation. This was brought home forcibly to Rocker while he was engaged in propagandising his *Jungen* brand of Socialism in country villages. He was driven off with sticks and stones. Reactionary priests had already put over the more convincing accusation that the Socialists were the servants of the Jews. A popular anti-Semitic ditty underlined the message:[2]

> Those who would all things destroy
> Into the Jewish trap must fall.
> Yes! Even the Socialist dreamers
> Are led by a Marx and Lassalle.

That Sunday, in a hired room on the first floor of a coffee house in the Boulevard Barbès, Rocker met, for the first time, a group of Jewish Anarchists. Scattered around tables, in small groups, he saw about fifty or sixty comrades of both sexes in lively discussion. A few were absorbed in reading journals printed in Hebrew, which he later recalled as the *Arbeter Fraint* and the *Freie Arbeter Stimme*. He noticed the absence of the Gentile caricature of the Jew. Some he would

2. Rudolf Rocker, *In Sturm*, London, 1952, pp.29-31.

have taken for Greeks or Italians, others, a minority, for Germans or Scandinavians, while the rest had the semi-Mongoloid features of the Slav. All spoke a German patois, which he followed with difficulty. What struck him forcibly was the active participation of women in large numbers, who, in accordance with Libertarian principles, operated as equals within the circle. He detected that although many adopted a Puritan mode, derived from their involvement in the Russian 'underground', this did not detract from their femininity. In every sense, relations between both sexes were free and without artifice.

> One could talk with these women, and forget that they were women. Yet they were no blue-stockings, nor were they the kind of feminists who aped mannishness. They were womanly, and motherly, but were conscious of their own equality, and of their human self-respect. It added to their charm.[3]

Modern Women's Lib could possibly have put it better.

The warmth and hospitality, the high-powered thrust in debate, appealed to Rocker. He returned often, and soon, on request, undertook to lecture to them in German. His audience provided him with the opportunity of testing his powers as a teacher. There was no doubting his success. He responded emotionally to these 'pariahs' who provided him with his first home. It was a case of mutual aid. Rocker insisted that he was the more fortunate recipient. 'A new world was opened up to me.' By their example they invalidated the myth that Jews were either bourgeois or parasites. Even those who had enjoyed the luxury of a profession back in Russia had chosen to learn and practise a trade in Paris. Thus they constituted a homogeneous working-class group.

For Rocker, all this was sound preparation for the London years. It was their diversity of character that fascinated him. His first friends were the Silbermans, who, in a small room in the Boulevard Menilmontant, ran a tailoring workship, without 'hands', on the principle of not employing others for profit. The couple had wandered round the world, taking in

---

3. Rocker, *The London Years*, p.61.

Palestine, Egypt, Turkey, Italy, and a short spell in the USA on the way, yet still retaining a natural innocence, being honest and generous to a fault. A contrasting pair were the Rodinsons who, at home, had been fellow students of Chaim Jitlovsky, and would later re-associate themselves with him in the Jewish nationalist movement. In Paris, Rodinson worked as a raincoat maker without neglecting his intellectual interests. His small flat in the Rue Sorbonne was a meeting-place for Russian *émigrés*:

> Every Sunday afternoon, ten to a dozen comrades would gather there — not all Jews. The walls were adorned with pictures of Russian revolutionaries, dominated by a large portrait of Bakunin. A circle of men and women were seated round a large broken table, on which a huge samovar smoked and bubbled. The Russians were strong tea drinkers, consuming up to a dozen glasses through pieces of sugar first placed in the mouth, which gave them relief as the sweat ran from their foreheads.'[4]

Rocker remained drawn to this novel milieu and, to the end, paid tribute to his early Russo-Jewish mentors. One of these, named Gordon, who, for harbouring illegal literature, had spent five years in a *katarg* near Irkutsk, spoke without emotion of the horrors endured in Siberia, exteriorising a cool detachment in adversity which Rocker would attribute to most Russian revolutionaries. He noted, too, that in spite of ideological differences and fierce arguments in debate, this did not in the least affect personal relationships. 'There was more tolerance here than I had ever found in Germany!'

For Rocker, one of the most gifted and attractive of his new comrades was Solomon Rappaport, who under the pseudonym 'Sh.An-ski' later made his debut in both Russian and Yiddish literature.[5] He leaves us with a deft sketch ('This tall, lean man with the pinched features and sad, dreamy eyes, sat quietly during discussions, silently watching but absorbing everything'), and recounts the circumstances which drew them together. On learning that Rocker was also a bookbinder and lacked adequate tools or workshop facilities,

4. Rocker, *In Sturm*, pp.36-7.
5. His play, *The Dybbuk*, has since been translated into many languages and acted in many countries around the world.

Rappaport invited him to move in. He lived in a cramped attic in the Rue St Jacques, which served as both living-room and work-place. Rocker found An-ski's tools no improvement on his own, and his partner an indifferent craftsman, having picked up his trade perfunctorily in between his revolutionary escapades in Russia. In effect Rocker came to his aid, and brought and shared his own work daily for three months, until a full-time job forced him to part company. Yet, in that short time, Rocker believed that he had found a comrade, endowed with those edifying qualities, which, for him, constituted the 'true' social revolutionary. Rappaport was not only living in utter privation, but seemed indifferent to material needs. He often subsisted on dry bread and tea, but never let on. Normally a shy, retiring man, he opened up to Rocker at the joint work-bench, recalling his involvement with the Narodniki and his personal effort to politicise Russian workers and peasants. He was convinced that the revolutionary potential of the peasantry would one day produce an upheaval whose consequences would surpass those of the French Revolution.

Rocker's first contact with London was derived from another quarter. In February, 1893, he had been invited by the West End 'Autonomie' group to discuss the prospects of smuggling their literature over the Belgian-German border. A previous plan had proved abortive, and the German section had chosen him to take charge of renewed operations. It proved a damp squib — but it gave Rocker his first feel of London which he adversely contrasted with Paris. But increased anti-Anarchist pressures in France forced him to reconsider his stay there. On New Year's Day 1895, he paid a second visit to London, ostensibly to establish his position with the German consulate as to the possibility of his return to Germany. He was brusquely ordered to go back and undergo compulsory medical examination, which any other German domiciled abroad could arrange locally. Rocker got the message. It meant continued exile or return to imprisonment. He was not overjoyed at the prospect of staying in London, but his election to Librarian of the famous First Section of the Communist Workers' Educational Union (Marx, Engels and William Liebknecht had been members) in

Grafton Street offered bread and an absorbing job. It was there that he met, for the first time, the two legendary figures who would have a profound influence on him: Louise Michel and Errico Malatesta.

A reluctant sojourner in London, he was resolved to adjust himself accordingly. He had gleaned some information about the *Arbeter Fraint* group from his Paris comrades, which was reinforced by a chance conversation with Yanovsky, with whom he had shared a platform at a Yom Kippur meeting. After his readings on 'Darkest London', particularly those of the anarchist John Henry Mackay,[6] he was moved to explore the East End and acquaint himself with the Jewish movement there. With a fellow *émigré*, Otto Schreiber, who had lived in London for years, he went on a series of expeditions on Saturday afternoons, into Tower Hamlets. It was a traumatic experience; but it helped shape his conviction that 'worse conditions mean better' (prospects for revolution) was a dangerous illusion.

> My wanderings through the distressed parts of London shook this early faith of mine, and finally destroyed it. There is a pitch of material and spiritual degradation from which a man can no longer rise. Those who have been born into misery and have never known a better state are rarely able to resist and revolt.
>
> There were at that time thousands of people in London who had never slept in a bed, who just crept into some filthy hole where the police would not disturb them. I saw with my own eyes thousands of human beings who could hardly be still considered such, people who were no longer capable of any kind of work. They went about in foul rags, through which their skin showed, dirty and lousy, never free from hunger, starving, scavenging their food out of dustbins and the refuse heaps that were left behind after the markets closed.
>
> There were squalid courts and alley-ways, with dreary tumble-down hovels, whose stark despair it is impossible to describe. And in these cesspools of poverty children were born and people lived, struggling all their lives with poverty and pain, shunned like lepers by all 'decent' members of society.
>
> Could anything spiritual grow on these dung-heaps? These were the dregs of a society whose champions still claimed that man was made in God's image, but who evaded meeting that image face to face in the slums of London.[7]

6. Author of *The Anarchists*, Boston, 1891. He gives an excellent description of contemporary Whitechapel and the Berner Street Club in 1887.

7. *The London Years*, pp.79-80.

What appalled him was the lack of sympathy for the indigent poor which he found in the most surprising quarters. He recalls the reply of Ben Tillett, to whom he posed the question of their rehabilitation. The dockers' leader considered them beyond the pale, a permanent threat to 'honest' labour. 'In times of revolution, he said, it was from these quagmires of degeneration that the hyenas of the revolution emerged. A Socialist government would therefore have to think of ways and means to get rid of this scum; false pity for them would harm the Socialist cause.'[8]

Returning from a tour of Poplar along the Commercial Road, Rocker bumped into L. Baron, whom he had already met at Grafton Hall. The latter took him home, where he was introduced to the local Jewish circle. In turn they invited him to join their meeting at the Sugar Loaf the following Friday. The visits were repeated, and soon he was asked to lecture to the group. He contrasted the audience with their counterparts in Paris, who, by comparison, were affluent. 'The Londoners looked sad and worn . . . half-starved. They sat crowded together on hard benches and the badly lit room made them seem paler than they really were.' They followed with rapt attention the fair, burly young German, who exuded warmth and generosity. His courteous and painstaking delivery, whether in explaining a theme, arguing his case, or answering questions, added a touch of civilised grace to the proceedings. At times he would, unconsciously, elevate his lecture to a stage act as though to accommodate an audience nurtured on rabbinical performances on the crude altars of the *stiebel*. It was not long before his charisma attracted a growing number of young enthusiasts. At last the radicals had acquired a personality who, as a popular spell-binder, would compete on equal terms with the 'imported' *maggidim*.

His involvement in the Jewish movement necessitated a

8. Ben Tillett's views are symptomatic of the fears of the local permanently or semi-permanently employed for the casual poor, which Stedman-Jones derives from 'a distinctive and self-conscious political tradition on one hand, a traditionalism punctuated by brute expressions of hunger and desperation on the other. In such a world, it was scarcely surprising that in the *grande peur* which followed the riots of 1886, homes were barricaded against the poor not only by capitalist London but also by its skilled working class.' (See Stedman-Jones, *Outcast London*, 'Socialism and the Casual Poor', pp.337-49.)

move to the East End. He found lodgings at the house of a comrade Aaron Atkin, who kept a small shop in Shoreditch. The shop parlour was used as a discussion centre by the local circle, among whom was Millie Witkop, an attractive young immigrant from Zlatopol in the Ukraine. Rocker first noticed her selling the *Arbeter Fraint* and collecting funds at Grafton Hall. 'She was [then] eighteen or nineteen, a slim young girl, simple and unaffected, with thick black hair and deep, large eyes, earnest and . . . zealous for our cause.' She had arrived in London alone in 1894, and was immediately forced into the netherworld of tailoring sweatshops, where by unrelenting labour and self-denial she saved sufficient money to bring over her parents and three sisters. The appalling conditions under which she lived and worked moved her to question her traditional faith. She viewed it as dead ritual, contributing nothing practical to the alleviation of want. A chance involvement in the bakers' dispute (September 1894) led her to an *Arbeter Fraint* meeting in the Sugar Loaf. 'Millie was one of those natures who cannot accept anything by halves.' Having lost the old religion, she embraced the new with almost fanatical zeal. It was a tremendous shock to her orthodox parents when they arrived from Russia; more so, when they learned that she had become intimately involved with an Anarchist 'goy'.

What the two did not bargain for was that, in choosing to live in 'sin', they would, for a brief spell, make top headlines in the US press. In December 1897, Rocker received a letter from a friend in New York advising him to come over, as job prospects were high, and offering to forward tickets for both. At first Rocker declined but, after losing his job with little hope of re-employment, decided to go. Millie agreed to accompany him. Registered as married in the passenger list of an old tub, the *Chester*, they sailed on 15 May, arriving in New York on 29th. Difficulties arose on Ellis Island, when they could not produce their marriage lines. They were hauled in front of a committee of officials to answer for their supposed negligence, and Rocker describes the dialogue which followed. In classic Libertarian terms they explained their rejection of 'legal' forms.[9]

9. Rocker, *The London Years*, p.103.

'We have no marriage certificate. Our bond is one of free agreement between my wife and myself. It is a purely private matter that concerns only ourselves, and it needs no confirmation from the law.'

The old lady looked straight at Millie, and said to her:

'But you can't as a woman agree with that. Don't you see the danger you are in? Your husband can leave you whenever he pleases, and you have no legal hold on him.'

'Do you suggest', Millie answered, 'that I would consider it dignified as a woman and a human being to want to keep a husband who doesn't want me, only by using the powers of the law? How can the law keep a man's love?'

'This is the first time I have heard a woman speak like that,' the old lady said reproachfully. 'If everyone ignored the law in respect of marriage, we should have free love.'

'Love is always free,' Millie answered. 'When love ceases to be free it is prostitution.'

By chance, a few journalists on hand became aware of the unusual happening, and next day the press turned up in force to interview the Rockers. The result was front-page coverage in both the local and national press — mostly in defence of the established Puritan ethic. The Yiddish Social-Democratic paper *Arbeter Zeitung* was almost a loner with its sympathetic heading 'Love without marriage or marriage without love?'. Officialdom was thrown into confusion. The case was unique. It could create a legal precedent unless quickly settled within normal procedure. The Commissioner-General of Immigration himself (T.V. Powderly, once President of the mighty trade-union organisation, The Knights of Labour!) intervened to break the impasse. He advised the Rockers to stop 'trying to break through a brick wall with your heads', and warned them of an ultimatum which came two days later: Get married legally or get out! The Rockers refused. They were immediately returned on board the *Chester*, and, as it steamed out of the Hudson, Rocker remarked, laconically, that the Statue of Liberty 'looked . . . as though she wore the dress of a nun'. When they arrived at Southampton they landed without incident. England, apparently, had heard nothing. But in America the affair was still causing a stir, as C.E. Walker in the Chicago *Lucifer* fanned the embers of debate with his polemics against the action of the immigration authorities.

Unemployment in London drove the returnees into the provinces, to Liverpool. An ex-Whitechapel comrade, Morris Jeger, who had established a small printing shop there, offered them both accommodation and persuaded Rocker, against his will, to become editor of a new Yiddish weekly called *Dos Freie Vort* (The Free Word). Rocker recalls that 'the offer hit me like a bolt from the blue. I objected that I could neither write nor read Yiddish. I had learned the Hebrew alphabet while I was in London. I could decipher the heavy type headings in the Yiddish papers, but that was all.' Little did he know then, that his reluctant decision would bind him irrevocably to the Jewish labour movement. Although the Liverpool sheet lasted for only eight issues,[10] it provided a fillip for the East End group to revive the *Arbeter Fraint*. The *Freie Vort* managed to pay its way, and this may have partly prompted Thomas Eyges, secretary of the *Arbeter Fraint* committee, to appeal to Rocker to return to London as editor of a resuscitated journal. Thus with a capital sum of barely twelve pounds, an unpredictable supply of good will (and dollars) from East side, New York, and the intervention of a flock of young Jewish zealots led by a German 'goy', the *Arbeter Fraint* was relaunched in its thirteenth year.

Frumkin had handed over to Rocker one asset — a caucus of enthusiasts. The circle of Jewish Anarchists in Tower Hamlets was far larger and, by definition, not organised into one particular group. Since the terms set by Lieberman they were almost, without exception, involved in trade-union activity. Their common focus was the Sugar Loaf. First dozens, later hundreds, converged on the outdoor meetings held by the *Arbeter Fraint*, as Rocker became the big draw. Volunteers undertook to spread the paper and pamphlets by selling at street corners and workshops. Its influence was extended by the policy of passing on copies after reading to non-buyers. Thus a whole workshop or household could share one copy weekly. It proved an efficient way of maximising propaganda while production was permanently

10. The first number of *Dos Freie Vort* appeared on 29 July, the last on 17 September, 1898.

limited by funds. Dependence on links with the USA where the only ideological equivalent in Yiddish was the monthly *Freie Gesellschaft*, proved rewarding, not only financially. Rocker assessed the long-term implications of the London movement, which went far beyond those envisaged by Lieberman.

> Most immigrants from Eastern Europe who came to Great Britain continued their journey sooner or later to America or to other countries overseas. They took with them to the United States, Canada, Argentine or South Africa the Socialist ideas they had first picked up in London. They formed groups in their new homes, and maintained contact with their original group in Britain, which remained the motherland of the movement. They imported the *Arbeter Fraint* and other literature, and when they could, sent us financial contributions. *London was the clearing house for the Jewish revolutionary labour movement.* The threads went out from London to all countries where there were large numbers of Jewish immigrants, and later even to their original homes in Russia and Poland, when the first anarchist underground groups began to form in Bialystock, Grodno, Vilna, Warsaw, Lodz and other places.

With natural humility he avoided reference to the contributory effects of his own voluntarism. The cards were stacked against him. 'I had all the material and other difficulties which had defeated my predecessors and, in addition, I had to devote myself to learning the Yiddish language.' He had first to come to terms with, and later adopt, a totally alien culture. While demands on him as a public speaker grew, the problem of attracting good writers to supplement his own weekly articles remained pressing. He had to impose a critical appreciation of their acceptability on the basis of a language he barely understood. Above all, he needed to educate the inner circle in the fundamentals of Libertarian ideology to equip them for their proselytising tasks, and win over a large peripheral body, who still posited Marxist doctrine at the weekly consortium in the Sugar Loaf.

It is through the voices of a diminishing breed of aged survivors, rather than the pages of *Arbeter Fraint* or *Germinal*, that we build up the mosaic of events which evolved around the prime character. The extraordinary rapport struck between Rocker and Jewish workers was ordained to last. The relationship sustained itself on a mutual feedback of ideas. Rocker delighted in the ferment of continuous, though tolerant, disagreement. He conceded that 'those talks over our various differences of opinion have remained among my most delightful memories of that early period of my work in the Jewish labour movement'. But this would depend on attracting and retaining those with high intellectual potential. There was never a dearth of these, according to Rocker.

> What amazed me was the thirst for knowledge among those ordinary working people who had received so little general education, yet had so much natural intelligence that they could easily grasp things about which they had been completely uninformed before. It made me happy to see with what zeal they pursued knowledge. I learned a great deal myself by accompanying them in their pursuit. I was inspired by them to discover new ideas, to think about things which, in a different environment less foreign to me, I would have taken for granted. I had to probe more deeply to think for myself.

The battle against 'historical materialism' was pursued through the pages of the *Arbeter Fraint*. During the first year of his editorship[11] he wrote twenty-five essays on the subject, presenting the Libertarian critique in a style and language intelligible to the ordinary worker. As far as is known, it was the first attempt to subject the Marxist interpretation to a critical examination in Yiddish.

The revived *Arbeter Fraint* maintained itself with difficulty as one financial crisis followed another. As editor, Rocker depended on the promise of a weekly salary of one pound. It was rarely kept. 'The amounts owing to me were entered in a book. When the total owing . . . became too large to consider ever paying so much, they put a pen through it and the debt was wiped out. It was a splendid way of keeping books . . .'[12] But it didn't pay the rent. Millie was highly skilled and less likely to be unemployed. It was her labour at the workbench, rather than Rudolf's odd jobs at bookbinding, that brought in the bread. The motivating force was the

11. 19 October, 1898 – 26 January, 1900.
12. Rocker, *The London Years*, p.138.

preservation of the paper and it called for continual self-sacrifice on the part of all members.

> Every penny these sweatshop workers gave us was something taken away from their own mouths. They denied themselves essentials; and they gave it willingly — gladly, ungrudgingly. If they didn't give more it was only because they hadn't more to give. They would have pawned their last few small possessions for us . . .

Equally important was the emergence of a core of good speakers, operating in both trade union and public meetings, of whom the most experienced was I. Kaplan.[13]

The paper's survival seemed assured when the blow fell from an unexpected quarter. Reluctantly the editorial had allowed advertisements from booksellers, photographers, shipping agents and the like, to acquire funds and meet overheads. An annual lump sum of fifty pounds had accumulated, and the comrade responsible for collecting it had spent it on personal debts. Once again the *Arbeter Fraint* was forced to suspend publication. Rocker made an immediate attempt to cover the loss by undertaking a lecture tour in Liverpool, Leeds and Manchester, but in vain. Neither was help forthcoming from the States, where the *Freie Arbeter Stimme* and the *Freie Gesellschaft* were emerging as competitive alternatives to the *Arbeter Fraint*. An offer to help, however, came from another source. In November 1899, Emma Goldman was in London, and Rocker met her for the first time at a meeting held at the South Place Institute, where she made a speech attacking national chauvinism to a hostile audience. (The Boer War had set off a wave of jingoism, not least among the workers.) She was

13. I. Kaplan was born in Sager, Lithuania. His early gift of oratory assured him the post of *maggid* at the local *stiebel*. On his arrival in England, he was employed in the same role by the Leeds Jewish community. Questioning his faith, he turned to the Leeds Anarchist group, who introduced him to the *Arbeter Fraint* and the *Freie Arbeter Stimme*. He learned English, and absorbed the current secularist literature which finally convinced him that his religion was no longer of any consequence. He entered a tailor's workshop as a machinist, and soon became a familiar and popular speaker in East London and after the 1890s. Rocker regarded him as an intellectual of the first rank (see *The London Years*, pp.139-41), perceiving that, had he had a systematic education, he would have proved an equally outstanding writer. Unfortunately his lack of a 'literary sense of words' and appreciation of aesthetics and literature denied him this.

intrigued with Rocker's involvement by choice in an exclusively Jewish environment, and when told of the *Arbeter Fraint*'s plight, volunteered to speak at three meetings to raise money: but the total funds collected barely covered the cost of hiring the halls and printing handbills. Another attempt was made to restart the paper, but, after ten issues, it was once more suspended (26 January, 1900).

Undaunted, the Rocker group were resolved to maintain some form of educative propaganda. The typesetting equipment had to be transferred to a ramshackle old shed in Stepney Green, adjoining some stables which exuded foul smells and were rarely free from 'swarms of flies and bluebottles'. In their hour of need the intercession of a new recruit – a young printer named Narodiczky – made continuity possible through the birth of the periodical *Germinal*. As an ex-rabbinical student with a taste for Hebrew literature, he embraced the Zionist cause and eschewed religion because of rabbinical opposition to Herzl. Rocker converted him to Libertarianism, which, for him, was not incompatible with nationalistic precepts. In return, Narodiczky claimed that he enhanced Rocker's knowledge of Yiddish through personal tuition. As for *Germinal*, it would provide a broader and deeper appreciation of Libertarianism in its application to contemporary literature and philosophy. It was to be a sixteen-page journal, published fortnightly and free of advertisements which might limit its scope. The first copy appeared on 16 March, 1900, advertised to replace the *Arbeter Fraint.*

Germinal presented the maturation of Rocker's ideology, by now Kropotkinist-oriented:

> I realised even then that all the ideas of mutualism, collectivism or communism were subordinate to the great idea of educating people to be free and to think and work freely. All the economic propositions for the future, which had still to be tested by practical experience, were designed to secure to man the result of his labour and to aim at a social transformation of life that would make it possible for the individual to develop his natural capacities unrestrained by hard and fast rules and dogmas. My innermost conviction was that Anarchism was not to be conceived as a definite closed system, nor as a future millennium, but only as a particular trend in the historic development towards freedom in all fields of human

thought and action, and that no strict and unalterable lines could, therefore, be laid down for it.

For Rocker, freedom in every area of activity could only survive and flourish under the auspices of flexibility and change. It was the ultimate deterrent against the atrophy of the human spirit resulting from the despotism of rigid ideas and immutable institutions.

> Freedom is never attained; it must always be striven for. Consequently its claims have no limit, and can neither be enclosed in a programme nor prescribed as a definite rule for the future. Each generation must face its own problems, which cannot be forestalled or provided for in advance. The worst tyranny is that of ideas which have been handed down to us, allowing no development in ourselves, and trying to steamroller everything to one flat universal level.[14]

Germinal survived its first three years (up to March 1903 when it was forced to suspend publication) under the most appalling conditions ('we were often without the barest necessities') thanks to the loyalty of Rocker's younger devotees. They continued to contribute both their meagre incomes and boundless energy to maintain it week by week. As a result, the London group was placed firmly on the map, with a range of readers extending to most of the larger cities of the USA and Paris, Berlin, Bucharest, Sofia, Cairo, Alexandria, Johannesburg, Cape Town, Buenos Aires, that is wherever there had been a recent settlement of Russo-Polish Jews. Tending to be more academic, even esoteric in parts, its propaganda value was more limited. Its initial appeal was to the *intelligent*, through whom it filtered down to the rank and file of each group. It was a source of cultural inspiration to individuals, who later branched off into non-political fields. One of these was the great actor Granach, who as a young immigrant baker in Germany was introduced to world literature through the pages of *Germinal*. He was 'discovered' reading prose at a meeting of Jewish anarchists in Berlin, recommended to join a drama school, and subsequently became one of the leading actors in the Weimar Republic. He

14. Rocker, *The London Years*, pp.144-5.

16. Dunstan Houses, the Yiddish anarchist quarter up to 1914.

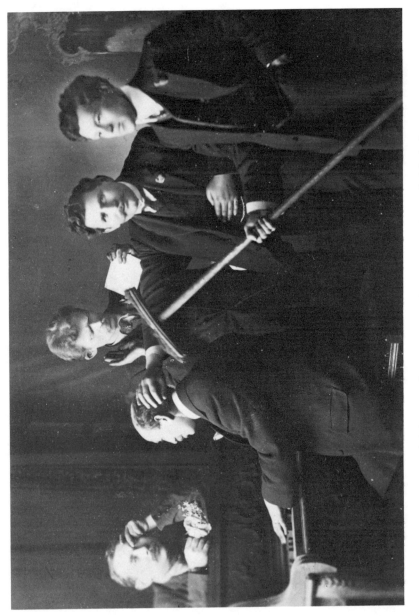

17. A group of *Arbeter Frainters* (1903). The young Sam Dreen holds the broom.

never denied his origins or the debt he owed to Rocker's journal.

By now the Rockers had moved to Dunstan Houses, Stepney Green, where a number of the *Arbeter Fraint* group had begun to congregate. These were located on the then eastern bounds of immigrant expansion, astride the Mile End Road, whose side streets were rapidly being filled up by Jews.[15] The march across Europe of thousands of young Rumanian Jews as a dramatic protest against home persecutions (1899-1900) brought 2,903 new immigrants into Britain, of which 1,504 stayed: the majority to swell the numbers in the East End.[16] From 1901 the volume of unemployment rose sharply. There were ominous signs of anti-alien sentiment reaching a new crescendo, locally and nationally. This time it could be forged into a movement under an effective leader and organiser — Major William Evans-Gordon, recently elected MP for Stepney. In December 1900, the British Brothers' League was founded by William Stanley Shaw, who knew little of East London, but was concerned that, although 'the immigration of destitute foreigners affects all classes . . . the working man is the most directly concerned. Consequently it was to the Working Men of East London that I first appealed.'[17] The next month an amendment proposing the implementation of promised anti-alien legislation was moved to the King's Speech (30 January, 1901) by Evans-Gordon. It sparked off a debate which demonstrated that a more potent spirit of exclusionism was abroad in the land. It is no surprise that Evans-Gordon could boast that he 'had no small share in the formation of the

15. See map showing the distribution of Jewish residents in Tower Hamlets about 1900, adapted from Russell and Lewis, *The Jew in London*, in Gartner, *The Jewish Immigrant in England (1870-1914)*, front and back covers. Rocker was living at 113 Stepney Green Dwellings in 1901, adjacent to Dunstan Houses; in March 1903 he was at 58 Dunstan Houses. Fermin Rocker suggests that the move to number 33 (the first flat he remembers with an inside toilet) took place about 1910.

16. The Census Return of Aliens in England and Wales for 1901 records totals of 61,789 Russians, 21,055 Russian Poles and 3,296 Rumanians and not listed, compared with totals 23,626, 21,448 and 734 respectively for 1891; that is, Jewish 'alien' numbers appeared to have almost doubled in ten years.

17. See *Eastern Post*, 23 November, 1901.

League' pledged to stop the alien 'invasion'.[18]

During these early manifestations of agitation for an Aliens Bill, the *Arbeter Fraint* was mostly out of circulation, and it is difficult to assess Anarchist response in East London, where the British Brothers' League's organisation was based. The first mass meeting sponsored by the League in Stepney was held on 11 May, 1901, and packed to overflowing. Others followed suit that year: 15 August again in Stepney, 15 October in Bethnal Green, 15 November in Limehouse, the movement reaching a peak at the monster gathering held at the People's Palace on 14 January, 1902.[19] During the last climactic session, in which an audience of over 4,000 had assembled, incidents were reminiscent of the Blackshirt tactics of the 1930s. Two hundred and sixty stewards — 'big, brawny stalwarts, dock labourers, chemical workers from Bromley, and operatives from Shoreditch, Bow, Poplar, Stepney, Bethnal Green and Mile End, whose duty it was to see that order was maintained' — moved in quickly when 'once or twice an alien angrily rose in his seat to protest' and bundled him unceremoniously outside. The old charges were voiced against the Jews by speakers led by the chairman, Evans-Gordon, from accusations of ousting the native Britisher from home and job, to being the major cause of crime and anti-patriotic activity. An excellent description of top members of the Central Committee of the British Brothers' League was given by a *Jewish Chronicle* reporter who attended their meeting in May 1901. He observed that by their 'focusing the growing sentiment against the Jews . . . it is clear enough, that in the turmoil of the general election in which party lines will be eliminated, in many ways a new catch cry will bring a new combination to the front'. As for the effect on the Jews locally, it was forcing them to begin 'a silent but deliberate attempt to move out of the district, and the Jewish landlords, whose rack renting is put down as the

18. For anti-alien movements prior to the Aliens Bill of 1905 see Gainer, *The Alien Invasion*, Chapter 4, 'Anti-Alien Societies in East London'; and Garrard, *The English and Immigration, 1880-1910*, pp.36-47.

19. See description of last meeting in *The Times*, 15 January, 1902, in article on 'Alien Immigration', and the *Jewish Chronicle*, 17 January, 1902. For a local report see the *East London Observer*, 18 January, 1902.

cause of the trouble, are beginning to sell out their property'.[20]

The temporary rehabilitation of the *Arbeter Fraint* took place on 8 February, 1901,[21] but its ploy was not conducive to attract readers at a time when Jews were on the defensive. It resumed its anti-monarchist, pro-Boer commentaries, providing such evidence required by the anti-alienists for their indictment of immigrants.[22] Union activities were covered in full, and the first of many great public meetings held by Rocker in front of the board school in Bucks Row, off Vallance Road, was announced for 28 April. The cessation of the *Arbeter Fraint* at this crucial time also saw Rocker away at Leeds for that year, which he considered the most difficult he had encountered since entering the Jewish movement.[23] It was not surprising. Most Jews would be reticent about associating themselves with subversives at a time, when, for example, in August 1902, the League could collect 45,000 signatures in Tower Hamlets alone for a petition demanding their exclusion.[24] It was left to the minority *Arbeter Fraint jungen* to continue their weekly campaign at open-air meetings to build union support and counter anti-alien propaganda. When Rocker returned (September 1902) he noted a new spirit in the London movement. Union activity was reviving from the doldrums of war and, notwithstanding the hostile milieu in which they had been obliged to function, his *Arbeter Fraint* circle had not only remained intact but had actually increased its strength. The courage and enthusiasm of Rocker's disciples had, in his absence, sustained the paradox of an Anarchist organisation which would continue to operate as a vanguard in Jewish labour struggles.

On 26 December an all-London conference of Jewish

20. *Jewish Chronicle*, 1 November, 1901: Article, 'British Brothers' League. A description, an analysis and a deduction'.

21. The *Arbeter Fraint* once more ceased publication from 10 May, 1901, to be revived permanently on 20 March, 1903.

22. See articles in *Arbeter Fraint*, 22 February and 1 March, 1901. They refer to the Boers' terrible suffering as a result of British barbarism under 'cannibal' Kitchener's policy of arson and pillage.

23. Rocker, *In Sturm*, pp.285-301.

24. *Eastern Post*, 17 August and 19 October, 1902.

Anarchists was called in Whitechapel. Four major items were discussed: the resurrection of the *Arbeter Fraint*, the problem of printing and distributing Anarchist literature, the formation of a Jewish Anarchist Federation in Britain, and the acquisition of permanent premises for a club. Rocker, who was the driving force throughout, elaborated the lessons they had learned from past failure. There must be some effective organisation, and clearly defined aims in the day-to-day-struggle. The Jewish movement would have to concern itself with the threefold task: to help organise and improve the conditions of Jewish workers and, in the process, break the back of the local 'sweating' industries; to implement improved social relations between Englishman and immigrant within the trade union movement; and, finally, to undertake the broader aim of educating all workers in the Libertarian creed. The first two, pragmatic responses to urgent needs of the day, were activated immediately.

On 20 March, 1903 the *Arbeter Fraint* reappeared as the 'Organ of the Yiddish speaking Anarchist groups in Great Britain and Paris'. This time it would continue without break until 1914. A permanent supply of cash to prevent stoppage was guaranteed by a non-stop series of concerts, fund-raising meetings and propaganda drives. An article in the second issue recalled the Christmas conference's conception of the *raison d'être* for the local group. 'Two things we lacked – a home and a paper. We couldn't get one place where we could hold our weekly meetings.' The paper was now out. The comrades were exhorted to 'devote their energies to the task of acquiring a club'. But there were more pressing demands on their attention.

The anti-alien movement was reaching its peak of intensity, as reflected in the amendment to the King's Address of February 1903, and the interim savage agitation which preceded the Royal Commission's Report on Immigration in August. In April, two editorial articles by I. Kaplan[25] posed some curious arguments on the motivation and purpose of the Commission. Herzl's evidence, labelling exclusionism as anti-Semitism which could only be overcome by government-

25. *Arbeter Fraint*, 3 and 17 April, 1903.

aided schemes to return the Jews to Palestine, is rejected on two counts. First, that the problem was one of immigration *per se* — whatever the creed of the immigrant. ('If instead of 120,000 Jews in London there were 120,000 Lithuanian gentiles, the Jewish question would not arise!'); second, that Jews were as much instigators as victims of anti-alienism.

> Who has spoken more about introductory measures in Parliament than the Jew? Who worked harder in the Committee of the British Brothers than the Jew? [reference to Harry S. Samuel, MP for Limehouse]. Who is blind to the foreign Jews, contemplating the newly arrived greener, murmuring between their teeth, 'Who wants them here? Why didn't they stay at home? How can we get rid of them?'
>
> The alien problem is not a Jewish problem, while they are not attacked personally, while it is stated by Jews to Jews.

Yet the second article is partially contradictory. By general consent, Kaplan suggests, the Jew is a special target for abusive treatment by the Englishman, although this can be explained by the Jews' traditional submissiveness in the face of violence.

> The ordinary Englishman, who lacks finesse, shouts at the foreigner, for the crime of being born, 'German sausage!' or 'Bloody Jew!' or occasionally, 'Why don't you go back to your own country?' And he is normally satisfied to limit himself to these insults. But the same man, when drunk, on meeting a frightened Jew on the way, will deal him a blow on the head. Let the same Englishman meet a Lithuanian gentile or an Italian ice cream vendor, a German or a Frenchman, who know how to deal with him, he will retreat singing quietly 'Rule Britannia' and so ends the affair. He (the Englishman) will bar him from his own factory or workshop, but he has never yet organised a mass attack on the foreigner.

In the final count, anti-alienism is conceived as a political measure by the Conservatives to counteract that moral 'pollution' introduced by the foreigner, which endangers the ruling class. Kaplan was convinced that the Commission 'would not harm a hair of the foreigner already in residence', but offered no advice on the means of combating local anti-Semitism. Rocker, the non-Jew who could stand back, would proffer the positive approach of bringing together

Jewish and Gentile workers by joint public meetings and co-operative action within the trade unions. With this in mind he continued to press for the acquisition of a club, in the Berner Street mould, that was open to all workers.

Reminiscences of aged survivors and a scrutiny of the *Arbeter Fraint* columns give evidence of the new dynamism which was infused into the East End movement. Successive public meetings would be followed by evening concerts on the same day. Members' personal contributions appear generously high, since, according to Sam Dreen, many of them offered most of their weekly pay to the paper's fund.[26] Every aspect of the immigrants' experience was a subject for involvement or debate. Kaplan followed up his articles on the Alien Commission with a public lecture at the New Alexander Hall, in Jubilee Street on 18 April. The first inclusion of a piece by the Yiddish and Hebrew folk writer I.L. Peretz was indicative of Rocker's concern with Jewish literature.[27] On the other hand the *Arbeter Fraint* noted with satisfaction the current *Daily News* report that only 26,162 out of a total 104,550 Jews in London attended the traditional first night Passover Service.

The outbreak of the Kishinev pogroms (April 1903) brought Rocker and his group to the forefront of the protest demonstrations. Even these were almost aborted by factional antipathies which continued to divide the Jewish labour movement. A separate Jewish demonstration, initiated by the Jewish Cabinet Makers' Union, was to be held at Hyde Park on 21 June, and an all-party delegation met to plan it. At the beginning the two representatives of the Social Democratic Federation rose and delivered an ultimatum. They would only participate on two conditions: first, that the Zionists must be barred from the conference and, secondly, that a resolution must be adopted expressing sympathy and support

26. *Arbeter Fraint*, 27 March, 1903, gives first indication of the membership of Sam Dreen, who contributed five shillings and H. Dubinski a pound. The same issue noted that an additional 500 copies (making a total of 3,000) had to be printed, which were 'all sold out and there was no more to meet even further demand'. Rocker wrote that the regular circulation increased from 2,500 to 4,000 within the year 1903-4 (*The London Years*, p.175). This was confirmed verbally by Sam Dreen.

27. *Arbeter Fraint*, 17 April, 1903.

for the Bund in Russia and Poland. This attempt at minority
dictation was ultimately rejected as an impertinence.

It was a presumptuous demand for an organisation which represented only a small minority of the Jewish working class in England.
*The Zionists had no following of any consequence at that time in
the Jewish working-class movement.* Besides the Zionist press had
accused the revolutionary movement in Russia of being in a way to
blame for the pogromist activity of the Russian government. For this
reason no invitation had been sent to the Zionists, and they for their
part had made no attempt to be represented at the conference . . . It
would have been absurd to adopt a resolution excluding an
organisation which was not seeking to be represented. The second
condition, too, was unacceptable, because the policy of the Czarist
government against the revolutionary movement in Russia was aimed
at the entire movement, not at one particular party. A special
resolution of sympathy with the Bund would have been a slap in the
face for all the other organisations.'[28]

It was Rocker's voice of censure that proved decisive. ('It was
an outrage that Socialists, no matter to what party they
belonged, should exploit the terrible tragedy of Kishinev for
their own party ends!') The SDF delegates' threat publicly to
accuse the London Jewish trade unions as enemies of the
Bund in the Russian press, if their resolutions were not
adopted, received short shrift from the majority.

There was more powerful opposition to the demonstration
emanating from the Yiddish daily press and the rabbinate.
The *Jewish Express* and *Jewish Telephone* regarded it as an
Anarchist plot, and the *Express* even voiced its suspicion of
Kropotkin's judophilia. It warned its readers that the meeting
was called for propagating Socialism rather than protesting
against Russian outrages. The Russian government had
charged the Jews with being agents of Socialism. Such a
demonstration would confirm that charge to the detriment of
further Jewish lives in the Pale. But the Sunday meeting took
place, in spite of the concerted pleas by the *rabbonim* from

28. *The London Years*, p.163, re Zionism in article by S. Freeman (*Arbeter
Fraint* 5 June, 1903). Zionism as a panacea for pogroms is strongly questioned.
Freeman argues, some would say prophetically, that 'the Zionists cannot
guarantee, that a Jewish rule or state, which must be founded on might as others
are, would handle its opponents differently from the present national governments'.

their pulpits, urging their congregants to boycott it. The largest gathering of Jews ever seen in London mobilised on the Mile End Waste and, with Rocker and his group at the head, marched off in close formation to Hyde Park. The London press estimated that there were at least 25,000 people assembled round three platforms to listen to speakers who included Rocker, Kaplan, Turner, Leggatt and Tcherkesov. Kropotkin, who arrived late, was recognised by the East Enders. He was lifted shoulder high, and passed over the heads of the crowds until he reached the main platform. Although ill and warned not to speak, he made two short speeches — one in Russian, the other in English — which were reported widely in the radical and daily press.[29] The success of this mighty demonstration sparked off a similar campaign in the provinces, in which Rocker emerged as the outstanding speaker at packed meetings in Leeds, Glasgow and Edinburgh. It would appear that, at last, the Jewish workers were beginning to appreciate their own strength in united action. It was time to direct their energies towards an assault on sweating. In preparing for the attack, Rocker's claim that 'all the Jewish trades unions in the East End, without exception, were started by the initiative of the Jewish anarchists', seemed valid. The ceaseless demands of their educational groundwork now made the need for acquiring a permanent institution more pressing.

Kishinev also meant a heavy inflow of refugees during the peak period of exclusionist sentiment. James MacDonald, Chairman of the London Trades Council, refused an invitation to speak at the Hyde Park meeting on the pretext that Jewish workers in London had blacklegged a recent tailors' strike. It was difficult to prove or refute this in a situation which demanded control of hundreds of small Jewish workshops which were proliferating in the ghetto. In article after article Rocker hammered home his theme: it was incumbent on the Jews to take the initiative in promoting comradely relations with the English workers. Although the latter continued to prove elusive, the Jewish movement

---

29. *Arbeter Fraint*, 19 June, 1903, editorial 'To Hyde Park'. *Arbeter Fraint*, 26 June, 1903 gives report on great demonstration in 'Noticebook'.

showed visible signs of growing strength. In March 1904
record sales afforded an increase in size of the *Arbeter Fraint*
to twelve pages, including four pages as a literary supplement.
The general strike, as a tactic to be employed for the
abolition of sweating, was reiterated as an article of faith. On
6 April, 1904 a mass meeting was called at the 'Wonderland',
Whitechapel, to propagate this. All the 5,000 seats were
occupied and the police were forced to close the doors
against an overflow crowd. Mowbray took the chair, and
besides Rocker and the Yiddish speakers, all the leading
orators of the movement then in London shared the
platform: Malatesta, Tarrida del Marmol, Mainwaring, Kelly
and Kitz. One result was a prelude to widespread strikes
when the Jewish Bakers' Union came out for improved hours
and working conditions. The test of public support was
gauged by the strike committee's additional demand that
each loaf be stamped with the union label to prove that it
came from a bakery that observed trade union conditions.

The immigrant housewives rose to the occasion. A few
days after the strike began, the smaller master bakers
attached the union label to their product, as the Jewish
women refused to buy any other. It was the custom of
grocers to stock bread. Women would first buy their
provisions, then ask for a loaf. If the label was missing it
would be handed back. The grocer was left with so much
unsold bread that he immediately switched to a union-based
supplier. It did not take long before the union's demands
were agreed to by every master. The workers here gained
conditions which were, for many years, in advance of those
prevailing amongst English bakers. Above all, it set an
example of the means to be employed in the coming assault
on the sweatshop system.[30] The anarchists who had dominated the action were riding high.

---

30. On 8 February, 1904 the *Arbeter Fraint* announced the bakers' strike, and
weekly reports were issued thenceforth. It constantly appealed for funds and aid
from other Jewish workers and organised mass rallies such as that in the
'Wonderland' on 18 June, with Rocker as prime speaker.

10. The Golden Years

He united us, filled us with revolutionary ardour, inspired us with his clear thinking and wide knowledge, his love and understanding of art and literature and the values of culture.

Rocker was our rabbi!

Sam Dreen

There is a danger of mouthing banalities when one persists in generalising conclusions derived from the study of some local movement. One needs to scrutinise the face in the crowd; to take account of the drives and responses of the individual. Until recently, in the case of the Rocker saga, there was a vast fund of information willingly offered by survivors. But there were no takers. Yet here, in a local setting, there emerged a common denominator of experience, defined by a unified purpose and life-style of its participants.[1]

Their accounts of the movement revolve around the personality of Rocker. They reflect his permanent effect on those young intelligent 'greeners' who drifted in casually out of the cold and stayed for good. Their recall is as much a revelation of their own talents as those of their guru — gifts which might have lain fallow but for his intervention. Let the chroniclers, the *chaverim* (comrades), speak for themselves.

Veteran Millie Sabel[2] remembered the dramatic impact of

1. I was fortunate in being able to interview some survivors who were close to Rocker both in and out of the movement including Sam Dreen, Joseph Leftwich (author and journalist), Aron Rollin (trade union leader and Jewish labour historian), Louis Bailey, Millie Sabel, Rose Robins, Polly Witkop, W. Kossoff, Karl Lahr, Fermin Rocker (Rudolf's son) and a variety of non-intimates in the USA who had heard him lecture in New York and California. I have been careful to confirm chronological and place accuracies by checking one against the other and omitted such information which lacked conclusive evidence. After all, much of historical data is based on the personal memories of old folk.

2. See my article 'Millie Sabel — Yiddish Anarchist', in the *East London Arts Magazine*, vol.4, no.1, winter 1967. She was first interviewed in June 1965 and on many subsequent occasions. A woman of rare beauty and intelligence, she

Rocker on her, when she was taken, almost unwillingly, to
the Sugar Loaf back in 1898.

Landsmen [countrymen] of mine would go to the Sugar Loaf public
house in Hanbury Street, and I accompanied them. Here I first met
Rudolf Rocker who had taken up our cause. He had a handsome
presence — tall, blonde, sturdy, recognisably German. He spoke
firmly and quietly but like an actor. He was wonderful. So I joined
the poor tailors, slipper and cabinet makers who came to listen to
him at the back of the pub. He would lecture to us and lead
discussions. He opened up to us the vision of a new society — no
persecution, no hunger, only warmth and generosity.

Four years later to the same Sugar Loaf came the small
seventeen-year-old immigrant from Vitebsk, Sam Dreen.[3] He
was brought along by one of his *landsfrau*'s (Chaie Beile's)
sons, one Friday evening, having already quit attending the
weekly Sabbath service.

I was terribly impressed by Rocker's delivery so I attended all his
lectures in future. I shall never forget his talk on Zola's *Germinal*,
which brought out Rudolf's great emotive sympathy with the
miners. It was moving and convincing and exemplified his uncanny
ability to maintain that pure mental and physical rapport with his
audience.

He spoke to us like a father to his child, like an elder brother. He
had time and patience for each one of us. We were not a crowd to
him but everyone was a separate person, an individual soul. Even at a
public meeting attended by hundreds of people, sometimes by
thousands, you felt that Rocker was speaking to you alone.

'Red' Rose Robins[4] confirmed this impression when,

---

remained the oldest surviving member of the *Arbeter Fraint* group until her death
in 1972 at the age of ninety-three — a Libertarian to the end.

3. First interviewed in Milwaukee on 18 October, 1969 and subsequently on
many occasions. Born in Vitebsk (1885), fled to England in 1900 and duly
ensconced in the East End as a trouser maker. He became one of the youngest
members of the *Arbeter Fraint* group, an intimate friend of Rocker's, and remains
a life-long disciple. At eighty-eight he still retains the hopes and enthusiasms of his
youth, and was primarily responsible for what he called 'his last tribute on this
earth', the Rudolf Rocker Centenary Celebration held at Toynbee Hall, East
London on the 9 September, 1973, which attracted both young and old who had
come to pay homage to Rocker.

4. 'Red' Rose Robins (born 1885 — died May 1971), interviewed on 5 March
and 15 April, 1971. Born in Valudeka in Kiev *guberni* and brought to London by

accompanying her brother and Millie Sabel to an *Arbeter Fraint* fund-raising *poiren* (peasant) ball at the Crown hall in Redmans Road, she first heard Rocker speak. Jacob Fine,[5] who was a newly arrived 'greener' that same year (1904), emphasised that from Rocker in the (later) Alexandra Hall, he received his formative education in western culture.

The *Arbeter Fraint* group, in spite of its dynamism and outward thrust, remained small, élitist, constituted of no more than two to three dozen members with little turnover up to 1914. External forces made it so. The non-politicised majority of immigrant *intelligent* persisted in their religious faith. The implications of supporting Anarchism were still frightening. Rocker's early lectures on free love attacked one of the fundamental bases of Judaism — the family. Dreen, in retrospect, suggests that this prevented wider support. 'There were too many traditional hangups — theological and otherwise — to accept free sex as a viable dictum of behaviour.' Rose Robins's parents tried desperately to stop her association with the *borveson* (barefooted) Anarchists, since girls who mixed with them presumably lost their most precious jewel, their virginity, and became prostitutes. The remedy, as prescribed by religious neighbours, was to lock her out all night when she attended the Jubilee Street Club. 'That would stop me? It didn't! After being nagged and persecuted by my parents, I moved out to my sister, who was already married and lived near by in Oxford Street.'

Perhaps the most fascinating pictures handed down to us were the community joy sessions, engendered by the Rockers, and intrinsic to the Libertarian style. They also served a practical purpose — to raise funds for the club. Two

her parents in 1901. Joined Rocker's group in 1904 (a daring venture for a young 'orthodox' girl) and remained a Libertarian. During her last year she derived much pleasure from relating the golden years of her youth with Rocker to British and American students who, in turn, were enthralled by the experience of a woman who had been 'liberated', in most senses, for nearly seventy years.

5. J.L. Fine, OBE, JP (1883-1971), interviewed July 1965. A Lithuanian Jewish immigrant of 1904, who in a long and colourful career, was in turn Trade Union administrator, municipal worker, magistrate and journalist. He recalled that his loneliness as a young 'greener' ended with his attendance at the Jubilee Street Club, where he was the recipient of the friendship and hospitality of the Rocker group, but where he also gained his formative western-style education.

of the inner group, Polly Witkop and Dreen, repeat the same theme. 'We were not just followers of a particular political trend. We were members of one family, brothers and sisters, so attached to each other that we simply could not part.' Even the editorial meetings were transformed into a weekly ritual of group dedication and self-sacrifice.

> Our comrade, Silberman, a manufacturer of handbags, allowed us the use of his workshop at the back of a house in Rutland Street. There, every Thursday evening, we would discuss articles and propaganda for the following week's issue and collect money to pay the printer. Often Lazar Sabelinsky and I would hand in almost all of our wages to the fund.

By 1904 the Jewish labour movement was growing fast. This was reflected in the sales of the *Arbeter Fraint*, now acknowledged as the most popular radical newspaper in Yiddish. The need for premises and therefore funds was pressing. Donations came in from a variety of sources.

> Young girls, who slaved in the sweatshops for a weekly pittance of ten or twelve shillings, literally took the bread from their mouths to give the movement a few pennies . . . In many workshops, the workers nailed a cigar box to the wall, and dropped their pennies in it: for the *Arbeter Fraint*.[6]

A major part of income was derived from the regular socials and balls organised by the group, which attracted hordes of young sympathisers and non-politicals who came to dance, sing and cavort to the early hours of the morning in the free atmosphere of the *chaverim*. Dreen recalls:

> We held social evenings regularly and two or three masked balls a year in peasant clothes, when prizes were presented for the gaudiest costume. We often hired the 'Crown Hall' in Redmans Road for concerts. One star attraction was a New York tenor, Svengali, who sang classical opera to an appreciative audience. I often used to sing Edelstadt's *lieder* accompanied by the Anarchist pianist, Berman. Always there would be an interval for refreshments when Rocker would stand up and there would be immediate silence. He would lecture to us on some literary or topical political interest. We sat

6. *The London Years*, p.175.

enthralled. It was as much due to him as to the musical performers that we always had a full house.

Which was also very profitable. Dreen noted that some weeks the treasurer, Lazar Sabelinsky, could stack away twenty-five to thirty pounds towards the club appropriation fund.

Youth's a stuff will not endure. The concerts and dances rarely ended before three in the morning.

> We younger ones never went home. Up to two dozen young men and women would troop off to one of our homes and there recline on cushions placed on the floor to talk throughout the night or pair off to embrace in the corners. Our favourite hosts were the old childless Anarchist couple, *chaver* Prusky and his wife, who plied us with coffee and pastries throughout the night.

The festivities would sometimes attract closer attention from other interested and opposing parties — the police (a permanent fixture, in and out of uniform, lurking outside) and continental revolutionists on the run. Rose Robins described an incident which she could never forget:

> I first saw Malatesta at the 'Crown Hall'. He had just escaped from Italy and plain-clothes men were on the prowl outside. He slipped in unobtrusively, a little dark man who looked like a Jewish cobbler. Suddenly he was recognised and everybody rushed to greet him. At the end he walked out casually by the side of Alexander Shapiro and I followed behind. Two plain-clothes men stepped out from the shadows between me and the comrades and assuming the same pace followed them through the Whitechapel streets . . . I understand that Shapiro helped to shake them off after an all-night pursuit.'

Other events underlined the necessity for acquiring permanent quarters. The Russo-Japanese war initiated a new influx of deserters, and the aftermath of the Russian revolution of 1905 a large crop of politicals. (Rocker relates a visit from Matuchenko, 'moving spirit' of the *Potemkin* mutiny, who had escaped to England and had been brought to Dunstan Houses by Kropotkin.[7]) These stimulated increased activity on the part of the Jewish labour movement with the Anarchists as its most vociferous advocates.

7. Ibid., p.173.

Violence erupted spasmodically as Jewish establishment interests attempted to subvert the radical groups. In 1904, gangs of thugs (*schlogers*) were hired to break up Anarchist and Social Democrat meetings. One such gang was the self-styled Bessarabian Fighters, who could be found playing cards at the Roumanian restaurant at the corner of Settles Street and Commerical Road. It was alleged by the *Arbeter Frainters* that, at least on one occasion, some official of the Federation of Synagogues had paid these mobsters to disrupt a mass meeting at Bucks Row, where Rocker and his bodyguard fought back with their fists and put them to flight. But young anti-religious militants were to blame for one annual fracas. It was occasioned by the Anarchist balls, deliberately held (against Rocker's wishes)[8] on Yom Kippur, the most solemn of Jewish festivals, which even marginal Jews respect. J.L. Fine was a regular observer of the tragi-comedy of young politicals who, flaunting their contempt for tradition, marched in column to the Spitalfields Great Synagogue (*Machzikei Ha Dath*) in Brick Lane, smoking or brandishing ham sandwiches as gestures of defiance and rejection of their creed. The service over, angry worshippers, sometimes in full regalia, swept out and attacked the scoffers with any weapon they could seize, while the local people gazed dumbfounded at the antics of the crazy foreigners. Fine also recalls a later incident when the Assembly Hall, paid for by Lord Rothschild as a centre for worship at High Holidays for poor Jews sponsored by the Jewish Board of Guardians, was the subject of a bomb hoax. The police received a warning that Anarchists had planned to blow up Rothschild at the service. All incoming congregants were searched and the hall cleared. There was no bomb.

In 1904, the annual affair provoked a full-scale riot in Spitalfields. The historian Rollin, then a Social Democrat, and Sam Dreen were both involved. In premises once used by Jacob Adler and his troupe, the Socialists had established a *Volkskuche* (People's Restaurant), which supplied cheap

---

8. Rocker stressed mutual non-interference according to the precept 'the right to act according to your own belief belongs to everyone. The place for a believing Jew on Yom Kippur is in Synagogue, not in the street trying to deny somebody else's right to do what he wishes on that day', and vice versa.

meals and was, therefore, heavily patronised. Prices, such as bread, a penny a piece, soup threepence a plate, sixpence for soup with meat, were half those charged by local private restaurateurs, who naturally resented this 'unfair' competition. Rollin suggests that, under the guise of protecting religion, the latter had prepared an attack on the *Volkskuche* on Yom Kippur, led by hired thugs. The *East London Observer*[9] reported what followed:

> Thousands of Jews were walking along the streets, when they were met by a body of Socialist Jews, who had driven a van containing food along the streets. All the Orthodox Jews were fasting and they at once resented this unseemly display. The Socialists being driven into their club responded by throwing glass bottles out of the windows. Several cases of minor injury occurred and the disorder thus started to spread quickly. Within half an hour the whole area round Princelet Street was in a state of great agitation. Excited groups of Orthodox Jews were parading the streets threatening the Socialists with dire penalties for their insults and stones were thrown at the home of prominent Socialists.
>
> ... It is alleged that the Socialists pelted a Synagogue which stands adjacent to their club, and that they had arranged a concert for the day of fasting — invitations to which they had sent to the principal Rabbis!

Rollin presents a different tale:

> I was making my way towards the Club with a young woman comrade in Princelet Street, where a threatening crowd had gathered. As we approached some men in front sprang at the girl like tigers, threw her to the ground and started beating her, whilst I was hurled against the wall and pinned there. The Club members, hearing our cries, rushed to our defence and brought us in. The girl was torn and bleeding and laid semi-conscious on the floor ... We sent a messenger begging help from the Anarchists, who were holding their ball in a hall at Rhondda Grove, Bow.

This brought Sam Dreen on the scene. He and a score of young bloods jumped a tram to Gardiners Corner, and rushed up Brick Lane in time to relieve the beleaguered Socialists. They apparently beat off the invaders, as a large force of police arrived and quickly dispersed the crowd, arresting

9. 24 September, 1904.

some men and boys in the process.

The magistrates attributed the cause of the disturbance to the so-called orthodox. Of the eight brought up for trial, two Socialists who declared that, being non-religious, they could not observe Yom Kippur, were summarily discharged; and the bench commented that it was deplorable 'that a class of persons who for centuries had been distinguished as the victims of the fiercest persecutions should, when in the one free country of the world, turn upon those who disagreed with them on religious points, their own co-religionists, and stone and persecute them'.[10]

In January 1905, *Germinal* was revived as a sixteen-page journal, swiftly reaching a circulation of 2,500 a year later, when its size was increased to forty-eight pages. At the same time, the *Arbeter Fraint* registered a peak demand for 5,000 copies weekly, now almost totally unopposed as the Yiddish radical organ in London. The Social Democrats, slightly boosted by immigrant Bundists, remained a small, esoteric group, more inward-looking in their concern for maintaining doctrinal purity. (Like Talmudists they debated endlessly, in public and private, on the correctness of theoretical interpretation, while the Anarchists were preaching to, and activating, the workers in the streets and factories.) Their party paper, *Die Neie Zeit*, founded by another Gentile, Beck, in 1904, struggled on as a weekly or fortnightly sheet until 1908. Many former Bundists, who had worked with the Social Democrats in Russia and Poland, soon took measure of the situation here and transferred their allegiance to the more practical body. The odd man out was Morris Myer, who continued to edit the *Neie Zeit* until its demise. He subsequently joined the Paole Zion, and founded the most successful non-political Yiddish daily — *Die Zeit* — which lasted for nearly forty years.[11]

10. Ibid., 24 September, 1904.

11. Morris Myer came to London from Rumania in 1902, where he had translated some of Rocker's articles in the Anarchist monthly *Revista Idii*, and continued to contribute several articles to the *Arbeter Fraint*. He became a Social Democrat, and with the end of *Die Neie Zeit* he joined the *Jewish Journal*. In 1913 he founded his own paper featuring news and romantic pieces (*Die Zeit*) which lasted until 1952. He became a prominent figure in the British Zionist movement.

By 1906 the Rocker group were ready to fulfil their hopes of a workers' club. Thanks to good housekeeping on the part of group treasurer Sabelinsky, there was enough money in the kitty to rent or lease their own premises. The fund had been created by the pennies and farthings of workers, plus income accruing from socials, dances, literature and the large personal subsidies offered by Lief (property owner), Freeman (glazier), and Silberman (handbag manufacturer). They agreed on a large two-storeyed building located at 165 Jubilee Street. It was originally the Jubilee Street Methodist Free Church, later used as a Salvation Army Depot, but currently hired out for meetings and dances. The proprietor had taken a shine to the group because of the civilised way they conducted themselves on the premises and was particularly drawn to Rocker's transparent honesty. He agreed to lease the building to a joint committee consisting of Sabelinsky, Prusky, Freeman and Schatz.

The weeks before the club opened were marked by frenzied activity, as volunteers poured in to redecorate and renovate the dilapidated interior. Not all were Anarchists. Artisan sympathisers brought their own tools and materials. A platform for a stage and a large wooden purpose-built refreshment counter were constructed in the great hall. Tables and chairs contributed by supporters added to those made on the premises. These were used to furnish the lower hall, which with the gallery could accommodate 800 people, and adjoining classrooms. The second floor housed a library with book shelves built in by the workers, and trestles covered with literature constituted a reading room. A small adjacent building (163 Jubilee Street) was also taken over to serve as permanent editorial and printing offices for the *Arbeter Fraint*. The whole was an extraordinary exercise in workers' self-help.

'A red letter day for Jewish comrades,' wrote Lillian Wess, of the opening of the Workers' Friend Club on Saturday, 3 February, 1906. The inside was packed from top to bottom as hundreds streamed in from the neighbouring Hawkins, Lindley and Smith Streets. Long before the start Rocker had to lock the doors, while outside in the cold, dozens more tried to push their way in: a remarkable display of support from a crowd of orthodox breaking their Sabbath ritual to welcome in an atheist establishment! Polly Witkop, Sam Dreen and Rose Robins, seated in front, concur in their description of the proceedings:

> The gas-lit lower hall was crammed with people on benches, or jostling each other against the walls. At the entrance sat the inseparable Tapler and Kerkelovich selling their *Arbeter Fraints*, *Germinals* and other group literature. Rocker mounted the stage. There was prolonged applause which was silenced by a quiet gesture of his hand.
>
> Comrade Rocker opened the proceedings and spoke of the many trials and persecutions which had been their experience during the last few years and how it had finally culminated in the determination to get a place of their own. This had now been accomplished by the Federation of Yiddish speaking Anarchist groups.

Rocker began to read out messages of support from Jewish trade unions, Malatesta, and Tarrida del Marmol, when he was cut short by a storm of clapping and cheering. Kropotkin, although warned by his doctor not to appear at any more public meetings because of his heart, had arrived. Rocker begged him not to speak, but Kropotkin waved him aside and ascended the platform. He

> congratulated the comrades in securing this fine hall for their new home . . . out of their own hard-earned pence without any middle-class assistance . . . He also made touching references to our comrades in Russia. 'The hearts of our brothers will be gladdened to know that here in London you have a home where they will be sure of finding a welcome waiting for them if circumstances force them to leave the land where they are now fighting so nobly for the cause of Liberty.'[12]

John Turner next reminded them of the old Berner Street Club, of which their venture was the more sophisticated, and richer endowed, successor. He hoped that it would finally prove the means of overcoming that which had hitherto eluded them: that by 'helping in both English and Jewish

12. Detailed accounts of the opening were given me by four survivors. Rose Robins recalls 'Mrs Kropotkin sitting next to me' ('I actually conducted her to the toilet!'). Also see *The London Years*, p.178 and report in *Freedom*, March 1906.

propaganda they would bring both sections in touch with each other'. Finally, Ted Leggatt, the burly Cockney carman, thundered his comradely greetings to the loud applause of a baffled audience. The speeches over, a vocal and instrumental recital followed; then the benches were cleared, a small band assembled on the stage, and to the strains of the *lazinki*, the Viennese waltz and the quadrille, old and young *chaverim* danced on through the night.

The club was also conceived as a focal point for all workers. For the next eight years it played a notable part in Jewish social and intellectual life, but not only did the Jews benefit. Rocker was concerned that its activities be open to everyone.

> Anyone could use our library and reading room, or join our educational classes, without being asked for a membership card. This made it impossible for us to sell drinks in the club, from which most of the other clubs got the greater part of their revenue. For the law restricted the sale of intoxicants to club members. We sold only tea, coffee and food.[13]

The dry bar was manned by volunteers — men and women. The latter mainly did the cooking, but all took turns at serving and scrubbing floors. Millie Sabel was pledged to prepare *gefilte* fish, chopped liver and pickled herring. She remembered some curious customers.

> I occasionally saw a small, intense man who sat alone at a table in the corner. He had slant eyes, balding reddish hair, drank Russian tea and spoke little. He was Lenin. There was also a handsome, dapper man who came later and helped paint the props at our theatrical — a quiet attractive comrade we called Peter the Lett. He was supposed to be Peter the Painter, although I personally doubt whether he was mixed up in the Sidney Street trouble.

Rose Robins throws light on the surreptitious antics of some of the orthodox on Kol Nidre night:

> It was an exhibition of hypocrisy. 'Shool' goers would creep furtively into the Club to snatch a meal with their *talusim* under their arms. On that night we were kept really busy preparing extra

13. Rocker, *The London Years*, pps.178-9.

food required, whilst Kaplan took advantage of the situation to lecture the invaders on the falsity of religion. It was a profitable night — for the *chaverim*!

Much of the cultural activity, initiated by Rocker, centred on the stage. Here, almost exclusively in the *mame loshen*, took place lectures, concerts, recitations, sketches (sometimes written by the performers themselves concerning current labour themes) and plays — classical and modern. Sam Goldenberg, erstwhile tailor turned star of the international Yiddish theatre, learned his stage craft in the Club, where he was seen by 'Red' Rose performing as a young amateur in *Andreiev* and sketches of Sholem Aleichem. Here young Leftwich watched rehearsals of a Yiddish production of Ibsen's *Ghosts* and observed the making of the future maestro of Shakespearian theatre, Abraham Teitelbaum, on the same boards.[14] Friday was carried over from Sugar Loaf days as lecture night. Speakers would include Rocker, Tcherkesov, Kaplan, Kropotkin, and Malatesta, on subjects ranging from world literature and science to modern political ideologies. Rocker had now matured into an orator of extraordinary power. Louis Bailey, member of the West End Wachruf (Awake and Call) group, was invited one Friday night in 1907 to hear Rocker lecture. It was on Hamlet, the first of what was to be his famous series, *Six Characters in World Literature*. Bailey, enthralled by the performance, returned to listen to a second, 'The Ninth Symphony of Beethoven'. Inspired by Rocker he thenceforth became a regular attender at the club. He tells of the variety of public discussions which took place there, where all opinions were open to free debate. One of the most absorbing was the long-remembered argument on 'Does God Exist?' between a *meshumed* (proselyte), Dr Levertov, and Kaplan. The incident is imprinted on W. Kossoff's memory, together with a learned commentary by Rocker on Maeterlinck's *Blue Bird* currently

14. Rose Robins recalls Yacov Gordon as a trainee actor in the club. Teitelbaum translated Shakespeare into Yiddish and wrote a Yiddish biography of the bard. He went to Russia in 1917, but left, disillusioned, for the USA where in New York, he joined the Jewish theatre company under Morris Schwarz, which then included Paul Muni.

being performed at Her Majesty's Theatre. Among the many historic personalities to be seen in the Friday audience, were Chaim Brenner[15] and Grigori Chicherin, future Soviet Foreign Commissar.

Social and cultural activities were interdependent. During winter, Sundays were set aside for a tea-cum-*conversazione*:

> In the lower hall tables were laid for tea and sandwiches. After tea Rocker would stand and lecture on some literary theme. He brought his subject to life, and we sat fascinated. I remember one clearly on 'Lilliput', whose allegory was made comprehensible to me by our fine teacher.
>
> (Rose Robins)

Summer brought the traditional trip to Epping Forest. Dreen describes what he regarded as the highlight of their lives, in contrast with the everyday gloom and drudgery of the sweatshop:

> Very early in the morning a hired horse and cart drew up at the Jubilee Street Club to transport tables, liquid refreshments, and sandwiches with Kerkelovich in charge of operations. He skilfully packed the food on the conveyance and took off with the driver to set up tables near High Beech in time to receive the crowd.
>
> The comrades arrived in Chingford by bus or in groups from Bethnal Green Station (where cheap tickets cost ninepence return). They then made their way through the forest to the meeting point. Some would bring their own food, but most bought refreshments at Kerkelovich's *ad hoc* bar, where the *Arbeter Fraint* treasurer, Sabelinsky, collected the money.
>
> Comrades would then gather in groups or young men and women would pair off and meander into the forest. Suddenly a loud call would announce that Comrade Rocker was about to address the crowd. All would swiftly converge to a glade at the edge of the wood. Some would lie down casually on the grass, others reclined against trees, as our teacher began his lecture.

---

15. Aron Rollin knew Brenner when he worked as a printer for Narodiczky at 44 Mile End Road (1905-6), and was literary editor of the Socialist *Freie Arbeter Velt*. Brenner lived in extreme poverty; half of his salary of one pound a week he invested in his Hebrew newspaper, *Hamorer*. When Lamed Shapiro came to London seeking work, Brenner handed over to him his literary editorship plus half of his current salary. Rollin regarded him as a *Tsaddik* — saintly, with a broad sense of humour devoid of any rancour.

In socio-educational terms the club's influence equalled, if not surpassed, that of Toynbee Hall. It was rarely empty, attracting the young (the majority) and old, the political and apolitical, the informed and the ignorant. It was sustained by a huge crowd of sympathisers who read the *Arbeter Fraint*, and while not engaged in outdoor agitation, except to provide front-line militants in strike action, gave regular support to social functions. Young boys and girls escaped from the restraints of patriarchal discipline into a freer milieu. There were recreational facilities to cater for all tastes. The open bar and cheap refreshments provided a centre for chess competitions, and heated debates. Over countless glasses of tea 'discussion would go on far into the night between Bundists, Zionists, Anarchists and Social Democrats, who argued excitedly together. We Anarchists were very tolerant. All workers were our comrades' (Sabel).

Rocker was resolved on the parallel duties of exposing the immigrants to western culture as well as stimulating trade union consciousness. The club, therefore, would not restrict itself to the propagation of ideology, but would develop as an all-embracing institute of education in the modern idiom. A wide curriculum was offered, open to all, whatever their creed.[16]

> The class included one in English, for the younger immigrants. I taught history and sociology. On Sunday mornings I took my classes to the British Museum, whose treasures richly illustrated what I had been trying to teach them . . . We also had speakers' classes, and a Sunday School, conducted by Nelly Ploshansky, her husband, Jim Dick, and my elder son Rudolf.[17]

He was a superb professional. His teaching method was evidently geared to mutual feedback techniques. Dreen echoes the sentiments one has heard from a dozen of his contemporaries:

16. Constantly advertised in *Freedom*, but few *goyishe* takers, as most of the teaching was conducted in Yiddish!

17. Rocker, *The London Years*, p.179. Mr W. Kossoff — the famous baker of the East End — informed me that he joined Rocker on his expeditions to the British Museum. 'He was my Rabbi! If it wouldn't be for the Club I might never have read a book.' Under Rocker he felt that he was part of a religious movement. (Interview 21 September, 1973.)

He acquainted us with Tolstoy and Dostoevsky, Ibsen and Strindberg and Maeterlinck, with Leonardo da Vinci, Michelangelo and Rembrandt. And with our great Yiddish writers, Mendele, Peretz, Sholem Aleichem, An-Ski, Reisen and Asch. This German *goy* had a thorough command of Yiddish . . . He was one of those who stood at the cradle of modern Yiddish literature.

He taught us history, philosophy, science, theatre, painting, music and acquainted us with the work of Marx and Proudhon, Bakunin, and Kropotkin, who was his close friend.

He was *our* teacher!

The club being run on co-operative and non-profit-making lines, its committee faced the continual problem of devising ways of meeting running costs. Dances, concerts, etc. helped somewhat, but not enough. The premises were thrown open for renting for the odd day or evening. 'Freedom', SDF and other English radical groups were among the hirers. The small trade unions, later branches of the Workers' Circle and a branch of the Russian Social Revolutionaries, enabled the club to keep its head above water by using it for their regular meetings.

Intimacies extended beyond the club into the homes of its creators. A quasi-Libertarian commune was now centred on the south-eastern wing of Dunstan Houses. The Rocker apartment, no. 33 on the top floor, was an ever open door.[18] Kropotkin's own *Lestki Chlieb i Volya* was printed in the block, and he was a regular visitor. So were the humbler fry. Whoever came, invited or not, would be welcome to share a meal, and the only large room of the three was automatically placed at the disposal of those seeking a bed for the night. The warmth of comradeship was such that the *chaverim* lived as a close-knit family, brooded over by their gentle and patient teacher. It was an unspoken assumption that all ages and sexes were treated equally, without patronisation. Unlike most ideologues, Rocker lived out his conviction that, in every sense, relations between the sexes should be free, and without artifice. Interchangeability of roles, therefore, came naturally to Rocker and his group.

18. On the same block, at various times, lived the Sabelinskys, Goldbergs, Hillmans, Liefs, Shapiros, Kerkeloviches, Linders, Polly Witkop and Rudolf Rocker, Jnr. Before 1914 the inner caucus of the *Arbeter Fraint* group formed what was virtually an Anarchist colony there. See Plate 16.

The club attracted a variety of eccentrics, strange off-beat characters who sought kindred spirits in this pocket of Bohemia. Small factions would assemble round a cult figure. Guy Aldred was intrigued by one Arnold Roller, pioneer advocate and pamphleteer of Direct Action:

> He spoke more than once at the Jubilee Street Club. He did not spend all his time in London but often disappeared mysteriously and as mysteriously reappeared in his old London haunts. I often saw him leave the club and turn into the Whitechapel highway, attended by a group of admiring supporters. His violent speech entranced them . . . He was arrayed in black, and wore an overcoat with a cape after the style of Edward VIII. On his head was a kind of black sombrero. He carried himself with a swagger and strode towards Aldgate like a king, guarded by his retinue, and disdaining all who passed him. He had all the flambuoyant grace of the traditional highwayman and might have been named Claude Duval.

It was his obsession with violence for its own sake that shocked Aldred:

> His case for direct action was sound, but what constituted direct action was menacing and absurd. It included every possible kind of social outrage under the heading of sabotage.[19]

Roller was one of many of that ilk who plagued Rocker and constituted a threat to the existence of the club. Being open to all, especially as a haven for foreign revolutionaries on the run, proved a mixed blessing. Young expatriates, from the Russian underground, were the most attractive and the most dangerous. They could not adjust to a freer life in London. Convinced that they were the vanguard in the battle against established society, they could see no difference between governments, Russian or British, since all bourgeois authority was the implacable enemy. They also provided an entrée into the revolutionary movement for Okhrana agents, double agents, spies and *agents provocateurs*. The Azev affair

19. Guy Aldred, *No Traitor's Gate*, Glasgow, 1955-6, part ix, pp.289-90. He first visited the club in February 1907 to attend a benefit social on behalf of the radical 'Voice of Labour'. There he met his future spouse, Rose Witkop, sister of Polly and Millie, herself an ardent women's liberationist and pioneer of birth control. In 1922 she was prosecuted for publishing Margaret Sanger's *Family Limitation*, which advocated and advised on contraception.

disclosed the depth of police penetration. Jubilee Streeters had to view newly-arrived politicals with caution. The group learned from some unpleasant experiences. One was the case of Tchishikoff, who, when engaged on 'expropri-ations'[20] in Russia, was caught and imprisoned in Vilna. While awaiting trial, he escaped by climbing over the prison wall, fell and broke his leg. Comrades on the outside managed to spirit him away, first for treatment, then safely across the border. He arrived in London with a limp. His revolutionary *élan* deceived everyone and using the club as a base, he committed a group of young enthusiasts to return with him on underground missions inside Russia. He was contemp-tuous of Rocker's open, peaceful propaganda, which to his mind contravened the basic precepts of revolutionism.

Rocker was repelled by his male-chauvinist attitudes. A womaniser, he won the love of a young girl, Zlatke, a dedicated worker, 'naive, impulsive, all heart'. She went to live with him, but after a couple of months Rocker learned that she had been thrown out by Tchishikoff and was pregnant. A few days later his legal wife arrived from Vilna, and they resumed their relationship in the very room in which he had co-habited with Zlatke. Rocker and the *Arbeter Fraint* group voted for his expulsion, but Tchishikoff's followers refused on the grounds that his private life was no concern to anyone, provided it did not interfere with his revolutionary activity. They collected money for him to return to Russia, where he acted as liaison officer in the underground and convened a secret conference attended by comrades from Poland and Lithuania. It was promptly raided by the police and all were arrested. Tchishikoff was the obvious traitor. Even his earlier prison escape had been engineered by the police in order that he might more easily gain the confidence of the revolutionaries. Fearing vengeance, he was permitted to escape in Switzerland, where he was soon discovered by a Russian student and shot.

The *Arbeter Frainters* were certainly haunted by the fear that 'propagandists by the deed' could, at any moment, place

20. Expropriations were armed raids on banks or commercial institutions to obtain funds for revolutionary activities. The maxim was 'the Tsar to pay for the Revolution'!

the whole London movement in jeopardy, and thereby threaten the existence of their club and paper. It was one of the penalties of maintaining an open door. Rocker, with an eye on current anti-alienism, continually argued that terrorism was criminally counter-productive. Such acts were manna for the exclusionists. His views were well known to the police, and, unwittingly perhaps, he proved useful to them in two ways: personally as a restraining force against the advocates of violence and through the club, which polarised the location of suspects. They therefore kept a close watch at Jubilee Street, but took no drastic action. In fact, the only time the club faced the possibility of closure was during the Houndsditch affair and the aftermath of the Sidney Street siege.

Yet the prospect of terrorist outrage remained a cause for concern. The German anarchist, Charles Lahr,[21] related the occasion when he was the subject of round-the-clock-observation in 1907. As an apprentice baker he often ate at the German restaurant in Leman Street, which was frequented by patriotic German butchers, bakers and the like. Lahr became incensed at the obsequious praise lavished on the Kaiser, and suddenly intervened shouting, 'The bastard ought to be shot!' He was quickly hustled to the door and flung out. The following day he found himself followed by two CID men. On confronting them he was informed that he was under surveillance, since they had information that an attempt would be made on the Kaiser's life. During the two weeks before the Kaiser's state visit (November 1907) the tail on Lahr was rigorously maintained. In 1914 Lahr was taken under guard to Alexandra Palace to be interned as an enemy alien. There one of the CID bloodhounds recognised him and called out, 'Hullo, Charles. Pity you *didn't* shoot the Kaiser.'

21. Charles (Karl) Lahr (1885-1971), born in Bad Nauheim, became, at the age of twenty, in turn Buddhist, then Anarchist. Fled from Germany on 1 October, 1905 to work as a baker's apprentice with a relative living in Sheridan Street, East London. Involved with a Hampstead Anarchist group prior to World War I, where he met Max Nomad and was helped and befriended by Guy Aldred. Interned with Rocker at the Alexandra Palace, he acted as his secretary. After the war he remained in London and became a bookseller of repute in the Gray's Inn Road. He was often seen, even as an octogenarian, cycling to work from his house in Highgate.

Unfortunately not all incidents ended in farce. On 23 January, 1909 the 'Tottenham outrages' shocked Britain. Two Letts from Riga, Jacob and Hefeld, snatched an eighty-pound payroll from a clerk returning to Messrs Schurmann's Rubber Factory in Chestnut Road, Tottenham. A tragi-comedy ensued. The robbers, who were armed, held up an electric tram and seized a milk van while trying to make their getaway. Pursued by the police, they opened fire. Armed police reinforcements were brought in and by the end of the day one constable (P.C. Tyler), shot in the head, lay dead and three others were wounded. Of the fifteen civilians injured in the fray one was a ten-year-old boy caught in the crossfire.[22] Neither of the would-be 'expropriators' lived to stand trial. Those who associated aliens with crime had a field day in the press. Even *The Times* was roused to voice its fears on the subject[23] which, as Rocker knew, were not without foundation. In November of the same year he discovered a plan by a group of young Russians to throw a bomb at the Lord Mayor's show. Fortunately one of the plotters had thought through the consequences of such an act, and begged Rocker to intervene. At a house in Whitehorse Lane, Mile End, he found a gang of four youths and a girl, and persuaded them to call it off. 'I said that I was sure some Russian police agent had incited them to such a stupid and senseless outrage, to discredit the whole revolutionary movement, and to close England to all political refugees.' Like incidents elsewhere had confirmed these as tactics of the Okhrana. The conspirators returned to Russia with the exception of the informant, who became a close friend of Rocker. Later he disclosed that the same group had planned to kill Kropotkin, on the principle that his influence as a moderate was holding back the revolutionary forces.[24]

Fortunately terrorists were the exception rather than the rule among the frequenters of the Jubilee Street Club. Most members adjusted to the new conditions and many rendered great service to the international labour movement as well as

22. A detailed account of the affair is reported in *The Times*, 25 January, 1909.
23. Ibid., 1 February, 1909, 'The Anarchists in London'.
24. *The London Years*, pp.192-3.

achieving personal fulfilment as free, rational human beings. S. Freeman, pioneer *Arbeter Frainter*, emigrated to New York, where he took over the management of the *Freie Arbeter Stimme*. Judith Goodman, a leading social revolutionary in Bialystock (who wore a wig permanently as a result of all her hair being torn out by Cossacks), thanks to the influence of the Rockers eschewed the practice of unmotivated terror before moving on to New York and non-violent agitation there. Baruch Rifkin, the great Yiddish littérateur, sharpened his wits against Rocker in never-ending discussions. From the latter's declaration of faith he learned of the innate flexibility of Anarchist ideology:

> There is never an end to the future, so it can have no final goal. I am an Anarchist not because I believe Anarchism is the final goal, but because I believe there is no such thing as a final goal. Freedom will lead us to continually wider and expanding understanding and to new social forms of life. To think that we have reached the end of our progress is to enchain ourselves in dogmas, and that always leads to tyranny.

Hence the group's involvement in diverse activities which aimed at improving the contemporary life-style of the immigrants. One of these was the establishment of the Jewish Workers' Circle. Conceived in the USA as a secular mutual aid organisation to protect its members in sickness and need, it operated in direct contra-distinction to the religious Friendly Societies, in that it was motivated by Socialist ideals. Members belonged to various Socialist groups, and each branch was free to conduct a cultural programme on its own terms. Any surplus cash was invested in progressive schools or adult educational schemes. The English group was founded in 1903 at the instigation of the *Arbeter Fraint*. By 1909 it was firmly established and grew steadily to a peak membership during the inter-war years.[25]

25. The first annual conference took place in London in May 1912, representing 814 members. By 1921 numbers had reached 1,103. As late as the 1950s there were still 12 branches in Britain bearing a total membership of over 1,200. Because of the challenges of alternative organisations and causes and the death of old members, the Workers' Circle in London has declined to a handful. Sam Dreen is one of the few survivors of the founding group. One of the *Arbeter Frainters*, Weiner, was general secretary for many years.

Rocker was not without enemies in the London movement. A Jewish *Freiheit* group led by his ex-comrades L. Baron and I. Rose parted company with him over ideological differences. Dreen recalls a campaign of hatred mounted against Rocker by his West End compatriots, in Dreen's view out of jealousy. Rocker agreed that he was rarely at ease in the company of fellow Germans, because of their authoritarian postures. (He later conceded that this was a 'national disease'.) In 1905 he was accused by them of being a German government spy, and a conference of London-based anarchists met in the public house on the corner of Old Montague and Osborne Streets (now The Archers) to which Rocker was called to answer the charge. Dreen, who was present, describes the scene:[26]

> A large room, at the rear, was packed with over fifty people. Amongst these were delegates from the *Freiheit, Arbeter Fraint*, and Solidarity groups. The last was an extremist faction led by comrades Greenstein and Ossip, who regularly indulged in punch-ups with the Social Democrats.
>
> A German delegate took the floor, and in strong terms questioned Rocker's career from his time with the 'Jungen' and in France, implying that he had evidence, which he could not produce, that Rocker was a police agent. The *Arbeter Fraint* group had requested Rocker not to speak. Others got up to support the accusation, although still without a shred of evidence. One of these was Morris Myer, a recent recruit to the *Freiheit* group, who hated Rocker because he had rejected some poems he had submitted to the *Arbeter Fraint*.
>
> Lief, acting as Rocker's advocate, treated the charge with the contempt that it deserved, and countered with a violent attack on the personal integrity of the chief accuser and Myer. The meeting ended in uproar. But it was already obvious, even to the prejudiced, that Rocker was innocent.

Except for the usual sporadic attacks against Socialists and atheists, who were lumped together with the missionaries, the Jewish press continued to ignore Rocker personally, as they were painfully aware of his influence in the East End. His public orations, sometimes attracting audiences of over a thousand outside Schneider's factory in Bucks Row, and the

26. As related by Dreen in an interview, 17 October, 1972.

ministrations of his acolytes in front of the Philpot Street missionary hall (and opposite the Great Synagogue!) on Saturdays, were thorns in the flesh of the *rabbonim* and local masters. By 1906, he could no longer be ignored as he directed himself towards a grand assault on the sweatshops.

11. Strikes and Sidney Street

Although most parts of Britain had established large-scale factorisation by 1900, East London was one area where the small workshop and outworkers not only persisted, but expanded their numbers. Factory owners geared their capital and labour input to the potentialities of continual production. The clothing industry operated according to seasonal demand, and it was therefore impossible for the small master to increase investment in machines and accommodation while they were subjected to periods of vacant capacity. As long as there was a constant inflow of immigrants into restricted areas of employment, the workshops could meet the optimum requirements of cheap labour and work loads. In that year (1900) the Medical Officer of Health for Stepney reported the existence of 1,778 small concerns in his borough, employing 20,000 people, of whom 75 per cent were Jews.

While the immigrants remained unorganised they remained exploited, and constituted a permanent threat to other workers in the industry. 1889 had registered a spate of new unionisation, not least among East End Jews. By 1896 there were 13 Jewish trade unions, rising to 32 by 1902, of which 26 had been founded in the last six years. This evidenced their instability. In 1898 the *Jewish Year Book* listed 15 unions, of which 2 had already disappeared by the following year. Unions rose and fell, a situation aggravated by the practice of treasurers absconding with the funds. (A legend that rendered all union officials automatically suspect as potential *ganoven* (thieves) or *drehkeppels* (twisters).) New immigrants were notoriously difficult to organise. Their will was undermined by permanent job competition, while the supply of labour, especially in the slack season, outstripped demand. At 'home' (Russia) they worked as artisans, one-

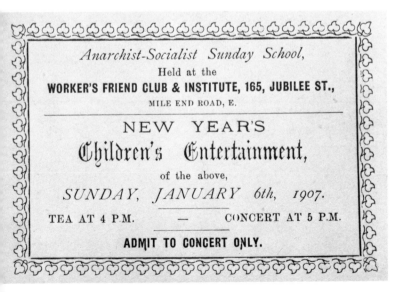

ANARCHIST-SOCIALIST SUNDAY SCHOOL.

AUGUST 22nd, 1906.

Bethnal Green Junction

to

Chingford.

———

CHILD.

Outward)   (half.

ANARCHIST-SOCIALIST SUNDAY SCHOOL

AUGUST 22nd, 1906.

Chingford

to

Bethnal Green Junction.

———

CHILD.

Return)   (half.

18. Railway and concert tickets for the Anarchist-Socialist Sunday School.

Anarchist-Socialist Sunday School,
Held at the
WORKER'S FRIEND CLUB & INSTITUTE, 165, JUBILEE ST.,
MILE END ROAD, E.

NEW YEAR'S

𝕮𝖍𝖎𝖑𝖉𝖗𝖊𝖓'𝖘 𝕰𝖓𝖙𝖊𝖗𝖙𝖆𝖎𝖓𝖒𝖊𝖓𝖙,

of the above,

SUNDAY, JANUARY 6th, 1907.

TEA AT 4 P.M.   —   CONCERT AT 5 P.M.

ADMIT TO CONCERT ONLY.

19. *Arbeter Frainters* Yud Kaplan and Rosa Kaplan (1900).

man or family concerns, or *luftmenschen*, where it had always been a day-to-day struggle for work and bread. For most, collective action within the economic format was outside their experience. Subjection of the journeyman to the unlimited power of his master gave rise to tension, but this was accepted by the former as a fact of life. He, in turn, would exercise his authority on a subordinate, when he became boss. Those who stayed in Russia would be confronted with rapid factorisation as late as the 1880s. Only then might organisation for collective action make sense.[1] In England, as we have seen, there were other factors which provoked it. After 1889 strikes were sporadic, and even if successful, resulted in short-lived gains. Cut-throat competition forced many a boss to renegue on agreements, since it was impossible to meet higher labour costs and remain in business. Dismissals, redundancies and closures through bankruptcy meant a restive work force, prone to radical influence.

How far were the *Arbeter Frainters* responsible for the growing militancy which culminated in the first great strike of 1906? It was not an overall principle to support trade union development *per se*. Club members were divided. For example, Alexander Shapiro opposed co-operation on the grounds of non-involvement in any centralised authority, but in defence of individual freedom of action (undetermined by majority pressure), agreed that comrades could engage, or not engage, in union activity, according to their own conscience. In retrospect Dreen considered that the group, as a whole, did not opt to act as union builders, but left it to the individual. It was a small caucus round Rocker, such as Dreen, Kaplan, Wess, Freeman, etc. who chose to participate. In doing so they gave the movement leadership, aim and direction.

By 1906 there were three independent Jewish tailoring unions whose strengths fluctuated, and whose influence, therefore, was minimal. Added to external factors was a quarrelsome leadership, which perpetuated their weakness.

---

1. For a discussion on this see Ezra Mendelsohn, *Class Struggles in the Pale*, London, 1970, in which the author concludes that 'the artisan composition of the Jewish proletariat, and the deteriorating economic conditions of that class . . . explain the labour movement's weaknesses as well as its strengths'.

Officials made little attempt to educate their members, and meetings often ended in chaos. Dreen's experience seems to exemplify this:[2]

> When I joined one of these three unions, the secretary was J.L. Sachs, a poor public speaker but a sincere and devoted worker. He had little contact, however, with his members, who didn't give him much respect and actually raised their fists against him sometimes. In the end he resigned. He was not strong enough for the job.
>
> The Chairman of my union was a presser, and his name was Berkovitch: a big, strong man who weighed sixteen stone. When some of the members came to blows at a meeting, as happened quite often, he would come down from the platform, get hold of the combatants and throw them out of the hall.
>
> The union work did not attract me. There was always a good attendance at the meetings which were held on a Saturday night or on Sunday, but the members came there mostly to meet their friends, to talk and quarrel and fight. Many of them came half drunk, spoiling for a fight. Usually the meetings ended in uproar.

The beginning of 1906 injected a sense of urgency into the Jewish campaign against the sweating system. Although the Aliens Bill had become operative in January, and was being implemented by a Liberal government, which in opposition had attempted to choke it by a mass of amendments, 'the Liberal consensus of opposition to it began to erode and the anti-alien faction to increase'.[3] Rocker appeared to be more sensitive to this than his comrades. As a gentile he could understand, though not condone, the sentiments of hatred and fear roused in the English workers by 'the development of new industries in the East End . . . which were not subject to trade union discipline and control, especially when those industries kept growing through the immigration of more foreign workers', an antipathy made more potent after the abortive attempts of some English unions to persuade Jewish workers to join them.[4] An assault on sweating by collective action was imperative.

---

2. From unpublished autobiography of Sam Dreen, Chapter 1, 'How I became an Anarchist'.
3. See Gainer, *The Alien Invasion*, Chapter 8, 'The Struggle for the Aliens Act'.
4. Rocker, *The London Years*, p.169.

It had already begun. On 7 February, the *Jewish Chronicle*'s Jewish labour news correspondent woke up to the fact that 'hardly a week passes without a fresh strike breaking out in one or other of the trades . . . Passing events in Russia and the wide publicity given to almost every detail by the Yiddish press have stimulated an interest in labour organisation unknown in the past.' By the beginning of February the stickmakers' union, having remained moribund for years, 'struck for the first time and cabinetmakers were out in London and Liverpool'. There was concern with 'rumours since October that the Jewish tailors will commence a general strike in the early Spring'. Who were the instigators? The correspondent confirms Rocker's claim that it was the Anarchists, rather than the Social Democrats, who were, according to him, no longer of any consequence:[5]

> To show that the increasing strike movement may be directly traced to the advanced propaganda, a brief review of its activity will not be out of place . . . The *extreme section* of Jewish Labour publishes one weekly and one fortnightly sheet besides a number of pamphlets in which the sociological speculations of Peter Kropotkin and advanced themes of other Continental Anarchists are exploited. It should be mentioned by the way, that although the two sheets have practically one faith and one desire in common, namely to bring about a state of society free from government, law, and social restraint of every kind, yet they occasionally turn round and rend each other whenever a trivial difference of opinion is manifested. Strange as this may seem, the sudden disappearance from the scene of their competitors, the Social Democrats, is even more remarkable. For while the latter have been engaged in tall talk, arranging for the extermination of Zionism, Territorialism and other isms on paper, and spreading the net of their propaganda in contemplation over a wider field, the advanced party had been 'up and doing'. Not only has their literary propaganda been considerably strengthened, but

5. The correspondent goes on to say: 'The Jewish labour movement appears to have entered a new era in history. The hitherto submissive Jewish workman . . . has been roused to a consciousness of his power resulting from combination with his fellows. Egoistic indifference in the masses generally is evidently destined to become a thing of the past giving place to courage, independence of character, and determination to secure freedom and human treatment in the proper sense of the term. Reinforced by new arrivals, fresh from the scenes of heroic struggle for liberty entailing enormous self-sacrifice the Jewish workers of the East End of London appear to have undergone a process of transformation.' (*Jewish Chronicle*, 2 March, 1906; *Jewish Labour News*, column 'Propagandist activity'.)

they have also quite recently secured the large and commodious Alexandra Hall (i.e. the Jubilee Street Club) as their club premises, and already rub their hands in glee at the possibility of carrying on a 'raging and tearing propaganda' of anarchism to their hearts content.

Tailoring being the major industry, it was there that the attack would be launched. Strikes and walk-outs in individual workshops were mounting, and in some places employers were giving way to the workers' demands on improved pay and conditions. The results of 'careless picketing' (according to the *Jewish Chronicle*), where blacklegs were physically assaulted, led to an increase in criminal charges and sentences imposed for 'watching and besetting', as evidenced by court reports in the local *East London Advertiser* and *Observer*. With agitation stepped up by the *Arbeter Fraint* and supplemented by mass public meetings, unrest reached a climax in June. Pushed from below, delegates from the three unions met to discuss strike action. A committee was drawn up and the twenty-one-year old Dreen elected treasurer, an appointment which, according to him, reflected the confidence in the integrity of Anarchists, since they were never known to make off with funds!

The strike developed its own momentum. On 8 June, the *Arbeter Fraint* announced a spontaneous mass walk-out, sparked off by a local lock-out ordered by the Master Tailors' Improvement Organisation, which assumed the character of a sympathy strike. Union groups began to concentrate in certain streets. Dreen, contemporary reporter for the *Arbeter Fraint*,[6] and sole survivor, conveys a lucid account of the affair. His own union members had mobilised at the confluence of Jubilee Street and Commercial Road. Hoisting improvised banners and shouting slogans, they marched off through the streets, stopping at each workshop and calling on the workers inside to come out and join them. One of the first to respond was Rose Robins, who started an exit of all hands.

> I got up and left. The governor's wife, a *hoiker* (hunchback) was shocked and screamed, '*Die* greener *geht oichet!*'[7] But I was glad to

6. *Arbeter Fraint*, 15 June, 1906. 'Tailors Strike in the East End', S. Dreen.
7. The 'greener' is also going!

join the strikers. My wages then was three shillings and sixpence a day, and never did I have a full week's work!

The strike committee set up their headquarters at the independent Tailor and Garment Workers' Union office located in a warehouse in Old Montague Street.[8] Their first task was to call a mass meeting of strikers to draw up demands and agree on tactics. On Sunday afternoon 10 June, the Wonderland theatre was packed with strikers, awaiting instructions from their leaders on the platform. Dreen notes in his report that those speakers advocating caution were shouted down, while a resolution moved from the floor was carried:

> The tailors' meeting declared unanimously not to return to work until the following are agreed:
> (1) All workshops to employ union members.
> (2) All shops to have a chairman other than the master.
> (3) Day work to replace piece work.
> (4) The working day to be from eight a.m. to eight p.m. with one hour for dinner and half an hour for tea.
> (5) Work to be equally divided amongst workers.
> (6) The master must give a week's notice and will give an acceptable explanation to the workshop chairman.
> (7) There must be humane treatment in the workshop.
> There was unanimous acclaim at the vote to strike with shouts of Long live the strike! Down with the Sweating System! The War is on!, culminating in the singing of the 'Marseillaise', as the members left the hall.

The contest between master and hand would be resolved on whose will and resources would break first. 'It is not only a general strike, but a general lock-out ... each party has entered in the fight with grim determination not to lay down its arms until the other party is vanquished.'[9] At strike headquarters the committee co-opted extra members to help in the drive to collect money and food for the men and to effect total stoppage. Among these were the old veteran Wess, Simon Freeman and Rocker — top *Arbeter Frainters.*

---

8. Located twenty yards West of Black Lion Yard, on the same side towards Brick Lane. The building was only recently demolished (1972).

9. *Jewish Chronicle,* 15 June, 1906.

Pickets were sent out from workshop to workshop, to plead with, cajole or threaten those still at work. Special watch was kept on nightworkers, some of whom were forcibly seized and frogmarched to headquarters, where they were promptly flung into a room, apportioned as a gaol for blacklegs.[10] Their family was notified, and the prisoner could be bailed out on payment of a fine by the wife or son, on the principle that money earned from blacklegging would be transferred to strike funds. It was extraordinary that no striker appears to have been prosecuted for such illegal action. Dreen suggests that this was due to the overwhelming public sympathy, so that the police left them well alone.

Rocker's intervention as propagandist and morale booster proved invaluable. Strikers gathered daily at Old Montague Street, where Rocker's orations helped sustain their enthusiasm. All over Stepney, open air meetings were called, notably at Bucks Row, addressed by leading Anarchists such as Freeman, Kaplan, and Jacob Solomon. Money was accumulated here and in daily house-to-house collections. Most East End Jews responded magnificently. The committee appealed to grocery shops to accept credit slips, issued by them to strikers, for the purchase of foodstuffs, which would be honoured in cash after the strike. Dreen, who as treasurer was responsible, recalls that most corner stores, being sympathetic and practical (there was little money around anyway) accepted this arrangement. Although the strike ended in failure, credit to the tune of £5,000 was redeemed in full from cash paid out by the unions. The AST sent a contribution of £1,000. It paid off, for both parties, in the long term. The hitherto independent Tailor and Garment Workers' Union felt duty bound to join the AST after the strike; and when the next great strike came in 1912, although emanating from the West End, it ensured the legal support of East End co-unionists.[11]

There were many moving incidents in which the solidarity of the Jewish poor, motivated by compassion, was mani-

10. The committee learned from the mistakes of 1889 and subsequent strikes and were resolved to deal firmly with 'black' labour.
11. The Jews also realised that they could no longer stand alone, and that success lay on the side of the big battalions.

fested. One was the continuous flow of donors, mostly shawled housewives, bringing *bagels*, brown herring, fruits, and home-made *gefilte* and fried fish to feed the strikers at the rendezvous in Old Montague Street. On the other hand a vicious hoax was played on them. At the point when funds were running out, the Committee suddenly received a cheque for £1,000, ostensibly from Rothschild. Distrustful of allowing one man to cash it (he might be tempted to abscond) a group of eight led by Dreen were elected to go to the bank and change it. 'Bitter was the disappointment on the faces, in the hearts of the delegates, when the bank manager informed them that the cheque was a dummy!' (Dreen). Money, that is a permanent strike fund, provided the key to possible victory.

The masters tailors knew this of old. On their part the problem was less keen. Individually, or as a body, they had immediate access to greater reserves. They met at the Jewish Working Men's Club in Great Alie Street on 17 June and threw down the gauntlet. Adopting the premise that the dispute was a lock-out, they laid down six conditions under which employees could return to work, all counter-proposals to those of the workers, with the last carrying the punch-line:[1][2]

> We further resolve not to make any settlement or enter into negotiations with our employees in a body, unless they are represented by properly recognised *English* Trade Union leaders, authorised with sufficient authority to enforce any decision arrived at. We further resolve, if our employees do not return to work within the next 48 hours, to resume work in the best possible way, in the interests of trade and for the convenience of the public at large.

In other words they would not negotiate with the Jewish strike committee, and intended, as in the past, to depend on blackleg labour to try and carry them through. They counted on the workers' low ceiling of resolve. When strike money ran out, they would be back. And the masters were right.

12. Reported fully in the *Jewish Chronicle*, 22 June, 1906, and briefly in the *East London Observer*, 23 June.

Work had also been transferred to outside centres, such as Leeds, Manchester and Liverpool, and a delegation was sent from East London to urge the provincial workers to extend the strike, but with little success. As the funds dwindled, and their families faced hunger, the strikers filtered back into the workshops, first singly, then in droves. By 29 June the *Jewish Chronicle* declared the strike at an end. *The Times* had it officially settled earlier at a meeting held at 69 Cannon Street 'between representatives of the Master Tailors' Improvement Organisation and the AST under the presidency of Mr Hardy, chairman and managing director of Messrs. Hyams and Co. (Ltd)'. Two days later it commented briefly on a mass demonstration in Trafalgar Square which took place on Sunday 24 June, in which the participants' are determined that the working day shall be from eight a.m. to eight p.m. with meal allowance of one hour and a half'.[13] The *East London Observer*, reporting on the march of a thousand from Whitechapel to Trafalgar Square, also thought that

> the strikers' demands have been conceded. They will work from eight to eight with an hour for dinner and a half hour for tea, and there will be no piece work. In the event of middlemen breaking these terms, the employers have promised to dispense with them and to establish direct indoor work. Questions of difficulty to be referred to settlement by the newly arranged board composed of representatives of employers and the executive committee of the AST.[14]

The *Jewish Chronicle* jubilantly noted that work would be resumed on 1 July. The agreement reached between master and men confirmed that 'the quarrels of friends are but a renewal of friendship'. It then proceeded to voice its own prejudices concerning the 'real' instigators of the dispute: 'We cannot too strongly condemn the action of a certain turbulent element in the East End who use strikes as a stalking horse for propaganda in the cause of a systematic subversion of law and order.' As for the previous Sunday's demonstration, it

13. See *The Times*, 23 and 25 June, 1906.
14. See the *East London Observer*, 30 June, 1906.

could redound little to the credit of the East End that crowds of Jewish young men and women, conspicuously more or less recent arrivals in the country should invade the westward thoroughfares, flaunting gaudy banners inscribed with revolutionary texts, and affrighting the decorous silence of a London Sunday with a blatant blare of brass.

What will the Sabbath-loving Gentiles think? Particularly the imposition of extra duties on the police 'who count many church-goers in its ranks, and the reflection that these men are compelled to forego their weekly hours of devotion for the purpose of controlling an alien mob is distinctly not a pleasant one!'[15]

Two weeks later an ambivalent labour correspondent was, on the one hand, indulging in some wishful thinking over the quick end of the strike, when the 'irresponsible propagandists'... pet theory of the General Strike has now received a blow, from which, among the Jewish workers, it is not likely to recover'; on the other hand, he was rightly dubious about the terms of settlement which were to become operative one month after the date of signing. Both parties had agreed on the abolition of piece work, a ten-and-a-half-hour working day, and trade union representatives in each shop allowed to collect subscriptions. His criticisms, on several scores, were perceptive: 'Some employees would refuse to abide by it when it results in actual loss of wages' and 'the inconvenience of taking their meals outside the premises'. The masters gained mainly from the *quid pro quo* that, while they must employ only union men, the union must only recognise employers who belong to the Master Tailors' Improvement Organisation. Victory for the workers was nominal, since it was dependent on the feasibility of a universal application of day against piece work. Finally, he noted that the general mood of the employees was one of despondency, 'regarding the settlement as a defeat and betrayal of their interests'.[16] Their bitterness was accentuated by the limited successes of parallel strikes waged by cabinetmakers, capmakers and the recently formed journey-

15. *Jewish Chronicle*, 29 June, 1906.
16. Ibid., 13 July, 1906.

man-butchers' union, in which all gained improved conditions.[17] Tailors quit their organisations in disgust, and union numbers fell dramatically. (The two top *Arbeter Frainters*, Dreen and Sabelinsky, departed for New York soon after the failure of the strike, but returned three years later to rejoin the Rocker group.)[18] There remained a staunch minority of workers, experienced in the field of labour struggles, who were dedicated to rebuild the union and renew the strike. It would take six long, hard years to fulfil this.

Notwithstanding defeat, the prestige of Rocker, his entourage and the club remained high. *Germinal* had projected their fame overseas, and Jubilee Street continued to attract a growing number of Jewish *intelligent* of diverse political creeds, who came to test their views against Rocker's. They found him a tolerant and gracious host. Paole Zion leaders became frequent guests who retained their friendship for the Gentile Anarchist, even though he continued to print anti-Zionist articles in the *Arbeter Fraint*. Among these were Kalman Marmor, then editing the Labour Zionist paper *Die Yiddishe Freiheit*, Dr Wortsman, publisher of the monthly *Die Yiddishe Zukunft*, and the noblest of them all, the Socialist and Nationalist philosopher, Ber Borochov. The latter, after a long and exhausting public debate with Rocker on 'Nationalism' at the club, was moved to embrace his opponent. Diverse cultural innovations continued to emanate from the club and its associated press. In addition to lectures and debates, members were exposed to a proliferation of printed materials: translations of the world classics, old and new, by A. Frumkin, whose versatility is evidenced by the Yiddish versions of Molière, Ibsen, Spencer, Gorky and Strindberg in *Germinal*. Both Anarchist papers opened up the world of Sholem Aleichem, Peretz, Asch, etc. to its readers. If the Rocker group had done nothing else, it certainly provided educational opportunities to the Yiddish-speaking

17. Ibid. The labour correspondent talked of strikes 'as a never-ending guerrilla warfare' which had also brought in the Jewish Trunk and Pursemakers' Union. The tailors regarded the settlement as dictated by the masters. Their own representative had been disregarded and there was no promise of pay rises.

18. Unpublished autobiography of Sam Dreen, Chapter 11, 'Memories of a Pioneer'.

workers, not only in London, but wherever the politicised immigrant could be found. One has only to talk to old survivors to catch the depth and permanency of their enlightenment, which they themselves attribute to the 'golden years' with the *chaverim.*

The club stood as an oasis in the desert of poverty and ignorance. For the *malheureux* who came here out of the sweat warrens, these were the nights of wine and roses. The *rabbonim* continued to thunder against the godless, but the *Arbeter Frainters* had won a grudging respect from some of their enemies – not least the police. Locally, Rocker had become a public figure. The burly figure, with the blonde leonine hair, could often be seen strolling casually along the Waste, to be halted every few steps by some acquaintance. There were periodical bleeps against Anarchists – a more strident chorus after the Tottenham outrages. Terrorism as a weapon was debated endlessly in the columns of *Germinal,*[19] and the *Arbeter Fraint* and on public platforms. By the end of 1910, the *meschuggena* (crazy) Anarchists were almost accepted as part of the East End landscape, until the Houndsditch murders projected them on the national scene.[20]

On 17 December, 1910, London awoke to the news of a triple murder of policemen in a cul-de-sac at the back of a jeweller's shop in Houndsditch.[21] It appeared that a neighbouring employee, Mr Max Weil, became alarmed at non-stop banging at the rear of the shop late at night, and notified a P.C. Piper, stationed at Bishopsgate. On investigating a ground floor flat at no. 11 Exchange Buildings in Cutler

19. See articles debating the issue between Dr Merison (New York) and Rocker in the columns of *Germinal*, vol. iv, 1907-8, nos. 9 and 12 esp. Rocker conceded that violence by terror was viable as a last resort against state violence, whilst Merison regarded any form of terrorism as a danger to the movement.

20. For details of contemporary accounts, see the local and national press. Perhaps the best is given by an author who had access to police files – J.P. Eddy, *The Mystery of Peter the Painter*, London, 1946. See also Rocker, *The London Years*, Chapter XII, 'Houndsditch'. An excellent, though imaginative, interpretation is the novel, *Death out of Season*, by E. Litvinoff, London, 1973, which presents a rare insight into Jewish immigrant life and illustrates the sometimes bizarre relationship between Okhrana agents and 'propagandists by the deed'.

21. Proprietor H.S. Harris at 119 Houndsditch. His son Harry was still operating the business in 1945.

Street, whose walls adjoined those of the jewellers, the constable had his suspicions aroused by the furtive behaviour of the 'foreigner' who opened the door, and he summoned the assistance of five other policemen led by a Sergeant Bentley. As they entered the premises they were greeted with a burst of gunfire. The gang leader, seized by a P.C. Choat, was mortally wounded by the bullets fired by his comrades to dislodge his captor. Choat and two others lay dead, as two men and a girl carried their dying accomplice through the side streets of Whitechapel to their destination at 59 Grove Street, off the Commercial Road.

There, on a bed in a small back room, he spent his last hours. Two women remained to minister to him — Sara Rosa Trassjonsky (apparently Peter the Painter's girl friend) and Luba Milstein. In desperation, and in defiance of strict orders left by the rest of the gang who had quit, Rosa called on a local Dr Scanlon, who soon caught on to the situation, and notified the police. The news broke with a police description in all papers of four men, including the dead one, who was quickly identified as George Gardstein, alias Poolka Kilkowitz, alias Muronzeff, who for some months had occupied a room at 44 Gold Street, Stepney Green. It appeared self-evident that there was some connection with the local Anarchist group, since in Rosa's flat were found copies of the *Arbeter Fraint* and *Germinal* as well as similar Russian and Yiddish publications underneath the dead man's pillow. The hunt was on for the remaining three: Peter the Painter or Peter Piatkov, alias Schtern (regarded as the brains behind the robbery), Fritz Svaas and the last, later identified as the limping man, Joseph Marx. What Rocker had always feared now happened.

At first, suspicion fastened on Malatesta, who on Siegfried Nacht's recommendation,[22] had sometimes allowed Gardstein access to his tools and machinery at his Islington workshop. He had also given him a personal card to present to his supplier, which was found on the body. Malatesta was promptly hauled into Scotland Yard for questioning and, his innocence proved, just as quickly released. The press,

22. Siegfred Nacht, alias Arnold Roller. See Chapter 10, p.269.

however, opened up full blast against Anarchists and political refugees, lumping them together in an all-out anti-alien campaign. The *Daily Mail* commented that 'even the most sentimental will feel that the time has come to stop the abuse of this country's hospitality by the foreign malefactors', a view shared by Robert Blatchford, Socialist editor of the *Clarion*. A number of Liberal and non-sensational papers maintained some balance, and directed attention to the root causes of such incidents. The weekly *Graphic* published at least two articles along these lines: Albert Kinross in 'The Letts, Their Land and Their Lawlessness' conceded that the criminals were 'products of the Russian system; no immigration laws will keep them out; so long as the Russian system of government is what it is, men desperate as these will be produced' — a hypothesis repeated by another contributor, Lucien Wolf, who re-emphasised that 'this type of desperado will only cease when the conditions in Russia have been swept away'. Like sentiments were, not unnaturally, voiced in the editorial of the *Jewish Chronicle*.[23]

For the first time, national attention was focused on Jubilee Street. 'Our club was presented as a meeting place of criminals, where only conspirators and initiates found admission by secret signs and passwords. It was a den of thieves and murderers. Peter the Painter had delivered lectures there to teach the use of explosives.'[24] This was counterbalanced by the more rational account given by novelist Sir Philip Gibbs as special reporter for the *Graphic*. He entered with some trepidation to find the group

in a large bare room furnished with a few wooden benches, a deal table and a number of wall posters in Yiddish. Here was the anarchists' club. I was a little assured and a great deal astonished when a number of women entered the room. They were all young women, most of them neatly dressed. One woman who sat behind the table where the pamphlets lay, and who seemed in some authority, had the face of a tragedy queen [i.e. Millie Rocker].

23. See *Graphic*, 14 January, 1911, article 'The Foreign Office Bag' by Lucien Wolf, and *Jewish Chronicle*, editorial of 6 January, 1911, which confirms Russian oppression as 'the root of the trouble'.
24. Rocker, *The London Years*, p.207.

He conversed with Rocker ('A tall, stout man with immense shoulders, and a big powerful head and a strong face, which might have been brutal but for the thoughtful look behind his spectacles') and concluded that his fears had been unfounded.

> These alien anarchists were as tame as rabbits. I am convinced that they had not a revolver among them. Yet remembering the words I heard, I am sure that this intellectual anarchy, this philosophy of revolution, is more dangerous than pistols and nitro-glycerine. For out of that anarchist club in the East End came ideas! [25]

Hardly had the hue and cry after Houndsditch begun to subside when the second drama broke. On 2 January, 1911, a Mrs Gershon, living at 100 Sidney Street (a house located about fifty yards from, and parallel to, the Anarchist Club) arrived at Arbour Square police station to report that two men, who had rented a room from her on the first floor, answered to the descriptions on the 'wanted' posters. The police surrounded the house and the tragi-comedy began. The men, sensing that they had been betrayed, seized their landlady and deprived her of her skirt and boots on the assumption that no religious Jewess would attempt to make a break in her underclothes. But Mrs Gershon was made of sterner stuff, and slid out while her captors' backs were turned. This set the scene for the first act in the affair of Sidney Street.

At seven-thirty next morning a policeman threw gravel at the first-floor window. There was a burst of gunfire, and a police Sergeant Leeson, posted opposite by the brewery wall, fell wounded in the chest. A gun battle ensued between police and desperadoes which continued for over two hours. At ten a.m., after an appeal to the Tower Garrison, a force of two squads of Scots Guards in battle regalia was brought up as reinforcements. A barrage of cross-fire was directed at the floor, where the besieged had erected a barricade of bedding and furniture across the windows. Meanwhile the Home

---

25. *Graphic*, 7 January, 1911, article 'An Evening in the Anarchist Club' by Philip Gibbs. See also follow-up article, 'A Night Down East', in the 14 January issue.

Secretary, Winston Churchill, had arrived on the scene ostensibly to direct operations. By lunch-time a whiff of smoke emerged from one of the windows on the first floor, and the return fire ceased abruptly. The house was soon immersed in flames. It is still an open question whether one survivor had set fire to it rather than surrender or whether it had been started by an incendiary device thrown from outside. When the firemen had finished (after five of them had been injured by falling masonry), two charred bodies were found and identified as those of Svaas and Marx. It was deduced that Marx died first since he had a bullet in the brain, while Svaas might have succumbed to suffocation after having started the fire. But the main police target, Peter the Painter, vanished; and so was born the second legendary anti-hero in East End folklore.[26]

What is certain is that while the Sidney Street terrorists were not Anarchists but Lettish Social Democrats, Peter was no myth. He had been a frequent visitor to the Jubilee Street club. How he eluded the police net is unknown. There have been a host of imaginative speculations: that he was an Okhrana agent who escaped with the connivance of the Russian police; that he fled with a fifth suspect, Joseph Levi, to France, and there was 'not sufficient evidence of murder to secure extradition' (Sir William Nott Bower, Police Commissioner). Some concrete evidence appears to emerge. J.P. Eddy suggests that correspondence from official Russian sources confirm that he returned to Russia in 1911. By December 1912 he was wanted by their police for evading military service, and absconded to Germany. Rocker offered what he felt was conclusive information on his whereabouts after 1917.

> It is certain that ... in the early days of the Russian Revolution, he appeared in Russia and was appointed by the Bolshevik government as an official of the terrible Cheka, becoming one of its most notorious agents. *Our comrade Alexander Shapiro, who had seen Peter in London, met him in Russia, working as an agent of the Cheka!*[27]

---

26. The first was, of course, Jack the Ripper.
27. Rocker, *The London Years*, p.212.

Sidney Street touched off some unpleasant sequels. Press agitation against Anarchists and 'criminal aliens' reached a new crescendo. Police watch on the club and individual members increased. In the eyes of the local public 'anyone who walked along in a Russian blouse was considered a suspicious character and sometimes assaulted'.[28] The most vicious attack on Anarchists was made by the Social Democrat organ *Justice* on 13 May. They were accused of promoting such crimes as Houndsditch, etc., since many of them were *agents provocateurs* who initiated terrorist acts to discredit Socialists generally, and to get the right of asylum withdrawn in England. It included the extraordinary charge that 'Emma Goldman is in the pay of the police . . . At one time she was employed by Mr A.E. Olarovsky, of the Russian Secret Police in San Francisco, as an agent and spy.' This could neither be proved nor disproved, since Emma Goldman would never make use of a state institution such as a court of law to defend herself. The editor, Harry Quelch, immediately found himself besieged by innumerable protesters ranging from *Freedom* to a number of SDP branches demanding that evidence for this charge be published. An editorial reply to the effect that it was revealed to him (Quelch) personally by the same police agent, Olarovsky, rendered the accusation even less credible.

Among the four arrested in connection with Houndsditch was the girl Nina Vasileva. The three men were members of the Lettish Social Democratic Party in London, and the party arranged counsel for their defence. Nina, who belonged to no organisation, had no one to turn to. It was Millie Rocker who took it upon herself to visit the prisoner, and found a young lawyer who would undertake Nina's defence gratis. The outcome was that the men were acquitted on insufficient evidence, while the girl was sentenced to two years' imprisonment — a heavy punishment for having an affair with Muronzeff. She served only three months, and was then released without explanation. Shunned by her own friends and *landsmen*, who, no doubt, were afraid of associating with someone who had been involved in the recent outrages,

---

28. According to Louis Bailey, veteran Anarchist.

in despair she turned to the Rockers. They took her in and kept her for a month until she found work and lodgings elsewhere. The postscript for Nina is recorded, with typical fairness, by Rocker:

> The London Press left her alone. Even the sensational papers which had featured her case, behaved decently in that regard. The issue of the political refugees and the right of asylum was dropped. I must say that in any other country the consequences would have been more serious.

The incidents at Houndsditch and Sidney Street did the movement no good. There is evidence that club attendance fell dramatically and outdoor speakers lost their audiences. The Jubilee club was linked irrevocably with the events of its neighbouring street, and it was reasonable to expect that those not politically motivated, and they were the majority, would opt out rather than risk being seen in a building, now under closer police scrutiny. But it was the activities of the Gentile workers which gave the Jewish movement a quick shot in the arm. Syndicalism, imported from France and already spelt out to the readers of the *Arbeter Fraint*, was coming into vogue. It preached that the trade unions were the germs of future democratic organisation, so that direct action via the general strike was the ultimate weapon in winning workers' control of industry and government.

On 14 June, 1911, the seamen and firemen, hitherto considered the most depressed and helpless of organised labour, struck for higher wages and overtime rates. By 27 June the shipping magnates of Southampton and Liverpool had conceded their demands. Other low paid workers took the cue, first those in engineering concerns, but especially in the docks. The Port of London Authority on 27 July granted its dockers a rise of a penny to sevenpence an hour. Those already on that rate with the shipping companies claimed eightpence an hour. On 1 August, 20,000 port workers came out and twenty ocean ships lay idle; but by 11 August the strike was settled to the men's advantage. Parallel activity in Liverpool was marked by violence, when troops brought in to quell the rioting fired on the crowd and killed two men. This provoked sympathy strikes in which the Amalgamated

Society of Railway Servants was involved. On 15 August, the day of the firing, Britain suffered a general railway stoppage, which was again marked by riots and bloodshed as troops intervened. It had been a long, hot summer, but strike fever continued unabated. On 20 December, a weavers dispute in Accrington against the employment of non-union labour led to a lock-out of 126,000 within the week. The new year brought long drawn-out discussions between miners and owners to a finale with a strike on 1 March, as 850,000 men left the pits. Dockers' leaders, spurred on from below by the easy victory of the previous year, were moved to confrontation with their employers over the employment of a foreman who worked without a union ticket. As in 1889, the East End was girding itself for a new round of industrial action.

In late April 1912 came the tailors' and militants' moment of opportunity, provided by a dispute in which 1,500 highly skilled West End tailors of international repute were demanding improved pay and working conditions. By 2 May, *The Times* reported on a strike meeting of 7,000 to 8,000 tailors out of a total of 50,000 employed in the London trade, with an ominous note by J. Blythe, Secretary of the London Tailors' and Tailoresses' Union, that 'employees in the East End remained at work', although he presaged that 'before many days . . . the strike would be general'. Four days later[29] an account followed of a conference held in East London on 5 May, to discuss the extension of the strike there. It ended with a statement by Kaplan (now Secretary of the London Ladies' Tailors' Union, numbering only 700 paid-up members) that the members decided to help the West Enders in the following ways: financially; all work from the West End now performed in Whitechapel to stop immediately; and members to have a free hand in joining the strike without consulting the executives of their union. He concluded that 'they could not agree to a general strike for the reason that over seventy per cent of the membership was engaged in the ready-made trade, which was not connected with the present dispute, and as a general strike would have

29. *The Times*, 6 May, 1912.

to include them, they did not think it advisable to call their members out'.

Kaplan really exposed what Rocker and the *Arbeter Frainters* feared; that it might be impossible to control work performed in the multiple sub-divisional sweatshops of the East End, which could then act as strike breakers against the rest. The lessons of 1906 were not lost on them. The *Arbeter Fraint* set its sights on a general strike in a passionate article by Rocker, who invoked support for a mass meeting called by the united Jewish tailoring unions for Wednesday 8 May. The response surpassed by far the Wonderland gathering of 1906. This time 'over 8,000 Jewish workers packed the Assembly Hall . . . More than 3,000 stood outside'.[30] Kaplan opened the indoor meeting by posing the question of a general strike. Blythe of the London Society of Tailors remonstrated that 'the struggle in the West End was not one of colour or creed but a fight between organised and a large proportion of unorganised labour and the domination of capital'. He warned: 'It was likely that trade would come down to the East End to be finished, and the tailors in East London must decline to finish that work or become blacklegs.' It was Rocker's moving speech in Yiddish which proved decisive. There was so much tension in the hall that no other speakers could get a hearing. A vote was immediately taken by asking those who favoured strike action to stand. The audience rose, as one, to their feet. The result communicated itself to the overflow who joined in a burst of cheering, which re-echoed along the Mile End Road. Within two days 13,000 immigrant tailors quit their workshops. The *East London Observer*[31] was incensed at the 'Gilbertian charade of a really stupid strike' adding, contemptuously that 'this last "ebullition" of unrest will present itself rather as a mild joke than a serious episode'. It was looking back on the fiascoes of the past. This was a more serious proposition.

There was organisation and direction from the start. A

30. Rocker, *The London Years*, p.220. *The Times*, 9 May, 1912, suggested that 'besides the gathering in the Great Assembly Hall an overflow meeting was held outside the hall where nearly 9000 people were addressed from six platforms'.

31. *East London Observer*, editorial, 11 May, 1912.

strike committee of fifty members representing the tailoring trades in the area was formed with appropriate sub-committees: negotiations — for finalising agreements with masters ready to accept the workers' conditions; finance — for raising funds to sustain the strikers, and finally a local strike committee of seven, which included Rocker and Kaplan, responsible for overall strategy. The *Arbeter Fraint* appeared as a four-page daily to keep the workers informed of up-to-date developments. Strike demands were drawn up. These included the recognition of a normal working day fixed at nine hours, the substitution of day for piece work, the abolition of overtime, higher wages (eventually fixed at a ten per cent increase), an end to disfunctional, unhygienic workshops, and the acceptance of closed union labour by the rest. Without recognition of the last by both sides, there could be no guaranteed maintenance of pay and working standards.

The strike brought Rocker his hour of glory. As chairman of the finance committee, he expended his Herculean energy, day and night, to raise money — the ultimate key to success or failure. Such was his stature that he was virtually besieged by an army of volunteers. He depended on the traditional response of East Enders to rally to the side of the strikers. Higher paid workers, with a little savings, not only refused strike pay, but contributed to the strike fund. Pennies and farthings flowed in from *ad hoc* outdoor meetings and door-to-door collections. Rocker needed to feed dozens of families who were absolutely destitute. He organised temporary canteens on trade-union premises, providing a minimum fare of tea, bread and cheese, with the occasional hot meal from meat contributions. The Jewish bakers' union and cigarette-makers offered free supplies. Other Jewish unions, such as cabinet-makers, slipper-makers and the like, placed a levy on their members for the tailors' strike fund. The Yiddish theatre put on several benefit performances and handed over the takings to Rocker, while individual sympathisers outside the area and the labour movement sent cash or cheques. This enabled Rocker to pay strikers a few shillings each, according to family needs, during the first week.

The Master Tailors' Association was as initially unprepared for the strike as the workers. Their association of about 300 members was a fraction of the hundreds more who ran small tailoring concerns in the East End. Moreover, they were dependent on the big City manufacturers for orders, and the City men refused to supply work to masters who submitted to the workers' demands. The old remedy remained. Convinced that without funds the strikers would be driven back to work by hunger, the masters retaliated with a three-week lock-out. To counteract public sympathy for the men, the masters' spokesman, Samson, gave out to the press that the workers had no real grievances, but were being manipulated by foreign Anarchists in a plot to disrupt industry; and reinforced his argument by producing some curious wage sheets, which purported to show that earnings by ordinary hands were anything between six and ten pounds a week. 'Reading the reports he put out, one got the impression that the infamous sweatshops of the East End were a Paradise!'[32] An old ploy of undermining the strike by playing on the fears of the womenfolk for their children proved equally abortive. Mass meetings of women were held in which they affirmed their determination to stand by their menfolk until the strike ended in their favour.

Rocker's duties within the leadership were tremendous. He attended all meetings of the strike committee, held the responsibility for all finances, as well as editing the *Arbeter Fraint*. In addition, he was in popular demand at strike meetings. He recalls his daily round of activity at the time:

> I worked on the paper from six in the morning till eleven. I addressed three or four strike meetings every day. I never got finished before two in the morning, which left me only three or four hours for sleep. Luckily I had a robust constitution. I wasn't the only one who worked all those hours. We were all at our posts day and night.

On 13 May East and West End organisations held a joint demonstration on Tower Hill[33] at which Rocker spoke. When that dispersed, hundreds of East Enders marched back to Stepney Green, where another monster meeting was

32. Rocker, *The London Years*, p.222.
33. See *The Times* report on 'The Tower Hill Meeting' on 14 May, 1912.

addressed by him. A parallel struggle, about to break out, helped maintain morale. Their docker neighbours were poised for a second great dock strike, and once again, as in 1889, suffering made strange bedfellows. Rocker was quick to use this opportunity to bring Jewish and Gentile workers together. In addition to his other undertakings, he chose to speak at joint strike gatherings, acting as the inspiring force behind the joint tailor and docker demonstrations on the Mile End Waste.

As far as the West Enders were concerned, the AST had refused to sanction the dispute and grant financial aid to striking members. This stance brought it in conflict with its London branch, who called a special protest meeting at Board Street, Soho, on 13 May. The AST was accused of endeavouring 'to break our ranks by secretly making overtures to the London master tailors'. A resolution pledged those present 'to do no work until the employers conceded our demands'. Three weeks after the strike started, it was ended by a settlement to the men's advantage, namely shorter hours, the abolition of piece work, improved sanitary conditions and the employment of union labour only. Direct action had triumphed. East End workers employed in men's tailoring and uniforms returned to work. This struck a psychological blow at the right time for the cause as a whole, although the dispute in the women's garment industry continued. The concept of a freely negotiated settlement was now acceptable to both sides, as both were getting desperate. The Masters' Association was facing the fact that its seasonal trade was almost ruined, the workers had no more funds. They agreed to confer, with the result that all the workers' demands were met except that of a closed union shop.

Rocker pleaded to the Committee that the last was imperative, the major objective in the conflict. Union recognition was some guarantee for workers' security, the strongest weapon in any future dispute. A mass meeting was called for 24 May at the Pavilion Theatre to settle the question. Rocker described the outcome in moving terms: [34]

---

34. The *East London Advertiser* of 1 June, 1912 incorrectly reported this meeting as the 'End of Strike'.

A murmur ran round the building when I stood up as the first speaker. I saw those pale, pinched, hungry faces, those thousands of people who had come together at midnight to decide what to do about this strike for which they had sacrificed so much. I felt that I dare not conceal anything from them . . . I explained the position to them. I said that if they held out a few more days I was sure that they would win. If they decided to go back now the masters would make them feel they had lost. But the decision, I said, 'rests with you. I am not going to tell you what to do. You must decide for yourselves.' There was a burst of applause, and from all sides came the cry: 'The strike goes on!'

The next morning, against their spokesman's advice, the masters capitulated. Negotiations began the same afternoon, and the workers were amazed to see Samson at the head of the queue to beg union permission to reopen his workshop. He was politely sent to the back. As the unbending opponent of the tailors' demands, he would wait to the last. Retribution was yet to come. He eventually signed the agreement but found that no one would work for him.

This, the most positive victory the tailors had won, was no death blow to the sweating system, as Rocker suggests.[35] It certainly dealt it a severe blow, which no act of Parliament could have rendered. For the practical necessity of unionisation was now firmly embedded among the immigrants; and recognised by the masters as a force, with which, in their own interests, they would have to co-operate. Thanks to the effects of the 1912 strike, J.L. Fine could build a united tailors' union.

Rocker emerged as the architect of victory, a Moses resurrected in Stepney. He was genuinely embarrassed.

I couldn't put my foot out in the street without becoming the object of a demonstration. One day as I was walking along a narrow Whitechapel street with Millie an old Jew with a long white beard stopped me outside his house, and said: 'May God bless you! You helped my children in their need. You are not a Jew, but you are a man!'[36]

---

35. Rocker, *The London Years*, p.224.
36. 'Man' here probably translated from the Yiddish *mentsch*, which really means a fine human being.

What was more important to him was that the view associating the Jews with strike-breaking was now invalidated. The dock strike was still dragging on and dockers' families faced starvation. In their hour of triumph the *Arbeter Fraint* called on the Jewish tailors to rally to the aid of the dockers. A committee was set up in conjunction with the Jewish unions, and Anarchists Ploshansky and Sabelinsky were elected secretary and treasurer respectively. It called on families to succour the children and offers of accommodation (more than could be accepted) and gifts poured in from Jews, many of whom could scarcely feed themselves. Local retailers subscribed shoes and clothing. Dockers, trade unionists and social workers spoke of the warmth and hospitality shown to their unfortunate charges by East End Jews. Rocker and Millie personally collected children from the docks, most of whom were reduced to 'a terribly undernourished state, barefoot and in rags'. Over three hundred children were taken into Jewish homes.[37] Such action was in accord with Rocker's aim of bringing about a more congenial relationship between Jewish and Gentile workers, and in this instance, it laid the foundations of many friendships which neither time nor circumstance could erase. The dockland slogan, 'No Jews allowed down Wapping', might persist. But it was the dockers of Wapping and St George's who constituted the militant vanguard of the movement which, in 1936, forcibly prevented the Mosleyite incursion into East London.

The two years between the 1912 strike and the outbreak of war registered the peak period of Anarchist activity, in which Rocker reached the zenith of his influence. Trade union membership expanded dramatically. Meetings were now called daily to propagate the creed or in response to local conflicts which continued to be fought out between masters and men. The *Arbeter Fraint* became a twelve-page sheet and sold out regularly. The club flourished with full attendances noted at lectures, dances, plays among the variety of social functions. The great Yiddish poet Abraham Reisen received a warm welcome at Jubilee Street, after

37. Millie Sabel informed me that she kept three children for nearly three weeks, which was not an uncommon act of mercy among the *chaverim* at that time.

which several of his new poems appeared in the *Arbeter Fraint*. When the Beilis ritual murder trial broke, the Anarchists were in the forefront of the Jewish protest movement, the *Arbeter Fraint* filling its editorials week after week with news and informed comment on the Tsar's insidious role in the current accusation. The Anarchists had achieved such popularity that they became almost respectable. A sympathiser could lay on his *tefillim* (phylacteries) on the morning of an Anarchist-sponsored strike, bless Rocker and still go off to evening service as an orthodox Jew. In 1914 the Jewish labour movement, primarily under Anarchist direction, reached its peak of activity. 'Who could have foreseen the collapse which followed the beginning of the Great War?' mused Rocker. But the seeds of dissolution were already there.

12. End of a Mission

In 1914 the Anarchists were the most dynamic element in East End political life. By the 1920s they were already an anachronism, shadowy ghosts of another era. Perhaps it would be pertinent to determine why they had achieved so much, before reconstructing causes for their ultimate failure.

Over the years they had never let up on propaganda and activism which was relevant to all facets of the immigrant's struggle to improve his quality of life. It would be reasonable to suggest, as they did, that Social Democrats, Bundists and the like were politicians first, in the sense that they were geared to long-term possibilities of remedying ills by party or parliamentary means, against direct action from below as initiated by the Anarchists. The latter responded to the immediate needs of the workers, placing no reliance on a future millennium. They were even more realistic by acting on root sentiments. While Anglo-Jewry rejected Yiddish and sought its demise, the Anarchists elevated it to the prime vehicle of communication as the *mame loshen* of the working masses, as well as conveying western culture through its medium. The immigrant was scarcely allowed to forget that he was an unwanted foreigner, and naturalisation was a long and costly affair. Many, at one time, had no vote, and were frustrated by their own impotence in attempting to gain political support on their behalf. In any case, very few had previously been exposed to a free society, and remained politically naïve. What was needed was an educational impetus towards social and economic consciousness. This they owed mainly to Anarchist voluntarism. The Jews of the *stetl* were forced into narrow egoism by Tsarist restrictions which meant a competitive, cut-throat existence. It was the paradox of stress on individual freedom within the context of a close-knit community reminiscent of the *stetl*, that drew the immigrant towards Libertarian associations.

In the long term the Jewish movement would not survive. The incident of the Sidney Street siege revealed the vital breach in Anarchist ranks. It focused the antithesis between the concept of educative growth combined with militant action conceived by Kropotkin and Rocker against the idea of 'propaganda by the deed' proposed by the advocates of violence. The terrorists embraced a *mélange* of fanatical idealists on the one extreme and criminal homicides on the other. Peter the Painter was representative of the latter, and it is symptomatic that he, the one who got away, should according to Shapiro re-emerge into history as an official of Lenin's Cheka and one of its most ruthless agents. Sir Philip Gibbs overestimated the power of 'intellectual anarchy', which he found 'more dangerous than pistols or glycerine'. A movement divided in itself cannot stand.

A mixture of saints and sinners drove it in many directions and confounded its disciples. The strength of religious orthodoxy accelerated the process of disintegration. Rocker was innately flexible, and later realised the danger of becoming identified as the advocate of free love, and opponent of marriage as an institution. By then it was too late. Dreen is convinced that it hampered wider support for their ideology. There were too many traditional hangups to accept free sex as a viable dictum, when it cut across the fundamental tenets of Judaism. Eulogies on terrorists such as Ravachol (which both Yanovsky and Rocker subscribed to in the earlier days) put off potential members, to whom violence, after their own experience in Russia, was anathema. There was no future in militant atheism with its Yom Kippur comedies, as a new generation of London-born Jews, over whom the lean years of suffering had passed less harshly, returned to the security and respectability of their ancient faith. And while the *Arbeter Frainters* had limited themselves to a self-perpetuating group under Rocker, their survival reached a crisis point with the internment of their leader, from which they never recovered.

But were those ideological *Arbeter Frainters* Libertarians *à l'outrance*? It is curious that some could reconcile their anarchism with entrepreneurship. Rocker's most devoted comrade Lief owned one of the fine Victorian houses in Bancroft Road, and later made a fortune by patenting a gyroscopic toy. Silberman, whose workshop had been used as *ad hoc* office and caucus headquarters, was a handbag manufacturer, and Freedman a successful bespoke tailor who chose to live in a more affluent area in Bow. Sam Dreen married in 1913 and left the group. Although he eventually became a Paole Zionist and master tailor, he still claims to remain true to those ideals derived from his teacher. (At eighty-eight he still retains that zest for life and generosity of spirit as a legacy from the golden years with the *chaverim*.) Alexander Shapiro, the movement's life-long professional, in his last years tried, albeit unsuccessfully, to run an import-export business in New York. There was, of course, the usual retinue of ersatz zealots, who, between heavy bouts of card-playing and swilling schnapps, engaged themselves as temporary actors in the Anarchist scene. By 1914 some of the old pioneers had lapsed, while others had departed for the USA and the prospect of the good life.

The 1870 Education Act cut off, in the long term, potential recruits to the movement. Second and third-generation children born to immigrants strove to become anglicised, that is integrated and therefore accepted by the host community. That they became 'English by a legal fiction'[1] is manifestly untrue. Even Arnold White, while regarding aliens as 'base coin', surmised that 'the second generation becomes English'.[2] Supporting evidence is given by headmasters of East End schools in a later report. J.M.P. Rawden of Deal Street Board School confirmed that in his school 'practically the whole of these children are of foreign parentage. Notwithstanding this fact, the lads have become thoroughly English. They have acquired our language. They take a keen and intelligent interest in all that concerns the welfare of our country. They are proud to be considered English boys.'[3] F.H. Butcher of Christian Street School regarded his Jewish boys as 'good educational material' and

---

1. According to W. Evans-Gordon, *The Alien Immigrant*, p.33.
2. Evidence before Select Committee on Sweating System, 1 May, 1888, no. 240, Min. 2300.
3. Royal Commission on Alien Immigration, 1903, cd. 1742, Min. 18,873.

'intellectually superior' to the rest.[4] W.A. Nugent of Betts Street School, St George's-in-the-East, informed the committee that his Jewish children were the cleanest, and their intelligence of the highest order. 'It is a remarkable fact that the foreign children show a better knowledge of English history than the English children themselves.'[5] It was part of a natural response by youngsters, who, sensitive to their position as outsiders, wanted desperately to be accepted; and consequently rejected much of their parents' adherence to the manners and customs of the *stetl*. Yiddish was a casualty on the way. By 1911, M.J. Landa[6] could suggest that 'few Jewish children in England wrote Yiddish; fewer still are to be seen reading a jargon sheet.' This is debatable, but it could demonstrate the desire of the new generation to identify themselves with the land of their birth. Both Yiddish and Anarchism were 'foreign' importations, and there could be no future for either among the recent breed of anglicised Jews.

The growth of alternative non-political institutions contributed to the erosion of the old radicals' influence. To combat the dangers of moral and religious laxity accruing from music hall, street life, atheists, and revolutionaries, leaders of Anglo-Jewry financed the setting up of youth organisations and staffed them with their sons. A Jewish Lads' Brigade was formed on the lines of the 'muscular Christianity' of its Anglican counterpart, the Church Lads' Brigade. Its first commander, Colonel Goldsmid, conceived it as 'ironing out the Ghetto bend'. A favourable British reaction could be expected to a movement which concerned itself with developing the physique and encouraging habits of cleanliness and restraint under military discipline. Clubs such as Brady Street (founded in 1896), followed by Stepney Jewish Lads and Victoria Boys, reached a more sophisticated standard with the foundation in 1913 of the later purpose-built Oxford and St George's Club by pioneer social worker Basil Henriques. Their function was ostensibly apolitical, but in fact they served to maintain the *status quo*. (Club leaders

4. Ibid., Min. 18863-65.
5. Ibid., Mins 18745 and 18757.
6. Anglo-Jewish author of *The Alien Problem and its Remedy*, London, 1911, p.146.

often preached at their evening assemblies against the dangers of anti-British, that is radical, ideas.) They certainly offered the young a more attractive alternative to the more rigorous demands of a radical commitment.

By 1914 religious tradition still prevailed, even where only surface rituals were observed. A further challenge to the radicals came from Herzl's political Zionism, which commanded Jews to fulfil the vision of an independent national future in Palestine. It was Lieberman who had first attempted to synthesise the opposite ideals of Socialism and Nationalism 'to amalgamate the struggles for working class and Jewish national independence'. This heady amalgam continued to hive off from Libertarian groups those who put greater emphasis on their Jewish identity. Leeds had already founded a small party of Paole Zionists (Workers of Zion) in 1905. The Aliens Act in Britain, and renewed Tsarist persecutions after the revolution culminating in the Beilis affair, strengthened the appeal to Jewish nationalism and fed the new movement for Zion, whose Messianic realisation would appear confirmed by the Balfour declaration of 1917.

On 4 August, 1914, Britain declared war on Germany. This was a death blow to East End Anarchism. Conflicting attitudes towards war split the leadership. Rocker and Malatesta opposed war on international principles, while Kropotkin supported it on the basis of historical necessity: that power on the Continent had fallen into the hands of a reactionary, military bureaucratic state, whose policy of violent expansionism must be opposed. On 7 August, Rocker's editorial in the *Arbeter Fraint* condemned the ineptitude of the Second International as a contributory cause, prophesying, against the optimists, a lengthy war, 'a period of mass murder such as the world has never known before'. Almost immediately, the vicious outpourings of the 'patriotic' press, such as the *Daily Mail, Daily Express* and *John Bull*, who had a field day conjuring up scare stories of subversive activities pre-planned by Germans settled here, hustled the Home Office into introducing registration of 'enemy aliens'. Rocker anticipated this as the first step to internment. It paralleled a wave of anti-German hysteria, which culminated in a pogrom in October, when Germans were beaten up in the street, German-owned butcher and baker shops pillaged, and their houses set on fire. Anti-Kaiser *émigrés*, who had worked at the same job for years, were promptly sacked. Englishmen no longer dared employ them.

Rocker featured in a last practical gesture to uphold international camaraderie. While French and German soldiers were killing each other on the western front, in London's West End, French and German Anarchists co-operated in opening up a Communist kitchen to feed unemployed German workers. Rocker followed suit in the East End. A house was rented and sympathisers brought in furniture and kitchen equipment, while volunteers brought and prepared food. There was no fixed price for meals. They were free to the many who couldn't pay, and comrades at work in London or the provinces sent money to meet the extra cost. The size of the *Arbeter Fraint* was reduced as demand fell. In October and November, its columns were thrown open to both pro- and anti-war elements. Rocker, in four articles opposing Kropotkin's stand, attacked the war 'as the contradiction of everything we had fought for'. It was a brave but dangerous opinion to express in print. On 2 December, 1914, Rocker was arrested in his flat at Dunstan Houses, to start the four long years of internment. He never returned; and his exit spelt finis to the group and the London Jewish movement.[7]

Why this dramatic end in 1914? The anglicisation of young Jews had taken root and drawn off a flood of volunteers into the armed forces. (Kaplan's only son joined the army and was killed in Flanders six weeks later.) Top activists were quickly interned, and immigration, which had fed the Libertarian movement with its most zealous followers, virtually ceased. Many of the older *chaverim*, still tied to the *heim*, saw their millennium in the advent of the Russian revolution. A Kerensky Commission in London, presided over by the old Narodnik, Zundelevich, sponsored passages back to the homeland, and hundreds flocked enthusiastically to join the great return (many eventually to disappear in the purges and

7. The next year the *Arbeter Fraint* office and press was closed by the police and the club ceased to exist. It became in turn a cheap cinema and then converted into the Jubilee Street Great Zionist Synagogue!

executions of the Cheka). In spite of political aberrations, the Bolshevik experiment appeared to confirm the viability of a worker-controlled state, and a generation of immigrants' sons embraced the new Communism from afar with a fanaticism more lasting than the old. The consolidation of Jewish trade unions without them deprived the Anarchists of another area of support. In the final count the triple pulls of Zionism, Orthodoxy and Communism after 1917, offered alternative challenges to the residual Anarchists, and eroded their ranks. By the early 1920s a few small esoteric groups remained, hovering on the periphery of the extreme Left, already functioning in obscurity.

For Rocker, the story did not end in London. It was only the beginning. Repatriated to Germany via Holland in 1918, he renewed his activities among the Jews there, fighting a heroic but futile battle against Nazi anti-Semitism, barely escaping with his life in 1933. His last years were spent writing contributory texts to Libertarian ideology[8] and campaigning for the Anarchist cause to the end. When his autobiographical piece, *The London Years*, appeared in 1956 it scarcely sold. Perhaps the *embourgeoisement* of a more secure Jewry made it inevitable that the pre-1914 story of Jewish working-class radicalism be consigned to oblivion. But a new generation of altruistic youth, Jew and non-Jew, emerged in the sixties rejecting the acquisitive and competitive *mores* of their parents. In doing so, a minority discarded the old authoritarian shibboleths for an alternative form of communal living, through which, in their terms, they could build from below to create a truly free, just and equitable society. And in their search for a continuing tradition, they have rescued from obscurity the story of East End Anarchism.

To-day a handful of survivors, old men and women, at the Workers' Circle, the cultural centre inspired by Rocker and the *Arbeter Fraint* group, recall with reverence the memory of a teacher who helped restore their dignity and self-respect after their debasement under Tsarist barbarism. Rocker

---

8. *Nationalism and Culture*, Los Angeles, 1937, is perhaps his greatest contribution to Libertarian historiography. His other classic is *Anarcho-Syndicalism*, which appeared in London in 1938.

20. Rocker with two group comrades, Lief and Dr Zhedlowski, in 1912.

21. Rocker with Polly Witkop, Sabelinsky with Millie, and three German comrades, in 1912.

would have none of that. The years of achievement were but a consummation of the work of his predecessors. Lieberman, Winchevsky, the Berner Streeters, Yanovsky, Wess and Frumkin were the pioneers, although the real creators were 'the ordinary rank and file, the men and women whose names are rarely mentioned, but without (whose) tireless day-to-day work there would be no movement'.[9] Out of the totality of their experience he proclaims a universal message:

> Social ideas are not something only to dream about for the future. If they are to mean anything at all they must be translated into our daily life, here and now; they must shape our relations with our fellow-man. It was this kind of human relationship that placed its seal on all the strivings and aspirations of the Libertarian movement of the Jewish workers in Britain.

9. Rocker, *The London Years*, p.57.

Appendix 1
'The Haunts of the East End Anarchist' (Evening Standard, 2 October 1894)

Just beyond the Proof-house of the Gunmakers' Company near the Whitechapel end of the Commercial Road, begins a series of narrow streets running at right angles to the main throughfare, and cutting Fairclough Street at the further extremity, where the Tilbury and Southend Railway passes through the district. More or less alike in appearance, these byways, for they are no more, consist entirely of small two-storeyed tenements with an occasional stable or cow-shed to' break the monotony, and a sprinkling of little shops devoted to coal and dried fish, stale fruit and potatoes, pickled cucumbers and salt herrings, shrivelled sausages and sour brown bread. There is Backchurch Lane, where the Irish resident still holds his own against the incoming Russo-Jewish settler, and Berner Street, where the window bills, written in Hebrew characters, inform you that there are 'loshings' or a 'bek-rum' (back room) to let, and thus proclaim the nationality of its denizens. There is Batty Street wholly given over to the foreign tailors, clickers and 'machiners'; Christian Street, long since an appanage of East End Jewry, and Grove Street, where the low-pitched tenements are so far below the pavement level that the passer-by can comfortably shake hands with the residents of the top floor through the bedroom windows. And intersecting all these are a number of courts, alleys, and passages, so dark and narrow, so dirty and malodorous, that the purlieus of Seven Dials and the backways of Clare Market may be called light and airy in comparison with them. Some are blind, others lead through to the adjoining thoroughfare. Some branch off to right and left, others conduct one to open spaces forming irregular quadrangles lined with houses below the street level, so small and snug that the occupier standing in his front parlour can open the door, stir the fire, reach the dustbin outside, or make the bed inside without stirring from the spot. Courts and alleys, streets and yards, all are densely packed, in many cases even to the cellars below lighted by small gratings in the

pavement. And the whole district, stretching from Backchurch Lane on one side to Morgan Street on the other, is the
resort and principal abiding-place of the East End Anarchists.
In the side streets and alleys hereabouts the majority of them
live and loaf; within a stone's throw are their favourite
haunts, the coffee-shops they patronise, and the private
gambling rooms where many spend their evenings, and close
by is their printing press, their temporary club and meeting-
house, and even the tavern where their Friday evening
discussions take place.

The Club and rallying place of the Russo-Jewish Anarchists
in East London was until lately in Berner Street. Recent
occurrences, however, rendered this an undesirable locality; it
was too well looked after by the authorities. So it was
transferred to a quieter and more obscure corner, where it
was less likely to attract the notice of outsiders; and it is now
by no means easy to find. Near the top of New Road which
opens into Commercial Road, there is a turning known as
Charlotte Street, at one corner of which is an oilmonger's and
at the other a tobacconist's. Three doors or so from the
former is a narrow archway, bricked over. The roadway
beneath is roughly paved, and the kerb is generally the seat of
some half-dozen unkempt and dishevelled gossips attended
by twice as many barefooted children. Passing under the arch
one emerges upon a lane or alley not more than nine to ten
feet wide. There is a row of small tenement houses on one
side, a dirty brick wall and some stables on the other. A few
costers' barrows are backed up against the wall, and the
uneven roadway and gutter are invariably sloppy and sloshy,
owing to the grooming of horses always going on, and the
practice the residents have adopted of emptying their waste
water from the upper windows. At the bottom of this
thoroughfare, and on the left hand side of it, is a small
building, half workshop, half warehouse, with a steep sloping
roof, the gable end facing the road. The lower part is entirely
boarded up, and tightly nailed-to. There is a large double
door on the first floor the entire width of the building, and
only the upper part of this is glazed so that it is impossible to
look in from without. Nor can the edifice be seen from the
streets at the end of the lane in which it stands. There are
two small doors, but without either bell or knocker, handle

or latch to them. A couple of posters are stuck on the doors, one in Hebrew characters, reading '*Arbeter Freund*', the other in English, 'Workers' Friend', thus announcing this to be the official headquarters of the East End Anarchist propaganda. Knock, kick, or batter at the side entry any afternoon or evening, and the big door on the upper floor will be cautiously opened, and you will hear a hoarse '*Khto tam?*' – 'Who's there?'. If you are unknown to the speaker, you will be told that no business is done there. If the questioner above recognises you, or you come with a friend, a string arrangement will open the side door on the left, and by means of a wooden staircase you can mount to the upper floor. Go up any afternoon or evening and you will hear the sound, not of political argument or Socialist debate, but of cardboard falling upon wood, and suppressed talk and laughter. The whole of the upper part forms a large oblong room, half office, half sitting-room, with a bench or two, upon which a score of young men and women are generally to be found seated, smoking and chattering away, while others are at a small table playing cards. As you enter you may catch one, watching the game, call out, in unctuous Yiddish, '*Dos kortel begrubt ach*', 'That card will bury you' – and the card apparently does settle the player, for he throws it down with an oath and a muttered '*Shwartz-mazel*', 'Bad luck', and tosses a couple of sixpences over to his companions. The young men usually present are well fed and dressed, belonging apparently to a comfortably-off class, and the young women are altogether comely specimens of 'fair Israel' in East London. But the visitors here are only new adherents, young converts. They are the idle drones of the Anarchist hive. The Club is but a rallying-place for such followers, and a blind for the outside public. For the workers we must look elsewhere. And these will be found in the smaller circles or branches which meet on Sundays, in their own appointed places.

One such branch, comprising a section of the women's organisation, has its meeting place in the very heart of the Anarchist quarter in the Commercial Road. Two or three doors from Morgan Street is a narrow passage by the side of the large public-house in the open thoroughfare. This is London Terrace, and leads to one of the darkest and most forbidding of the alleys that abound in the vicinity. There are houses on one side only, on the other a wall, which effectually prevents any glimmer of sunlight from reaching the tenements. So bad is the reputation of the terrace that none but residents would willingly go through it after dusk, and even those take care to keep their lower window-shutters close-barred and their doors locked as soon as twilight sets in. At the further end the wayfarer down there is as far from help and hearing, if attacked or molested, as though he were a hundred miles instead of a hundred paces away from one of the busiest thoroughfares in London. Half-way along the passage we enter an open doorway, and are ushered down a short flight of stairs by an associate, to whom we have letters of introduction, then across a yard communicating, seemingly, with the block of houses facing Umberstone Street only to find ourselves in an ordinary-aired room filled by two and twenty persons seated like those attending a spiritualist séance, men and women ranged alternately round the wall. They are all Jews and Jewesses, but markedly different from the ordinary stock types encountered in the East End of London. None of the men are over forty, and only two of them wear beards — the rest moustaches and side-whiskers. They are neatly and quietly dressed, and, were it not for their Jewish features, would pass unnoticed in any ordinary assembly of Englishmen. The women are, all of them, taller than the average, strongly built, and plain-looking, with the heavy features of Russian Jewesses. They wear their own hair — which East End Jewesses generally cover with a *sheitel*, or wig — and none of them have wedding rings. Their expression of face is not prepossessing for the eye-brows are unusually bushy, and there is an ominous 'v' fold in the depression above the nose of several of them. Their peculiar utterance of certain consonants marks them out as Courlanderinnen, natives of Courland.

In presence of visitors properly vouched for, the proceedings at the meeting go on as usual, at least, so it is said. The programme consists of readings from advanced thinkers, with comments by the members, recitations of poems calculated to foster the spirit of Anarchism, and songs having the same tendency. The readings for the day are from Herbert Spencer, and the criticisms, with the frequent references to the

abolition of marriage as an institution, the destruction of
capital, and the good times coming when their revolutionary
links will 'spew cartridges', are by no means milk for babes.
The poems recited are decidedly strong meat. What do
English readers say to this for a specimen verse or two? The
original is, of course, in Judeo-German, and it is rendered
rough and ready from the original, the raciness of which
however, it is impossible to reproduce:

> If I dig in the mines of the frozen north,
> I'll dig with a will: the ore I bring forth
> May yet make a knife — a knife for the throat of the Tsar.
> If I toil in the south, I'll plough and sow
> Good honest hemp; who knows, I may grow
> A rope — a rope for the neck of the Tsar.

Sarah Bernhardt might envy the fire and verve with which
this recitation is given by one of the Jewesses, and there can
be no possible mistake about the sentiments of the speaker
and her auditory, whatever there may be about the merits of
the verses. And the same fiery stuff, or fiery stuff of the same
description, is being spouted about the same time at half a
dozen other branches of the Anarchist League in the district
between Backchurch Lane and the New Road, that runs up
to Whitechapel. Everything is turned to account, too, for the
purposes of its mischievous propaganda. Why, before the
meeting is closed one member produces and sings an
Anarchist version of 'After the Ball', with a finely-buttered
moral drawn from the contrast between the wealthy dancers
inside and the shivering poor outside, winding up with an
Anglo-Yiddish chorus in which all join.

Of course, all those frequenting the Anarchist resorts of
East London are not of the same temper and class as the
foregoing. On the other side of the Commercial Road, in
Greenfield Street, and about two doors down, is a small,
squalid-looking shop, with a window on each side, a door in
the centre, and panels painted a dull dirty yellow. The
appearance of the whole place is fly-blown and untidy, from
the torn curtains that conceal the interior to the shabby
hangings that decorate the glass door. There are two rows of
brown leather-covered seats running lengthwise inside, some
little tables in front of them, a fly-specked mirror with the

gilding cracking off, and a battered-faced clock against the side wall. Bills in each of the windows, in Hebrew characters, inform the Yiddish public and passers-by that 'here can be had coffee', also what they spell and call *tie* (tea), and *alle ort von refreshments* which every one will easily construe to mean all kinds of refreshments. This is a coffee-house much patronised by the great bulk of the poorer East End Anarchists and Socialists who live in the district, and here some distinct classes and types may be seen. One soon learns to distinguish them — one, that is, who has some knowledge of the foreign settlers and their dialects, for there are several forms of Yiddish which the accustomed ear as readily discriminates as an educated Englishman the brogue of an Irishman from the *lingua Cockneyana* of the born East Ender. Here may be noted the restless-eyed Galician, thin and lanky and flat-chested, his head cropped quite close, and remains of his ear-ringlets just showing; there the sly and foxy-looking Lithuanian, whose tongue instantly betrays him, for, like the Ephraimites of old in Judea, he cannot pronounce the 'ah', and says to this day and hour, *Sibboleth* for *Shibboleth*. There the restless Pole hobnobs with the muddle-headed German, each styling the other *genoss*, 'associate', for which privilege the foolish wretches pay their few pence weekly to the astute rascals who run the branches of which they are members. Only a few minutes' walk from the Commercial Road are the King's Arms (closed lately), in Fieldgate Street, and the Sugar Loaf, in Hanbury Street, both favourite resorts of the East End Anarchists, who get up the weekly discussions that tempt poor flies into the trap. Too lazy to work, they find in the mischievous propaganda they spread a capital means of bringing grist to their own particular mills. When not engaged in this work, the leaders and followers of East End Anarchism have only one resource, what they term *Klein Shas*, literally the 'little Talmud', a euphemism for card-playing; and they spend night after night in the haunts mentioned and the card rooms that abound in the neighbourhood, gambling away the last coin that should have gone to their underfed wives and children, and returning home to rave afresh against society and the iniquities of those who do not go and do likewise.

Appendix 2
Four strike and protest leaflets

1. 1889 strike leaflet.
2. Balance sheet of the great strike of 1889.
3. Leaflet advertising a mass protest meeting, 1890.
4. Leaflet advertising a meeting called to protest against the TUC's anti-alien resolution of 1895.

NOTICE

to

TAILORS & TAILORESSES !

As the employees of

MESSERS HEBBERT & Co.,

35 & 37, Bethnal Green Rd., E.

are on

STRIKE,

All Workers belonging to the Tailoring trade are requested to

KEEP AWAY from that place.

Tailors' Strike Committee

**"White Hart," Greenfield Str.
Commercial Rd,. E.**

Worker's Friend Printing Office, 40, Berner St., Commercial Rd. E.

BALANCE SHEET

OF THE

GREAT STRIKE OF EAST LONDON TAILORS,

For 10¼ hours per day.

EXTENDING FROM AUGUST 27th. to OCTOBER 2nd, 1889.

Introductory Note by the Secretary on behalf of the Strike Committee.

In presenting this Sheet before the attention of the public, we beg to take the opportunity of offering our heartiest thanks to all sympathisers who so readily and freely responded to our appeal for help, and more so to those who did not even wait for our appeal. And while, considering the importance of monetary assistance in such critical times to save the struggling soldiers from bending before the whip of starvation, we express our utmost appreciation at the way in which sympathisers of all grades, rich and poor, laborers and manufacturers, subscribed to our funds, we cannot refrain from emphasizing with great pleasure the fact that the readiness and fraternal spirit shown to us by the various Trade Organizations and other English Working Men's Bodies armed us with a most effective weapon to carry the fight to victory. We only hope that our brethren all over the Globe will not fail to take a grand lesson of solidarity from the Dock Labourers' Strike, as well as from this of the Tailors and of others, which will mark a new and splendid epoch in the history of Labour; a lesson that will lead the workers of all countries to their complete emancipation and real happiness.

INCOME.

	£	s.	d.
Half Balance from Joint Fund of Tailors and Cabinet Makers	6	5	8¼
Collections in the Streets	47	18	4¼
Do. in West London Shops, by West London District, A.S.T.	44	3	10
Do. by the Machinists' Society	0	10	0
Do. do. Pressers' Society	0	10	0
Executive Council Amalgamated Society of Tailors	25	0	0
Collection by Mantel Makers' Co-operative Society ...	0	7	2
Per Mr. Rabin, List No. 9	0	5	6
,, L. Biemshitz ,, 5	0	8	5
,, W. Wess ,, 8, 14, 20, 43 & 48	3	0	10
,, W. Rosenthal ,, 12	0	4	0
,, Cohen ,, 44	1	14	6
,, Connor, Jun. ,, 2	0	2	6
,, Cohen ,, 44	0	2	0
,, Moses Frankel ,, 24 & 25 ...	1	0	0
,, S. Goldberg ,, 2	0	2	3
,, Goldstein	0	3	0
,, Goldberg	0	4	3
Per "Jewish Standard"	4	13	6
Per Mr. Fisher	0	9	1
Employés of Messrs. Hunter, Wiltshire & Co. Cigar Manufacturers	0	11	0
Do. of Mr. Van Oestren, Cigar Manufacturer ...	0	8	4
Do. of Mr. Charles Baker	0	12	6
Amalgamated Society of Boot and Shoe Makers	10	0	0
Cigar Makers Provident Society	2	0	0
London Society of Compositors	10	0	0
Cigar Makers Mutual Association	5	0	0
Dock Labourers Strike Committee	100	0	0
Mr. Jacob Her-bman	1	0	0
City Clothing Manufacturer	10	0	0
Mr. S. Montagu, M.P.	30	10	0
Mr. Goodman	1	1	0
Mr. John Piggott	1	1	0
Anonymous Friend, per Mr. Montagu, M.P. ...	5	0	0
Lord Rothschild	73	0	0
Mr. N. L. Cohen, per Mr. Montagu, M.P. ...	5	5	0
Per "Star" Office, from Finsbury R.F., and others ...	4	3	0
Manchester International Working Men's Club, per "Worker's Friend"	1	18	8
Total	**£398**	**15**	**5**

EXPENDITURE.

	£	s.	d.
ORGANISING.			
Printing	10	2	0
Postage and Telegrams	1	17	3
Stationery	0	16	7
Banners	1	4	0
Bands	29	0	0
Vans for Demonstrations	2	3	0
Caretakers and Porters of Meeting Places ...	2	4	6
Fares of Deputations	2	4	11
Bill Posting	0	17	9
Pickets	1	14	4
Collection Box and Banner Bearers	2	10	2
RELIEF.			
In Cash	54	17	6
In Tickets	212	9	6
In Cash taken home to sick cases	1	19	0
Bread and Cheese to Strikers at Demonstrations ...	3	18	7
Refreshment to Box and Banner Bearers ...	2	10	10½
DEFENCE.			
Towards legal expenses of Asher Cohen... ...	3	0	0
Police Court Expenses to Lewis Winter ...	0	4	6
RENT AND DAMAGES.			
Proprietor "White Hart"...	5	0	0
GENERAL.			
Committeemen and Chairman	39	2	6
Treasurer for time lost and travelling	0	13	2
Secretary's Salary	6	10	0
Sundry Expenses, (including Collecting Boxes) ...	6	18	1½
Granted to Secretary in recognition of good services rendered...	5	0	0
Audit Expenses	0	15	0
	397	13	3
* Balance in hand	1	2	2
	£398	**15**	**5**

* This Balance, or whatever may come in, will be handed over to the Silvertown Strike Fund, in accordance with the decision of the Committee.

Audited and found correct,

H. COOMBE, West End Branch, Amalgamated Society of Tailors.

J. T. JEWELL, Dragon Branch, Amalgamated Society of Tailors.

H. J. CLARKE, Dock, Wharf, Riverside & General Labourers' Union.

W. PARISH, Treasurer.

WILLIAM WESS, Secretary,

October 22nd, 1889.

40, Berner Street, Commercial Road, London, E.

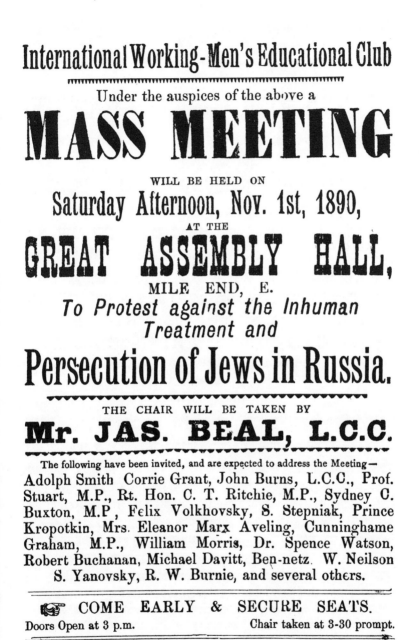

International Working-Men's Educational Club

Under the auspices of the above a

MASS MEETING

WILL BE HELD ON

Saturday Afternoon, Nov. 1st, 1890,

AT THE

GREAT ASSEMBLY HALL,

MILE END, E.

To Protest against the Inhuman Treatment and

Persecution of Jews in Russia.

THE CHAIR WILL BE TAKEN BY

Mr. JAS. BEAL, L.C.C.

The following have been invited, and are expected to address the Meeting—
Adolph Smith Corrie Grant, John Burns, L.C.C., Prof. Stuart, M.P., Rt. Hon. C. T. Ritchie, M.P., Sydney C. Buxton, M.P , Felix Volkhovsky, S. Stepniak, Prince Kropotkin, Mrs. Eleanor Marx Aveling, Cunninghame Graham, M.P., William Morris, Dr. Spence Watson, Robert Buchanan, Michael Davitt, Ben-netz. W. Neilson S. Yanovsky, R. W. Burnie, and several others.

☞ COME EARLY & SECURE SEATS.

Doors Open at 3 p.m.   Chair taken at 3-30 prompt.

Communications respecting this meeting to be addressed to the Sec., W. WESS, Int. Working-Men's Club, 40, Berner Street, Commercial Road, E.

Worker's Friend Printing Office, 40, Berner Street, Commercial Road, E.

אידען! גרייסט אסעמבלי האל

גרויסער פראטעסט מיטינג

אייני׳צ׳רופען פון דיא צעהן אידישע יוניאנס אין לאנדאן

ווירד שטאמפינדען

נעקסטען שבת 7 דעצעמבער פון 1 ביז 6 אוהר

צו פראטעסטירען גענען דיא קארדיווער רעזאלוציאן.

דיא ענגלישע אנטיסעמיטען האבען אזוי ווייט געבראכט
דאס דיא ענגלישע ארגאניזירטע ארבייטער פארדערען פון
דיא רעגיערונג צו פערמאכען דיא טויערן פון ענגלאנד
פא־ פרעמדע ארעמע לייטע, מיינענדיג הויפטזעכליך דיא
אידען. אידישע ארבייטער, איהר מארט יעצט ניט שווייגען
איהר מוזט קומען אין אייערע טויזענדע צום מיטינג אין

דיא גרייט אססעמבלי האל

מייל ענד רויד

דער טשעהרמאן וועט זיין דאקטאר אוועלינג

פאלגענדע רעדנער וועלען רעדען אין ענגליש און אידיש:—

הערבערט בוראס (ט־עושירער פון מעסש־גירלס יוניאן), דזן. מאקדאנאלד
(סעק. אמאלגאם. סאסייעטי אף טיילארס), מרם. עלינאר מארקס (קארל
מארקס טאכמער) גענו ואו־ק. און דועגערל לייבאר. יוניאן), ס. מענדעלזאן,
קראפאטקין, מערנער (שאף אססיסטנגמס יוניא), דזש. נראה (פרעזידענט
קעב מענס יוניא׳), וועפמ (סעקרעטער־ אליינגם קאבינעט מייקערס) קאפלאן
(סעקרעטער קעפ מיקערס), שייניר (פרעזידענט אמאלגאמיסטער שניידערס),
פין (סעק. מענטל מיקע־ס), סטעפאניאק, גאלדבלאט, ערא׳, אין פ׳עלע אנדע־ע.
פיעלע מעמבערס אף פארליאמ׳אנט זיינען גענען אוא געזעטמץ אין אונטערשטיצען
אונז. אזוי א מיטינג ווי דער אין גרייט אססעמבלי האל וועט זיי נעבען מעהר
מוטה אונז צו פערטיידיגי׳ן. אידען קומט אין מאסען און פילט אן דיא האל.

דיא אידישע ארבייטער פערטהיידיגונגס קאמטע.

דרוקעריי פאן א.וו. ראבכינזאוויטש, 64 היא סטריט ווייטשעפעל.

Bibliography

1. Documentary/Government Sources

John Burnett, Report to the Board of Trade on the Sweating System at the East End of London, by the Labour Correspondent of the Board, PP 1887, vol.lxxxix.
Board of Trade, Memorandum on the Immigration of Foreigners into the United Kingdom, 1887, PP, vol.lxxix.
House of Commons Select Committee on Alien Immigration, Report and minutes of evidence, vol. i., 27 July, 1888; vol. ii., 8 August, 1889 (SP 1888, ix, p.419; 1889, x, p.265).
House of Lords Select Committee on the Sweating System, Report and minutes of evidence, vol. i., 11 August, 1888; vol. ii, 20 December, 1888; vol. iii, 24 May, 1889; vol. iv, 17 August, 1889; vol. v., Appendix and Proceedings, 1890 (SP 1888, xx, xxi; 1889, xiii, xiv; 1890, xvii, p.257).
Royal Commission on Alien Immigration, vol. i., Report, cd. 1742, 1903; vol. ii, Minutes of evidence, cd. 1742, 1903; vol. iii, Appendix, cd. 1741, 1903; vol. iv, Index and analysis to minutes of evidence, cd. 1743, 1904, (SP 1903, ix).

2. Trades Union Congress Reports

1892, 1894, 1895, debates on anti-alien resolutions.
1902-1910, naturalisation and anti-sweating resolutions.

3. An extensive bibliography is given in Professor Lloyd Gartner's *The Jewish Immigrant in England* (1870-1914), London, 1960 (pp. 285-308); to which can be added the

following books and documentary sources — published and unpublished.

General

Demidoff San-Donato (Prince), *The Jewish Question in Russia*, London, 1884.
Joll, J. *The Anarchists*, London, 1964.
Mendelsohn, E., *Class Struggles in the Pale*, London, 1970.

Biographies and autobiographies

Dreen, S., *Autobiography* (unpublished).
Eyges, T., *Beyond the Horizon*, Group Free Society, Boston, 1944.
Gordin, A., *S. Yanovsky, his Life, Struggles and Achievement, 1864-1939*, S. Yanovsky Memorial Committee, Los Angeles, 1957.
Rocker F., *Autobiography* (unpublished).
Rocker, R., *The London Years*, London, 1956.
Winchevsky, M., *Stories of the Struggle*, Chicago, 1908.

Fiction and semi-fiction

(invaluable for their insight into the immigrant and Anarchist milieu)
Litvinoff, E., *A Death out of Season*, London, 1973.
Meredith, I., *A Girl among the Anarchists*, London, 1903.
Mackay, J.H., *The Anarchists*, Boston, 1891.
Zangwill, I., *Children of the Ghetto*, London, 1909.

Articles, papers, diaries

Finestein, I. (QC), *Jewish Immigration in British Party Politics in the 1890s*. Paper delivered to the Jewish Historical Society of England, 12 July, 1970.
Rocker, R., Correspondence, unpublished material, etc., in the institute for Social History, Amsterdam.
Rollin, A.R., 'Russo Jewish Immigrants in England before 1881', article in *Transactions of the Jewish Historical*

Society of England, vol. xxi, pp. 202-13.

Tcherikover, E., Minutes of the Hebrew Socialist Union, reproduced from 'The Beginnings of the Jewish Socialist Movement (Lieberman's Period)', *YIVO Historische Shriften*, I, Vilna, 1929, cols. 469-532, translated from the Yiddish by W.J. Fishman.

4. *Major newspapers, periodicals, etc, relating to the Jewish Socialist and Anarchist movements*

Yiddish radical press
   Arbeter Fraint, London, 1885-1932. After 1892 Anarchist.
   Die Freie Welt, London, 1891-2. Socialist.
   Germinal, London, 1900-8. Anarchist.
   Die Neie Zeit, London, 1904-8. Socialist.
   Die Poilishe Yidl, London, 1884. Mainly Socialist.
   Die Tsukunft, London, 1884-9. After 1886 non-radical.
   Die Yiddishe Freiheit, London, 1905. Socialist-Zionist.

English radical press sporadically reporting on the Jewish movement includes *Commonweal, Freedom, the Anarchist*, the *People's Press, Reynolds News, Justice*, and the *Social Democrat*.

Jewish non-political press making critical commentaries on Jewish radical activism:

Yiddish
   Die Yiddish Express, Leeds, 1896-9, London, 1899-?
   Die Yiddish Telefon, London, 1897-9.
   Die Yiddish Zhurnal, London, 1907-44.
   Die Zeit, London, 1913-52.

English
   Jewish Chronicle, London, 1841 on.
   Jewish Year Book, London, 1896 onwards — gives information on community's response to the 'aliens question'.

Index